Verissimo Toste

OXFORD
UNIVERSITY PRESS

Based on an original concept
by Tom Hutchinson

OXFORD
UNIVERSITY PRESS

Great Clarendon Street, Oxford, OX2 6DP, United Kingdom

Oxford University Press is a department of the University of Oxford.
It furthers the University's objective of excellence in research, scholarship,
and education by publishing worldwide. Oxford is a registered trade
mark of Oxford University Press in the UK and in certain other countries

© Oxford University Press 2019

The moral rights of the author have been asserted

First published in 2019

2023 2022
10 9 8 7 6 5 4

No unauthorized photocopying

All rights reserved. No part of this publication may be reproduced, stored
in a retrieval system, or transmitted, in any form or by any means, without
the prior permission in writing of Oxford University Press, or as expressly
permitted by law, by licence or under terms agreed with the appropriate
reprographics rights organization. Enquiries concerning reproduction outside
the scope of the above should be sent to the ELT Rights Department, Oxford
University Press, at the address above

You must not circulate this work in any other form and you must impose
this same condition on any acquirer

Links to third party websites are provided by Oxford in good faith and for
information only. Oxford disclaims any responsibility for the materials
contained in any third party website referenced in this work

ISBN: 978 0 19 425618 6	Teacher's Guide
ISBN: 978 0 19 420490 3	Teacher's Online Practice Access Card
ISBN: 978 0 19 421286 1	Teacher's Online Practice
ISBN: 978 0 19 421235 9	Classroom Presentation Tool: Student's Book
ISBN: 978 0 19 421253 3	Classroom Presentation Tool: Workbook
ISBN: 978 0 19 421280 9	DVD-ROM

Printed in China

This book is printed on paper from certified and well-managed sources

ACKNOWLEDGEMENTS

Based on an original concept by Tom Hutchinson

The Museum of the Strange by: Paul Shipton (pp.32–33, 58–59, 84–85)

Tests by: Sage Stevens

Photocopiable worksheets by: Barbara Mackay

Culture video scripts by: Kiki Foster

Online Practice exercises by: Sarah Bennetto

The authors and publishers are very grateful to all the teachers who have offered their comments and suggestions which have been invaluable in the development of Project Explore. We would particularly like to mention those who have helped by commenting on Project Explore:
Croatia: Branka Plećaš, Ivan Štefanić
Czech Republic: Martin Hrdina, Kateřina Hurtíková
Hungary: Király Ildikó
Serbia: Vojislava Koljević, Jagoda Popovic
Slovakia: Jana Krídlová, Jana Hrianková
Slovenia: Vojko Jurgec, Mina Mazouzi

The authors would like to thank the editorial and design teams at Oxford University Press who have contributed their skills and ideas to producing this course.

Back cover photograph: Oxford University Press building/David Fisher.

Commissioned photography by: MM Studios

Illustrations by: Adam Horsepool/Advocate Art pp.12 (ex.1), 28, 57, 81; Alleanna Harris/The Bright Agency pp.11, 21, 80; Jennifer Naalchigar pp.64, 74, 76; Lila Kalogeri/Advocate Art pp.12 (ex.2), 18, 47, 55; Marco Marella/Advocate Art pp.48, 50; Mark Duffin pp.13, 53; Nan Lawson/Advocate Art pp.27; Parwinder Singh/Advocate Art pp.34, 42, 71; Peter Nagy/Beehive illustration pp.10.

The publisher would like to thank the following for permission to reproduce photographs: Advertising Archives pp.65 (John West TV advert); Alamy Stock Images pp.6 (ROWAN ATKINSON BEAN/A.F Archive), 6 (Rogue One/BFA), 6 (La La Land/Moviestore Collection), 6 (Toy Story 3/Entertainment Pictures), 6 (The Hunger Games: Mockingjay Part 1/Moviestore Collection), 6 (Rupert Grint/Entertainment Pictures), 20 (Museum of Math, New York/MShieldsPhotos), 20 (Musee des arts forains/Hemis), 24 (Hiking/Roberto Fumagalli), 29 (Film crew and actors/PearlBucknall), 29 (Charville Castle/scenicireland.com/Christopher Hill Photographic), 30 (The Metropolitan Museum of Art of New York/Mauritius images GmbH), 45 (Titan triggerfish, eating a plastic bottled lid/Paulo Oliveira), 50 (Lachlan Smart/Xinhua), 56 (Mini/Ernie Jordan), 67 (Margaret Mead/Everett Collection Inc), 67 (George Bernard Shaw/Archive Pics), 69 (St. George´s Day, Barcelona/Age Fotostock), 70 (Molly Malone statue/Simon Reddy); Bridgeman Images pp.31 (Impression: Sunrise/Claude Monet), 31 (The Proxy Marriage of Marie de Medici (1573-1642) and Henri IV (1573-1642/Peter Paul Rubens), 31 (Don Sebastian de Morra/Diego Rodriguez de Silva y Velazquez), 31 (Hands of God and Adam, detail from The Creation of Adam, from the Sistine Ceiling/Michelangelo Buonarroti), 31 (The Last Supper/Leonardo da Vinci), 31 (The Starry Night/Vincent van Gogh); Getty Images pp.6 (Graham Butler/Robbie Jack), 19 (Faces on discs/Dimiti Otis), 20 (Cirque du Soleil/Didier Messens), 22 (Media student/Sturti), 23 (Cleaning forest/Klaus Vedfelt), 25 (Volo dell'Angelo/READA&CO), 27 (Hikers/Aleksander Rubtsov), 29 (Jesse Rose/Kieran Frost), 40 (Interview/Track5), 40 (Conference/Caiaimage/Rafal Rodzoch), 50 (Laura Dekker/AFP), 63 (Friends eating/White Packert), 65 (John West salmon/Education Images), 69 (Castellers/Guillam Lopez), 70 (Cast of Riv/Torsten Blackwood), 70 (The Dublineers/Ollie Millington), 72 (lonelygirl15/Bloomberg), 74 (Sales/LeMusique), 74 (Man buying ukuele/Peter Cade), 76 (The Tonight Show/NBC), 79 (Teens In booth/Tony Anderson), 82 (CHAMPS/Bernard Weil), 82 (Usain Bolt/Franck Fife), 82 (Auckland junior rugby/Phil Walter), 83 (Teens on bikes/Westend61), 86 (Bobsleigh/Clive Mason); Oxford University Press pp.8 (Happy girl/Fizkes), 18 (On the Origin of the Species/Oxford University Press), 24 (Praa Sands Beach/Ian Woolcock), 46 (Great Wall of China/Yuri Yavnik), 46 (Moai statues/Kovgabor), 60 (Red watch/Alex Roz), 60 (Tablet/Thaiview), 60 (Video game/Ballball74), 60 (TV/Scanrail1), 61 (Laptop/Segey Peterman); Press Association pp.50 (Tom Davies/Yui Mok); Shutterstock pp.5 (Students/Monkey Business Images), 6 (Murder on the Orient Express Movie Poster/Faiz Zaki), 6 (Robin Hood/Universal/Kobal/REX), 8 (Skateboarding/Lzf), 8 (Sunglasses/Kostenko Maxim), 8 (Girl with crown/Veles Studio), 8 (Star pattern/Janna Mudrak), 8 (BMX cyclist/Zeber), 8 (Bear with headphones/Olga Angelloz), 8 (Daisy pattern/Kate Inspiration), 8 (Flowers/Vectrogirl), 8 (Teen boy with headphones/Lightfield Studios), 9 (Karate/BRG Photography), 10 (Chimps/Catherine D Sales), 10 (Group of teens/Iakov Filimonov), 12 (Drug test/Image Point Fr), 12 (DNA/Vitstudio), 12 (3D globe/Brovkin), 14 (Emojis/Carboxylase), 16 (Working in library/Mind and I), 17 (Teen boy/WaiveFamiscoCz), 17 (Students/Rawpixel.com), 17 (Male obstetrician/Monkey Business Images), 17 (Female student/Monkey Business Images), 17 (Young woman/Avelina), 17 (black hole background/Pavel Ignatov), 18 (Edinburgh University/STLJB), 18 (HMS Beagle/Granger/REX), 20 (Big Apple Circus/A Katz), 21 (Emojis/Carboxylase), 21 (Magician/Strandret), 22 (Climber/Akif Oztoprak), 22 (Harvesting vegetables/AYA images), 22 (Climber/Vitalii Nesterchuk), 22 (High school/Syda Productions), 23 (Smelling flowers/Elipetit), 23 (Volunteers/Mangostock), 23 (Beach cleaning/Africa Studio), 24 (Bungee jump/Vitalii Nesterchuk), 24 (Kayak/Kuznetcov Konstantin), 24 (Throwing oranges/Paolo Bona), 24 (Climber/Inu), 26 (Seychelles/Simon Dannhauer), 26 (Skiers/Iofoto), 26 (Restaurant/Prasit Rodphan), 27 (Sailing boat/Kite rin), 27 (Beijing/Zhao Jian Kang), 27 (Egypt/WitR), 29 (Presentation/Syda Productions), 29 (black hole background/Pavel Ignatov), 30 (Brooklyn Bridge/Uwe Kraft), 30 (Statue of Liberty/Erik Pendzich), 35 (Walking teens/Monkey Business Iamges), 36 (The Zimmers/Ken McKay/Thames), 37 (New driver/SpeedKingz), 37 (Female executive/Wavebreakmedia), 37 (Nanny/Mangostar), 37 (Heart tattoo/Africa Studio), 37 (Wedding/Happy image), 37 (Riding a scooter/Tiffany Bryant), 38 (Friends in corridor/Monkey Business Images), 39 (Customer experience/Black Salmon), 40 (Building/Han871111), 43 (Industrial area/Mike Mareen), 43 (black hole background/Pavel Ignatov), 44 (Wombat/Covenant), 44 (Camels/Stanislav Fosenbauer), 44 (Red fox/Milosz Maslanka),44 (Kangaroo/John Crux), 44 (Emu/Colacat), 44 (Koala/Yatra), 44 (Baby rabbits/Houshmand Rabbani), 45 (Yokohama/Voyata), 46 (Christ Redeemer/Dmitry Islentev), 46 (Burj Khalifa/Tomasz Czajkowski), 46 (Pisa/Deyan Georgiev), 46 (El Castillo/Paulcreative), 46 (Taj Mahal/Olena Tur), 46 (Temple in Petra/Kanuman), 46 (Djenne mud mosque/Trevor Kittelty), 47 (Golden Gate bridge/Travel Stock), 47 (Rainforest/Filipe Frazao), 47 (Panama/Fotos593), 47 (Table mountain/Adnrea Willmore), 47 (Sagrada Familia/Mapies), 52 (Mars/Jurik Peter), 54 (Athens/Dimitris Panas), 54 (Al-aqsa mosque/Vadim Petrakov), 54 (Stairs/Karel Gallas), 54 (Arch/Carlos Caetano), 54 (Statue of Liberty/Matej Hudovernik), 54 (Siem Reap/Della Liner), 55 (black hole background/Pavel Ignatov), 56 (Fish and chips/SADLERC1), 56 (Marks and Spencer/Moomusician), 60 (Smart phone/Fad82), 60 (Electric cars/Dimitris Leonidas), 61 (Rusty bucket/Eva B), 61 (Plastic bucket/Sergey Maksimov), 61 (Antique shoes/Tadija Savic), 61 (Blue shoes/Fortton), 61 (Carved thrones/Dimitris Panas), 61 (Grey chair/Marina D), 61 (Microwave/MrGarry), 61 (Fridge/Nerthuz), 61 (Washing machine/Pro3DArtt), 64 (Street art/Tala Natali), 64 (Times Square+C151/Travelview), 66 (Smiling woman/Dean Drobot), 67 (Oscar Wilde/Everett Historical), (black hole background/Pavel Ignatov), 72 (Dead fairy/Dan Baines), 74 (Woman buying dress/Kokulina), 74 (Seamstress/UfaBizPhoto), 75 (Clothing store/Creative Lab), 75 (Modern window/Fiphoto), 75 (Display window, sale/Nampix), 75 (Macy's store/Alexander Image), 77 (Before and after/Kotin), 81 (black hole background/Pavel Ignatov), 82 (All Blacks/Paolo Bona), 83 (Party/Syda Productions)

Project Explore

Teacher's Guide 4

Contents

Student's Book Contents	Tiv
Introduction	Tvi
Level planner	Txiii
Teaching notes	
Introduction	T4
Unit 1	T8
Unit 2	T20
Unit 3	T34
Unit 4	T46
Unit 5	T60
Unit 6	T72
Student's Book audio scripts	T86
Workbook answer key	T94
Workbook audio scripts	T104

Student's Book contents

Page		Grammar	Vocabulary
	Introduction		
4	**A** Keeping in touch	Present tense review	Phrasal verbs for relationships
6	**B** Stories	Pronouns and possessives	Genres
1	**Social circles**		
8	**A** Classmates	Present perfect	Relationship adjectives
10	**B** Group instinct	Past simple and past continuous	Relationship expressions
12	**C** Starting points	Conjunctions	Origins
14	**D** A piece of cake		**Everyday English:** Expressing opinions
	Revision: 16	**My project:** My social circle 17	**Culture:** Charles Darwin 18
2	**New horizons**		
20	**A** Awesome	*will* and *going to*	Day trip attractions
22	**B** Collaborate	Present tenses for future arrangements	Volunteering verbs
24	**C** Taking a risk	First conditional	Adjectives to describe places
26	**D** Sorted!		**Everyday English:** Expressing preferences
	Revision: 28	**My project:** Our town 29	**Culture:** The smart tourist's guide to New York 30
	The Museum of the Strange Episode 1 32		
3	**Respect**		
34	**A** Testing	Modals – advice, obligation and necessity	Practical science nouns
36	**B** Young at heart	Permission: *can, could, be allowed to*	Phrasal verbs for socializing
38	**C** Finding solutions	Possibility: *can, could, may, might*	The scientific method
40	**D** Emil's petition		**Everyday English:** Expressing advantages and disadvantages
	Revision: 42	**My project:** Read all about it! 43	**Culture:** Australia under attack 44
4	**Travel**		
46	**A** Wonders of the world	Second conditional	Buildings
48	**B** Ticket to ride	Comparatives and superlatives; *too/enough*	Train travel
50	**C** Off the beaten track	Adverbs of frequency, manner, place and time	Phrasal verbs for travel
52	**D** Hard to believe		**Everyday English:** Expressing belief and doubt
	Revision: 54	**My project:** The trip of a lifetime! 55	**Culture:** As British as…? 56
	The Museum of the Strange Episode 2 58		
5	**Heritage**		
60	**A** Surviving the test of time	The passive	Verbs and dependent prepositions
62	**B** Globalization	Defining and non-defining relative clauses	Compound nouns
64	**C** Modern life	Countable and uncountable nouns and determiners	Modern life nouns
66	**D** Stereotypes		**Everyday English:** Agreeing and disagreeing
	Revision: 68	**My project:** Celebrations in Barcelona 69	**Culture:** Irish heritage 70
6	**Our world**		
72	**A** Online hoaxes	Reported speech	Digital media
74	**B** Shopping	Reported commands and requests	Shopping nouns
76	**C** Fashion	Subject and object questions	Fashion adjectives
78	**D** Life hacks		**Everyday English:** Giving instructions
	Revision: 80	**My project:** Creating a video 81	**Culture:** Small nations, sporting giants 82
	The Museum of the Strange Episode 3 84		

Tiv   Project Explore

Reading/Writing	Listening/Speaking	Pronunciation
R A dialogue: Friends online	S Welcoming a new student	
R W Film posters and characters		
R A forum: What makes a good classmate	L S Talking about activities	
R An article: The Dunbar number	L S Storytelling	
R W An online article	L A podcast	
R A dialogue: A team project	L S Using online material	Silent or pronounced 'e'?
Song 19	Learn through English: Six degrees of separation (Citizenship) 19	
R Reviews: Day trips/Online chat	L A monologue / L S Previewing	
R W A website: Citizenship project	L Garden project plans / S Community activities	
R W Travel blogs	L An advertisement	
R A dialogue: Honeymoon plans	L S Types of holidays	Linking
	Learn through English: Art styles and periods 31	
R UK Science lessons / W A lab report	L A monologue: An experiment / L S Animals in medicine	
R An article: As young as you feel	L S A podcast: Is it legal?	
R A website: The scientific method / W Reporting conclusions	L S A dialogue: A problem	
R A dialogue: Save our park!	L S A campaign	Sentence stress
Song 45	Learn through English: Water (Science) 45	
R An advertisement: The New Seven Wonders of the World	L S A dialogue: A travel competition	
R A leaflet: Interrail advice / W A journal entry	L A dialogue: Identifying a route / S Role-play: Train information	
R An article: The modern Phileas Foggs / W A tourist leaflet	L Talking about trips	
R A dialogue: Off to Mars!	L S Transport for the future	/aɪ/ /i/ /j/
	Learn through English: The invention of travel (History) 57	
R A museum guide: Inventions that have stood the test of time	L S A dialogue: Guessing an object	
R Forum posts: Globalization / R W Quiz and report	S Are you global or local?	
R Has life changed? (Mind maps)	L S Describing adverts	
R A dialogue: I completely disagree!	S A discussion: Teenage stereotypes	Word stress
Song 71	Learn through English: Techniques from literature 71	
R Articles: Was it true? / W A review of digital media	S Talking about digital media	
R Forum posts: Bargain hunting	L S My best bargain / S A sales campaign	
R A dialogue: A guessing game	L S A quiz show / S Describing clothing / Your image	
R A dialogue: Trust me!	L A dialogue: TV series / S Choosing a life hack	/ʌ/ /uː/
	Learn through English: Be active! (Physical Education) 83	

Activities for student A and B 86

Project Explore Tv

Introduction and methodology

Overview

Project Explore is a five-level course aimed at international English language students aged 10–14/15 years old. The course combines the tried and trusted, successful methodology and structure from previous editions of *Project* with 100% brand-new content from a new author team. It offers clearly structured, bright, dynamic lessons, and exciting new characters and stories.

Project Explore engages students with its diverse, motivating topics and realistic, relatable contexts. It systematically develops students' linguistic and 21st century skills, to help prepare them for the world beyond school.

Methodology

Project Explore is an easy-to-use course, with a syllabus based on a traditional structural progression. It guides and supports both students and teachers, by providing a highly structured learning environment. In each unit, grammar and vocabulary is broken down into manageable chunks and presented through engaging, meaningful tasks. The language acquired is then assembled and applied to a real-world, communicative outcome: the project. The focus on progressive language development is coupled with a systematic focus on skills development. The lesson contexts are contemporary, diverse and entertaining, which ensure that student interest and involvement are maximized.

A flexible approach

Project Explore is designed to include a high level of flexibility to help meet the individual needs of all students. Each component of the Student's Book has a tangible outcome, meaning that you can choose what to include, in which order, and also which elements may be better suited to homework tasks.

To supplement the Student's Book, there is a wide range of additional material to select from, such as the closely integrated Workbook exercises, varied photocopiable worksheets, online practice material and extensive video content.

Improved grammar and vocabulary support

The vocabulary and grammar input in the course is structured in a way that allows students to gradually progress from understanding to acquiring and finally to using the language with confidence. Each Vocabulary section starts with visual and audio input, often accompanied by a short task, followed by a communicative activation task. In the Grammar sections, the target language is first seen in a real context. The subsequent exercises then encourage students to take an active role and discover the grammar for themselves. Students then complete tasks which allow for controlled and freer practice of the new language.

Skills development

From the outset, a high profile is given to the development of skills. To recreate authentic usage of language, skills are often integrated. For example, students read and complete a quiz and then listen to check their answers. Not only is this blending of skills more natural, but it also helps keep students curious and engaged.

A systematic approach has been taken to developing written and oral skills. Students first spend time on the 'Get ready to…' stage, working with a model or preparing notes. This support and preparation means students are then able to accomplish the main productive task effectively and confidently. With the writing tasks, students also have the option to complete Workbook exercises, which provide further guidance and practice, prior to writing their own text.

In addition to the main speaking tasks, there are numerous opportunities to practise oral skills and, to further enhance spoken language, each unit has a dedicated pronunciation focus in the form of an entertaining, memorable chant.

Revision, Project, Culture and Learn through English

Revision

These pages serve to review and consolidate each unit's Vocabulary, Grammar and Everyday English expressions. The exercises can either be integrated into class time or assigned as homework. They can be used as an indicator of how well students have assimilated the new language and highlight any areas which may require further reinforcement.

Project

These pages give students the opportunity to use the unit's language to complete a personalized, creative task. The projects focus on a variety of means of presenting information and call upon students to exercise research, IT, written and oral communication skills.

Culture

Each Culture page centres on an aspect of the English-speaking world connected to the topic of the unit. These sections aim to broaden students' knowledge and understanding of diverse cultures and invite them to draw comparisons with their own. There are also related short films for extension purposes.

Learn through English

These pages provide a cross-curricular focus and give students the chance to learn about a range of other school subjects through English.

Student's Book and Workbook integration

The Workbook provides extensive additional write-in activities to reinforce and consolidate the content of the Student's Book. The course is designed so that the two books can be used in close tandem in the classroom. The Workbook exercises mirror not only the unit and section structure of the Student's Book, but also each discrete stage of the lesson. To ensure a seamless transition between the two resources, at the appropriate points, there is clear signposting in the Student's Book to direct learners to the relevant Workbook exercises. Once they have completed these exercises, there is signposting back to the Student's Book.

To support differentiation, the Workbook tasks are graded by difficulty and clearly marked with between one and three stars, with one being the easiest. This ensures that in a mixed-ability class, all students can tackle a task and gain a sense of accomplishment.

Characters and context

In *Project Explore* Level 4, there are characters who appear regularly throughout the course.

Students will quickly get to know school friends Liza, Erika, Danny and Oliver. We encounter them in the unit photostories, whose function is to present Everyday English language in contexts students can comfortably relate to, such as collaborating on school projects, or dropping a phone in water.

Students will also grow familiar with the characters in the three-part mystery story *The Museum of the Strange*. The episodes appear at the end of every two units and consolidate the language students have learned. The fact that the story is told in parts adds to students' feelings of anticipation and excitement.

Tour of the Teacher's Guide

For ease of use, the Teacher's Guide notes are interleaved with the corresponding Student's Book pages. In addition to task instructions, answer keys and audio scripts at the back of the book, the Teacher's notes also include the following features for each unit.

Unit objectives

The main aims of each unit are clearly stated at the start. This allows you to see at a glance what your students will be working towards in the coming lessons and will be able to do on completion of the unit.

Language summary

This is a clear list of the grammatical structures, vocabulary and Everyday English expressions which are presented in the unit. Also outlined here are the themes for the Project, Culture and Learn through English pages.

➡ Reference to supplementary materials

A list of the related Workbook pages and photocopiable worksheets and online practice material are supplied at the beginning of each lesson to help you prepare all the material you need for class. There are also further references within the notes, to indicate at what stages in the lesson these exercises and activities may best be used.

EXTRA IDEAS These notes include practical suggestions for how a task may be extended, to allow for further practice of the focal language point or vocabulary. There are also ideas for how some tasks could be approached in an alternative way and some suggestions for ways to encourage students to respond personally to the input.

In addition, after each Writing and Project task there is a suggestion for what could be done with the work the students have produced. Ensuring that students' writing has a readership is important, as it gives them a real purpose and can motivate them to try harder. Seeing their work on display in the classroom or elsewhere can give students a sense of achievement and pride.

EXTRA SUPPORT These notes offer tips on how to stage, adapt or follow up a task to cater to the needs of weaker students or classes. In a mixed-ability class, these graded tasks will help lower-level students to participate more actively and confidently.

EXTRA CHALLENGE These notes suggest ways in which a task may be exploited to ensure that more able students or classes remain engaged and challenged. In a mixed-ability class, these tasks will help to ensure that stronger students maximize their potential and, by keeping them actively involved, will also limit the possibility of boredom and disruption to the lesson.

LANGUAGE NOTE These notes provide clear explanations and support for dealing with grammatical, lexical or pronunciation points which students may find difficult or confusing.

CULTURE NOTES These comprehensive notes provide additional background information related to the content of each Culture page. They can be used to further broaden students' knowledge and understanding of aspects of culture in the English-speaking world, with which they may be unfamiliar.

There are also shorter notes at times which highlight potential cultural differences between the way things are said or done in English-speaking countries and in your students' home country.

Additional grammar notes

These are extended grammar explanations which fine-tune or supplement those given in the grammar summary pages of the Workbook. They will be useful when addressing the problem areas of particular grammar points and also provide something additional for higher-level, more aspirational classes.

Additional pronunciation notes

These are extended explanations which focus on the discrete pronunciation point being taught. They offer practical advice on how to assist students in understanding and correctly producing the relevant sounds.

Additional subject notes

These in-depth notes are included in the page corresponding to the cross-curricular Learn through English lessons. They expand on the school subject the page relates to and equip the teacher with extra knowledge of and useful lexis related to the focal subject area.

Suggested activities for using the video in class

1. When playing the video through for the first time, pause it at appropriate moments and ask students to predict what's going to happen next. You could divide the class into teams to discuss the options, watch the next scene, and then award a point to the team with the closest prediction to what actually happened. This is a good way to focus students' attention and generate interest in the story.
2. Get students to sit in pairs, one facing the screen and the other with their back to the screen. Turn the sound off and play a section of the video. The person facing the screen describes to their partner what's happening. Students then swap places, so they both get a turn at describing and listening. They can then watch the whole section and see how good their partner's description was. This is a fun activity and a great way to practise present continuous verb forms.
3. Play the video and get the students to say 'Stop!' every time a new character appears. Pause the video and get students in pairs to describe what the character looks like and what he/she is wearing. This is a good way to review appearance language and clothes.
4. Pause the video after each section and give a false sentence, e.g. *The Museum of the Strange Episode 1*: 'Declan likes museums.' 'The museum has a collection of animal paintings.' Students have to correct the false information. With stronger classes, this could be done as a pair activity.
5. Pause the video at intervals and get students in pairs to ask and answer questions.
6. Students work in a group and choose a scene from the video to act out. Give them time to practise and then get each group to present to the class. Alternatively, allocate a different scene to each group and then the class acts out the whole story. This is a dynamic, creative activity and a good way for students to practise some of the key language and grammar from the previous two units.

Mixed-ability support

In every class, students learn at varying paces and present a range of learning styles, needs, interests and motivations. In classes where the scope of abilities is broad, this can pose a challenge for the teacher. For this reason, *Project Explore* offers strategies and materials to help teachers tailor lessons to meet the needs of individual students.

In the Student's Book, at the end of every lesson in each unit, there is an *Extra* task. These can be given to fast finishers in class and can mostly be done either individually or in pairs as a communicative addition. Alternatively, these tasks can be set as homework.

In addition to the core material, the course also includes supplementary worksheets and online practice with reinforcement and extension activities, to be used as and when required.

The Project pages in every unit are also very well suited to classes with mixed-ability learners. Students can work at their own pace, in their own way, towards an achievable goal and produce something purposeful and personalized.

The Tour of the Teacher's Guide section on page Tvii outlines further how mixed-ability classes are supported.

21st Century skills

In addition to academic knowledge and understanding, students these days require a broad spectrum of skills which they can apply to a wide range of real-life situations. The tasks in *Project Explore* are designed to help students develop some of these vital skills, such as collaboration, creativity, communication and critical thinking. The Level Planners indicate the tasks and activities in each unit which require these skills to be utilized.

Special Educational Needs in the ELT classroom

Adapted from Into the Classroom: Special Educational Needs by Marie Delaney (Oxford University Press, 2016)

What is SEN?

Special Educational Needs (SEN) is the term used to refer to the requirements of a student who has a difficulty or disability which makes learning harder for them than for other students their age. Note that gifted and talented students are also considered to have special needs as they require specialized, more challenging materials.

Strengths, not just weaknesses

Of course, students make progress at different rates and vary widely in how they learn most effectively. Although students with special needs may have difficulties in some areas, there will also be areas of strength. Recognizing and utilizing these strengths is important to the students' academic development as well as their self-esteem. Your daily contact with these students will help you understand what works best for each individual student and determine your choice of the most appropriate techniques.

You can do it!

You might be worried about trying to include students with SEN in your class. It can feel like it requires specialist knowledge and extra work for you, the teacher. This does not have to be the case. As a teacher, you are used to dealing with different personalities and abilities in your class. You are probably continually adapting to the widely differing needs of your students each day. Students with SEN are simply part of this variety and challenge. In addition, the teaching techniques which help to support students with SEN are good, practical techniques which will benefit all the learners in your class.

Top tips for creating an inclusive classroom

You do not need to be an expert in SEN to teach students with SEN. You do need to want to work with these students and to be prepared to learn from them.

Tip 1: Be a role model

Students will take their lead from their teacher. It is important to show that you respect and celebrate differences between people. For example, if you notice some students do not want to work with a particular member of the class, ensure you talk to those students privately about their behaviour. Draw attention to appropriate behaviour by giving positive reinforcement to students who are working well together.

Tip 2: See the person not the label

It is very important to get to know each student individually and to not label them according to their SEN. If you have students who wear glasses in your class, you do not assume that they have all got the same personality. In the same way, you should not assume every student with SEN is the same. Find out their interests and their strengths. Remember also that the range of SEN is wide, so take time to find out the level of a student's difficulty. Do not assume, for example, that a visually impaired person cannot see anything – they may have some sight.

Tip 3: Avoid judgements of behaviour

Do not label a student as lazy or not trying. Students with SEN are often trying really hard and get criticized unfairly by teachers. They might look like they are daydreaming in class, but their brains might be overloaded with information which they cannot process and they need a short brain break. These students also need positive feedback on appropriate behaviour, so make sure that you notice when they are behaving appropriately. Many students with SEN and behavioural difficulties only get noticed negatively by the teacher.

Tip 4: Celebrate difference and diversity

The classroom and the world would be a boring place if everyone was the same. You can use the differences between students to learn from each other and about each other.

Tip 5: Cater to different learning styles

As students with SEN tend to find it difficult to learn in traditional ways, it is important to integrate different approaches into lessons to help each student maximize their potential. Visual learners relate well to illustrated tasks, picture stories, video input and clear board work. Those who favour an auditory style benefit from listening to the teacher, as well as varied audio input, such as dialogues, stories and songs. Kinaesthetic learners are innately active students, who tend to find it difficult to sit still for extended periods. They respond well to hands-on involvement in activities like role-plays and mime games.

Tip 6: Plan ways to adapt your lesson plan

You will need to sometimes adapt your lesson plans. This is called 'differentiation'. Differentiation means planning and teaching to take account of all students in the class, whatever their level or capability. The students can make progress in their learning wherever they start from. All students should achieve the same main aim, but may do this in different ways.

Tip 7: Work on classroom management

Clear, consistent classroom management is a key consideration for students with SEN. They often have problems understanding and following rules and instructions, so it is important to think about the best way to present these. For example, considering your seating plan carefully can help with general class discipline.

Tip 8: Work cooperatively with adults and students

Teamwork is the best approach to teaching students with SEN. It is particularly important to work with parents/carers, as they know their child best and will often have helpful strategies to suggest. Other people who can help you include school psychologists, counsellors, speech and language therapists, occupational therapists, and SEN organizations and charities. Try to find out what's available in your local area and keep a list of useful contacts.

Tip 9: Work with students' strengths

Try to find out what each student's strengths and interests are and include these where possible in your teaching. Students who have problems reading may have strong creative skills and excel at project work. Students who find it difficult to sit still might be good at role-play or problem-solving activities. Learners who are struggling academically might be very kind and helpful to other students. Identifying and exploiting individuals' strengths can help boost motivation and self-esteem and also create a cooperative, productive classroom environment.

Course overview

For students

Welcome to **Project Explore**. Here's how you can link learning in the classroom with meaningful preparation and practice outside.

Student's Book

All the language and skills your students need to improve their English, with grammar, vocabulary and skills work in every unit. Also available as an e-book.

AUDIO   ACTIVITIES   VIDEO   WORDLISTS

Workbook

Exclusive practice to match the Student's Book, following the grammar, vocabulary and Everyday English sections for each unit. Students can use their Workbook for homework or for self-study to give them new input and practice.

Online Practice

Extend students' independent learning. They can do extra **Grammar**, **Vocabulary** and **Skills** activities, and **Test yourself** with instant feedback. Students can also access all the Workbook audio on the Online Practice.

Workbook audio

Full Workbook audio is available on the Online Practice.

projectexploreonline.com

Tx   Project Explore

For teachers

Teacher's Guide

Prepare lessons with full teaching notes for each unit and get ideas on how to adapt and extend the Student's Book material, access photocopiable activities, and deal with potential problems.

DVD-ROM

All the videos and songs, plus photocopiable activities to help you exploit the songs and videos.

ACTIVITIES   TESTS   TRACKING   RESOURCES

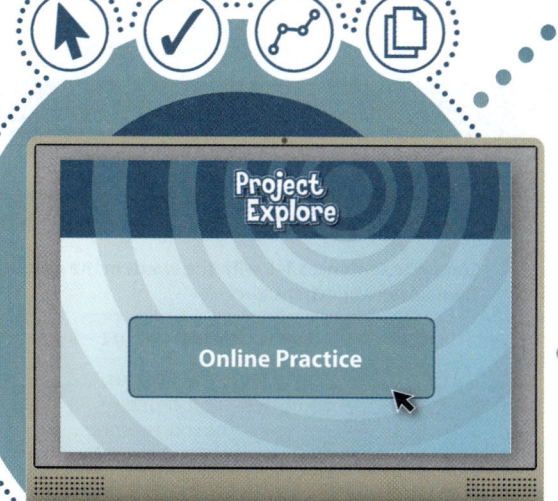

Teacher's Resource Centre

All your *Project Explore* resources, stored in one place to save you time. Resources include:

Student's Book and Workbook audio, videos, scripts, photocopiable activities, tests, wordlists and more.

Use the Learning Management System to track your students' progress.

Classroom Presentation Tool

Use in class to deliver heads-up lessons and to engage students. Class audio, video and answer keys are available online or offline, and updated across your devices.

Class Audio

Full course audio is available on the Teacher's Resource Centre, and on audio CDs.

To log in for the first time, teachers use the Access Card in the front of the Teacher's Guide for the Teacher's Resource Centre, and students use the Access Card in the front of the Workbook for Online Practice.

Project Explore Classroom Presentation Tool

Deliver heads-up lessons

Engage students in your blended learning classroom with easy-to-use digital features. Download to your tablet or computer, connect to an interactive whiteboard, projector or screen, and teach lessons that run smoothly – every time.

Play audio and video at the touch of a button, launching activities straight from the page. Answer keys reveal answers one-by-one or all at once to suit your teaching style. Capture your students' attention with the Focus tool – activities fill the screen so that everyone can participate, even in large classes.

Take your classroom presentation tool with you and plan lessons online or offline, across your devices. Save your weblinks and make notes directly on the page – all with one account.

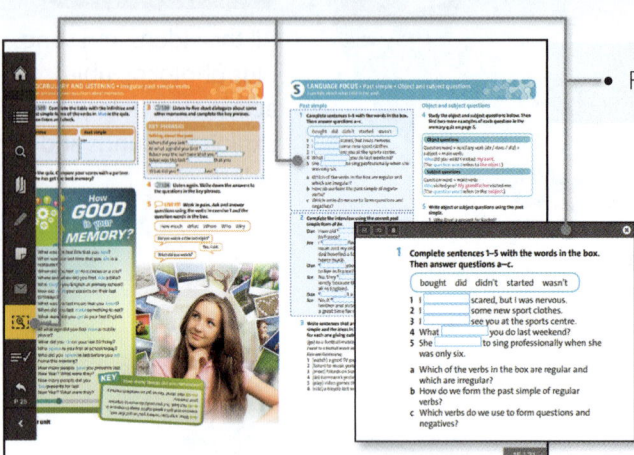

- Focus your students' attention on a single activity.

- Play audio and video at the touch of a button.
- Speed up or slow down the audio to tailor lessons to your students' listening level.

- Save time in class and mark answers all at once.
- Reveal answers after discussing the activity with students.
- Try the activity again to consolidate learning.

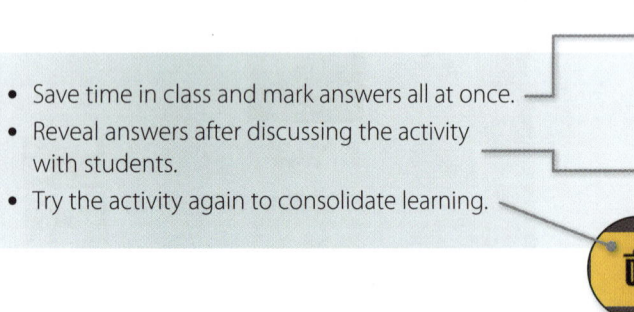

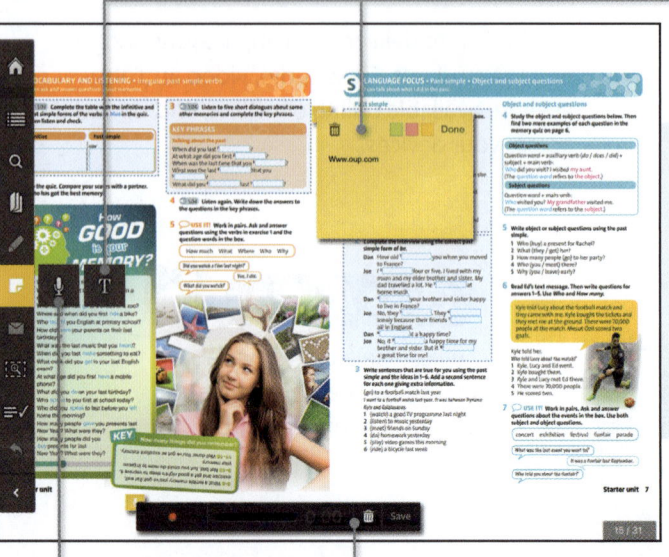

- Save your weblinks and other notes for quick access while teaching.
- Save your notes, and access across devices using one account so that you can plan your lessons wherever you are.
- Work on pronunciation in class: record your students speaking and compare their voices to *Project Explore* audio.

Planner – *Project Explore* Level 4

Introduction

Curriculum	Outcomes	Topics, Culture overlap with other subjects, competencies
Vocabulary • phrasal verbs for relationships • genres **Grammar** • present tense review • pronouns and possessives **Text types** • dialogue • webpage • email • photo story **Communication** • discussing options for keeping in touch with friends • discussing ideas on how to make new students welcome • describing a film or a book	**Receptive skills** • understand the main points and ideas from reading or listening to a dialogue • find information in reading and listening texts and use it to answer questions • read and listen to decide whether statements about what you have heard are true or false • read and understand short texts **Productive skills** • complete sentences with missing words • write a short paragraph on how to make a new student feel welcome • match words to their definitions • replace words with possessive pronouns **Interactive skills** • give your own and listen to others' opinions • share ideas and decide as a class • ask for and give opinions about films and characters	**Collaboration** • work with a partner to write some notes on a character from a book, film or TV series **Critical thinking** • analyse input to determine grammar rules **Creativity** • role-play discussing how to make a new student feel welcome

Planner – *Project Explore* Level 4

Unit 1

Curriculum	Outcomes	Topics, Culture overlap with other subjects, competencies
Vocabulary • relationship adjectives • relationship expressions • origins **Grammar** • present perfect • *How long* • *for, since, ever, never, just* • past simple and past continuous • conjunctions **Pronunciation** • silent or pronounced 'e' **Text types** • forum posts • article • online article • podcast • fact file • dialogue • photo story **Communication** • discussing what makes a good classmate • exchanging opinions on how many friends one needs • telling short stories • discussing why people move to or leave a town • talking about your family and your ancestors • discussing where to find information • expressing opinions	**Receptive skills** • read information in a text and give an opinion • listen to check predicted answers • understand the main points and ideas from reading or listening to texts • seek detailed information from reading or listening texts **Productive skills** • complete sentences with missing words • listen to conversations and complete the table with the missing information • write some *How long* questions • choose the correct alternatives to complete sentences • listen to and repeat words and phrases using the correct pronunciation and intonation • complete the table with the correct conjunction • join the sentence halves with conjunctions • put sentences in the correct order to write a paragraph • write some biographies **Interactive skills** • give your own and listen to others' opinions • discuss what adjectives you would use to describe yourselves • talk about activities and say how long you have done them • discuss what you know about DNA • ask for and give opinions about when and how to use online material for your schoolwork	**Collaboration** • discuss positive and negative personal qualities • write short dialogues with a partner • practise dialogues with a partner **Critical thinking** • analyse input to determine grammar rules • evaluate using online material from different sources • compare two different experiments **Creativity** • tell a short story • project – write about your social circle **Civic studies/critical thinking** • Charles Darwin – analyse the impact of modern life on the human body **Social studies** • six degrees of separation – understanding how people are connected **Learning to learn** • formal and informal English

Planner – *Project Explore* Level 4

Unit 2

Curriculum	Outcomes	Topics, Culture overlap with other subjects, competencies
Vocabulary • day trip attractions • volunteering verbs • adjectives to describe places **Grammar** • *will* and *going to* • present tenses for future arrangements • first conditional **Pronunciation** • linking **Text types** • reviews • text messages • website • blogs • dialogue • advertisement • email • photo story • cartoon story **Communication** • talking about day trips • exchanging opinions about volunteering • describing photos • talking about the type of holiday you prefer • discussing how couples celebrate getting married • expressing preferences	**Receptive skills** • understand the main points and ideas from reading or listening to texts • seek detailed information from reading or listening texts • listen to check predicted answers • read and understand exchanges of text messages • listen to information and use it to answer questions • understand quiz questions and give the correct answers **Productive skills** • listen to and repeat words and phrases using the correct pronunciation and intonation • complete sentences with missing words • write a short description on one of the community activities • match adjectives to their definitions • write a blog entry for a holiday activity • make notes about your holiday preferences **Interactive skills** • ask for and give opinions about day trip attractions • present your community activity to the class • ask and answer questions about each other's community project • exchange opinions about dangerous activities	**Collaboration** • plan a day trip to a place in your country with a partner • do some research with a partner on community activities that young people can do in your town • role-play a discussion about community projects • create a poster with a partner • practise dialogues with a partner **Critical thinking** • analyse input to determine grammar rules • evaluate the usefulness of different community activities • analyse and evaluate others' blog entries to understand what makes a good description **Creativity** • plan a day trip to your town • create a poster for a famous tourist site • write a blog about a holiday • project – make a presentation of your town **Civic studies/critical thinking** • New York – evaluate a list of activities **Art** • styles and periods **Learning to learn** • taking risks

Planner – *Project Explore* Level 4

Unit 3

Curriculum	Outcomes	Topics, Culture overlap with other subjects, competencies
Vocabulary • practical science nouns • phrasal verbs: socializing • the scientific method **Grammar** • modals: advice, obligation and necessity • permission: *can*, *could*, *be allowed to* • possibility: *can*, *could*, *may*, *might* **Pronunciation** • sentence stress **Text types** • article • lab report • website • dialogues • monologue • podcast • questionnaire • newspaper report • photo story **Communication** • exchanging opinions about experiments • interviewing people • discussing how to raise awareness of issues that affect you • expressing advantages and disadvantages	**Receptive skills** • understand the main points and ideas from reading or listening to a text • find information in reading and listening texts and use it to answer questions • listen to check predicted answers • understand information in an article • read and understand a personality questionnaire • read and listen to decide whether statements about what you have heard are true or false **Productive skills** • match words to their definitions • listen to and repeat words and phrases using the correct pronunciation and intonation • write a lab report • complete sentences with missing words • make notes in favour of and against various topics • ask your partner questions in order to find the missing information • listen to a podcast and complete the table with the missing information • complete sentences with the correct modal verb • write a report **Interactive skills** • talk about your experiment • discuss various topics and agree or disagree with your partner • talk about a typical weekend	**Collaboration** • discuss various topics with a partner • practise phrasal verbs with a partner • interview an older person • draw and compare conclusions from an experiment • do a class survey on social media usage and write up findings **Critical thinking** • analyse input to determine grammar rules • compare arguments for and against • analyse data from experience and draw conclusions • write up a report on a survey about social media usage • analyse and evaluate others' articles and choose some interesting facts **Creativity** • think of arguments for and against topics • project – write an article about an important issue **Civic studies/critical thinking** • Australia under attack – identify elements of the natural world in own culture **Science** • water – the essential ingredient to life and the Great Pacific Garbage Patch **Learning to learn** • brainstorming

Planner – *Project Explore* Level 4

Unit 4

Curriculum	Outcomes	Topics, Culture overlap with other subjects, competencies
Vocabulary • buildings • train travel • phrasal verbs for travel **Grammar** • second conditional • comparatives and superlatives • too / enough • adverbs of frequency, manner, place and time **Pronunciation** • /aɪ/ /i/ /j/ **Text types** • advertisement • webpage • leaflet • article • dialogues • photo story **Communication** • discussing which famous buildings and monuments you know • describing famous places • talking about travelling by train • describing a building or a monument • exchanging opinions on why people like to travel • talking about time and space travel • expressing belief and doubt	**Receptive skills** • understand simple information from a short passage • listen to and understand a dialogue • find information in reading and listening texts and use it to answer questions • understand the main points and ideas from reading or listening to a text • seek detailed information from reading or listening texts • listen to check predicted answers • understand information in an article **Productive skills** • listen to and repeat words and phrases using the correct pronunciation and intonation • complete sentences with missing words • make notes about a monument, a building or a natural wonder • match words to their definitions • write a short journal entry about the last two places that you visited • write a leaflet for tourists visiting your capital city • make predictions about a story • make mind maps about possible forms of transport in the future **Interactive skills** • present your list of seven wonders • talk about a trip you would most like to go on • talk about various forms of transport	**Collaboration** • make a list of seven local wonders with a partner • work in a group to agree on one place to visit • interview someone about their interrail trip • compare symbols for your country **Critical thinking** • analyse input to determine grammar rules • identify and select the most interesting places to visit • analyse and evaluate others' leaflets and decide which is the most interesting **Creativity** • think about what you would do in various situations • write a journal comparing two different places • create a leaflet about your capital city • take part in role-play activities • make a mind map • project – plan an interrail trip **Civic studies** • Cultural symbols of Britain – evaluate cultural symbols of own culture **History** • the invention of travel **Learning to learn** • English in the real world

Planner – *Project Explore* Level 4

Unit 5

Curriculum	Outcomes	Topics, Culture overlap with other subjects, competencies
Vocabulary • verbs and dependent prepositions • compound nouns • modern life nouns **Grammar** • the passive • defining and non-defining relative clauses • countable and uncountable nouns and determiners **Pronunciation** • word stress **Text types** • museum guide • forum • dialogues • article • webpage **Communication** • talking about personal objects • talking about globalization • discussing differences between the lives of teenagers now and a hundred years ago • discussing what adults think of young people • agreeing and disagreeing	**Receptive skills** • listen to information and use it to answer questions • listen to check predicted answers • find information in reading texts and use it to answer questions • understand the main points and ideas from reading or listening to a text • read and understand a questionnaire • read a text and complete a mind map • listen to a text and decide whether statements about what you have heard are true or false **Productive skills** • match the prepositions to the verbs • complete sentences with missing words • rewrite sentences using the passive • write a report on globalization • listen to and repeat words and phrases using the correct pronunciation and intonation • prepare a short lecture • write some stereotypes about teenagers **Interactive skills** • talk about inventions • talk about common objects • talk about important aspects of modern life • talk about stereotypes	**Collaboration** • agree on three interesting / surprising objects in a group • play a guessing game with a partner • complete a quiz and compare with a partner • prepare a short talk on an aspect of modern life • discuss stereotypes with a partner and in a group **Critical thinking** • analyse input to determine grammar rules • analyse and evaluate others' reports and decide whether the class is local or global • evaluate and agree on the three worst stereotypes • organize notes into paragraphs before writing a report **Creativity** • write a report on whether you are local or global • make some notes with a partner about an important aspect of modern life • project – write a report about celebrations **Civic studies/critical thinking** • Irish heritage – identify an important aspect of own heritage **Literature** • literary techniques – simile, metaphor and hyperbole **Learning to learn** • expanding ideas

Planner – Project Explore Level 4

Unit 6

Curriculum	Outcomes	Topics, Culture overlap with other subjects, competencies
Vocabulary • digital media • shopping nouns • fashion adjectives **Grammar** • reported speech • reported commands and requests • subject and object questions **Pronunciation** • /ʌ/ /uː/ **Text types** • articles • online forum • dialogues • quiz show **Communication** • talking about the trustworthiness of information that you can find on the internet • talking about shopping • discussing why people follow fashion • describing a piece of clothing that you really like wearing • giving advice • giving instructions	**Receptive skills** • find information in reading texts and use it to answer questions • understand the main points and ideas from reading or listening to a text • listen to information and use it to answer questions • read information in a text and give an opinion • seek detailed information from reading or listening texts • listen and complete missing information **Productive skills** • match words to their definitions • listen to and repeat words and phrases using the correct pronunciation and intonation • complete sentences with missing words • write a review of the apps or websites your partner uses • complete the reported commands and requests **Interactive skills** • ask and answer questions about a website or a vlog you visit frequently • interview your partner about their use of smartphone apps and websites • describe your favourite possession • present your sales campaign to the class • talk about life hacks	**Collaboration** • interview your partner on apps and websites • compare ideas on a sales campaign and create a new campaign together • play a guessing game with a partner • think of a life hack with a partner **Critical thinking** • analyse input to determine grammar rules • evaluate others' sales campaigns to choose the best • evaluate comments on image and give reasons **Creativity** • create a sales campaign • describe a piece of clothing • project – create an online video • write a review of a video **Civic studies/critical thinking** • small nations, sporting giants – comparison with own culture **Science** • health education – be active **Learning to learn** • flashcards

Introduction

A Keeping in touch

 How easy is it for young people to keep in touch with friends in other towns or countries? What should a new person to your town do to make new friends?

1 a 🔊 **1.02** ▶ Read and listen. What is the relationship between Liza and Emil?

1

Danny	Hi Liza.
Liza	Oh…hi Danny.
Danny	Who are you texting?
Liza	Oh, just Emil.
Danny	Emil? That Danish guy you met in Paris last summer?
Liza	Yep.
Danny	You still keep in touch?
Liza	Oh yeah! We get on very well. We're into all the same things.
Danny	Sounds like you really hit it off.
Liza	We did. He's a really nice guy.
Liza	This is him now!
Danny	OK, see you later.
Liza	No, talk to him. I'm sure you'll get on!

2

Emil	Hi Liza! I see you're with a friend!
Liza	This is Danny.
Danny	Hello.
Emil	Ah, Danny! Liza has told me a lot about you!
Danny	Really?
Liza	Er, yeah, er…I told him about…how much you like playing video games. What are you playing now, Emil?
Emil	Oh, I'm not playing anything exciting. Just *Mission Accepted* for the fiftieth time!
Danny	*Mission Accepted*?! I love that game! I often play it at the weekends if I don't hang out with my friends.
Emil	Me too! Do you like playing online?
Danny	Yeah!
Emil	Let's arrange something!
Liza	Emil, let's catch up later… about that thing.
Emil	Thanks, Liza. See you, guys!
Danny	What's 'that thing'?
Liza	Nothing…

3

Danny	Hello?
Liza	Hi Danny. Erm, are you playing with Emil?
Danny	Yeah…
Liza	Let me guess, *Mission Accepted*. I wondered why I couldn't get through.
Danny	Yeah.
Liza	Can you ask him to call me?
Danny	Yeah.
Liza	Promise?
Danny	Yeah…yes, I will. We never play after eight, so he'll ring you then.
Liza	OK. Bye, Danny!
Danny	Bye!

Introduction

Unit objectives
- use phrasal verbs to talk about relationships
- review the present tense
- discuss ways to welcome a new student
- identify film and book genres
- use pronouns and possessives
- write about book, film or TV characters

Language
Grammar: present tense; pronouns and possessives
Vocabulary: phrasal verbs: relationships; genres

A Keeping in touch

Supplementary materials
Photocopiable worksheets: Grammar and Vocabulary, Communication
Online Practice

Note
The story can be used in class as a reading and listening task, a video task or both.

You First

Sts write some notes to answer the questions.

Then, in pairs, ask Sts to discuss the second question. Get feedback and write their suggestions on the board. Ask Sts to rank the three best suggestions. Discuss their reasons.

EXTRA IDEA To get Sts thinking about how to keep in touch with people, ask them to list all the different ways you can keep in touch, both now (texting, voice clips, etc.) and also those from the past (letter writing, telegrams, pigeon courier). Give Sts a time limit to come up with the strangest ways people keep / kept in touch. Then, ask them to tick the ways they use the most. Compare as a class.

1a 1·02

- Dialogue 1: Ask Sts to look at the photo. Ask *Who do you see?* (*Liza and Danny*), *Where are they?* (*At school*), *What are they doing?* (*Danny is watching Liza texting on her phone.*), *How do they feel?* (*Liza looks happy, Danny looks a bit cross.*)
- Dialogue 2: Ask *Who are the people?* (*Liza's friend Emil, Liza and Danny*), *Where are they?* (*Emil is probably at home, Danny and Liza are at school.*), *How does each person feel?* (*They all look happy.*)
- Dialogue 3: Ask *Where is Danny?* (*At home*), *What is he doing?* (*Playing a video game and talking on his phone*), *What about Liza?* (*She's at home / in her bedroom, talking on her phone*) *Where is Emil?* (*Sts will find this out in the text. He's at home, playing an online video game with Danny.*)
- Tell Sts these characters will appear throughout the book.
- Play the audio for Sts to listen, follow and answer the question. Alternatively, show the class the video of the story from the DVD-ROM.

Liza and Emil are friends.

Note
To further exploit the video in class, you could use some or all of the suggested activities from page Tviii.

Project Explore T4

b
- Sts read and listen to answer the question.

Liza and Danny are friends.

c
- Give Sts time to complete the exercise.
- In pairs, Sts compare answers and correct any mistakes.

1 T
2 F (Liza told Emil a lot about Danny, including how much he likes playing video games.)
3 T
4 DK
5 DK

EXTRA SUPPORT Ask Sts to explain their answers with examples from the dialogues.

EXTRA IDEA In groups, ask Sts to write three sentences about the dialogue: one true, one false and one they are not sure about. They then read their sentences to another group. The other group decides if the sentences are true, false or they don't know.

d
- Sts find examples of the expressions in the dialogues.
- Sts translate the expressions into their own language. Give them time to complete the task.
- Sts compare answers in pairs to make sure they agree.

a guy = a boy or man (informal)
Let me guess. = Here, Liza is joking – she's quite sure the boys were playing *Mission Accepted*. (informal)
we're into = we're interested in (informal)
I couldn't get through. = His phone was busy, so I couldn't talk to him.

EXTRA CHALLENGE In pairs, Sts write a short two-line dialogue using each expression. Then, pairs act out their dialogues for the class.

Vocabulary Phrasal verbs for relationships

2a
- Write on the board: 'Do you agree with the advice?' 'Why? / Why not?'
- Give Sts time to read the text to answer the question.
- Get feedback from the class.

EXTRA SUPPORT Encourage Sts to ignore the gaps and focus on the questions on the board. This will develop their skimming skills in reading.

When they have completed the exercise, remind Sts they didn't need the words in the gaps to answer the questions.

b
- Give Sts time to complete the exercise individually, then compare answers in pairs and discuss any differences.

Note
Prepositions can be challenging, so encourage Sts to discuss when they disagree. This will give them a stronger reason to listen for the answers in the next exercise.

c 🔊 1·03
- Play the audio for Sts to listen and check their answers.

1 in 2 up 3 off 4 out 5 up 6 into 7 on

Grammar Present tense review

3a
- Give Sts time to complete the exercise.

EXTRA SUPPORT Get Sts to write the answers in their notebooks. Tell them to draw two columns, headed **Present simple** and **Present continuous**, and write the sentences in the correct column. Tell them to underline the verbs.

1 **Present simple:** I see you're with a friend., I love that game., I often play it at the weekends if I don't hang out with my friends., Do you like playing online?, We never play after eight.
  Present continuous: Who are you texting?, I'm not playing anything exciting.
2 I often play it at the weekends if I don't hang out with my friends., We never play after eight.
3 Who are you texting? I'm not playing anything exciting.
4 We often play it at the weekends., We never play after eight.
5 *see*, *love*, and *like*

EXTRA SUPPORT Write on the board: 'We use adverbs of frequency when we talk about…' (*habits*) Ask Sts to complete the sentence. Elicit the rules for adverbs of frequency, e.g. before the verb or after *be*. Elicit more examples of stative verbs, e.g. *know*, *think*, *want*, *prefer*, *hate*, *understand*, *hear*, *taste*, *smell*, *feel*.

LANGUAGE NOTE Stative verbs are often connected with thinking / opinions and feelings / emotions.

b
- Give Sts time to complete the exercise. Check answers.

1 'm writing 2 have 3 'm waiting 4 are (you) enjoying
5 text 6 get

Speaking

4a
- Give Sts time to discuss the question with a partner.

b
- Put Sts in groups to make a list of the best ideas.

EXTRA IDEA Sts write their six ideas in order of importance (1–6, with 1 being the most important). Encourage Sts to discuss and agree with each other.

c
- Groups explain their ideas to the class.
- Decide as a class on the best ideas. Get Sts to argue why their idea is the best.

EXTRA SUPPORT Write one or two of their ideas on the board and get Sts to explain what's good about them. Write their reasons on the board. Sts can use your notes to help them write the paragraph in the next activity.

Extra
Sts can either do this in class or as a homework task.

Project Explore

b What is the relationship between Liza and Danny?

c Decide if the sentences are true (T), false (F) or don't know (DT).
1 Liza and Emil have similar interests.
2 Emil hasn't heard anything about Danny.
3 Emil and Danny like doing the same things.
4 Liza and Danny have started playing online during the week.
5 Danny wants to go out with Liza.

d Spoken English What do these expressions mean? How do you say them in your own language?

Vocabulary Phrasal verbs for relationships

2 a Read the advice about what a student at a new school should do. Do you agree with it? Why? / Why not?

New friends

You should keep ¹___ touch with your old friends and catch ²___ with what they're doing, but you should also get to know your new classmates.

You might not hit it ³___ with people immediately. Be patient and hang ⁴___ with your new classmates and put ⁵___ with conversations about people and things that you don't know anything about. You soon will!

If you fall out with someone, try and make up with them soon. Of course, it depends on the problem, but most arguments are about unimportant things and it's better to try to find out what people are ⁶___ and get ⁷___ well with everybody.

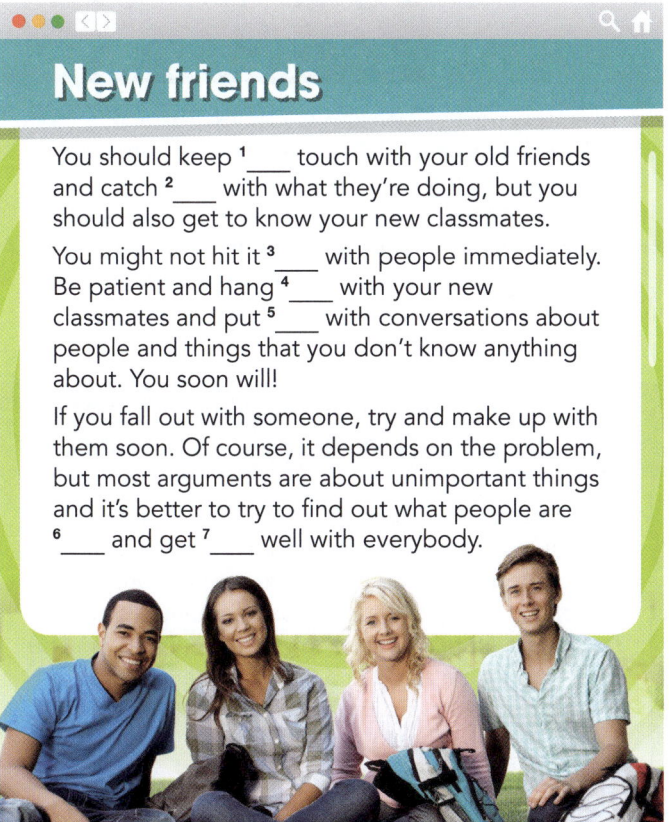

b Complete the phrasal verbs with the prepositions. Use the dialogue in exercise 1a to help you.

in off on out up (x2) into

c 🔊 **1.03** Listen and check.

Grammar Present tense review

3 a Read the underlined sentences in exercise 1a and answer the questions.
1 Which sentences are in the present simple and which are in the present continuous? Find examples of the affirmative, negative and question forms for each tense.
2 Which sentences talk about habits?
3 Which sentences talk about activities that are happening now?
4 Can you find adverbs of frequency in the sentences?
5 Which verbs do we always use in the present simple and never in the present continuous?

b Complete the email with the correct form of the verbs in the box.

enjoy get have text wait write

Hi Tom, how are you? I ¹___ to you during my first week at my new school! To be honest, I was nervous the first day, but my new classmates are great. I ²___ lunch with them every day and they tell me everything about the school. Actually, at this moment I ³___ for my new classmates outside the cinema because we're going to see a film together. Anyway, ⁴___ you ___ the first week back after the summer holidays? I often ⁵___ Emer and Jake and they said we should meet up next Saturday. We ⁶___ lots of homework every day but I'll do it on Friday so I can see you. See you then! Jasmine

Speaking

4 a Work with a partner. Discuss the question: what can you do to make a new student welcome?

b Work in a group. Make a list of the six best ideas.

> I think we should introduce new students to our friends.

> Good idea. We should also show them around the school.

c Explain your group's six ideas to the class. Decide on the best from the whole class.

 Write a short paragraph about the best ideas.

Introduction **5**

B Stories

What is the best story that you have read or seen at the cinema or at home during the summer? What did you like about it?

Vocabulary and Reading Genres

1 animation, comedy

2 _____   3 _____   4 _____   5 _____   6 _____

1 a Match the films to the genres. Some films match more than one genre.

action and adventure   animation   comedy   crime drama   musical   sci-fi

MY FAVOURITE CHARACTER

KATNISS EVERDEEN

My favourite character of all time is Katniss Everdeen from the series of fantasy novels The Hunger Games. The action takes place in the country of Panem. Its capital is wealthy but there are also 12 poor districts and every year they have to send a group of their children to participate in a televised fight to the death: the winner is the last child alive. You could say that The Hunger Games are also horror stories because they are really frightening at times. One of the children is 16-year-old Katniss. She is poor but she is a survivor and ready to fight for what is hers. However, things become difficult for Katniss when her friendships with a boy, Peeta, from District 12 and a girl from District 11, Rue, become strong. The book plays with your feelings because you want Katniss to win but at the same time you don't want her to kill her friends! In the end, Katniss is a real hero and she leads them all to victory.

CHRISTOPHER

A character that I really like is Christopher from the novel The Curious Incident of the Dog in the Night-time. The novel is a mystery and a drama but it's also like a detective story because 15-year-old Christopher investigates the death of a dog and why it happened. The action takes place in Christopher's home and school and on a train journey. Christopher lives in a world that is different to ours. He is excellent at maths but he has problems with relationships. His dad tells him that his mum died two years ago but when he discovers it isn't true, he tries to find her. He goes on a journey to London that becomes a dangerous adventure because of his problems. I admire Christopher because he is determined to find answers to the mysteries that he finds around him and although he has problems, in the end he helps his parents with theirs.

RON WEASLEY

Ron Weasley from the Harry Potter stories is a favourite character of mine. The stories take place at a special school, Hogwarts, and its students all have unusual powers. The Harry Potter stories are examples of fantasy literature and although each story is a separate mystery they are also all connected. The hero of the stories, Harry, and the very intelligent Hermione always solve them, but they need Ron's help to do it. I think that I like Ron because of his loyalty to Harry and Hermione, his bravery and his sense of humour. These are qualities that we would like all our friends to have. Ron sometimes feels jealous about Harry's skills but he is a true friend to Harry and even when they fall out, he isn't angry for very long and they soon make up.

6 Introduction

B Stories

You First
Give Sts some time to think about the question. Then, Sts talk to a partner about their stories. Get some feedback.

EXTRA IDEA Brainstorm: In one minute, ask Sts to list different film and book genres. Then give them one minute to list words to discuss films or books, e.g. *plot*, *characters*, *special effects*, *style*, *exciting*, *realistic*.

EXTRA IDEA To lead into exercise 1a, ask Sts to look at the film posters. In pairs, Sts talk about which films they have seen and what they thought about these films. If they haven't seen these films, ask them to talk about which one(s) they would like to see, and why.

Vocabulary and Reading Genres

1a
- Give Sts time to complete the task.
- Get Sts to compare with a partner, then check answers.
- Encourage Sts to explain their choices.

> 1 *Toy Story* – animation, comedy
> 2 *Rogue One: A Star Wars Story* – sci-fi, action and adventure
> 3 *Bean* – comedy
> 4 *Murder on the Orient Express* – crime drama
> 5 *The Adventures of Robin Hood* – action and adventure
> 6 *La La Land* – musical

EXTRA IDEA Ask Sts what their favourite film is, and why. Elicit the genre of their favourite film.

B

b
- Give Sts time to complete the exercise.

1 mystery   2 drama   3 horror   4 fantasy   5 detective story

EXTRA SUPPORT Before doing exercise 1b, ask Sts if they know the characters in the photos.

c
- Give Sts time to complete the exercise.

d
- Give Sts time to complete the exercise.

EXTRA IDEA Give each student a genre. You can repeat genres. Sts think of the best story / film for their genre.

Write Sts' choices for one genre on the board. Have a class discussion, then vote on the best story / film in that genre. Do this for each genre.

2a
- Put Sts into three groups, **A**, **B** and **C**. Each group reads the same text, e.g. group **A** reads about Katniss Everdeen.
- Give Sts time to read and answer the question.

Possible answers
Katniss: She's a survivor and ready to fight for what's hers.
Christopher: He's determined to find answers to mysteries around him.
Ron: He's loyal, brave and funny.

EXTRA SUPPORT Read the texts and decide if you need to pre-teach any new vocabulary before Sts do exercise 2a.

EXTRA SUPPORT Before reading the text, ask Sts if they know the characters in the photos. Ask *Why do you think…is their favourite character?* Ask Sts to read the texts quickly to check if their predictions are correct. Remind Sts that they do not have to understand every word.

b
- Put Sts into new groups of three. Each group should have one student from groups **A**, **B** and **C**.

EXTRA SUPPORT Sts can discuss the answers to the questions in their groups from exercise 2a before joining their new group.

- In their new groups, Sts take turns asking and answering the questions.

Katniss Everdeen: 1 *The Hunger Games*   **2** fantasy, action and adventure   **3** Peeta and Rue   **4** Panem   **5** She participates in a televised fight to death.   **6** because she's a hero and leads them to victory
Christopher: 1 *The Curious Incident of the Dog in the Night-time*   **2** mystery, drama, detective story   **3** his dad and mum   **4** at home and on a train   **5** He goes on a journey to London to find his mum.   **6** because he's determined to find answers to mysteries
Ron Weasley: 1 Harry Potter stories   **2** fantasy   **3** Hermione and Harry   **4** Hogwarts school   **5** He helps solve mysteries   **6** because of his loyalty, bravery and sense of humour

EXTRA CHALLENGE Sts think of one or two extra questions to ask about each text.

c
- Write the questions on the board.
- Give groups time to discuss.

EXTRA CHALLENGE Ask Sts if they have read a book and seen a film for the same story. Write on the board: 'Which is better, the book or film of a story? Why?', 'How are they different?'

EXTRA IDEA Ask Sts to each tell the class a sentence about one of the characters. The class guess the character.

EXTRA IDEA Ask Sts to write two sentences about one of the characters. One of the sentences should be false. Sts say one of their sentences for the class to guess if it's true or false.

Grammar   Pronouns and possessives

3a
- Give Sts time to complete the exercise.

A Subject   **B** Object   **C** adjectives   **D** Possessive

b
- Give Sts time to complete the exercise.

1 it   2 her   3 them   4 my   5 his   6 yours   7 ours

c
- Give Sts time to complete the exercise.

1 my   2 theirs   3 her   4 ours   5 our   6 they

EXTRA SUPPORT Sts compare their answers with a partner. Discuss any differences.

d
- Give Sts time to complete the exercise.

2 Is it hers?   3 Yours is on the table.   4 They're theirs.
5 It's his.   6 No, mine is really old!   7 Yes, they're ours.

EXTRA CHALLENGE Put Sts into pairs. Allocate each pair a sentence (1–6). Each pair writes a further two lines to continue their dialogue.
Example:
A Is that Sam's book?
B No, it's mine.
A Oh, can I borrow it?
B Yeah, sure.

Note
Providing a context for possessive pronouns will help Sts remember them better.

Writing

4a
- Give Sts time to discuss and write their notes.

EXTRA CHALLENGE In their pairs, Sts work alone to write their own notes on the same character. They then compare their notes with their partner, and decide which notes they are going to include in their paragraph.

b
- Give Sts time to write their paragraph.

EXTRA CHALLENGE Display Sts' paragraphs around the classroom. The class reads the paragraphs and decides who they agree with.

Extra
Sts do the activity in pairs in class.

T7   Project Explore

b Match the definitions to the highlighted words in the text.

A film, book or play…
1 often about an activity that is not legal or a murder, with a surprise ending that explains all the events
2 with an exciting story and a lot of action
3 about frightening things such as dead people coming alive again
4 about an imaginary world
5 about the search for information and clues to solve a crime

c Make a list of examples for each type of film in exercises 1a and 1b.
Animation – Cars

d Work with a partner. Compare your lists. Do you agree with the examples?

2 **a** Work in groups of three and read about your character. What is special about them?
Group A Read about Katniss Everdeen.
Group B Read about Christopher.
Group C Read about Ron Weasley.

b Work in new groups of three with students from groups A, B and C. Ask and answer questions about your article.
1 Which novel or series does the character appear in?
2 What kind of story is it?
3 Who are the other characters in the story?
4 Where does the story take place?
5 What does the character do?
6 Why does the writer like the character?

c Work in groups of three. Answer the questions.
• Which story do you think is, or sounds, the most interesting or boring? Why?
• Which is best, the book or film of a story? Why?

Grammar Pronouns and possessives

3 **a** Complete A–D with the words in the box.

adjectives   Object   Possessive   Subject

A ___ pronouns	B ___ pronouns	Possessive C ___	D ___ pronouns
I	me	4 ___	mine
you	you	your	6 ___
he	him	5 ___	his
she	2 ___	her	hers
1 ___	it	its	its
we	us	our	7 ___
they	3 ___	their	theirs

b Complete 1–7 in the table.

c Complete the text with pronouns and possessive adjectives.
I'm always arguing with ¹___ best friends about books and films and my ideas are very different to ²___ . I love Jane Austen's stories and I think we can learn a lot from ³___ characters. I know that 200 years ago they lived a very different life to ⁴___ , but ⁵___ relationship problems today are not so different. Strangely, although my friends don't read Jane Austen's books, ⁶___ all love the film versions of her novels!

d Replace the underlined words with a possessive pronoun.
1 Is that Sam's book? No, it's <u>my book</u>.
   No, it's mine.
2 Whose rucksack is this? Is it <u>Hannah's rucksack</u>?
3 Where's my mobile? <u>Your mobile</u> is on the table.
4 Whose tickets are these? They're <u>Alex and Mia's tickets</u>.
5 Whose jacket is this? It's <u>Harry's jacket</u>.
6 Is that your laptop? No, <u>my laptop</u> is really old!
7 Tom and Zac, are these your pens?
   Yes, they're <u>our pens</u>.

Writing

4 **a** Work with a partner. Write some notes on a character from a book, film or TV series that you like.
• What's the name of the book, film or TV series?
• What type of book, film or TV series is it?
• Where does the action take place?
• Who is the character?
• What does he / she do?
• What is he / she like?
• Why do you like him / her?

b Write a paragraph about the character with the information from your notes.

EXTRA Describe a film or book. Guess the film or book that your partner describes.
Describe…
• the type of film or book it is
• the characters
• what happens

> This film is an animation and the two most important characters are a cowboy and an astronaut.

Introduction 7

1 Social circles

1A Classmates

YOU FIRST! What makes a good classmate? Work with a partner and make a list of as many qualities as you can.

Reading and Vocabulary
Relationship adjectives

1 Read the forum posts. Which posts do you agree with the most? Why?

2 a Complete the table with the highlighted adjectives.

Positive	Negative	Both

b 🔊 1.04 Listen and check, then repeat.

3 **Over to you!** Discuss with a partner. Which three adjectives would you like people to use about you? Which three wouldn't you like them to use? Why?

> I would like people to say that I'm loyal. I think it's important to help your friends when they need you. I would also like…

▶ **Workbook** page 2, exercises 1–2

WHAT MAKES A G👍👎D CLASSMATE?

SkaterJack 12th September 3.55 p.m.
A good classmate…
doesn't get jealous if I do well in an exam.

CharlieBoy 12th September 5.23 p.m.
is sensitive to people's feelings and doesn't make cruel jokes.

HarryK 12th September 4.05 p.m.
isn't selfish and shares their ideas when we do group projects.

DaisyS 12th September 5.32 p.m.
is sensible most of the time, but knows how to have fun!

QueenChloe 12th September 4.13 p.m.
is caring when someone has a problem.

Freya 12th September 5.49 p.m.
understands that some people are moody and can quickly change from happy to sad for no reason at all!

RubyStar 12th September 4.45 p.m.
is self-confident enough to believe in themselves and their abilities.

MrLogan 12th September 6.02 p.m.
is loyal to their friends and doesn't leave them to hang out with the cool guys.

Noah365 12th September 5.10 p.m.
knows the difference between being aggressive and being competitive.

MaxOut 12th September 6.27 p.m.
is honest and someone that I can trust.

Unit 1 · Social circles

1 Social circles

Unit objectives
- use words to describe relationships
- use words to describe the origins of people
- use the present perfect
- use the past simple and past continuous with *when* or *while*
- use conjunctions correctly
- express your opinions about a topic
- write a fact file about a famous person using conjunctions

Language
Grammar: present perfect; present perfect with *How long*, present perfect with *for*, *since*, *ever*, *never*, and *just*; past simple and past continuous; conjunctions
Vocabulary: relationship adjectives; relationship expressions; origins
Everyday English: expressing opinions
Project: My social circle
Culture: Charles Darwin
Learn through English: Six degrees of separation (Citizenship)

1A Classmates

Supplementary materials
Workbook: pages 2–3, exercises 1–8
Workbook: Grammar summary Unit 1
Photocopiable worksheets: Grammar and Vocabulary, Communication

You First
Give Sts one minute to write a list of what qualities make a good classmate. Then, write their adjectives on the board. Which are the most common? Do any appear in the texts?

EXTRA IDEA Ask Sts to rank the three most important qualities of a good classmate. Discuss their reasons.

Reading and Vocabulary Relationship adjectives

1
- Give Sts time to read the forum posts and decide on the posts they agree with.
- Get feedback.

2a
- Sts complete the task individually.
- Sts compare their answers and discuss any differences. Encourage them to give examples when they disagree, e.g. How is being competitive positive? How is it negative?

EXTRA CHALLENGE Ask Sts to choose an adjective from the **Positive** column and another from the **Negative** column, and write a sentence using each adjective.

EXTRA CHALLENGE Sts choose an adjective from the **Both** column and write two sentences using that adjective, one positive and the other negative.

b 🔊 1·04
- Play the audio for Sts to listen and check their answers.
- Play the audio again for Sts to repeat.

EXTRA SUPPORT Ask Sts to identify where the stress falls. Then get them to repeat the words, paying attention to the correct stress.

Positive: caring, self-confident, sensible, loyal, honest
Negative: jealous, selfish, aggressive, cruel, moody
Both: competitive, sensitive

EXTRA SUPPORT Get Sts to match the positive characteristics to their classmates. Write on the board 'I think ____ is ____ because…'

EXTRA CHALLENGE Ask Sts to think about the characteristics of members of their family and other people they know, and add one more characteristic to each column.

LANGUAGE NOTE Make sure Sts are clear that *sensible* refers to a person having good judgement while 'sensitive' refers to a person having delicate feelings.

3
- Give Sts time to think about the questions individually first, then discuss with a partner.
- Get feedback.

➡ **Workbook** page 2, exercises 1–2

1A

Reading and Grammar   Present perfect

4a 🔊 1·05
- Write the question on the board to help Sts focus.
- Play the audio for Sts to answer the question.

> He didn't enjoy sports like football, and he wanted to do something different.

EXTRA SUPPORT Sts compare their answers. Play the audio again to confirm.

b
- Ask Sts to find examples of the present perfect in the conversation and complete the rule.

> To form the present perfect, we use the verb **have** and the **past participle**.

EXTRA SUPPORT On the board, write examples of the present perfect from the dialogue. Ask Sts to point out, or come to the board and underline, *have* and the past participle.

5
- Sts look back at the conversation and answer the question.

> 3 We use *How long* to talk about time.

EXTRA CHALLENGE Write these questions on the board: 'How long have you lived here?' 'How long have you known me?' 'How long have you been interested in (e.g. music)?' Put Sts in pairs and give two questions to each pair. Sts take turns to ask and answer the questions as well as some follow-up questions.

6a
- Give Sts time to complete the task.
- In pairs, Sts compare their answers and try to correct any mistakes before you check answers with the class.

> 1 just   2 for   3 ever   4 never   5 since

EXTRA CHALLENGE In pairs, Sts think of a famous person and write sentences with *for*, *since*, *ever*, *never* and *just*. They then read their sentences to another pair who try to guess who the famous person is.

EXTRA IDEA Sts think of five *Have you ever…?* questions. They then ask other Sts their five questions. The aim is to find five different students who can answer *Yes, I have* to the questions.

b
- Give Sts time to complete the task.
- In pairs, Sts compare their answers and discuss any differences.

> 1 A   2 D   3 B   4 E   5 C

EXTRA SUPPORT Encourage Sts to use examples from the dialogue to support their answer.

7a
- Give Sts time to complete the task.
- Sts compare answers with a partner.

b 🔊 1·06
- Play the audio for Sts to listen and confirm their answers.

> 1 How long, for   2 ever, just   3 just   4 How long, since
> 5 ever, never   6 How long, since

- Play the audio again for Sts to listen and repeat.

EXTRA SUPPORT Divide the class in half. In chorus, one half repeats the questions, the other half repeats the answers.

EXTRA CHALLENGE Give each pair of Sts one of the dialogues and ask them to write two more lines. Then, they act it out for the class, e.g.:
A How long have you been in this class?
B I've been in this class for three weeks.
A Oh, do you like it?
B Yes, very much.

EXTRA CHALLENGE In pairs, Sts create two mini-dialogues for another pair of Sts to complete, e.g.:
A Have you ever…?
B Yes, I have.
A How long has…?
B …for three years.

➤ **Workbook** pages 2–3, exercises 3–6
➤ **Photocopiable** Grammar and Vocabulary

Listening and Speaking

8 🔊 1·07 Audio script pT86
- On the board, write the headings 'Activity', 'How long?' and 'Good about it?'.
- Ask Sts what activities they expect to hear. Write their ideas under **Activity**.
- Then ask them about **How long?** and **Good about it?**

> **Note**
> Predicting what they will hear will improve Sts' listening skills.

- Play the audio for Sts to listen and complete the task in their notebooks.
- Sts compare their answers with a partner.
- Play the audio again to check answers.

> **Jake:** basketball, two years, he's learnt about team work
> **Ruby:** chess, since she was a child, it really makes you think
> **Lucy:** gymnastics, since she started primary school, she's become more self-confident / she feels she can do well at other activities, too

EXTRA SUPPORT Read the script and decide if you need to teach any new lexis before Sts listen.

9a
- Give Sts time to add two more activities to the list and write their notes to answer the questions.

EXTRA IDEA Ask Sts to share their activities with the class. Write them on the board, and ask Sts which activities they think are the most and least popular.

b
- Put Sts in pairs to talk about their activities.
- Get Sts to complete the table for their partner's activities.

➤ **Workbook** page 3, exercises 7–8

Extra
Sts can either do this in class or as a homework task.

T9   Project Explore

1A

Reading and Grammar Present perfect

4 a 🔊 **1.05** Read and listen to the conversation. Why did Max decide to take up judo?

Amy   Hi Max, where have you been?
Max   I've just finished judo training. I'm a member of the martial arts club.
Amy   Wow, I'm impressed! How long have you been a member?
Max   I've been at the club for about three years. Have you ever tried martial arts?
Amy   No. Why did you join?
Max   I've never enjoyed sports like football, so I decided to try something different and I'm glad I did. It's a competitive sport, but everyone can take part. I've felt more self-confident since I started judo and I love it.
Amy   What are the other club members like?
Max   Very friendly. They've become my best mates.
Amy   You make it sound great. I think I'll have to come and see what it's like.
Max   Good idea! I'm sure you'll want to join when you've tried it!

b Read the conversation again and complete the rule.

> To form the present perfect, we use the verb ____ and the *past/present* participle. We use it to give information about recent events or about past events when the time is not specified.

Present perfect with *How long*

5 Look at the conversation. When do we use *How long*?

> To talk about: **1** cost   **2** distance   **3** time

Present perfect with *for, since, ever, never* and *just*

6 a Complete the sentences from the text with *for, since, ever, never* and *just*.
1 I've ____ finished judo training.
2 I've been at the club ____ about three years.
3 Have you ____ tried martial arts?
4 I've ____ enjoyed sports like football.
5 I've felt more self-confident ____ I started judo.

b When do we use *for, since, ever, never* and *just* with the present perfect? Complete the rules. Write A–E.
1 We use *for* ____ .
2 We use *since* ____ .
3 We use *ever* ____ .
4 We use *never* ____ .
5 We use *just* ____ .

> A to talk about how long something has happened
> B to ask if an event has happened at any time in the past
> C to say something took place a short time before now
> D to talk about when something started
> E to say an event hasn't happened at any time in the past

7 a Complete the dialogues.
1 A ____ have you been in this class?
   B I've been in this class ____ three weeks.
2 A Has Hannah ____ lived in another town?
   B Yes, her family has ____ moved here.
3 A Where have they been?
   B They've ____ had lunch in the canteen.
4 A ____ has Poppy had a dog?
   B She's had a dog ____ Christmas.
5 A Have you ____ run a marathon?
   B No, we've ____ run more than 5 km!
6 A ____ has Joe been in the chess club?
   B He's been in the club ____ September.

b 🔊 **1.06** Listen and check, then repeat.

▶ **Workbook** pages 2–3, exercises 3–6

Listening and Speaking

8 🔊 **1.07** Listen to three conversations and complete the information.

	Jake	Ruby	Lucy
What is the activity?			
How long have they done it?			
What is good about it?			

9 a Get ready to speak Look at the list. Add two more activities. Which things do you do? How long have you done them? What is good about these activities? Write some notes.

play a sport   play an instrument
do voluntary work   do art classes

b Work with a partner. Talk about the activities in exercise 9a that you do.

▶ **Workbook** page 3, exercises 7–8

Write some *How long* questions that you would like to ask a celebrity. Use the verbs in the box.

> be   have   know   live   want

Unit 1 · Social circles

1B Group instinct

 How many friends do we need?

Reading and Listening

1 Look at the photos. Describe what you can see. What are the similarities?

2 a 🔊 1.08 Read and listen to the article. Complete the infographic with the correct numbers.

  b According to Dunbar, what do we need to make real friendships? Do you agree? Why?/Why not?

THE DUNBAR NUMBER

When Robin Dunbar invented the Dunbar number, he was studying the social habits of monkeys. The Oxford University professor was watching the way monkeys clean each other when he realized that intelligent animals have big social groups. He found that this was true for humans, too. Dunbar also discovered some unknown facts about our past while he was studying relationships between humans. While humans were living in small communities thousands of years ago, they were more successful when the group had 150 members. That was the Dunbar number: 150. The perfect number for a group of humans to work and socialize with each other.

One hundred and fifty, however, was not the only Dunbar number; there are others. The smallest is five. This is the number of people that we trust the most and they are usually the members of our families and our best friends. The next group has 15 members and they are people that we are fond of. These people won't let you down and they will keep their promises. Then there is a group of 50 people that you have something in common with such as studying, working or playing sports together. Finally, there is the biggest group, 150 people. You might not be keen on all of them and might even hate one or two of them. However, because they include your friends' friends or their boyfriends or girlfriends, you accept them all.

Of course, thanks to social media we can easily get in touch with old friends, like and dislike the things they do and get to know new friends all over the planet. Dunbar says, however, that we need real contact with people to build real relationships. We might fancy a boy or girl in a photo, but we have to meet them to find out what they are really like. We have to do things with someone if we want to become true friends. We can share photos and videos through social media, but we can't share real experiences together online: at least not yet.

1 ____
The perfect number for humans to work and socialize together.

2 ____
The people that you have something in common with.

3 ____
The people that you are fond of.

4 ____
Family members and best friends.

10 Unit 1 · Social circles

1B Group instinct

Supplementary materials
Workbook: pages 4–5, exercises 1–9
Workbook: Grammar summary Unit 1
Photocopiable worksheets: Grammar and Vocabulary, Communication

You First

Tell Sts to write the number of friends they think people need on a piece of paper, making it large enough for the rest of the class to read. Once everyone has finished writing, ask Sts to hold up their piece of paper and give them a moment to compare their answers. Discuss the numbers as a class, asking Sts to give reasons for their answers.

EXTRA IDEA Ask Sts to discuss the question in small groups and agree on a number. Write the numbers on the board and discuss them as a class, asking Sts to give reasons for their answers.

Reading and Listening

1
- Sts look at the photos individually, then discuss the similarities in pairs.

EXTRA IDEA Give Sts 15 seconds to look at the photo at the bottom of the page. Then, have them close their books. Get ideas from Sts about what they saw. Then, give them another 15 seconds to look at the photo and add more information.

EXTRA SUPPORT Elicit or teach the meaning of *socialize, trust, fond of, keen, real contact, have in common with, fancy*. Tell Sts they are from the article. Add any other words your Sts may find difficult.

EXTRA CHALLENGE Sts look at the two photos. Ask *How do you think the photos relate to the text?* Discuss ideas as a class.

2a 1·08
- Play the audio for Sts to listen and follow.
- Give Sts time to complete the infographic.

EXTRA SUPPORT Sts find the sentences to justify their answers in the text. Remind Sts they are looking for a number.

1 150 **2** 50 **3** 15 **4** 5

b
- Set a time limit of one minute for Sts to find the answer.

We need real contact with people.

EXTRA IDEA Sts write five sentences from the article, removing an important word from each sentence. Then, they swap with another student and complete the sentences.

EXTRA CHALLENGE Ask *What else do we need to make real friendships?* Sts discuss in small groups.

EXTRA IDEA Sts complete the numbers in the infographic for 2–4 about themselves. Encourage them to consider their use of social media.

EXTRA CHALLENGE Sts make two infographics: one for the people they know face-to-face and another for the people they know on social media. Sts discuss the differences in pairs and then as a class.

EXTRA CHALLENGE Write on the board 'Social media gets in the way of making real friendships.' Tell half the class to think of arguments in favour of the statement, and the other half to think of arguments against. Then hold a class debate.

1B

Vocabulary Relationship expressions

3a
- Give Sts time to complete the task.
- Get them to compare with a partner before you check answers.

1 'm not keen on   2 gets in touch with   3 fancied   4 hate
5 've got a lot in common   6 let me down   7 dislikes
8 is fond of   9 socialize   10 got to know

EXTRA CHALLENGE In pairs, Sts change the sentences with the alternative expressions. E.g. 1 *I got in touch with Alex because I wanted to invite him to my party.* 2 *My dad is fond of his friends on the internet.* Ask Sts to share their sentences with the whole class and choose the best ones.

b
- In pairs, Sts ask and answer the questions.

EXTRA SUPPORT Elicit the questions from the class and write them on the board.

➡ **Workbook** page 4, exercises 1–3

Grammar Past simple and past continuous

4a
- Sts read the article to find the missing words.

1 When   2 when   3 while   4 While

EXTRA CHALLENGE Get Sts to complete the exercise before reading the article again. Give them time to compare their answers in pairs.

EXTRA SUPPORT Tell Sts that all the words can be found in the first paragraph of the article.

b
- Give Sts time to complete the rules, referring back to the article if necessary.

1 past continuous   2 past simple   3 while   4 when

c
- Give Sts time to complete the task.

1 While, was driving, had   2 socialized, while, was visiting
3 didn't get on, while, were studying   4 While, was waiting, didn't think / wasn't thinking   5 Were, having, when, heard
6 When, broke down, weren't travelling

EXTRA IDEA Ask Sts to write two similar sentences, one true and one false, about themselves and their friends. Sts say a sentence to the class and the class guesses if it's true or false.

➡ **Workbook** pages 4–5, exercises 4–6
➡ **Photocopiable** Grammar and Vocabulary

Listening and Speaking

5a 1•09 Audio script pT86
- Play the audio for Sts to listen and answer the question.

Don't go out onto a busy street and let your dog, even the world's smallest dog, run free!

EXTRA SUPPORT Read the script and decide if you need to teach any new lexis before Sts listen.

EXTRA SUPPORT Ask Sts to look at the pictures and try to predict what the audio will be about.

b 1•09 Audio script pT86
- Before you play the audio again, ask if anyone can tell you which picture shows Alex's story, and why it isn't the other picture. <u>Don't</u> confirm or deny at this stage. Get Sts to listen again to confirm the answer.

EXTRA IDEA Put Sts into pairs and give them a time limit of two minutes to find the differences.

EXTRA CHALLENGE Put Sts into two or three teams and ask them to cover the pictures. Ask questions about the pictures. Each team can get one point for every correct answer.

Picture A shows Alex's story.
In picture A, we can see more traffic and more people than in picture B.
In picture B, the dog is big and on a lead, but in picture A, the dog is small and isn't on a lead.
In picture B, the dog is barking, but in picture A, the dog isn't barking.
In picture A, the teenager is talking to the dog and he is listening, but in picture B, the dog isn't listening.

EXTRA IDEA In small groups, Sts re-tell Alex's story based on what they remember. Then, they listen again and add more information they have heard to their story.

EXTRA CHALLENGE In small groups, each student re-tells Alex's story, but says one thing that is false. The rest of the group listens to find the false statement.

➡ **Workbook** page 5, exercises 7–9

6a
- Give Sts about five minutes, individually, to think of a short story and make notes about it.

b
- Put Sts in small groups to tell each other their stories.

EXTRA CHALLENGE Get Sts to tell their story without reading their notes. Encourage them to look up while they are speaking, which will make them sound more natural. If they forget what they want to say, they can briefly look at their notes, then look up again to tell the story.

c
- Have a class discussion to find out which story Sts liked the most. Ask them to give reasons.

EXTRA CHALLENGE In pairs, Sts take turns telling their story. One student says a sentence from their story, the other continues the story with another sentence, and so on until they finish the story.

Extra
Sts do the activities in pairs in class.

1B

Vocabulary Relationship expressions

3 a Choose the correct words to complete the sentences.
1. I *got in touch with* / *'m not keen on* Alex because of the cruel jokes that he often makes.
2. My dad *gets in touch with* / *is fond of* his best friends on the internet every weekend.
3. I *fancied* / *disliked* him until I spoke to him! He really loves himself!
4. I *socialize* / *hate* people that take football so seriously!
5. We *'ve got a lot in common* / *let each other down* and like doing things together.
6. I asked Ann to keep my secret, but she *got to know* / *let me down* and told everybody!
7. Sam *dislikes* / *fancies* people that don't share his interests.
8. Kate *is fond of* / *hates* Harry and she enjoys his company.
9. We're all good friends in the basketball team and we always *have got a lot in common* / *socialize* together after every match.
10. I started a new school this year, but I *'m not keen on* / *got to know* my classmates quickly and made friends.

b Work with a partner. Ask and answer questions.

> get to know / this school
> socialize with / at the weekends
> get in touch with / by text message (phone / email)

> Who did you first get to know when you started at this school?

▶ **Workbook** page 4, exercises 1–3

Grammar Past simple and past continuous

4 a Find the missing words in the article.
1. ___ Robin Dunbar invented the Dunbar number, he was studying the social habits of monkeys.
2. The Oxford University professor was watching the way monkeys clean each other ___ he realized…
3. Dunbar also discovered… ___ he was studying…
4. ___ humans were living in small communities…

b Choose the correct words to complete the rules.

1. We use the *past simple* / *past continuous* to talk about an action in progress when another action happened in the past.
2. We use the *past simple* / *past continuous* to talk about one or more completed actions in the past.
3. We usually use *when* / *while* with the past continuous.
4. We usually use *when* / *while* with the past simple.

c Choose *when* or *while* and complete the sentences with the correct past form of the verbs in brackets.
1. *When* / *While* Dad ___ (drive) home, he ___ (have) an accident.
2. Chloe ___ (socialize) with Tom for the first time *when* / *while* she ___ (visit) her cousins.
3. I ___ (not get on) well with your mum *when* / *while* we ___ (study) at university together.
4. *When* / *While* I ___ (wait) for my friends at the cinema, I ___ (not think) about buying the tickets.
5. ___ we ___ (have) lunch *when* / *while* we ___ (hear) the news?
6. *When* / *While* the coach ___ (break down), we ___ (not travel) on the motorway.

▶ **Workbook** pages 4–5, exercises 4–6

Listening and Speaking

5 a 🔊 1.09 Listen to Alex's story. What did he learn?

b 🔊 1.09 Listen again. Which picture shows Alex's story? What are the differences between the two pictures?

A

B

▶ **Workbook** page 5, exercises 7–9

6 a **Get ready to speak** Tell a short story. It can be true or invented.

b Work in a group. Explain your story to your group.

c Which story did you like best? Why?

 Write three true sentences and two false sentences about things that happened while you were doing something last weekend. Listen to your partner's sentences and decide which are true and which are false. Explain why you think two sentences are false.

Unit 1 · Social circles

1C Starting points

YOU FIRST! When did your family move to your town? Do you know why? Why do people move to or leave your town?

Vocabulary and Reading Origins

1 a Read the online article. Why did people leave Africa 200,000 years ago?

Thanks to science, we can now look at people's DNA, information about their ¹____, and say where their families and older ²____ came from. The *National Geographic* magazine organizes the Genographic Project, which helps people find this information. Over 700,000 people have taken part since the project started. We now know that the first humans lived in Africa 200,000 years ago, but then there was a big ³____ and a lot of people travelled north, east and west. Scientists think that there were not enough ⁴____ such as food and water, so some people decided to leave. While the people from Africa were looking for new ⁵____ to live in, they met the Neanderthals. The humans and the Neanderthals probably became good friends because today most of the world's ⁶____ has between 1% and 2% Neanderthal DNA. Africans don't have any Neanderthal DNA because Neanderthals never lived in Africa.

Glossary
DNA   Neanderthal

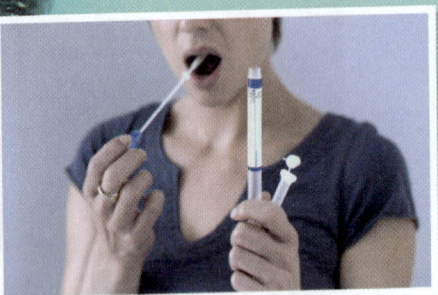

b What information surprised you the most?

c Match the nouns (1–6) to the definitions (a–f). Check your answers with a partner.

1 Ancestors
2 Genes
3 Habitats
4 Migration
5 Population
6 Resources

a is the number of people that live in a place.
b is the movement of large numbers of people.
c are things such as water, wood, etc. that people can use.
d are people in your family who lived a long time ago.
e are places where a type of plant or animal is found.
f are parts of cells that parents pass onto their children.

d 1.10 Complete the online article with the nouns. Listen and check, then repeat.

> ancestors   genes   habitats
> migration   population   resources

▶ **Workbook** page 6, exercises 1–2

Listening

2 a 1.11 Listen to the podcast. What did the *National Geographic* look at to discover where the Darwins came from?

b Listen again and look at the map. Which is the Darwins' route?

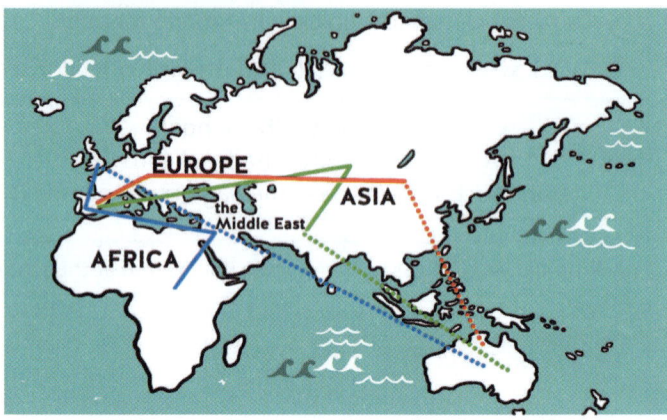

c 1.11 Listen again. Complete the fact file.

THE DARWIN FAMILY

Charles Darwin, famous ¹____ who was born in 1809 and died in ²____.
His book, *On the Origin of Species*, says people and animals have the same ³____.
Chris Darwin, great-great-⁴____ of Charles Darwin. Lives in ⁵____ where he works for the Charles Darwin Reserve that protects plants and ⁶____.
The Darwins left Africa ⁷____ years ago and arrived in Britain ⁸____ years ago.

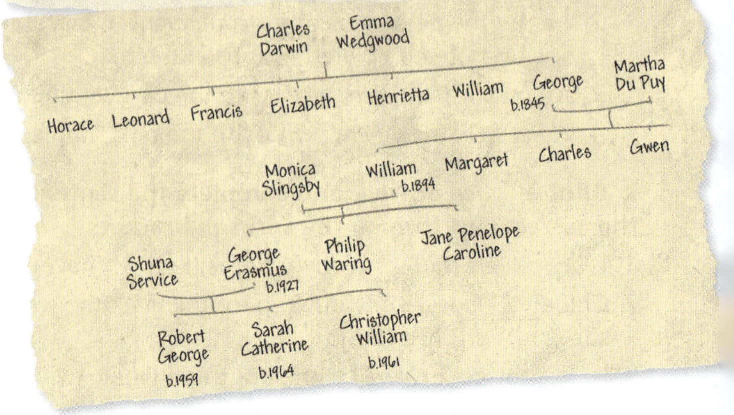

3 Over to you! What do you know about the history of your family or your ancestors? Tell a partner.

12   Unit 1 · Social circles

1C Starting points

Supplementary materials
Workbook: pages 6–7, exercises 1–8
Workbook: Grammar summary Unit 1
Photocopiable worksheets: Grammar and Vocabulary, Communication

You First
Ask Sts *Who has lived here all of their life? If you haven't, when did you move here? Why did you move here?* Write some of their reasons on the board. Discuss the last question as a class.

Vocabulary and Reading Origins

1a
- Discuss some possible answers to the question. Write Sts' ideas on the board.
- Get Sts to read the article to see if any of their ideas were correct. Tell them not to worry about the missing words for the moment.

> **Note**
> Remind Sts they don't have to understand every word in the text in order to complete the task.

There weren't enough resources such as food and water.

EXTRA CHALLENGE Set a time limit of one minute for Sts to find the answer. This will help to develop their reading skills.

EXTRA IDEA Discuss Sts' ideas on the board. Compare their ideas with the reason given in the text.

b
- Ask Sts if anything in the text surprised them. If so, what was it?
- Ask in what way the information surprised them, e.g. Did they not believe it? Did they think something else was true? Were they not aware of this at all?

EXTRA SUPPORT Sts make notes of the information that surprised them the most. This will help them with the class discussion.

c
- Give Sts time to complete the task.

1 d **2** f **3** e **4** b **5** a **6** c

EXTRA SUPPORT Understanding from context: Ask Sts to find the words in the text and read the sentence in which they are used. This should help them better understand the word and complete the exercise.

d 🔊 1·10
- Get Sts to read the article again and complete the task.
- Play the audio for Sts to listen and check their answers.

1 genes **2** ancestors **3** migration **4** resources
5 habitats **6** population

EXTRA CHALLENGE Get Sts to write sentences using some of the words in the box.

➡ **Workbook** page 6, exercises 1–2

Listening

2a 🔊 1·11 Audio script pT86
- Ask Sts what they know about Charles Darwin. Ask *Where was he from?* (*England*)
- Discuss the question with the class before they listen. Elicit ideas from Sts and write the possible ones on the board.
- Play the audio for Sts to listen and answer the question.

Chris Darwin's DNA

EXTRA SUPPORT Read through the script and decide if you need to teach any new lexis before Sts listen.

EXTRA SUPPORT For more information about Charles Darwin, look at the Culture note on page T18.

LANGUAGE NOTE Tell Sts that 'geographic' refers to features on a map. 'Genographic' refers to the mapping of DNA.

EXTRA IDEA Before listening again, ask Sts to tell a partner what they can remember about the podcast.

b 🔊 1·11 Audio script pT86
- Play the audio again for Sts to determine which is the Darwins' route.
- Sts discuss their answer with a partner.
- Check answers.

The blue line beginning in Africa shows the correct route.

EXTRA SUPPORT Play the audio and pause at important points to allow Sts to follow the route.

c 🔊 1·11 Audio script pT86
- Ask Sts to complete as much as they can of the fact file with information they remember.
- Give them time to compare and discuss their answers with a partner.
- Play the audio for Sts to check or complete their answers.

1 scientist **2** 1882 **3** ancestors **4** grandson **5** Australia
6 animals **7** 45,000 **8** 12,000

3
- Individually, Sts write some notes about their family's history.
- Sts share their information with a partner.

EXTRA CHALLENGE Sts tell the class about their partner's family history. What did they find most interesting / most surprising?

EXTRA IDEA Sts draw their family tree as far back as they can remember. Encourage them to talk to their family about it and to include photos. Display their work in the classroom and discuss.

Project Explore T12

1C

Grammar Conjunctions

4a
- Sts complete the table with the underlined words.

2, 3, 4 While, until, When **5, 6** but, although **7** so

EXTRA SUPPORT Write on the board 'I'm very tired today…' and elicit possible endings with the different conjunctions, e.g. *I'm very tired today because I went to bed late last night.*

b
- Give Sts time to read the text and complete the task.
- Check pronunciation of *Denisovan* /dəˈniːsəvən/.

1 While **2** Although **3** When **4** Until **5** because **6** so **7** but

EXTRA CHALLENGE Ask Sts what they know about Neanderthals. If possible, put a picture up on the board, or refer Sts to the image in the text. Ask *How were they different from us (Homo sapiens)?*

EXTRA IDEA Ask Sts about the text *What did you find the most interesting? What surprised you the most?*

EXTRA CHALLENGE Sts write 1–2 questions on what they would want to know about the discovery of the Denisovans. Encourage them to find the answers to their questions online.

➡ **Workbook** page 6, exercises 3–5
➡ **Photocopiable** Grammar and Vocabulary

Writing

5a
- Put Sts in pairs and give them time to complete the task. Elicit or explain that we can join two sentences by adding something at the beginning, as well as in the middle, as in the example for sentence b.
- Get pairs to compare their answers with another pair.

b Although we have a negative image of the Neanderthals, they had a culture and looked after the sick members of their group. / We have a negative image of the Neanderthals, **but** they had a culture and looked after the sick members of their group.
c When the first humans came from Africa, they lived with the Neanderthals.
d Today, **although** all Europeans have about 1% Neanderthal DNA, some people in South East Asia have between 3% and 5% Denisovan DNA. / Today, all Europeans have about 1% Neanderthal DNA, **but** some people in South East Asia have between 3% and 5% Denisovan DNA.
e While the Neanderthals were hunting in Europe, the Denisovans were doing the same in Asia.
f The Neanderthals didn't have much imagination, **so** their culture didn't change in 170,000 years.
g Scientists thought the Neanderthals were alone **until** they discovered the Denisovans in 2008.

b
- In pairs, Sts put their sentences in a logical order, starting with sentence c.
- Encourage Sts to discuss their choices before writing out their paragraph. Get them to compare in groups to see if there were any differences between the paragraphs.
- Check answers.

Possible answers
c, b, f, g, e, a, d

When the first humans came from Africa, they lived with the Neanderthals. Although we have a negative image of the Neanderthals, they had a culture and looked after the sick members of their group. (OR We have a negative image of the Neanderthals, but they had a culture and looked after the sick members of their group.) The Neanderthals didn't have much imagination, so their culture didn't change in 170,000 years. Scientists thought the Neanderthals were alone until they discovered the Denisovans in 2008. While the Neanderthals were hunting in Europe, the Denisovans were doing the same in Asia. Humans survived and the Neanderthals and Denisovans disappeared because humans were more competitive for resources. Today, although all Europeans have about 1% Neanderthal DNA, some people in South East Asia have between 3% and 5% Denisovan DNA. (OR Today, all Europeans have about 1% Neanderthal DNA, but some people in South East Asia have between 3% and 5% Denisovan DNA.)

EXTRA SUPPORT
1 Write letters a–g on seven pieces of paper.
2 Ask a student to come to the front of the class and read sentence a. The student holds up the letter a.
3 Ask another student to read sentence b. Ask this student to come to the front and stand next to the first student, either before or after. Ask the class *Before or after?* The student holds up the letter b.
4 Ask another student to read sentence c. Ask this student to come to the front and stand next to or between the two Sts standing. Ask the class *Before or after?* This student holds up the letter c.
5 Continue until all the sentences have been read and are in the correct order.

c
- Give Sts time to read the information in exercise 2c again and write their two fact files.
- In pairs, Sts compare their fact files and make any changes.

EXTRA CHALLENGE Get Sts to note down questions for anything else they would like to know about either person. They then search for the information online and add it to their fact files.

➡ **Workbook** page 7, exercises 6–8

d
- Based on their notes, Sts decide on the topic of their paragraphs and organize their notes.
- Sts check on the conjunctions they have used and see if they could include others.

Extra
Sts can either do this in class or as a homework task.

1C

Grammar Conjunctions

4 a Read the sentences from the online article and the podcast. Complete the table with the underlined words.

Africans don't have any Neanderthal DNA <u>because</u> Neanderthals never lived in Africa.

<u>While</u> the people from Africa were looking for new habitats to live in, they met the Neanderthals.

Charles Darwin died in 1882, <u>but</u> he has a great-great-grandson.

Chris lived in Britain <u>until</u> he was 25.

<u>When</u> Chris heard about the *National Geographic* project, he wanted to take part.

He wanted to take part, <u>so</u> the *National Geographic* looked at his DNA.

Most of the family stayed in Britain, <u>although</u> Chris is now in Australia.

Conjunctions	
reason	¹because
time	² ___ , ³ ___ , ⁴ ___
contrast	⁵ ___ , ⁶ ___
result	⁷ ___

b Choose the correct answers.

WHO ARE YOUR ANCESTORS?

THE NEANDERTHALS...

OR

THE DENISOVANS?

¹*Until / While* scientists were studying human bones from a cave in Siberia, Russia in 2008, they discovered a small bone from a girl's finger. ²*Although / So* the bone didn't look very different to the others, they decided to do a test on its DNA. ³*Because / When* the results of the test came back, the scientists realized the bone was from a new type of people: the Denisovans. ⁴*Until / But* the discovery of the Denisovans, scientists believed that early human populations only shared the planet with Neanderthals. Now scientists are studying people's DNA ⁵*although / because* they want to discover where the Denisovans lived on the planet. Lots of people from South East Asia have some Denisovan DNA, ⁶*so / while* they know that the Denisovans lived in Asia, ⁷*when / but* few Europeans have Denisovan DNA; they have Neanderthal DNA.

▶ **Workbook** page 6, exercises 3–5

Writing

5 a Get ready to write Work with a partner. Join the sentence halves with conjunctions. You can use more than one conjunction for some sentences.

The history of human life

a humans survived and the Neanderthals and Denisovans disappeared / humans were more competitive for resources

Humans survived and the Neanderthals and Denisovans disappeared because humans were more competitive for resources.

b we have a negative image of the Neanderthals / they had a culture and looked after the sick members of their group

c the first humans came from Africa / they lived with the Neanderthals

d today, all Europeans have about 1% Neanderthal DNA / some people in South East Asia have between 3% and 5% Denisovan DNA

e the Neanderthals were hunting in Europe / the Denisovans were doing the same in Asia

f the Neanderthals didn't have much imagination / their culture didn't change in 170,000 years

g scientists thought the Neanderthals were alone / they discovered the Denisovans in 2008

b Work with a partner. Put the sentences in exercise 5a into the correct order to write a paragraph. Use capital letters and the correct punctuation.

c Look at the fact file in exercise 2c. Use the information to write short fact files of Charles and Chris Darwin.

Include information about…

- dates of birth (and death of Charles)
- the relationship between the two Darwins
- where they were born and where they lived / live
- what they did / do now

▶ **Workbook** page 7, exercises 6–8

d Write the biographies.

- Organize your notes into paragraphs.
- Use as many conjunctions as you can.

EXTRA Do some research on DNA.
- What is DNA?
- Who discovered it?
- In what ways can we use the information from DNA?

Unit 1 · Social circles 13

1D A piece of cake

YOU FIRST! Where do you find information for school work? Do you find information in different places for different subjects?

1 a 🔊 1.12 ▶ Read and listen. What do Liza, Danny and Oliver disagree about?

Danny ...so what do you think about this project for Miss Hamilton?
Liza I'm not sure. It could be interesting...
Oliver Interesting? It's a project about searching online!
Liza Not exactly...
Oliver Well, I think I can use a search engine!
Erika So you'll get an 'A' then?
Oliver Look, I grew up with the internet. I go online all the time. We all do!
Erika That's a good point.
Liza I see what you mean, but I feel we should be open-minded. We can always learn more.
Oliver As far as I'm concerned, I already know it all.
Liza Oh, come on! You don't really think that.
Oliver That's exactly what I think!
Danny I'm not sure about that, Oliver.
Oliver OK look, Erika, you be on my team. I'll do all the work and we'll definitely get an 'A'.
Erika Hmmm...
Oliver And we'll beat these two as well!
Erika OK – let's do it!
Danny Sounds good to me.

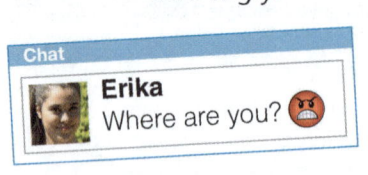

b Answer the questions with the names *Liza*, *Oliver*, *Danny* or *Erika*. Who…?
1 doesn't think they will learn anything
2 thinks there is more to learn about searching online
3 makes the project into a competition
4 seems happy to let another person do all the work
5 thinks of three words to get information online

2

Liza OK, what's your opinion on 'ancestors', 'genes' and 'Neanderthals' as search terms? Do you think they work?
Danny Yeah, my view is that we try those first. OK, let's check this one out…*Live Science*.
Oliver What's up, guys? Still doing your project? Wow, you're slow.
Danny Have you finished?
Oliver Yep.
Liza How?
Oliver It was a piece of cake! Three words: Find. Copy. Paste.
Liza You copied!
Danny You can't do that!
Oliver Oh, yes, I can. You wait and see. Erika and I will get an 'A' on our project.
Liza I think you're in for a surprise, Oliver…

3 Liza What's up?
Oliver It's Erika. I think she's angry.

Chat
Erika Where are you? 😠

2 a Spoken English What do these expressions mean? How do you say them in your own language?

- Check…out
- Wow!
- What's up?
- A piece of cake!
- Oh, come on!
- You're in for a surprise!

b Work with a partner. Write short dialogues for three of the expressions from exercise 2a. Role-play the conversations for another pair. Decide if the conversations use the expressions correctly.

▶ Workbook page 8, exercise 1

14 Unit 1 • Social circles

1D A piece of cake

Supplementary materials
Workbook: pages 8–9, exercises 1–6
Photocopiable worksheets: Everyday English, Pronunciation
Online Practice

> **Note**
> The story can be used in class as a reading and listening task, a video task or both.

You First

In pairs, Sts discuss the questions, making a list of the different places they find information. Encourage them to think beyond online sources, e.g. books and magazines, other teachers, family, etc. Elicit feedback. Which sources do they find the most useful?

EXTRA CHALLENGE Sts discuss how reliable online information is compared to books or people they know.

1a 1·12

- Play the audio for Sts to listen, follow and answer the questions. Alternatively, show the class the video of the story from the DVD-ROM.

> They disagree about whether they can learn more about searching for information online (*Liza and Danny*) or whether they already know everything about using the internet (*Oliver*).

b

- Sts read, listen or watch again to complete the exercise.

1 Oliver **2** Liza **3** Oliver **4** Erika **5** Oliver

EXTRA SUPPORT Ask Sts to support their answers with examples from the text.

EXTRA CHALLENGE Ask Sts who they agree with, Liza and Oliver or Danny. Encourage them to discuss why.

2a

- Give Sts time to complete the task.
- Ask them to find the expressions in the dialogue.
- Model and drill the phrases, using the audio.

> **Check…out** = look at something that seems interesting (informal)
> **Wow!** = an expression of surprise (informal)
> **What's up?** = Here, it means 'What are you doing?' (informal)
> **A piece of cake!** = very easy (informal)
> **Oh, come on!** = 'Are you being serious?' It shows that Liza doesn't believe what Oliver has just said. (informal)
> **You're in for a surprise!** = Things are not going to turn out the way you think they are. (informal)

EXTRA IDEA In pairs, Sts write short dialogues for three of the expressions. Ask each pair to act out one of their dialogues.

> **Note**
> To further exploit the video in class, you could use some or all of the suggested activities from page Tviii.

➡ **Workbook** page 8, exercise 1

1D

3a
- Elicit some ideas, but don't tell Sts if they are right at this stage.

b 🔊 1•13 ▶ Audio script pT86
- Play the audio for Sts to listen and check their prediction. Alternatively, show the class the video of the story from the DVD-ROM.
- Make sure Sts understand what happened. Ask Sts how they feel about it.

EXTRA IDEA Before they listen, ask Sts to re-tell what happened in the first part of the story.

4
- In pairs, Sts discuss the first two questions.
- Discuss question 3 as a class. Encourage Sts to share any experiences they have had.

Everyday English Expressing opinions

5a
- Give Sts time to complete the task.

LANGUAGE NOTE We use *opinion on* when referring to issues, e.g. *What's your opinion on climate change?* We use *opinion of* when referring to people, e.g. *What's your opinion of that actor in the film?*

b 🔊 1•14 Audio script pT86
- Play the audio, pausing for Sts to listen and repeat.
- Model and drill the phrases, using the audio.

LANGUAGE NOTE Remind Sts that using the correct intonation and stress is very important in English. They should pay special attention to this when practising.

EXTRA IDEA Ask Sts to change the intonation of the phrases, or model this yourself. Can they hear a difference? Do the same with the stress pattern. Can they hear the difference?

EXTRA IDEA Give Sts an emotion (sad, angry, excited, embarrassed, etc.) and ask them to repeat the phrases with that emotion.

EXTRA CHALLENGE Divide Sts into groups of three. Student **A** asks for an opinion, Student **B** gives an opinion, Student **C** agrees or disagrees. Give Sts time to prepare their dialogues, then act them out for the class.

➡ **Workbook** pages 8–9, exercises 2–4
➡ **Photocopiable** Everyday English

Pronunciation Silent or pronounced 'e'?

6a 🔊 1•15
- Play the audio for Sts to listen to the words.
- Play it again and get Sts to listen and repeat each word and decide if the underlined 'e' is silent or not.

b
- Ask Sts to say each word to a partner, then add it to the correct column in the table.
- In small groups, Sts check their answers and discuss any disagreements.

c 🔊 1•16
- Play the audio for Sts to listen and check.
- Check answers.

Silent: finished, online, paste
Pronounced: exactly, internet, project

➡ **Workbook** page 9, exercise 5
➡ **Photocopiable** Pronunciation

Listening and Speaking

7a 🔊 1•17 Audio script pT86
- Give Sts time to read the three rules.
- Play the audio for Sts listen and answer the question.

Rule 2

EXTRA SUPPORT In pairs, Sts discuss examples of each rule. Then, discuss these as a class.

b 🔊 1•17 Audio script pT86
- Give Sts time to read through the questions.
- Ask them to discuss questions 1 and 2 with their own ideas.
- Play the audio for Sts to listen again to answer all four questions.
- In pairs, Sts discuss the answers to the questions. Play the audio again if there is any doubt or disagreement.

1 On their websites and blogs   **2** To make their ideas public
3 A list of rules   **4** Copy our work

➡ **Workbook** page 9, exercise 6

8a
- Give Sts time to think about the questions and write down their ideas.
- Encourage them to give examples based on a personal experience.

b
- Put Sts in pairs to discuss their opinions. Encourage them to use the expressions in exercise 5a.
- Get them to tick an expression when they use it correctly.

EXTRA CHALLENGE Give Sts a new topic to discuss, e.g. air pollution, space travel, unhealthy food. Give each student an expression from exercise 5a to use with the new topic.

Extra
Sts can either do this in class or as a homework task.

T15 Project Explore

1D

3 a What do you think will happen next?

  b 🔊 1.13 ▶ Listen and check.

4 Over to you! What do you think?
  1 Is the bad grade only Oliver's fault or does Erika have some responsibility, too?
  2 Why is 'Find. Copy. Paste.' not a good idea?
  3 What should you do when you include other people's ideas and work in your schoolwork?

Everyday English Expressing opinions

5 a Look at the useful phrases. Find examples in the dialogue in exercise 1a.

Useful phrases: asking for opinions
What do you think about…?
What's your opinion on / of…?
Do you think it works / they work?

Useful phrases: giving opinions
As far as I'm concerned…
My view / opinion is that…
I feel we should…

Useful phrases: agreeing and disagreeing with opinions
That's exactly what I think.
That's a good point.
I see what you mean, but…
I'm not sure.

  b 🔊 1.14 Listen and repeat the phrases. Try to copy the intonation.

▶ Workbook pages 8–9, exercises 2–4

Pronunciation Silent or pronounced 'e'?

6 a 🔊 1.15 Listen and repeat the words in the box.

  ancestors   copi<u>e</u>d   exactly   finish<u>e</u>d
  int<u>e</u>rnet   onlin<u>e</u>   past<u>e</u>   proj<u>e</u>ct

  b Decide if the underlined letter 'e' is silent or pronounced.

silent	pronounced
copied	ancestors

  c 🔊 1.16 Listen and check.

▶ Workbook page 9, exercise 5

Listening and Speaking

7 a 🔊 1.17 Listen. Which rule do they talk about?

○ **Can I use material I find online for schoolwork?**
  Today, we can find digital material everywhere, but if we use it in our work, we have to say where it comes from. Use these three rules to help you:

○ 1 If the material comes from different pages of a website, give the address of the website, e.g. http://global.oup.com/

○ 2 If the information is from one page or one article on a website, a book, a newspaper, etc., give the name of the author, the date, the title and the website, e.g. Stephen S. Hall, October 2006, *Last of the Neanderthals*, http://ngm.nationalgeographic.com

○ 3 If there is no author and date, include the other information. You can also have a link in your document so readers can click on it and go to the document.

  b 🔊 1.17 Listen again. Answer the questions.
  1 Where are people happy to share their ideas?
  2 What do people use the internet for?
  3 What has Miss Hamilton given the students?
  4 What don't we want people to do?

▶ Workbook page 9, exercise 6

8 a 📝 **Get ready to speak** Make a note of your opinions about using the following online material for your schoolwork. When do you think it is right / wrong to use it?

  an essay from a homework site
  material from an e-book
  a YouTube video made by students
  articles from news / magazine sites
  photos from a social networking site

  b Work with a partner. Discuss your notes from exercise 8a.

  What's your opinion of using an essay from a homework site?

  My view is that it's dangerous! The essay might be wrong!

  That's a good point.

EXTRA Think of three tasks to give a student who copies material and doesn't say where it is from.

Unit 1 • Social circles **15**

1 Revision

Vocabulary Relationships

1 Choose the correct adjectives to complete the sentences.
1 I think the *caring/sensible/sensitive* thing to do is to ask your teacher for help.
2 Children are sometimes very *jealous/cruel/self-confident* to each other and say unpleasant things.
3 Kate is quite *moody/honest/sensible* and can go from happy to sad in seconds!
4 Andy is really *loyal/selfish/sensitive* and only thinks about himself.
5 They're a *cruel/jealous/competitive* team and they always try hard to win.
6 My grandmother is very *self-confident/caring/aggressive* and always looks after us when we are ill.

2 Complete the text with the words in the box.

> common   fancied   fond   keen   know   socialized

My mum and dad got to ¹___ each other at university, although at first my mum wasn't very ²___ on my dad. They didn't have a lot in ³___ and when they ⁴___ at student parties, he only talked about football. My dad, however, really ⁵___ my mum and he found out she loved dancing, so he learned to dance! They started going to dances together and my mum soon became ⁶___ of my dad and they fell in love!

Origins

3 Complete the sentences with the words in the box.

> ancestors   genes   habitat
> migration   population   resource

1 The birds' ___ has disappeared because they have cut down the forest.
2 There was a big ___ of agricultural workers from the countryside to the big cities in the 1990s.
3 There are pictures of his grandparents and other ___ on all the walls of the house.
4 Saudi Arabia's main natural ___ is oil.
5 The ___ of Tokyo is over 33 million!
6 Eye colour is controlled by the DNA in our ___ .

Grammar Present perfect

4 Complete the conversation.
Anna   ¹___ have you been at this school?
Martin   I've been here ²___ I was six.
Anna   Have you ³___ studied at a different school?
Martin   No, I've ⁴___ been to another school. And you? You've ⁵___ started here, haven't you?
Anna   No, I haven't. I've been here ⁶___ a year!
Martin   Well, we've ⁷___ met before because it's a big school!

Past simple and past continuous

5 Complete the sentences with the correct form of the verbs in brackets. Then choose when or while.
1 We ___ (not chat) *when/while* the head teacher came into the library.
2 *When/While* we were watching the film, Dad ___ (cook) dinner.
3 We ___ (take) videos on our phones *when/while* we were visiting Paris.
4 Jack ___ (wear) his new suit *when/while* he dropped food on it.
5 ___ Sam ___ (fall) asleep *when/while* we were listening to the presentation?
6 *When/While* my brother ___ (live) in Washington, he met the president.

Conjunctions

6 Complete the text with the conjunctions.

> although   because
> but   so   until   while

¹___ I enjoy studying, I don't like spending *every* weekend in the library! I often stay there ²___ they close ³___ I have a lot of work. ⁴___ I'm working, my sister is having fun. It's the same every weekend, ⁵___ the next one is going to be different. It's my 17th birthday, ⁶___ I'm organizing a party!

Everyday English Expressing opinions

7 Complete the dialogue with the words in the box.

> exactly   far   feel   mean   opinion   point

A What's your ¹___ of our new coach?
B As ²___ as I'm concerned, she's great.
A That's ³___ what I think, but the others ⁴___ she shouldn't make us train so hard.
B I see what they ⁵___, but if we want to win games, we have to be fit.
A That's a good ⁶___. I think you should make it clear to the others.

Learning to learn Formal and informal English

When we write letters or emails to people that we don't know, or essays, we usually use formal English with longer sentences and linking words.

When we speak or write to friends (text messages, emails, etc.) we use informal expressions, contractions and shorter sentences.

▶ **Workbook** pages 10–11, exercises 1–9

Unit 1 · Social circles

Revision

Supplementary materials
Workbook: pages 10–11, exercises 1–9
Online Practice
Unit test 1

Vocabulary Relationships

1

> 1 sensible 2 cruel 3 moody 4 selfish 5 competitive 6 caring

2

> 1 know 2 keen 3 common 4 socialized 5 fancied 6 fond

Origins

3

> 1 habitat 2 migration 3 ancestors 4 resource 5 population 6 genes

Grammar Present perfect

4

> 1 How long 2 since 3 ever 4 never 5 just 6 for 7 never

Past simple and past continuous

5

> 1 weren't chatting, when 2 While, cooked (*was cooking* is also possible) 3 took, while 4 was wearing, when 5 Did, fall, while 6 While, was living

Conjunctions

6

> 1 Although 2 until 3 because 4 While 5 but 6 so

Everyday English Expressing opinions

7

> 1 opinion 2 far 3 exactly 4 feel 5 mean 6 point

Learning to learn Formal and informal English

- Divide the board into two columns. Label the columns 'Formal English' and 'Informal English'. Write these expressions on the board:
  'Good morning, how are you?'
  'Hey, how's it going?'
  'I'll be at the meeting.'
  'I will attend the meeting.'
  'Sorry I'm late.'
  'I apologize for being late.'
  'I would like to see you again.'
  'I wanna see you again.'

- Tell Sts to write the expressions in the correct column. Then, discuss the differences between formal and informal English. Finally, ask Sts to add some of their own expressions to each column.

- Discuss if each of the following relates to formal or informal English. Ask Sts to give examples. They could use the expressions from the activity above.
  uses a relaxed tone (*informal*)
  used when you want to be very polite (*formal*)
  uses contractions and slang (*informal*)
  more commonly used in writing work emails or letters (*formal*)
  uses phrasal verbs (*informal*)
  used at work / in business meetings (*formal*)
  used a lot on social media (*informal*)
  used more when speaking (*informal*)
  uses a serious tone (*formal*)

▶ **Workbook** pages 10–11, exercises 1–9

▶ When Sts have finished the **Revision** page, tell them to go to the **Workbook Progress Check** *p.11* and complete the **Your progress** table.

1

My project

Project checklist

Before the lesson
- Ask Sts to bring in photos of friends and family for their social circle.

Materials for the lesson
- A3 paper (1 sheet per student), glue, colour pens
- Photos

You First

Sts read the questions and consider the different relationships in their lives. Discuss the questions with the class.

EXTRA IDEA Sts discuss their relationships in pairs and then in small groups. Then, they add anyone else to their list of relationships.

1a 1•18
- Play the audio for Sts to listen, follow and write the names in the circle.

| 1 Laura | 2 dad | 3 classmates from class 10B | 4 Andy Barton |

b
- Sts complete the **Look!** box.

| 1 extremely | 2 really | 3 quite | 4 a bit |

EXTRA SUPPORT Write the highlighted adverbs on the board in mixed order. Ask Sts to write them in the correct order in the triangle, starting with the strongest.

c
- Sts make a list of the different people they see frequently.
- Encourage them to think about people they see often but are not friends with; someone in the school canteen, for example, or someone in their local area.

EXTRA SUPPORT Sts discuss their lists in pairs and then in small groups. This will give them an opportunity to see other relationships and make any changes to their lists.

d
- Elicit what the Dunbar Number is and the different categories. Write them on the board. Ask Sts to look at page 10 if necessary.
- Using the Dunbar Number, Sts organize the people on their list into different social groups.

2a
- First, ask Sts to write short sentences about the people on their lists.
- Then ask them to go back to their sentences and use adjectives to describe the people.

EXTRA SUPPORT Tell Sts to consider these questions for their sentences: *How close are they to me? How do I feel about them? How long have I known them? Using adjectives, how would I describe our relationship?*

EXTRA SUPPORT Sts share their sentences in pairs and small groups to get ideas from other Sts.

b
- Give each student an A3 sheet of paper.
- Give Sts time to draw their social circles, following the example, and write in the names.
- Get them to add some photos to their circles.
- Encourage Sts to make their social circles attractive, with colours and photos.

c
- Using the notes they wrote in exercise 2a, Sts write the first draft of their text.
- Get them to look at the example text on page 10 to help them organize their paragraphs.

d
- Encourage Sts to use adverbs of degree and the language they have learned in the unit:
- **Unit 1A** the present perfect (*page 9*)
- **Unit 1b** words relating to relationships and the past simple and past continuous (*page 11*)
- **Unit 1C** conjunctions (*page 13*)

3a
- Sts complete the project, adding any final photos.

EXTRA SUPPORT If there is time, ask Sts to show you their projects before the presentation.

EXTRA SUPPORT Give Sts time to read their texts at least once in order to remember what they are going to say.

b
- In pairs, Sts practise their presentations with each other. Encourage them to look at their partner and speak rather than just read their texts.
- It is important to listen actively. Get Sts to ask two questions about each other's social circles.

c
- Presenting the projects to the class:
  1. Ask half of the class (the presenters) to stand around the room with their presentations.
  2. Ask the other half of the class (the listeners) to go and stand by a presenter, so they are in pairs, one presenting and one listening.
  3. Tell the presenters to talk about their social circles. The listeners should listen actively, asking at least two questions.
  4. After a few minutes, tell the listeners to move to the presenter to their right. (Sts don't need to have finished their whole presentation.) Repeat the process.
  5. Repeat the whole process one more time.
  6. Sts switch roles – the listeners become the presenters and the presenters become listeners. Repeat the process.
- Discuss with Sts which adjective is used most.

EXTRA IDEA Ask Sts to present their projects in small groups.

Project Explore

My project   1

YOU FIRST! Who would you speak to if you had a problem? Who do you see when you want to have a good time? Are they the same or different people? What different types of relationships do they represent?

A presentation

³___, Mrs Fenchurch
everybody else at school, my ex-boyfriend ⁴___

²___, the volleyball team

Mum, Granny, Chloe, ¹___

MY SOCIAL CIRCLE

There are four people that are **really** close to me: my mum, my sister Chloe, my granny Sandra, who has lived with us since my parents divorced, and my best friend Laura. My sister Chloe and I are really different; I'm shy and she's **extremely** sociable and has lots of friends, but we get on very well. Laura and I go to the same school and we have lots of things in common!

In my second circle, I've put my dad. I love my dad, but I don't see him very often and we don't always agree on things! I've also included the girls from the school volleyball team. They're **quite** competitive when they play games, but they are really loyal friends.

In my third social circle, I've got all my classmates from class 10B. I've been with some of them since we started primary school and there's a good atmosphere in the class; nobody is ever aggressive and there's no bullying. I've also included our class tutor, Mrs Fenchurch, because she wants everybody to do well.

Finally, in my last circle, I've put all the other people that I know at school. There's also my ex-boyfriend, Andy Barton. He's **a bit** selfish, but I've included him because he was my first boyfriend and he's still in my group of friends!

1 a Get ready to write 🔊 **1.18** Read and listen to the student's project. Complete the social circles with the names of the people.

b Read the Look! box. Complete it with the highlighted adverbs from the text above.

Look! Adverbs of degree
We can use adverbs of degree with adjectives to express how strongly we feel about something.

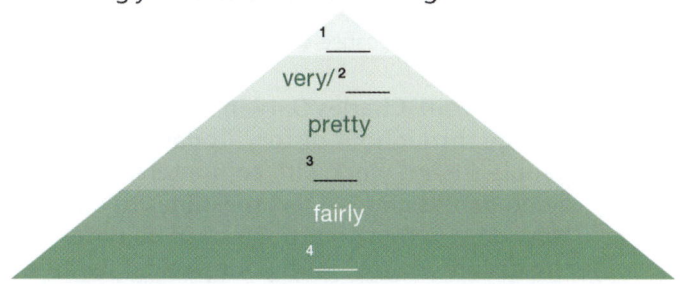

1 ____
very/ ² ____
pretty
3 ____
fairly
4 ____

c Make a list of the people that you see frequently.

d Organize the people in your list into different groups according to the Dunbar Number (see page 10).

2 a Start writing Make notes about the relationship that you have with each person. Think of an adjective or adjectives to describe each person.

b Draw your circles and write the names in them.

c Use your notes to prepare what you are going to say.

d Try to use some adverbs of degree.

3 a Complete your project Try and include a photo in each social circle.

b Practise your presentation.

c Present your project to the class. Listen to them and discuss your classmates' presentations. Which adjective is used most?

Unit 1 · Social circles   17

1 Culture

YOU FIRST! What can we learn when we travel to different towns, regions or countries?

Charles Darwin

EARLY YEARS

Charles Darwin was one of six children from a wealthy family. His grandfather and father were doctors and the young Darwin went to Edinburgh University to study Medicine. However, he hated the sight of blood and he soon realized that he couldn't be a doctor. He was also bored by the lectures! He then went to Cambridge University and discovered that he had a great interest in studying plants, insects and animals. Fortunately, one of his university professors recommended Darwin for the perfect trip for a biologist: a voyage around the world to investigate nature.

THE BEAGLE

In 1831, Charles Darwin left Plymouth on *The Beagle*, a ship that took him around the world for five years. While he was travelling, he studied the plants and animals in the countries and on the islands that the ship visited. He also ate quite a few of them! As a student, he was a member of a university club that ate unusual animals and on *The Beagle* he tried armadillo, ostrich and puma! Darwin also spent his time on *The Beagle* in his cabin writing notes about the things he had seen and when he finally arrived back in Britain, Darwin was already starting to create his famous theory that all living things had a common ancestor.

DOWN HOUSE

At home at Down House, a place that you can still visit today, Darwin wrote many articles and books about his travels, but he didn't want to publish anything about his theory. He worked in his study, where he wrote 250,000 words about his theory of evolution, but he was frightened about what people might say about his idea that monkeys were the ancestors of humans. He expected the public and the Church to be against it and became so frightened that he became ill with worry. However, when another scientist started to write about similar ideas, Darwin decided to publish his book, *On the Origin of Species*. Most scientists accepted Darwin's theory and they continue to accept it today.

A

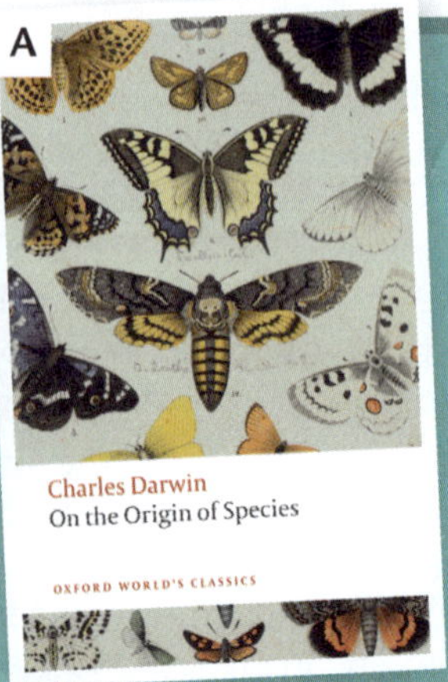

B

C

Glossary

| lectures | armadillo | puma | theory |
| voyage | ostrich | cabin | publish |

1 Look at the photos. What can you see?

2 a Read the article and match the photos to the sections.

b Work with a partner. Discuss and decide if these facts are true (T) or false (F).
1. Charles Darwin changed his mind about his future at Edinburgh University.
2. Darwin received help to get a place on a voyage around the world.
3. Darwin didn't have time for study on the ship.
4. The trip gave Darwin ideas about the beginnings of human life.
5. He thought that people and the church would support his ideas.
6. Darwin finally published his famous book because of another scientist's work.

c 🔊 1.19 Listen and complete the fact file.

ASCENSION ISLAND
Ascension is a ¹____ island.
In the 19th century, ²____ didn't want to visit it.
No ³____ water or plants.
Thanks to Darwin and Hooker, it now has a nice habitat and a population of over ⁴____ people.
Scientists study it because of possible future visits to ⁵____.

3 Over to you! Charles Darwin said that animals change throughout history. Today, more and more people sit and work with computers. We play video games and we text messages to our friends. How do you think our bodies will be different in the distant future? With your partner, write a list of ideas. Use the words in the box to help you. Discuss your ideas with your classmates.

| brains   eyes   fingers and thumbs   legs   muscles |

18 Unit 1 · Social circles

▶ Emmeline Pankhurst: a biography

Culture

Supplementary materials
Photocopiable worksheets: Culture, Culture video

CULTURE NOTES Below are some additional notes on Charles Darwin which you may want to share with your Sts.

As a young boy, Charles Darwin loved dogs. He became one of the first scientists to write about emotions in non-human animals.

Darwin did not focus on his school work. His father, Robert, became worried. He told his son that he 'cared for nothing but shooting, dogs, and rat-catching, and you will be a disgrace to yourself and all your family.'

At school, he was a slow learner. He described himself as lazy, clumsy, and naughty.

Darwin first went to Edinburgh University to study medicine. That didn't last very long because he hated the sight of blood.

He then went to Cambridge University to study Divinity, but he was more interested in studying about nature.

Darwin suffered from a mysterious illness for much of his adult life, with symptoms such as blisters, headaches, insomnia and vomiting. He tried to fight this by following a strict daily schedule in his later years, which featured a lot of time reading and researching at home. It also included two games of backgammon with his wife, Emma, every night between 8:00 and 8:30. He kept score of their games. He once bragged that he had won '2,795 games to her piddling 2,490'.

Darwin was very organized and analytical, even when it came to marriage. He wrote a list of advantages and disadvantages of marriage.

His advantages included children, having a constant companion, as well as the charms of music and 'female chit-chat'. His disadvantages were loss of time, and less money for books.

Darwin and Emma were married for 43 years, until he died in 1882. They had ten children.

Darwin Day is celebrated around the world on 12th February, the day he was born. The aim of Darwin Day is to encourage curiosity about the natural world.

You First

Divide the board into three columns and add the headings 'Towns', 'Regions', 'Countries'. Ask the class to tell you where they have travelled to. Write the places in the columns. Sts discuss the question in pairs. Elicit ideas based on the places on the board.

EXTRA IDEA Show Sts images of places you have been to. Get them to ask questions about the places and what you learned by travelling there.

1
- Sts look at the photos and answer the question.
- Write Sts' ideas on the board.

2a
- Give Sts time to read the article and complete the task.

Early years: B **The Beagle:** C **Down House:** A

EXTRA SUPPORT Read the text and decide if you need to teach any new lexis before Sts do the task. Refer Sts to the **Glossary**.

b
- Put Sts in pairs to read the facts and decide if they are true or false.
- Encourage them to find the sections in the article which gave them the answers.

1 T (He hated the sight of blood and he soon realized that he couldn't be a doctor.)
2 T (Fortunately, one of his university professors recommended Darwin for the perfect trip for a biologist: a voyage around the world to investigate nature.)
3 F (While he was travelling, he studied the plants and animals in the countries and on the islands that the ship visited.)
4 T (When he finally arrived back in Britain, Darwin was already starting to create his famous theory that all living things had a common ancestor.)
5 F (He expected the public and the Church to be against it.)
6 T (However, when another scientist started to write about similar ideas, Darwin decided to publish his book.)

EXTRA IDEA In groups of three, each student reads a section and finds something interesting to share with the group.

c 1•19 Audio script pT87
- Play the audio for Sts to listen and complete the fact file.

1 volcanic **2** sailors **3** fresh **4** 800 **5** Mars

3
- In pairs, Sts think about how people might be different in the future, based on the words in the box, and make a list of ideas.
- Ask pairs to join with another pair and discuss their ideas.

EXTRA CHALLENGE
1 Divide the class into five groups.
2 Give each group one of the items in the box.
3 The groups prepare a brief presentation on how humans will change in the area they were given (brains, eyes, fingers and thumbs, legs, or muscles). Encourage Sts to give reasons and examples of current behaviour.
4 The groups present their predictions to the class.
5 Class listens, asks any questions and agrees or disagrees with the predictions.

▶ Video Emmeline Pankhurst: a biography

As an extension to the Culture topic, Sts watch a short film about Emmeline Pankhurst and do the accompanying photocopiable exercises. You can either do this in class or set it as optional homework. The film is available on the DVD-ROM or on the Online Practice.

1

Learn through English

Supplementary materials
Photocopiable worksheet: Song

Additional subject notes

The topic of this lesson is the idea that all people are six, or fewer, social connections from each other. This means you can connect two strangers through a chain of a friend of a friend of a friend, and so on. Below are some more examples of theories on how people can be linked.

Erdős number
Erdős Paul was a famous Hungarian mathematician who wrote over 1,500 mathematical papers with over 500 different collaborators. The Erdős number counts the number of connections needed to link the author of a paper back to Erdős. Due to the amount of collaboration between different fields of study, it is possible for people who are not mathematicians to have an Erdős number; for example, the American linguist Noam Chomsky has an Erdős number of 4.

Morphy number
Paul Morphy was an American chess player, who died in 1884. Many people believe that he was the greatest chess player of his day. It takes four connections to link Paul Morphy to more recent Grandmasters, such as Garry Kasparov, Polgár Zsuzsa, Ljubomir Ljubojević and Szabó László.

Bacon number
Kevin Bacon is an American actor who has acted in nearly 100 TV programmes and films. He had worked with so many actors in Hollywood by the 1990s that a game was created called 'Six Degrees of Kevin Bacon'. In the game, you compete to link actors back to Bacon using the shortest number of connections possible. Elvis Presley and Ian McKellen both have a Bacon number of 2.

Facebook
Mathematicians have looked at how many connections it takes to link one person to any other person on Facebook, and have calculated that the number is, on average, just over three connections.

You First

Give Sts time to think about who they would like to meet and what they could do to meet them. Then, discuss their choices as a class.

1 🔊 **1·20** Audio script pT87
- Ask Sts, in pairs, to try to complete the sentences before listening.
- Play the audio for Sts to check their ideas and complete the sentences.

1 introductions **2** short story **3** computers **4** messages
5 illness(es)

2a
- Before Sts read about the two experiments, show them Boston on a map of the United States and Kenya on a map of Africa.
- Put Sts in pairs and give them time to read their texts.

b
- Sts find two similarities and two differences between the two experiments, and discuss with their partner.

Possible answers
Similarities: Boston was common in both experiments; the post was used in both experiments.
Differences: The Milgram experiment was in one country; the Kenya experiment was between countries. The Milgram experiment was based on many letters; the Kenya experiment was based on one package.

EXTRA CHALLENGE In both experiments, modern digital media was not used. Ask Sts to discuss how social media could affect the six degrees of separation.

3
- Ask Sts, in pairs, to each write the name of a famous person.
- Sts discuss the first thing they would do to meet a famous person.
- Ask Sts to share their ideas with the class.

4a
- Sts make a list of five people they know. Encourage them to list people from different activities in their life, school, clubs, social events, etc.

b
- Ask Sts to draw a diagram like the one in exercise 4c.
- Sts write their names and the names of their friends on the diagram, indicating how they know the person.
- Ask them to think about any possible connections between the people.

c
- Sts explain the relationships and consider the connections between the different people.

EXTRA IDEA In pairs or small groups, Sts explain their relationship to the different people. Encourage them to ask questions to get more information about the relationships.

EXTRA CHALLENGE In new pairs, Sts tell their new partner about the relationships of their previous partner. Encourage them to ask each other questions.

🔊 **1.21 Song** *Let's Work Together*
- Play the audio for Sts to listen to the song and complete the Song photocopiable worksheet.
- Check answers.

Learn through English

YOU FIRST! Have you or your friends ever met anyone famous? Who would you like to meet? What could you do to meet them?

1 🔊 **1.20** Listen and complete the sentences.

Six degrees of separation – the facts!

- A theory that we are six ¹___ away from every person on the planet.
- In 1929, Hungarian writer Karinthy Frigyes wrote a ²___, *Chains*, where he talked about the theory for the first time.
- Mathematicians have used ³___ to show it is possible.
- Researchers showed that that we are all six ⁴___ or fewer away from any person in the world.
- Scientists are interested because they can use the theory to understand how ⁵___ and disease move and they can also use it to stop terrorism.

2 a **Get ready to speak** You are going to discuss two experiments.

Student A Read about The Milgram Experiment.   **Student B** Read about The Kenya Experiment.

b Work with a partner. Discuss the similarities and differences between the two experiments.

THE MILGRAM EXPERIMENT

In the late 1960s, psychologist Stanley Milgram did an experiment to discover just how close the connections between humans are. Milgram asked people in different US states to send a letter to a businessman in Boston. He gave letters to 160 people and asked them to send them to friends who they thought could help get the letters to Boston. The people who received the letters had to do the same thing: send the letters to someone who could help get the letters to Boston. The letters reached the businessman in five or six steps. Milgram's experiment demonstrated that the six degrees of separation theory worked in one country.

THE KENYA EXPERIMENT

A few years ago, a TV company decided to see if the six degrees of separation theory would work between countries. They asked Nyaloka Auma, who lives in a small village in Kenya, to send a package to a scientist in Boston, USA. Nyaloka could only send the package to someone that she knew well. At first, she had a problem passing it on. Nyaloka couldn't think of anybody who could take the package out of her village, which was a closed social circle. Then an aunt from the capital of Kenya, Nairobi, visited her and provided the solution. She had a friend in New York and she promised to send the package to her. Nyaloka's aunt sent it to her friend in New York, who then sent it to a friend in Boston and the package arrived at the scientist's house in six steps.

3 Work with a partner. Look at your answers to the YOU FIRST! questions. What would be the first step that you would take to meet a famous person?

4 a Make a list of five people that you know from different places: school, a sports club, etc.

b Draw a diagram with you at the centre and the names of the five people around your name. Are there any connections between these people?

c Explain the relationships. How did you meet these people? Which ones know each other? How?

Chloe my best friend at school
Mr Bennett my next door neighbour
Alice my best friend in the basketball team
Harry my boyfriend
Sam my basketball coach

ZOE

I'm Zoe. I met Harry at a friend's party and we've been going out for a year. He introduced me to Sam, who is his best friend, and he invited me along to the basketball team that he trains.

▶ **Song** 🔊 **1.21** *Let's Work Together*

Unit 1 · Social circles

2 New horizons

2A Awesome

YOU FIRST! What was the last day trip that you went on? Would you recommend the place to friends? Why? / Why not?

Reading

1 Read the reviews. Which trip would be best for the following people?
1 Matt loves wild animals.
2 Alice really likes science.
3 Andy likes nature and wild places.

⭐⭐⭐⭐⭐   12:35

MUSEUM OF MATHEMATICS, *NEW YORK*

When you visit New York, this isn't the first place that you think of, but it's fun and full of great ¹____ and lots of ²____ that you can do. You can ride a bike with square wheels, participate in a car race and make designs with different shapes! There's also a ³____ that uses artwork and light to show the importance of maths in art. It's awesome!

⭐⭐⭐⭐⭐   14:55

BLUE ⁴____ OF BISEVO, *CROATIA*

We got up early to visit one of the most popular ⁵____ on the Croatian island of Vis. We went on a ⁶____ by boat from Vis to the island of Bisevo and the ⁷____ was incredible as we travelled along the coast. We changed to a smaller boat so that we could get through the ⁸____ to the cave. I couldn't believe how beautiful it was when we got inside. If you are in Croatia, you have to go!

⭐⭐⭐⭐⭐   08:14

LONGLEAT SAFARI PARK, *ENGLAND*

We went to Longleat for my younger brother's birthday and had a great time watching the lions, tigers and other animals as we drove through the park. The only problem was that the monkeys tried to take the car mirrors off! Later, we visited the ⁹____ and my dad needed an hour to find his way out! My brother also went on a few ¹⁰____ , such as a children's railway, and then we stayed for the ¹¹____ of light at night. It was a fantastic ¹²____ that involved the use of lights in the trees and on the buildings to tell stories. It was a great day out and I'd recommend it to everybody!

Vocabulary Day trip attractions

2 a 🔊 1.22 Choose the correct answers to complete the reviews. Then listen and check.

	A	B	C
1	scenery	entrances	exhibits
2	activities	tours	mazes
3	ride	gallery	festival
4	Exhibit	Cave	Gallery
5	attractions	mazes	shows
6	activity	scenery	tour
7	scenery	gallery	cave
8	entrance	festival	maze
9	tour	entrance	maze
10	exhibits	shows	rides
11	festival	activity	scenery
12	gallery	show	entrance

b 🔊 1.23 Listen and repeat.

3 a 🔊 1.24 Listen and choose the correct photo.

b 🔊 1.24 Listen again and complete the review.

⭐⭐⭐⭐⭐   11:06

MUSÉE DES ARTS FORAINS, *PARIS*

This is a fantastic museum of ¹____ and rides from old amusement parks in Europe. There are lots of ²____ that you can do and you can even go on some of the rides. The man who started the museum said that there are lots of museums about ³____ , but none about people having a good time and ⁴____ . The museum is very ⁵____ and you should book tickets on their ⁶____ as soon as you can.

4 Over to you! Put the four activities on this page in order of preference. Compare your lists. Do you agree / disagree?

▶ **Workbook** page 12, exercises 1–3

20   Unit 2 · New horizons

2 New horizons

Unit objectives
use words to talk about day trip attractions
use verbs to talk about volunteering
use adjectives to describe places
use *will* and *going to* correctly
talk about future arrangements using present tenses
use the first conditional with *if* and *unless*
express preferences
write a blog entry

Language
Grammar: *will* and *going to*; present tenses for future arrangements; first conditional
Vocabulary: day trip attractions; volunteering verbs; adjectives to describe places
Everyday English: expressing preferences
Project: Our town
Culture: The smart tourist's guide to New York
Learn through English: Art styles and periods

2A Awesome

Supplementary materials
Workbook pages 12–13, exercises 1–9
Workbook: Grammar summary Unit 2
Photocopiable worksheets: Grammar and Vocabulary, Communication

You First
Ask the first question to the class and get feedback. Then put Sts in pairs to tell a partner about their day trip, and whether or not they would recommend it. After they finish, get them to tell the class about their partner's trip.

EXTRA IDEA In pairs, Sts recommend their own trip to a different partner and say why.

Reading
1
- Divide the class into three groups. Ask group 1 to read the sentence about Matt, group 2 about Alice, and group 3 about Andy. Get them to read the reviews and choose the best place for their person to visit.
- Tell Sts they don't need to know the missing words to make their choices.

1 Longleat **2** Museum of Mathematics
3 Blue Cave of Bisevo

EXTRA CHALLENGE To practise scanning skills in reading, divide the class into three groups and give each group one of the sentences. Give Sts one minute to find the answer.

EXTRA SUPPORT Ask Sts to justify their choices with examples from the reviews.

Vocabulary Day trip attractions
2a 1·22
- Give Sts time to complete the task.
- Get them to compare their answers with a partner.
- Play the audio for them to listen and check their answers.

b 1·23
- Play the audio again for Sts to listen and repeat.

1 C **2** A **3** B **4** B **5** A **6** C **7** A **8** A **9** C **10** C
11 A **12** B

3a 1·24 Audio script pT87
- Discuss the photos with the class. Ask *What can you see?* (*two trapeze artists; fairground carousel; pantomime horses*)
- Ask Sts if they have been to an amusement park. Ask *What rides did you go on? What was your favourite ride? How do amusement parks today differ from fairgrounds in the past?*

EXTRA SUPPORT Read the script and decide if you need to teach any new lexis before Sts listen.

- Tell Sts they are going to listen to a conversation between two people, and they must choose which of the three photos the conversation is about.
- Play the audio for Sts to listen and choose the correct photo.

B

Note
Encourage Sts to focus on choosing the correct photo. Ignoring information that doesn't help them is an important listening skill; here they are listening for gist.

b 1·24 Audio script pT87
- Sts listen again to complete the review. Tell them they are now listening for details. Tell them to read the text first to help them focus on what they are listening for.

1 exhibits **2** activities **3** wars **4** laughing **5** popular
6 website

EXTRA CHALLENGE Sts try to complete the text before listening again, then discuss their answers with a partner.

4
- Ask Sts to look back at the three trips in exercise 1 and the trip in exercise 3a and put them in order of preference.
- With a partner, Sts compare their lists and discuss their preferences.

➡ **Workbook** page 12, exercises 1–3

Project Explore T20

2A

Reading and Grammar will and going to

5
- Ask Sts if anyone has been to a magic show, or if they know of any famous magicians, e.g. Houdini, David Blaine, Derren Brown, or anyone from their country. Can anyone in the class do any magic tricks? What tricks?
- Give Sts time to complete the task.

> c

> **EXTRA CHALLENGE** Ask Sts to explain their answer and find the evidence for it in the chat. Encourage them to explain why the other options could not be correct.

6
- Give Sts time to complete the task.

> **1** e **2** c **3** b **4** d **5** a

> **EXTRA SUPPORT** On the board, write 'will / going to' next to the meanings in exercise 6. E.g. 'a going to', 'b will', 'c will', 'd will', 'e going to'. Then write the blue sentences on the board and underline keys parts to help Sts find the meanings, e.g. 'I'm <u>sure</u> we're going to <u>enjoy</u> it!'

7
- Give Sts time to complete the task.
- Ask them to compare their answers and discuss any disagreements.
- Check answers.

> **1** I'll, c **2** I'm going to, e **3** I'll, b **4** will, d **5** isn't going to, a

> **EXTRA CHALLENGE** Sts write similar sentences with *will* and *going to*. Sts read the sentences to the class. The class matches the sentences to the meanings from exercise 6.

➡ **Workbook** pages 12–13, exercises 4–7
➡ **Photocopiable** Grammar and Vocabulary

Listening and Speaking

8a 🔊 **1·25** Audio script pT87
- Write the question on the board to help Sts focus.
- Play the audio for Sts to listen and answer the question.
- Give Sts time to compare answers in pairs before checking as a class.

> **EXTRA SUPPORT** Read the script and decide if you need to teach any new lexis before Sts listen.

> Hungary, the United States, Argentina, London (England)

> **LANGUAGE NOTE** *London town* is a colloquial expression to refer to modern London in a way that evokes traditional sentiments, to a time when it wasn't as populated.

> **Note**
> The Magic Circle is an organization in London that promotes the art of magic.

b
- Ask Sts to read the questions first, as this will help them to know what they are listening for.
- Play the audio again for Sts to listen and answer the questions.

> **1** He promises the four magicians will really entertain everyone with their incredible magic.
> **2** a different type of magic
> **3** with the power of his thoughts
> **4** He is confident they will amaze everyone with their awesome talents.
> **5** There is going to be a break for 15 minutes.

> **EXTRA SUPPORT** Divide the questions among the class. Sts listen to answer their question. Distribute the questions again to different Sts. Sts listen to answer their question. This helps weaker Sts focus on one question. They don't need to listen to all of the content.

> **EXTRA SUPPORT** Play the audio for Sts to answer the questions. As an answer comes up, raise your hand with the number of fingers for the question being answered at that point.

> **EXTRA CHALLENGE** Get Sts to try to answer the questions before they listen again.

9
- In pairs, Sts make notes to answer the questions.
- Tell them to decide when they will use *going to* and when they will use *will* in their presentation.

10a
- Put Sts in new pairs. Tell them to present their day trip to their partner without saying where it is, to see if their partner can guess the place.

> **EXTRA IDEA** Pairs decide which day trip is better.

> **EXTRA CHALLENGE** When Sts have heard their partner's description, they ask follow-up questions to find out more about their partner's choice of place.

b
- Ask Sts to present their descriptions to the class.
- When they have finished, list their places on the board and have a show of hands to find out which is the most popular.

> **EXTRA IDEA** Ask *Who do you think would enjoy this trip?* Sts choose a classmate they think would enjoy the trip, and explain why.

> **EXTRA CHALLENGE** Ask Sts to choose a place they have never been to but would like to visit. They write about their proposed trip and give it to you. Read the accounts to the class for Sts to guess who wrote them.

➡ **Workbook** pages 13, exercises 8–9

Extra
Sts do the activities in pairs in class.

T21 Project Explore

Reading and Grammar will and going to

5 Read the chat. Which diagram illustrates the show?

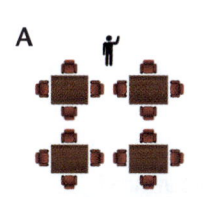

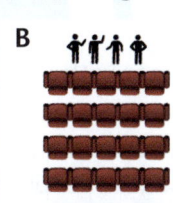

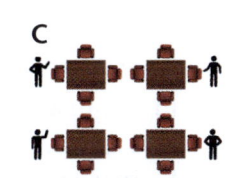

A   B   C

Julia

Plans for Saturday? I'm buying tickets from the website of the Magic Circle. Interested?

Sounds cool! ¹ What are you going to see exactly?

The magic museum and a show in the evening.

I'm really into magic.

That's why I'm texting you!!! 😀

How much?

£20.

Two minutes! ² I'll ask my mum.

Buy me one! ³ I'll give you the money tomorrow – promise! 😁

You will!

What's in the museum?

⁴ I think we'll see things that magicians use for tricks – not sure – website says it's a 'mystery'! 😉

And the show?

They divide the audience into four groups and you sit at a table with your group. Each group has a different magician. They change after 20 mins.

We're going to see four different magicians?

👍

Wow! ⁵ I'm sure we're going to enjoy it!

👍👍👍

6 Look back at exercise 5. Match the items in blue to the meanings a–e.
  a a prediction based on what we know or can see
  b a promise
  c a spontaneous decision
  d a prediction based on what we think is true
  e a future plan or intention

7 Choose the correct answers. Match each sentence to one of the meanings in exercise 6.
  1 That suitcase is heavy. *I'll / I'm going to* carry it for you.
  2 The school rugby coach has asked me to play for the team next year! *I'll / I'm going to* play in defence.
  3 Sorry, I forgot your book. *I'll / I'm going to* bring it for the next class. I promise.
  4 Do you think people *will / are going to* live on Mars?
  5 Look at that sky. It *isn't going to / won't* rain today.

▶ **Workbook** pages 12–13, exercises 4–7

Listening and Speaking

8 a 🔊 1.25 Listen to the presenter of the *Magic Circle* show. Where do the four magicians come from?

  b Answer the questions.
  1 What does the presenter promise?
  2 What is each magician going to show?
  3 How is Henry going to make things move?
  4 What is the presenter confident about?
  5 What is going to happen after the first two acts?

9 Get ready to speak Work with a partner. Read the questions and make some notes.
  • Choose a place in your country for a day trip.
  • Decide what you are going to do there.
  • Make predictions about the things that you think you will enjoy.

10 a Over to you! Present the place from exercise 9 without naming it for a new partner to guess. Then change roles.

> We're going to visit a place that is in the capital city. It isn't very famous, so I don't think you will know it. We're going to...

  b Listen to other descriptions. Which places would you like to visit on a daytrip?

▶ **Workbook** page 13, exercises 8–9

EXTRA Make a list of the five best places to visit for a day trip in your town, region or country. Compare your list with other students.

Unit 2 · New horizons

2B Collaborate

YOU FIRST! What do you think of volunteering? Do you know anyone who has helped in the community? What did they do?

Reading and Vocabulary
Volunteering verbs

1 a Check the meaning of the verbs in the box. Use some of the verbs to describe the photos.

> build   create   collaborate   deliver
> develop   improve   monitor   organize
> participate   plan   protect   raise

> The young people are chatting with the business people because they want to collaborate with them and…

b Read the text. Match the photos (A–E) to Phases 1–3.

c 🔊 1.26 Choose the correct verbs to complete the text. Then listen and check.

d 🔊 1.27 Listen and repeat.

▶ Workbook page 14, exercises 1–3

2 Answer the questions with the numbers 1, 2 and 3. In this phase, you will…
a learn how to participate in meetings
b provide something for people in your area
c learn something new
d do physical activities
e decide on how to do something
f learn how to work with others

Writing and Speaking

3 a Work with a partner. Do some research and discover the type of community activities that young people can do in your town or region. Use the words in the box to help you.

> animals   children   culture
> elderly people   environment   sport

b Write a short description of one of the community activities that you found in exercise 3a. Use some of the verbs from exercise 1a.
- What is the community activity?
- Who does it want to help? / What does it want to improve / protect?
- Who participates in it?
- Who organizes it?
- When do volunteers participate?

4 Over to you! Explain your community activity to the class. Which community activity do you think is the most useful? Why?

NATIONAL CITIZEN SERVICE

Life is too short to spend it at home! NCS is a great chance for 14–18-year-olds to [1]*participate / monitor* in amazing activities together and to [2]*plan / improve* their communities at the same time! Your National Citizen Service experience has three phases:

PHASE 1 ADVENTURE

You'll spend five days living with a team of 12–15 young people that you've never met before! Our team leaders [3]*organize / build* adventure activities such as rock-climbing, hiking and abseiling that will encourage you and your new friends to work in a team. The team leaders will [4]*deliver / monitor* everything you do and make sure that everybody enjoys the challenge.

PHASE 2 DISCOVERY

Time to study! This is where you and your team [5]*collaborate / create* to learn a new skill in media, photography, business, music, drama or art. You'll also [6]*organize / develop* your confidence, leadership and communication skills, and meet organizations and important people from your community.

PHASE 3 SOCIAL ACTION

Time to make a difference! You and your team will put your new skills to good use and [7]*participate / deliver* a social action project for your community. First you have to [8]*plan / raise* the project, then show you can pay for it and finally carry it out. Will you [9]*protect / build* a space that blind people can enjoy, [10]*raise / improve* money for homeless people, or [11]*create / participate* a campaign to help [12]*collaborate / protect* the environment?

Unit 2 · New horizons

2B Collaborate

Supplementary materials
Workbook: pages 14–15, exercises 1–9
Workbook: Grammar summary Unit 2
Photocopiable worksheets: Grammar and Vocabulary, Communication

You First
Ask Sts to discuss the questions in pairs, then get feedback from the class.

EXTRA CHALLENGE Ask *What does 'collaborate' mean?* Encourage Sts to give some examples of good collaboration, e.g. a successful sports team or a harmonious music band.

Reading and Vocabulary Volunteering verbs

1a
- Ask Sts to use the verbs to describe the photos.

EXTRA IDEA Ask Sts to look at the photos for 30 seconds, then close their books. What did they see? Then, ask them to look at the photos again for 30 seconds. Encourage them to say something no one else will say.

EXTRA SUPPORT Write on the board: 'Example sentence', 'Meaning', 'Translation'. Ask Sts in turn to give one of these for a word in the box.

b
- Give Sts time to read the three phases.
- Tell them not to worry about the alternative verbs yet, they just need to find enough information to match the photos to the phases.

Phase 1: A, D   **Phase 2:** B, E   **Phase 3:** C

EXTRA SUPPORT Ask Sts to write a sentence from the text to support their choice.

c 🔊 1·26
- Give Sts time to complete the exercise.
- Point out that the first two items in the task are within the introduction to the text.
- Get them to compare with a partner.
- Play the audio for Sts to listen and check.

1 participate 2 improve 3 organize 4 monitor
5 collaborate 6 develop 7 deliver 8 plan 9 build
10 raise 11 create 12 protect

EXTRA CHALLENGE Sts explain the difference between both word choices in each item, justifying the correct answer.

d 🔊 1·27
- Play the audio again for Sts to listen and repeat, paying attention to the correct stress.

➡ **Workbook** page 14, exercises 1–3

2
- Explain that Sts need to decide in which phase 1–3 the given activities will take place.
- Give them time to complete the task, then check answers.
- Ask Sts to find the information in the text which gave them the answer.

a Phase 2 **b** Phase 3 **c** Phase 2 **d** Phase 1 **e** Phase 3
f Phase 1

Writing and Speaking

EXTRA SUPPORT Sts can do the research at home before the lesson if there is no internet access in the classroom.

3a
- In pairs, Sts research the type of community activities that young people can do in their area. Get them to suggest possible sources and websites.
- Ask Sts to share their results with the class.

EXTRA CHALLENGE Pairs prepare a brief presentation on a community activity and present it to another pair.

b
- Ask Sts to use the questions to discuss one community activity from exercise 3a with a partner.
- Sts write about their community activity based on the questions and their discussion.

EXTRA CHALLENGE Sts write their description as if it were a promotion for the activity. Their text will be used to convince young people to volunteer for that activity. Display the descriptions in class. Let Sts read them and decide which they would volunteer for.

4
- Sts explain their community activity to the class.
- Have a class discussion on which is the most useful, and why.

EXTRA CHALLENGE Sts present their activity to the class as a promotion (using their written texts from exercise 3b). Sts decide which activity they would volunteer for. Discuss any differences between the Sts' vote for the written texts and the oral presentations.

Note
Sts write better when they have a purpose and an audience. Writing or presenting their chosen activity as a promotion / publicity for it provides Sts with both of these: they are writing to persuade their classmates to volunteer.

2B

Listening

5a 🔊 **1·28** Audio script pT87
- Discuss the photos with the Sts. Ask *What can you see? Is there a common theme?*

> **Note**
> Discussing the photos gives Sts an idea of what they are going to listen to. This helps them listen better.

- Play the audio for Sts to listen and choose the correct photo.
- Ask Sts to say what helped them choose the photo.

B

> **EXTRA SUPPORT** Read the script and decide if you need to teach any new lexis before Sts listen.

b 🔊 **1·28** Audio script pT87
- Play the audio again for Sts to complete the task.

> **1** 31st August **2** this week **3** tomorrow **4** ten o'clock
> **5** Tuesday afternoon **6** every month

> **EXTRA SUPPORT** Tell Sts to read the sentences before they listen again.

> **EXTRA IDEA** Check comprehension further with these questions:
> *What does the director of the Bilton Savings Bank advise?*
> *Why are they speaking to the manager of the Bilton Garden Centre?*
> *What kind of plants do they need?*
> *Who does the land belong to?*

> **EXTRA CHALLENGE** Sts complete the sentences before they listen again.

> **EXTRA CHALLENGE** Ask *Who do you think will benefit from this project?* (Possible answer: blind people – 'we want plants that produce strong smells, and trees that are interesting to touch'; 'the council has a piece of land next to the home for the blind that we could use.')

Grammar Present tenses for future arrangements

6a
- Give Sts time to complete the task, then check answers.

> **1** Present simple **2** Present continuous **3** Present continuous **4** Present simple **5** Present continuous **6** Present simple

b
- Sts complete the rules, referring back to their conclusions about the sentences in exercise 6a.

> **1** We can use the present **simple** to talk about future events which are part of a timetable. We often use **dates** / **times** and **times** / **dates** in these sentences.
> **2** We can use the present **continuous** to talk about fixed plans for the future. We have often arranged to do these things with other **people**.

> **EXTRA CHALLENGE** Ask Sts to write true sentences about themselves using each tense.

> **Note**
> When Sts write true sentences about themselves, they remember the language better, because it has meaning for them.

c
- Give Sts time to complete the task, then compare with a partner.
- Check answers.

> **1** start **2** finish **3** is arriving **4** are delivering **5** opens **6** are coming

> **EXTRA SUPPORT** Sts work in pairs to complete the exercise.

➡ **Workbook** pages 14–15, exercises 4–7
➡ **Photocopiable** Grammar and Vocabulary

Speaking

7a
- Divide the class into **A** and **B**.
- Sts **A** read the information on page 86.
- Sts **B** read the information on page 87.

> **EXTRA SUPPORT** Answer any questions Sts have about their texts to make sure they understand.

> **EXTRA CHALLENGE** With their books closed, in small groups of Sts **A** and **B**, Sts tell each other what they can remember about their texts.

b
- Put Sts in pairs, **A** and **B**, to ask and answer questions about each other's activity.

> **EXTRA IDEA** Sts suggest questions they want to ask the other group. Write the questions on the board.

➡ **Workbook** page 15, exercises 8–9

Extra

Sts can either do this in class or as a homework task.

T23 Project Explore

2B

Listening

5 a 🔊 **1.28** Which community project are they doing? Listen and choose the correct photo.

A

B

C

b 🔊 **1.28** Listen again and complete the sentences.
1 This National Citizen Service project ends on ____ .
2 What are you doing ____ , Adam?
3 Eva and I are meeting local business people ____ .
4 The meeting starts at ____ .
5 I'm giving a presentation with Lucas to the council on ____ .
6 The council holds a meeting on the first Tuesday of ____ .

Grammar Present tenses for future arrangements

6 a Say if the sentences from exercise 5b are in the present simple or present continuous.

b Complete the rules with the words in the box.

> continuous   dates   people   simple   times

1 We can use the present ____ to talk about future events which are part of a timetable. We often use ____ and ____ in these sentences.
2 We can use the present ____ to talk about fixed plans for the future. We have often arranged to do these things with other ____ .

c Complete the email with the correct present simple or present continuous form of the verbs.

We've only got one week to build the garden. We ¹____ (start) on Monday 27th August and ²____ (finish) on Friday 31st! On Wednesday a lorry ³____ (arrive) to take all the rubbish away, so we've got to work hard to clean it up by then! Gardeners from the Bilton Garden Centre ⁴____ (deliver) the plants and trees on Thursday morning. Then on Saturday 1st September at five o'clock the garden ⁵____ (open)! The Mayor and her husband ⁶____ (come) to open it and we've also invited the local media, so it has to be ready!

▶ **Workbook** pages 14–15, exercises 4–7

Speaking

7 a **Get ready to speak** You are going to talk about the two other community projects in the photos.
Student A Look at page 86.
Student B Look at page 87.

b Ask and answer questions to find out more about each other's project.

> What's your project about?

> In the first week we are creating a campaign to tell people about…

▶ **Workbook** page 15, exercises 8–9

EXTRA 📝 Write a short paragraph explaining which of the three community projects on this page you would like to do.

As far as I'm concerned, the community project that I would like to do is…

Unit 2 · New horizons   23

2C Taking a risk

YOU FIRST! Which type of holiday do you prefer? Why? Why do some people do activities such as climbing, bungee jumping or kayaking on holiday?

Reading

1 a 🔊 1.29 Read and listen to the blog. Answer the questions.

Which activity takes place…?
1 during seven days
2 in the dark   3 once a year

b Which activity do you think is the most dangerous? Which activity would you like to try?

Vocabulary   Adjectives to describe places

2 a Match the highlighted adjectives to the definitions.
1 offering a wide view
2 far away from places
3 something from the past
4 full of people
5 something you will always remember
6 not changed or damaged
7 bright and full of colour
8 important in history
9 connected to the area
10 attractive in an old-fashioned way

b Complete the sentences with the adjectives from above.
1 Although the mountain village is ___ and hard to get to, you should go to see the ___ views of the valley.
2 They've preserved the ___ buildings and they build all new buildings in the ___ style of the region, so the town streets have an old-fashioned feel.
3 They can't build on the coast, so the beaches are ___ . The fields, the sand and the sea create a colourful and ___ sight!
4 I think it's a good restaurant because it's always ___ with a lot of ___ people from the town.
5 Scuba diving was so exciting; swimming with the ___ tropical fish and the sharks was an ___ experience!

WILD ITALY!

Let our local bloggers show you the Italy that your parents don't want you to see!

PLACE: BRENTA DOLOMITES   **BLOGGER:** GIANNA   **POSTED:** AUGUST 25TH

If you like adventure holidays in unspoiled environments, try the Via Ferrata in the remote Dolomite Mountains. The Via Ferrata, 'iron road' in Italian, is a climbing and walking route through some of the most incredible scenery that you'll ever see. Italian soldiers opened the first Via Ferrata during the First World War and today trekkers and climbers spend a week on the same route. However, unless you feel comfortable in high places, you won't enjoy looking at the panoramic views! Many of the paths are cut out of the rock and although you're connected to a rope so you can't fall, the view down the sides of the mountains is frightening!

PLACE: IVREA, PIEDMONT   **BLOGGER:** PAOLA   **POSTED:** AUGUST 17TH

Like a lot of Italian towns, the town of Ivrea has a picturesque centre with lots of historic buildings. However, a month before Easter, it becomes a war zone! Thousands of local people meet in the town square to throw oranges at each other: 200,000 kilos of oranges! The town is crowded for three days as the fight takes place and unless you want to get hit by an orange, you'll feel safer watching from a balcony. Local people say that the traditional Battle of the Oranges represents a 13th century fight between the rich and the poor of the town, although they probably used something even more dangerous than fruit!

PLACE: STROMBOLI, AEOLIAN ISLANDS   **BLOGGER:** GIULIANI   **POSTED:** AUGUST 13TH

If you want to feel the power of nature, walk up the volcano on the island of Stromboli. Stromboli is one of the world's most active volcanoes. There's volcanic activity every 30 minutes and you'll have to join an official group if you want to go. On the day I went, we left at 6 p.m. and it took three hours to climb the 924 metres to the top. I've never been on such a frightening walk: I could feel the mountain shake as I was going up it! Stromboli threw fire and burning rocks into the night sky four times while we were there…a colourful sight and an unforgettable experience!

2C Taking a risk

Supplementary materials
Workbook: pages 16–17, exercises 1–9
Workbook: Grammar summary Unit 2
Photocopiable worksheets: Grammar and Vocabulary, Communication

You First
Ask the class what type of holiday they prefer, and discuss their reasons. Write the different holiday types on the board. Remind Sts of the activities they saw and read about in this lesson (abseiling, climbing, hiking). Write 'kayaking' and 'bungee jumping' on the board. Discuss what they are. You could also teach or elicit *scuba diving*, as it comes up in exercise 2b. Ask *Has anyone tried these? If not, would anyone like to?*

EXTRA IDEA Ask Sts to think of one type of holiday for a classmate. Encourage them to explain their choice. Then, ask the classmate if they agree. Encourage them to explain why or why not.

EXTRA IDEA Ask Sts to imagine a conversation in each photo. E.g. *What are some of the people on the beach saying? What is the person jumping saying?*

EXTRA CHALLENGE Ask Sts to discuss why each type of holiday might be better than the others. Why do some people prefer a beach holiday? Or an adventure holiday?

Reading
1a 🔊 1·29
- Elicit or explain that a 'via ferrata' is a mountain route that is accessible to climbers and walkers by using ladders, cables and bridges.
- Play the audio for Sts to listen, follow and answer the questions.

> 1 walking and climbing the Via Ferrata   2 seeing Stromboli volcano   3 orange fight in Ivrea

EXTRA SUPPORT Before they listen, get Sts to read the texts through quickly to name the three activities.

EXTRA SUPPORT Ask Sts to choose three words that are specific to each text. Then, ask them to say one of the words. The class matches the word to the text and finds the sentence.

EXTRA IDEA With a partner, ask Sts to imagine they are on one of the holidays. Tell them to describe what they see, how they feel and what they can hear.

b
- Sts discuss which activity is the most dangerous.
- Encourage Sts to explain their choices with examples from the texts.

EXTRA IDEA Tell Sts there is going to be a secret vote to find out the most popular choice of activity to try. First, ask Sts to guess which will be the winner. Then, ask them to close their eyes and vote with a show of hands for the activity they'd like to try. Tell them the results and then have a class discussion.

Note
In British English, many words ending in -ed can be spelled in two ways. For example, *spelled* and *spelt*.

Vocabulary   Adjectives to describe places
2a
- Give Sts time to complete the task, then compare their answers with a partner and discuss any disagreements.
- Model and drill pronunciation of any difficult adjectives, e.g. *panoramic* /ˌpænəˈræmɪk/ and *picturesque* /ˌpɪktʃəˈresk/.
- Check answers.

> 1 panoramic   2 remote   3 traditional   4 crowded
> 5 unforgettable   6 unspoiled / unspoilt   7 colourful
> 8 historic   9 local   10 picturesque

EXTRA CHALLENGE Ask Sts to write their own sentences using the highlighted words.

EXTRA CHALLENGE Ask Sts to read one of their sentences to the class. Instead of saying the highlighted word, they should substitute it with the word 'buzz'. The class listens and guesses the missing word.

b
- Give Sts time to read through the sentences and complete the task.
- Get them to compare with a partner before you check answers.

> 1 remote, panoramic   2 historic, traditional
> 3 unspoiled / unspoilt, picturesque   4 crowded, local
> 5 colourful, unforgettable

EXTRA SUPPORT Sts work in pairs to complete the exercise.

EXTRA IDEA Ask Sts to make a word search puzzle with the words. Then, give their puzzles to other Sts to solve.

EXTRA IDEA Put Sts into teams and ask them to close their books. Write one of the adjectives on the board and ask Sts to give a short definition. The first team to give a correct definition gets a point.

Project Explore   T24

2C

3
- Put Sts in pairs and tell them they are going to make a poster for a famous tourist site.
- Give them time to agree on a site.
- Sts follow the instructions to make their poster.

EXTRA IDEA Sts plan their poster. Give them each a piece of paper. Write on the board 'Where are you going to put the name of the place?' 'How many photos will you use?' 'Where will you put them?'

EXTRA IDEA Display the posters around the class. Have a class vote for the best photos, best text, and best overall poster. Get Sts to discuss the reasons for their choices.

> **Note**
> If you don't have access to the internet or a printer, you could bring in brochures from a travel agency. Alternatively, after Sts have planned their poster, they could bring in the photos they need from home.

➡ **Workbook** page 16, exercises 1–3

Grammar First conditional

4a
- Give Sts time to complete the task.
- Check answers.

1 walk **2** 'll have **3** Unless **4** try **5** won't enjoy

EXTRA CHALLENGE Ask Sts to complete the exercise without looking back at the blog.

b
- Give Sts time to read through the sentences.
- Tell Sts to look at the sentences in exercise 4a to help them decide which ones are true, and to correct the false ones.
- Sts compare and check answers with a partner.

1 T
2 F (The *if*-clause can also go in the middle of the sentence.)
3 T
4 F (We use a comma when the *if*-clause comes at the beginning of the sentence, but not when it comes in the middle.)

EXTRA SUPPORT Ask Sts to find a sentence from exercise 4a to show an example of each rule.

c
- Sts complete the exercise.

1 take **2** they'll **3** Buy **4** unless **5** hotel **6** If

EXTRA CHALLENGE Get Sts to rewrite the correct sentences by swapping the order of the *if* / *unless* clauses. Tell them to pay special attention to their use of commas. They could do this in pairs or on their own. E.g.:
1 Take an umbrella unless you want to get wet.
2 They'll enjoy it more if they go with a guide.

d
- Sts complete the sentences about themselves and their friends.

EXTRA IDEA Divide the class into five groups. Give each group one of the sentences. Ask Sts in each group to complete the sentence. Then, Sts read their sentences and decide on the two they agree with the most.

➡ **Workbook** pages 16–17, exercises 4–6
➡ **Photocopiable** Grammar and Vocabulary

Listening

5a
- Use the photo to introduce *zip wire*.
- Ask Sts if they have ever done this activity, or would like to do it.
- Give Sts time to read the advertisement and choose *if* or *unless*, ignoring the gaps.

EXTRA IDEA Elicit other extreme activities from this unit, and the verbs used when doing the activities (*go* + [activity]*ing*) and point out that *zip wire* is not used as a verb in this way: *go on a zip wire* NOT ~~*go zip wiring*~~.

> **Note**
> Sts improve their listening skills by thinking about the topic they are going to listen to.

b 🔊 1•30
- Discuss as a class what the missing numbers might be. Encourage Sts to give reasons for their answers.
- Play the audio for Sts to listen, check and complete the advertisement.

1 If **2** If **3** 1,000 **4** 120 **5** If **6** Unless **7** 16
8 unless **9** 10

Writing

6a
- Write on the board, 'Wild _____!' and tell Sts they are going to write a blog entry with this title.
- Put Sts in pairs to look at the questions and plan their blog entry.

EXTRA SUPPORT Encourage Sts to make notes for each question. They can then use their notes to write their blog entry.

➡ **Workbook** page 17, exercises 7–9

b
- Sts write their blog entry.
- Encourage Sts to look at the blog entries on page 24.
- Remind them to use the first conditional and some of the adjectives from exercise 2a.

c
- Sts exchange their blog entries with other Sts.
- Sts answer the questions about each other's blog entries.

EXTRA IDEA Display the blog entries in the classroom. Let Sts walk around and read them.

d
- When Sts have read all the blog entries, get the class to vote for the three they like best.

Extra
Sts can either do this in class or as a homework task.

2C

3 Over to you! Work with a partner. Create a poster for a famous tourist site you know.
- Find suitable photos
- Research information about the site
- Write short explanations for the photos
- Use some of the adjectives on page 24
- Present your poster to the class

This place is unspoiled because it is quite remote. In the summer...

▶ **Workbook** page 16, exercises 1–3

Grammar First conditional

4 a Complete the sentences from the blog.
1 If you want to feel the power of nature, ___ up the volcano on the island of Stromboli.
2 You ___ to join an official group if you want to go.
3 ___ you want to get hit by an orange, you'll feel safer watching from a balcony.
4 If you like adventure holidays in unspoiled environments, ___ the Via Ferrata...
5 Unless you feel comfortable in high places, you ___ looking at the panoramic views!

b Are the sentences about the first conditional true (T) or false (F)? Correct the false sentences.
1 *Unless* + affirmative verb has the same meaning as *if* + negative verb.
2 *If* must come at the beginning of the sentence.
3 Instead of *will* + verb, we can use an imperative to give advice and make recommendations.
4 We always use a comma.

c Choose the correct answers.
1 Unless you want to get wet, *take/ you'll take* an umbrella.
2 If they go with a guide, *they/ they'll* enjoy it more.
3 *You'll buy/ Buy* tickets for the museum online if you want to avoid queues.
4 We'll have a great time in Ivrea *unless/ if* we get hit by oranges.
5 We'll eat at the *hotel,/ hotel* if we arrive late.
6 *Unless/ If* you are fit, you'll be able to complete the historic Via Ferrata route.

d Complete the sentences so that they are true for you and your friends. Use commas when necessary.
1 Unless you study hard ___ .
2 If we go to bed late tonight ___ .
3 ___ unless we get up early.
4 Unless we get fit ___ .
5 ___ if we save some money.

▶ **Workbook** pages 16–17, exercises 4–6

Listening

5 a Read the advertisement. Choose the correct answer: *if* or *unless*.

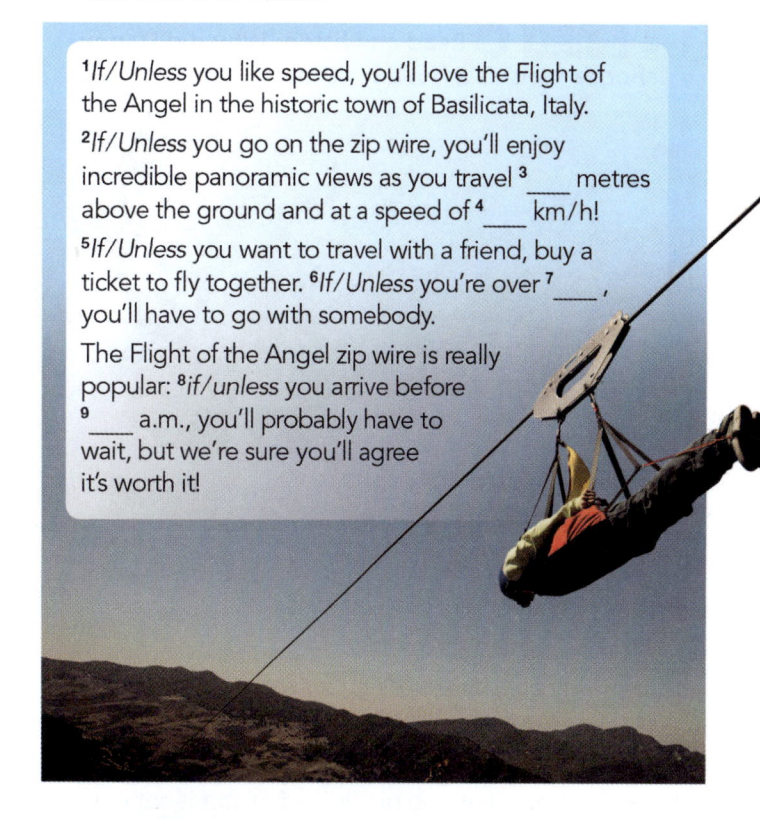

¹*If/Unless* you like speed, you'll love the Flight of the Angel in the historic town of Basilicata, Italy.
²*If/Unless* you go on the zip wire, you'll enjoy incredible panoramic views as you travel ³___ metres above the ground and at a speed of ⁴___ km/h!
⁵*If/Unless* you want to travel with a friend, buy a ticket to fly together. ⁶*If/Unless* you're over ⁷___ , you'll have to go with somebody.
The Flight of the Angel zip wire is really popular: ⁸*if/unless* you arrive before ⁹___ a.m., you'll probably have to wait, but we're sure you'll agree it's worth it!

b 🔊 1.30 Listen, check and complete the advertisement with numbers.

Writing

6 a Get ready to write Work with a partner. You're going to write a blog entry called 'Wild ___ !' for a holiday activity in your town, region or country.
- Which place are you going to write about?
- What can you do there?
- What will visitors experience if they do the activity?
- What advice or recommendations can you make?

▶ **Workbook** page 17, exercises 7–9

b Write the blog entry and choose a photo or photos to illustrate it. Use the first conditional and adjectives to describe places.

c Exchange your blog entries with other students. Would you like to try the activity? Have you already tried it? Is the blog entry a good description?

d Vote on the best three entries for a 'Wild ___ !' blog about activities in your country.

EXTRA Create an advertisement for a risk-taking activity for your parents. Explain what will happen and how they will feel if they do it.

Unit 2 · New horizons 25

2D Sorted!

YOU FIRST! How do couples celebrate getting married in your country? What events do they organize just before and just after the wedding?

1 a 🔊 1.31 ▶ Read and listen. Why did Danny choose Paris as a holiday destination?

1

Liza Hi Danny. Are you OK?
Danny My sister is getting married.
Erika So, what's the problem?
Danny My parents are paying for their honeymoon and I volunteered to plan it!
Liza Oh. I see.
Erika What? That's no big deal – just sort it out online.
Danny I have no idea what kind of holiday they want. My sister just said 'something unforgettable'!
Erika Ah...
Danny Exactly! I need some ideas!

2

Erika Oh, I'd love to go on a beach holiday. Could that work?
Danny A beach holiday? I'd prefer not to play it so safe.

b Answer the questions.
1 What did Danny volunteer to do?
2 Where does Erika say Danny can organize it?
3 What's more interesting than a beach holiday?
4 Who got married last year?
5 What is expensive?
6 What is stressful?

3

Liza What about skiing? I'm not very keen on it, but some people love it.
Danny That sounds more interesting than a beach holiday...but for a honeymoon? No way!
Liza OK, let me ask Emil. His brother got married last year.
Danny Emil! That's it! You met him in Paris, didn't you? The city of love!
Liza Isn't Paris too full of tourists? I think I'd rather go somewhere quiet for a honeymoon.

4

Erika And isn't it really expensive? I'd rather not worry about money on my honeymoon!
Danny It's a bit pricey...
Liza And Emil says a honeymoon should be relaxing.
Danny I reckon Paris is a great idea. It's romantic! It sounds much better than a beach or skiing holiday.
Liza We *are* trying to help, you know.
Danny I'm sorry. It's so stressful! My parents need to know soon. I'd prefer just to decide on Paris now!
Liza If you're sure...
Danny I am! Sorted!

26 Unit 2 · New horizons

2D Sorted!

Supplementary materials
Workbook pages: 18–19, exercises 1–6
Photocopiable worksheets: Everyday English, Pronunciation
Online Practice

Note
The story can be used in class as a reading and listening task, a video task or both.

You First
Write some questions on the board, e.g. 'Where is the wedding ceremony?' 'How long is it?' 'Who are the guests?' 'What happens in the celebration of the marriage?' 'Do you like going to weddings?' Then, have a class discussion. If you have students from different countries, get feedback about any different traditions.

1a 1·31
- Ask Sts to look at the photos. Ask *What is Danny doing? What does Erika suggest? What does Liza suggest?*
- Play the audio for Sts to listen, follow and answer the question. Alternatively, show the class the video of the story from the DVD-ROM.

It's romantic.

Note
Discussing the photos helps Sts know what to expect. At this point getting the right answers is not as important as Sts having an idea about the context for the conversations. This will engage them in the activity and help them when they listen to the audio.

EXTRA SUPPORT Read the script and decide if you need to teach any new lexis before Sts listen, e.g. *pricey*.

EXTRA CHALLENGE Sts discuss the things they like best about weddings based on their own experiences.

b
- Give Sts time to answer the questions.
- Play the audio or video again for Sts to check their answers.

1 plan his sister's honeymoon 2 online 3 a skiing holiday
4 Emil's brother 5 Paris 6 planning the honeymoon

EXTRA SUPPORT Play the video or audio. As Sts listen, raise your hand when a question is answered.

EXTRA SUPPORT Divide the questions among the class, giving one question to each student. Sts listen to answer their question.

EXTRA IDEA Write some extra comprehension questions on the board: 'What's wrong with a beach holiday?' (*too safe*) 'What's wrong with a skiing holiday?' (*not appropriate for a honeymoon*)
'What's wrong with Paris'? (*too many tourists / too expensive*)
Let Sts try to answer the questions from memory, then play the audio or video for Sts to listen and confirm their answers.

EXTRA CHALLENGE Sts suggest a destination for the honeymoon. Encourage them to give their reasons.

Note
To further exploit the video in class, you could use some or all of the suggested activities from page Tviii.

Project Explore T26

2D

2a
- Sts read the expressions and find them in the dialogue.
- In pairs, they discuss what the expressions mean.
- Sts translate the expressions into their own language. Discuss any disagreements as a class.
- Check answers.

> **That's no big deal** = that isn't difficult, not a big problem (informal)
> **sort it out** = organize it (informal)
> **play it safe** = not take any risks (informal)
> **No way!** = there's no possibility of that (informal)
> **It's pricey** = it's expensive (informal)
> **I reckon…** = I think (informal)
> **Sorted!** = the problem is solved (informal)

EXTRA CHALLENGE Give one expression to each pair. In pairs, Sts write a short dialogue using the expression. Each pair acts out their dialogue.

b
- Put Sts in groups of three to practise speaking the dialogue, beginning with Erika's line in frame 2 and ending with Danny's second line in frame 4.

➡ **Workbook** page 18, exercises 1–2

3a
- Write the question on the board.
- Discuss the question based on the two pictures. As a whole class, elicit some ideas, but <u>don't</u> tell Sts if they are right at this stage.

EXTRA CHALLENGE Tell Sts Danny's sister has been on her honeymoon in Paris. Ask *What do you think they liked and didn't like about Paris?*

b 🔊 1·32 ▶ Audio script pT87
- Play the audio for Sts to listen and check their answers. Alternatively, show the class the video of the story from the DVD-ROM.

> **Possible answer**
> Not very successful

4
- Ask Sts to discuss the first two questions with a partner. Play the audio again if necessary.
- Discuss the third question as a class.

> **1** The traffic was bad, there were a lot of tourists, and the hotel was expensive.
> **2, 3** Students' own answers.

EXTRA CHALLENGE Divide Sts into groups of three. Each student tells a story, either true or made up, of a surprise present. The class decides if the story is true or false.

Everyday English Expressing preferences
5a
- Give Sts time to find the expressions in the dialogue.

b 🔊 1·33 Audio script pT88
- Play the audio, pausing for Sts to listen and repeat the expressions.
- Model and drill the pronunciation, paying attention to intonation and stress.

EXTRA IDEA Give Sts an emotion and ask them to say the phrases with that emotion, e.g. happy, sleepy, sad, stubborn, angry, etc.

EXTRA CHALLENGE Divide Sts into groups of three. Give each group an expression. Sts write a dialogue using their expression and an emotion. Sts act out their dialogues for the class to guess the emotion.

➡ **Workbook** pages 18, exercises 3–4
➡ **Photocopiable** Everyday English

Pronunciation Linking
6 🔊 1·34
- Play the audio once for Sts just to listen.
- Now play the audio again, pausing for Sts to repeat, paying attention to the linking.

EXTRA IDEA Get Sts to say the sentences with and without linking, and ask them if they can hear the difference.

EXTRA CHALLENGE Sts write a sentence to practise linking words. They could choose any sentence from the **Student's Book** and write it out, adding appropriate linking marks as in the **Pronunciation** box.

➡ **Workbook** page 19, exercise 5
➡ **Photocopiable** Pronunciation

Listening and Speaking
7a 🔊 1·35 Audio script pT88
- Make sure Sts understand *peer-to-peer travel site*. Ask if they have heard of any, or used them (e.g. Airbnb).
- Play the audio for Sts to listen and answer the questions.

> a city break in Madrid

EXTRA SUPPORT Teach any new lexis before Sts listen.

b
- Sts answer the questions. Play the audio again if necessary.

EXTRA CHALLENGE Ask Sts to answer the questions before playing the audio again.

> **1** They feel too old for that type of accommodation.
> **2** He isn't keen on sharing a room with strangers.
> **3** It sounds more interesting because of all the art galleries, restaurants, and the Real Madrid stadium.

➡ **Workbook** page 19, exercise 6

8a
- Ask Sts to choose a holiday based on the photos.
- Write on the board 'Why do you prefer it?' 'Why would you rather not do the others?'
- Get Sts to write down their ideas.

b
- With a partner, Sts explain their preferences and agree on one of the holidays.

EXTRA IDEA Discuss preferences as a class. The class agrees on one of the holidays.

Extra
Sts do the activity in pairs in class.

T27 Project Explore

2D

2 a Spoken English What do these expressions mean? How do you say them in your own language?

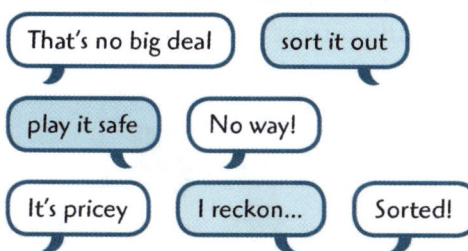

- That's no big deal
- sort it out
- play it safe
- No way!
- It's pricey
- I reckon…
- Sorted!

b Work with a partner. Practise the dialogue from 'I'd love to…' to '…better than a beach or skiing holiday'.

▶ Workbook page 18, exercises 1–2

3 a How successful do you think the honeymoon was?

b 1.32 ▶ Listen and check.

4 Over to you! Answer the questions.
1 What were the three problems with the honeymoon?
2 How do you think Danny's sister felt about going to Paris?
3 What are the dangers of giving and receiving surprise presents? Have you ever done it? What happened?

Everyday English Expressing preferences

5 a Look at the useful phrases. Find examples in the dialogue in exercise 1a.

Useful phrases: expressing preferences
I'd prefer to…
I'd love to…
I'd rather…
I'd prefer not to…
I'd rather not…
I'm not very keen on…
It sounds much better than…
That sounds more interesting than…

b 1.33 Listen and repeat the phrases. Try to copy the intonation.

▶ Workbook page 18, exercises 3–4

Pronunciation Linking

6 1.34 We link the consonant at the end of a word onto the next word if it starts with a vowel. When you speak, imagine that the consonant is at the beginning of the next word. Listen and repeat the expressions.

What's‿up?
What‿about skiing?
I'm not very keen‿on‿it
for‿a honeymoon
That's‿it!
better than‿a beach‿or skiing holiday
they enjoyed‿it

▶ Workbook page 19, exercise 5

Listening and Speaking

7 a 1.35 Listen. What type of holiday do they choose and where do they decide to go?

b Answer the questions.
1 Why would Mark's mum and dad rather not stay at a youth hostel?
2 What is Mark not keen on at the youth hostel?
3 Why does Madrid sound more interesting?

▶ Workbook page 19, exercise 6

8 a Get ready to speak Choose one of the holidays in the photos. Make notes about why you would prefer it. Make notes about why you would rather not do the others.

b Work with a partner. Explain your preferences and try to agree on one of the holidays.

EXTRA Talk about what you would like to do next weekend and the things that you don't want to do.

Unit 2 · New horizons

2 Revision

Vocabulary Day trip attractions

1 Choose the correct answers.

We went on ¹*a ride / an exhibit / a tour* of the Scottish Highlands last year. We didn't see the Loch Ness monster, but we did see beautiful ²*mazes / scenery / activities*! We also visited a ³*festival / tour / scenery* of Scottish culture. There was music and dancing and a sound and light ⁴*show / entrance / cave*. There was also an art ⁵*ride / gallery / maze* and museum with ⁶*festivals / exhibits / tours* about the Highlands in the past. Life was very hard – I'm glad it's changed!

Volunteering verbs

2 Replace the underlined words with the correct form of the verbs.

> collaborate improve monitor organize participate protect

1 We need to <u>look after</u> the environment, not destroy it.
2 I hope my English will <u>get better</u> when I'm in London.
3 A 'cobot' is a robot that <u>works</u> with humans in the same place.
4 He <u>watched and checked</u> the children while they were working.
5 Who is <u>preparing and arranging</u> the school trip to Milan?
6 Alice never <u>takes part</u> in the after school activities.

Adjectives to describe places

3 Complete the sentences with an adjective.

1 The river in the town isn't polluted. It's clean and ___ .
2 It isn't a new festival. It's a ___ one that they've celebrated since the 17th century.
3 The show is on at a ___ theatre, only ten minutes from home.
4 The village isn't near any towns. Actually, it's very ___ .
5 The shops weren't empty! In fact, they were really ___ .
6 Our school isn't in a modern building. It's in a ___ one.

Grammar will and going to

4 Choose the correct answers.

A We're lost, aren't we? Where are we? I ¹*'ll / 'm going to* ask that man.
B Wait, I ²*'ll / 'm going to* use my smartphone. Look, it says we're 3 km from the hotel.
A Hmm, we don't want to go to the hotel. We ³*'ll / 're going to* meet the others at Piccadilly Circus at 7 p.m. How far is it?
B Two kilometres.
A But it ⁴*'ll / 's going to* rain any minute. Look at those clouds!
B I think we ⁵*'ll / 're going to* get there before it rains if we hurry.

Present tenses for future arrangements

5 Complete the sentences with the correct present simple or present continuous form of the verb in brackets.

1 What time ___ the train ___ (leave)?
2 We ___ (have) dinner at Luigi's on Saturday evening.
3 Dad's flight ___ (arrive) at 9 a.m. tomorrow morning.
4 Our holidays ___ (start) on 22nd December this year.
5 Luca ___ (not see) his girlfriend at the weekend.
6 Our Maths teacher ___ (get) married next month.

First conditional

6 Complete the sentences with *if*, *unless* or the correct form of the verbs in brackets.

1 ___ we hurry up, we'll miss the plane!
2 If Alex gets up early, he ___ (not have) to queue at the ski station.
3 Take a map ___ you want to get lost.
4 I won't have enough money for the trip unless I ___ (get) a job.
5 ___ you want to practise your English, speak to local people.
6 What ___ (they / do) if it rains?

Everyday English
Expressing preferences

7 Match the sentence halves.

1 I'm not very keen
2 We'd
3 My sister would rather
4 I'd prefer
5 That sounds much better

a prefer to visit museums.
b read all day.
c than a tent.
d on crowded places.
e not to go to the beach.

Learning to learn Taking risks

Studies have found that teenagers who take risks in their learning can make more progress. This is especially true of learning a language. Try these things:

- Tell the class about a time when you learned something from a mistake.
- Work with different partners for pair or group work. You can learn new things by working with different people.
- Think of a question about a hobby, interest, etc. and find an online forum in English to answer it. However, don't take risks with safety by giving too much information about yourself on the forum.

▶ Workbook pages 20–21, exercises 1–8

Revision

Supplementary materials
Workbook: pages 20–21, exercises 1–8
Online Practice
Unit test 2

Vocabulary Day trip attractions
1

1 a tour 2 scenery 3 festival 4 show 5 gallery
6 exhibits

Volunteering verbs
2

1 protect 2 improve 3 collaborates 4 monitored
5 organizing 6 participates

Adjectives to describe places
3

1 unspoiled / unspoilt 2 traditional 3 local 4 remote
5 crowded 6 historic

Grammar *will* and *going to*
4

1 'll 2 'll 3 're going to 4 's going to 5 'll

Present tenses for future arrangements
5

1 does, leave 2 're having 3 arrives 4 start 5 isn't seeing
6 is getting

First conditional
6

1 Unless 2 won't have 3 unless 4 get 5 If
6 will they do

Everyday English Expressing preferences
7

1 d 2 a 3 b 4 e 5 c

Learning to learn Taking risks
Mistakes
- Ask Sts to write two mistakes they have made as English Sts. Encourage them to think about when they first started lessons.
- Ask them to tell a partner what they did about their mistakes.
- Get feedback from the class about how they overcame their mistakes. Make a list of strategies for taking risks and overcoming mistakes and display it in the classroom.

Pair and group work
- Ask Sts to write two things they like about group work and two things they don't like.
- Ask them to share their list with the class.
- Finally, get the class to agree on a list of how to make pair and group work better.

Online
- Sts think of questions about a hobby to research online.
- Have a class discussion about online safety, and what they can do to keep themselves and their details safe.
- Sts discuss in class the sites they found useful and how it answered their question.

▶ **Workbook** pages 20–21, exercises 1–8

▶ When Sts have finished the **Revision** page, tell them to go to the **Workbook Progress Check** *p.21* and complete the **Your progress** table.

2

My project

Project checklist

Before the lesson
- Organize for Sts to be able to use computers with access to the internet and Microsoft Office PowerPoint or a similar program to make a presentation with slides.
- If you cannot organize for computer access, Sts could do internet research about their chosen place before the lesson. Alternatively, they can get information from the tourist office or ask friends and family, and bring books, magazines, photos, or other resources to the lesson.
- Ensure the materials listed below are available for use in the lesson.

Materials for the lesson
- Photos
- Computers with internet access and a program, e.g. PowerPoint, to make a slide presentation (optional)
- Without computer access, Sts can create their presentations on paper. You will need: A3 paper (one sheet per 'slide' for each presentation)
Coloured pens and pencils.

You First

Sts make a list of the most popular places in their town or region. Then, they make a list of less known places worth visiting. Encourage them to think of places that people their age would like to visit.

EXTRA IDEA Sts work in groups of three or four. Groups decide on one to three places they will write about for their project.

1a
- Put Sts in pairs to make their list.

b 🔊 1·36
- Play the audio for Sts to listen and decide on the order of the photos.

    1 C   2 A   3 B

EXTRA SUPPORT Get Sts to discuss the photos before they listen to the presentation. What do they see?

c 🔊 1·36
- Play the audio again for Sts to listen and tick the topics they hear.

    buildings, music, events / festivals, history, famous people

EXTRA SUPPORT Sts look at the photos again. What topics do they think they are they going to hear about?

2
- In their pairs, Sts choose a topic from exercise 1c for their presentation and write some notes.

EXTRA SUPPORT Sts think about the places they discussed in **You First**. Include these in their notes.

3a
- Sts read through their notes and decide each part they are going to present.
- Then they write their text.

EXTRA SUPPORT Sts look at the text on page 29 to help them write their own.

EXTRA SUPPORT Sts share their text with their partner and discuss any changes.

b
- Tell Sts they should include adjectives in their texts to describe their place. Check that they remember the correct order when they use more than one adjective in a description.

EXTRA SUPPORT Write the correct order on the board: quantity, value/opinion, size, temperature, age, shape, colour, origin, material.

c
- Sts choose photos to show during their presentation and decide when they will show them.

EXTRA CHALLENGE Sts make a PowerPoint presentation for the class. They should use no more than five slides:
1 Title: Introduction to the place and some general information
2 First photo: Information related to the photo
3 Second photo: Information related to the photo
4 Third photo: Information related to the photo
5 Conclusion: Sts finish their presentation.

d
- In their pairs, Sts practise their presentation.

4a
- Sts present to other groups, on paper (showing their photos) or using a computer.
- Encourage them to use language from the text:
  Hello, and welcome to…
  There are lots of good reasons for…
  As you can see,…

EXTRA CHALLENGE Ask Sts to each at least one follow-up question about each presentation.

b
- Write on the board, 'What have you learned about your town?'
- Sts listen to the presentations and make notes to answer the question.
- Have a class discussion about what they have learned.

T29 Project Explore

My project

YOU FIRST! Which places in your town or region are most popular with visitors? Which less known places do you think people should visit?

OUR TOWN

A team presentation

Tullamore

Orla Hello and welcome to our town, Tullamore. It has a population of just over 14,000 and it's right in the middle of Ireland. You can get to anywhere in the country from Tullamore in about two hours! However, there are lots of good reasons for staying here and we're going to introduce you to one, a place that we love in our town. Now over to Liam.

Liam Here you can see historic Charleville Castle. It's a large, grey castle that was built in 1814. It's just outside the town and it was home to a number of wealthy people, including the famous English poet Lord Byron, who organized some incredible parties there. However, the castle was empty for many, many years and after a long time nobody wanted a forgotten, old building.

Orla Today, volunteers have repaired the castle and it's started a new life. As you can see, it's been used in films and TV shows, and lots of tourists come to visit the castle and the gardens during the day. They also visit at night. If you visit, you'll have to stay at the castle during a 'fright night'. They say there's a ghost, a young, blonde girl, who walks around the castle only when it's dark. On 'fright nights' people stay to try and see her. A lot of people say that they've heard laughing and screams, and a few say they've seen the girl in a long, blue and white dress!

Liam If you don't like ghosts, visit the castle in July, when there is, according to the media, the 'best little music festival in Ireland'. For three days you can hear some of the best musicians in the country. So there you have it. Charleville Castle: just one of many reasons why you should visit our town, Tullamore!

1 a Get ready to write Work with a partner and make a list of five interesting things about your town, city or region.

b 🔊 **1.36** Read and listen to the presentation. Put the photos in the order that the speakers talk about them.

c 🔊 **1.36** Listen again and tick (✓) the topics that you hear.
- buildings
- history
- music
- famous people
- sport
- environment
- events / festivals
- industry

2 Choose one of the topics from exercise 1c for your presentation. Make some notes.

3 a Start writing Look at your notes in exercise 2 again. Divide the bullet points into two and decide which of you is going to present each point. Write full sentences.

b Check you use adjectives in the right order.

c Choose some photos to show during the presentation. Decide when you will use them.

d Practise your presentation together.

4 a Complete your project Give your presentation to other students. Use some of the presentation expressions that Orla and Liam used.

b Listen to and discuss your classmates' presentations. What have you learned about your town?

Unit 2 · New horizons

2 Culture

YOU FIRST! Which places can people visit for free in your town? What events or festivals are free?

THE SMART TOURIST'S GUIDE TO
NEW YORK

WHAT DO YOU KNOW ABOUT THE CITY THAT NEVER SLEEPS?

1 Which singer is from New York?
- A Taylor Swift
- B Selena Gomez
- C Lady Gaga

2 Which film series does New York appear in?
- A *Spider-Man*
- B *Batman*
- C *Wonder Woman*

3 There are five boroughs in New York: the Bronx, Brooklyn, Queens, Staten Island and…
- A Washington
- B Manhattan
- C Chicago

4 Which building is the tallest in New York?
- A One World Trade Center
- B Rockefeller Center
- C Empire State Building

5 What is the name that people sometimes give to New York?
- A The Big Orange
- B The Big Apple
- C The Big Banana

1C 2A 3B 4A 5B

Although New York is the most expensive city in the USA, that doesn't stop people from wanting to visit it. However, unless you're on a big budget, you'll be happy to hear that there are still some things in the city that are free…or at least, almost free!

THE BEST VIEW IN TOWN
Everybody wants to see a panoramic view of the New York skyline, but a trip to the top of the Empire State Building, The Rockefeller Center or One World Trade Center is expensive. The solution? For the price of a drink, you can sit in the bar on the roof of the Standard Hotel and admire the Manhattan skyscrapers as you relax and drink.

FOR ART LOVERS
The Metropolitan Museum of Art in Central Park attracts art lovers for two reasons. First, it has incredible collections of Greek, Roman, Egyptian, European and American art. Secondly, it's almost free! If you enter the museum, you'll see a sign that says that it costs $25 to go in, but that is just a recommendation! You can pay as much…or as little…as you like!

FREEDOM FERRY
Can you imagine going to New York without seeing the Statue of Liberty? No, we can't either! You can get great views and photos of the statue and Ellis Island from the ferry that travels between Manhattan and Staten Island. The ferry goes back and forward across New York Bay all day and it's free for all passengers.

ROCK AND POP IN THE PARK
If you want to chill out after a hard day in New York in the summer, go to Prospect Park in Brooklyn and watch a free concert. Folk, rock and pop are just some of the sounds that New Yorkers and visitors can listen to while they lie on the grass and relax.

THE BRIDGE OF SELFIES
Are you looking for the perfect selfie? Then walk across the Brooklyn Bridge as you return to Manhattan from Prospect Park. The city opened the bridge in 1883 and it is one of New York's best. From the Brooklyn side of the bridge, you'll have the skyline of Manhattan in front of you: turn around and you've got the perfect background for that special selfie that you can upload to your social media page! However, be careful with the cyclists…they don't like anybody standing in the cycle lane and they'll let you know if they're angry!

Glossary
budget   skyscraper   chill out
skyline   ferry   cycle lane

1 Work with a partner. Answer the quiz questions. Then check your answers.

2 Read the online article. Which place(s) or event(s) would you recommend to someone who likes…?
1 culture
2 seeing the city
3 taking photos
4 relaxing

3 Work with a partner. Discuss which activities from the article you would most / least like to do. Why?

4 Over to you! Write five sentences about what you'll do in New York if you travel there in the future.

30 Unit 2 · New horizons

▶ Heading west from New York

Culture

Supplementary materials
Photocopiable worksheets: Culture, Culture video

CULTURE NOTES Below are some additional notes on New York City you may want to share with your Sts.

Le Bain rooftop bar, the Standard Hotel: The views from the Standard Hotel are fantastic. You can see the skyline and also the view across the Hudson River to New Jersey. There is a discotheque at the top with world-famous DJs. In the summer, there is a pool for young people.

Liberty Helicopters: For the best views, take a helicopter ride. It's expensive, but you can see amazing views. A tour lasts 12 to 15 minutes and costs $150. You'll see the Statue of Liberty, Ellis Island and the World Trade Center, as well as the Chrysler Building, the Empire State Building and the Woolworth Building along the way. You'll also see the George Washington Bridge and green Central Park.

The Statue of Liberty: The Statue of Liberty was a gift from France to the United States. It was sent to New York in 350 different pieces. It stands in New York Harbor, and is a symbol of welcome for all the immigrants going to America. It is a universal symbol of freedom.

Brooklyn Bridge: The Brooklyn Bridge opened to the public on May 24, 1883. Only a few days after it opened to the public, disaster struck. The many people crossing the bridge thought it was going to collapse, and they ran to escape. Twelve people died in the crush, and 36 were seriously injured. No one knows the reason for the panic. In May 1884, 21 elephants marched across the bridge to show that the bridge was safe.

You First
Ask the two questions to the class and make a list on the board of free (or very cheap) places to visit.

1
- Ask Sts what they already know about New York City and the United States. Ask if anyone has ever been there.
- Put Sts in pairs to do the multiple-choice quiz about New York.
- Sts check the answers at the bottom of the page.

1 Lady Gaga   2 *Spider-Man*   3 Manhattan
4 One World Trade Center   5 The Big Apple

EXTRA IDEA Ask Sts to find photos of New York, either in magazines / brochures or online. Discuss the photos in class.

EXTRA IDEA Tell Sts some of the extra information in the **Culture notes**. Write on the board 'Would you like to visit New York City?' 'Why? / Why not?' Sts discuss the questions. Encourage them to use some of the things they have just learned about New York.

2
- Ask Sts to read the article and make recommendations based on the four topics.

1 The Metropolitan Museum of Art, Prospect Park
2 The Standard Hotel, the Staten Island Ferry, Brooklyn Bridge
3 The Standard Hotel, the Staten Island Ferry, Brooklyn Bridge
4 The Standard Hotel, Prospect Park

EXTRA SUPPORT Read the text and decide if you need to teach any new lexis before Sts do the task. Refer Sts to the **Glossary**.

EXTRA IDEA Get Sts to recommend one of the areas for a classmate. Encourage them to explain their answer.

3
- In pairs, Sts discuss the activities in the article and say which ones they would like to do, and which they would prefer not to do.
- Encourage them to give their reasons.

EXTRA IDEA Sts answer the question for you, imagining what they think you would answer. Then, they explain their choice. Tell them your choices at the end of the discussion.

4
- Give Sts time to write their sentences.
- If you have chosen to give them the additional information in the **Culture notes**, they can include this if they want to.

EXTRA IDEA Read out some of the Sts' sentences, but without saying whose they are. See if the class can guess who wrote each sentence. When they have identified the writer, briefly discuss it.

▶ Video Heading west from New York

As an extension to the Culture topic, watch a short film about heading west from New York and do the accompanying photocopiable exercises. You can either do this in class or set it as optional homework. The film is available on the DVD-ROM or on the Online Practice.

2

Learn through English

Additional subject notes
Renaissance: This started as a cultural movement in Italy in about 1400, which brought about a new style of art characterized by realism. Artists such as Leonardo da Vinci and Michelangelo studied human anatomy and the mathematical laws of perspective to paint scenes that had realistic depth. At first, the subjects were mostly from biblical stories, but later they included portraits, episodes from classical Greek history and mythology, and even events from contemporary life.

Baroque: The Baroque period followed the Renaissance and spread across Europe from its origins in Rome, Italy. The word 'baroque' comes from a French and Portuguese jewellery term meaning 'imperfect pearl'. Baroque art is noted for the use of clear details, exaggerated motion, and light and shadow to create a sense of drama. Two of the best known Baroque artists are Peter Paul Rubens and Diego Velásquez.

Impressionism: This movement started in France in the 19th century and takes its name from Claude Monet's painting titled Impression, Sunrise. Impressionist artists painted directly from life, in the open air, and tried to capture the momentary effects of light and movement. Well-known Impressionists include Claude Monet, Auguste Renoire, and Edgar Degas.

Post-Impressionism: This term is normally used to describe the work of artists such as Paul Cezanne, Paul Gauguin and Vincent van Gogh who worked during the late 19th century. These artists still painted real-life subjects like the earlier Impressionist artists, but they experimented with shapes and colours to represent their subjects in new, bolder ways.

You First
Write the questions on the board. Give Sts time to think about their answers. Then, discuss as a class.

1a
- Give Sts time to match the artists to their paintings, and decide which artist's work is not shown.
- Get them to compare with a partner, then check answers.
- Ask if Sts have seen any paintings by Picasso, and if they know what style of painting he is best known for (*Cubism*).
- Ask Sts which painting they like best, and why.

A Monet **B** Van Gogh **C** Da Vinci **D** Velázquez
E Rubens **F** Michelangelo
Not shown: Picasso

EXTRA IDEA Ask Sts to research one or two paintings they like. Tell them to bring to class one or two facts they found interesting.

CULTURE NOTE Name the artist of each painting:
1 *Impression, Sunrise* – Claude Monet
2 *The Starry Night* – Vincent Van Gogh
3 *The Last Supper* – Leonardo Da Vinci
4 *Portrait of Sebastián de Morra* – Diego Velázquez
5 *The Wedding by Proxy of Marie de Medici to King Henry IV* – Peter Paul Rubens
6 *The Creation of Adam* – Michelangelo Buonarroti

b
- Ask Sts to match the styles and periods to the paintings.

Baroque: Velázquez, Rubens
Impressionism: Monet
Post-Impressionism: Van Gogh
Renaissance: Da Vinci, Michelangelo

EXTRA IDEA Ask Sts to look up some interesting information about each art style and when it was popular. Tell them to show the class another painting from the style.

2a 1•37
- Play the audio for Sts to listen and follow.
- Play the audio again, or get Sts to read the text again, to match the artists from exercise 1a to the notes.
- Make sure Sts understand that they should consider all seven of the artists in the box in exercise 1a for their answers.

1 Van Gogh **2** Picasso **3** Da Vinci, Michelangelo

EXTRA SUPPORT Pre-teach or elicit any difficult or new vocabulary. Refer students to the **Glossary**.

b
- Give Sts time to read the questions and find the answers in the text.

1 They supported artists like Leonardo da Vinci or Michelangelo. (paragraph 2)
2 They started buying art to improve their social status. (paragraph 2)
3 Favourable reviews and positive comments in the media and from the public (paragraph 3)
4 An artist's biography (paragraph 4)
5 They want visitors to recognize the paintings that they have bought. (paragraph 5)

EXTRA SUPPORT Tell Sts which paragraph holds the answer to each question.

EXTRA SUPPORT Divide the class into five groups. Ask each group to answer one of the questions. Then, groups share their answers with the class. Encourage groups to say where they found the answer in the text.

3a
- Give Sts time to prepare their descriptions, based on the questions.

b
- Put Sts in pairs. They read their descriptions to each other, without saying which painting they are describing.
- The listening partner identifies the picture.

EXTRA CHALLENGE Sts find a picture online of a painting they really like and bring it to class. Display the pictures. Let Sts briefly talk about why they chose it.

T31 **Project Explore**

Learn through English

2

YOU FIRST! Which are the most famous art galleries in your region or country? What type of paintings can you see in them? Which is your favourite painting? Why?

A B  C  D 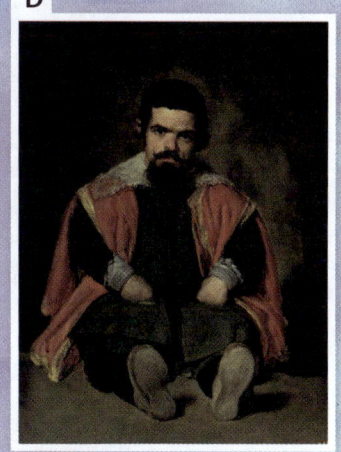 E  F

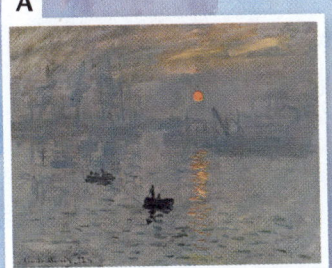

Art styles and periods

Art galleries are popular places for family and school day trips, but they're also a key part of one of the world's most important businesses – the buying and selling of art. However, what makes one piece of artwork more valuable than others?

Art and artists started to attract the interest of wealthy Europeans during the Medieval and Renaissance periods. Many of the works of Leonardo da Vinci or Michelangelo, for instance, were created thanks to the support of families such as the Medici of Florence. Wealthy people wanted to improve their social status by buying art and this resulted in an increase in the value of art. It also made some artists famous and everything that they painted had a high price. Buying art became a way of investing money.

So what makes a painting valuable today? Works by Velázquez, Rubens, Monet and other famous painters are always going to be popular and so there will always be wealthy people happy to buy them. However, tastes in the art world change just as in any field. This can happen when a painting attracts the attention of art critics. For contemporary artists, it is particularly good news when their work is displayed in a top gallery. Furthermore, if the media and public are enthusiastic about it, then the value of their work immediately increases.

The artist's biography can also affect the price of a painting. One of the most obvious examples is the Dutch painter Vincent Van Gogh, whose problems with mental illness had an important influence on his artistic production and on public interest. Other life events that seem to have a positive effect on how an artist's work is viewed include unhappy love affairs and even lawbreaking!

Finally, one of the most important factors for buyers is the artist's style. If someone spends millions of dollars on a Picasso, they want it to be immediately clear to visitors in their home or office that it is a Picasso. If people don't recognize it, they will feel that they have wasted their money.

Glossary
valuable	field	contemporary
social status	critics	affair

1 a Match six of the artists in the box to their paintings. Whose work is not shown? Have you seen paintings by this artist?

> Da Vinci   Michelangelo   Monet
> Picasso   Rubens   Van Gogh   Velázquez

b Match the styles and periods in the box with the paintings in exercise 1a.

> Baroque   Impressionism
> Post-Impressionism   Renaissance

2 a 🔊 **1.37** Read and listen to the article. Match four of the artists from exercise 1a to the notes.
1 health problems
2 a way of painting
3 helped create the art business

b Read the article again. Answer the questions.
1 What did the Medici family do?
2 Why did people start buying art?
3 What can increase the value of a work of art?
4 What can affect the price of a painting?
5 What do owners of famous paintings want?

3 a Prepare a description of one of the paintings that you like on this page.
- Which colours did the painter use?
- What can you see in the picture?
- Why do you like it?

b Work with a partner. Take it in turns to describe your painting and identify your partner's.

Unit 2 · New horizons

The Museum of the Strange   Episode 1

1 🔊 1.38 ▶ Read and listen to the story.

'It's raining,' said Laura. 'Again!'
Declan laughed. 'Don't you like the rain?'
'It hasn't stopped since we arrived,' said Ben.
The friends were on a school trip in the north of England. They were in a small town by the sea.
'Look.' Laura pointed at a building on a little side street. 'There's a little museum. Why don't we look around?' she said.
'A museum?' Declan shook his head. 'No, thanks! I'll see you later!'

Inside the museum a tall man sat at the front desk. He looked up and a big smile appeared on his face.
'Welcome to the Museum of the Strange,' he said.
'You'll want to spend a long time here, I'm sure.'
Laura tried not to laugh. 'Um – thanks.'
'I'll give you a tour, of course,' continued the tall man.
'No, that's OK,' said Ben, but the man was already standing.
'If I don't give you a full tour, you'll miss our best exhibits.'

A sign in the museum's first room said THE PAST. The room was full of things from all different times and places – a sword, an old watch, an early bicycle, clothes from many years ago …
Laura stopped in front of a very simple painting of a horse.
'This looks *really* old,' she said. 'Is it?'

The museum guide's smile grew wider. 'I'll tell you the story of our famous cave painting. A few years ago there was a young man called Dan. His family moved to a small village near here and Dan wasn't happy about it. He didn't have any friends. He didn't know what to do with his life when school finished.

One afternoon Dan was walking when he saw some kids from his school. They were at the railway bridge.

'Hey, I know you. You're the new kid at school!'

'That's right – my name's Dan. What are you all doing?'

'We're going to make this boring old bridge look much better. More colourful.'

'Hey, I saw you at Art in school – you're good. Why don't you spray something for us?'

Dan just looked at the can of red spray-paint.

'Sorry, I won't do that. I like art, but I don't like graffiti.'

Dan started to walk away but then he heard a shout.

'Hey, you kids! You can't do that!'

32 The Museum of the Strange • Episode 1

The Museum of the Strange Episode 1

Supplementary materials
Workbook: pages 22–23, exercises 1–9
Online Practice
Progress test 1

Note
The story can be used in class as a reading and listening task, a video task or both.

1 🔊 1·38 ▶

- In pairs, get Sts to look at the pictures on page 32 and predict what they think will happen in Episode 1. Elicit some ideas, but don't tell Sts if they are right at this stage.
- Play the audio for Sts to listen and follow. Alternatively, show the class the video of the story from the DVD-ROM.
- Ask Sts how similar their predictions were to what happens.
- Give Sts time to retell the story about Dan in pairs. You could write the words from the pictures on the board to help, e.g. '1 walking, bridge' '2–3 art, graffiti' '4 shout' '5 questions, ran' '6 ground, hole' '7 cave, light' '8 painted, thousands' '9 running, phoned' '10 centuries, artist'
- Elicit parts of the story from different pairs.

EXTRA SUPPORT Pre-teach or elicit from the pictures *tour*, *exhibits*, *cave*, *shout*, and *graffiti*.

EXTRA SUPPORT Play the audio again for Sts to listen and follow again before doing the task. They could also retell the story with their books open, using the pictures to help.

EXTRA CHALLENGE Tell Sts to close their books. In pairs, Sts take turns to say what happened in all the pictures, e.g. *Laura, Declan and Ben were on a school trip in the north of England. It was raining, so they went into a small museum…*

➡ **Workbook** pages 22–23

Notes
The story can be further exploited by doing the tasks from these pages in the **Workbook**. These can be done in class or set as homework.
The tasks in the **Workbook** review the following language points covered in **Units 1–2** in the **Student's Book**:
- Verb forms (*pp. 9, 11*)
- Conjunctions (*p.16*)

1
- Sts complete the sentences, using the correct form of the verbs in the box.
- Get Sts to compare their answers and discuss any differences. Encourage them to look at the story.

2 hasn't stopped **3** saw **4** went **5** sitting **6** offered
7 said **8** gave **9** looked **10** told

EXTRA IDEA Ask Sts to look back at the story and compare their answers.

EXTRA IDEA Sts go back to the story and choose five sentences. They rewrite the sentences without the verb, leaving a gap. They give their sentences to a partner to complete.

EXTRA IDEA In pairs, Sts take turns to say a sentence in the past tense about the events in the story. Their partner says if the sentence is true or false and corrects any false information, e.g.:
A The friends were on a school trip in the south of England.
B False! They were in the north of England.

2
- Ask Sts to read the definitions in the exercise and complete the ones they know.
- Then, ask Sts to look back at the story to complete the ones they don't know.

1 artist **2** exhibits **3** graffiti **4** bridge **5** cave **6** guide

EXTRA IDEA Sts choose six words that are specific to the story, e.g. *museum*. Then, they write a definition for the word, similar to the definitions in the exercise, e.g. *The place the children visit*. Next, they give their definitions to a partner to solve. Sts could also do this orally, saying their sentence to the class for them to guess the word.

3
- Ask Sts to read the sentences and correct the false information in each one.
- Encourage them to look back at the story to check their answers.

2 Dan **didn't have any** friends.
3 He was walking in the country, when he saw some **children / students** from his school.
4 They were **sitting on a bridge**.
5 One of the kids wanted Dan to spray graffiti on the **bridge**.
6 Dan ran because **he didn't want to answer a lot of questions**.
7 He **fell** into a cave.
8 The paintings in the cave were **thousands** of years old.
9 That day, Dan decided to become **an artist**.

EXTRA IDEA Ask Sts to look at the story again and choose two sentences they like. Then, ask them to make one of the sentences false by changing it slightly. Finally, have Sts read one of their sentences to the class. The class decides if it is true or false and corrects the false information.

4
- Ask Sts to put the words in the correct order to make sentences.
- Then, ask them to match each sentence to the speakers in the pictures.

2 I'll give you a tour, of course. A **3** I like art, but I don't like graffiti. B **4** This looks really old. E **5** Someone is coming to get you out. C

Project Explore   T32

1

EXTRA IDEA Ask Sts to choose something that one of the characters in the story says, then say it to the class. The class guesses who the speaker is. Encourage Sts to use different voices and emotions to make it more fun.

EXTRA CHALLENGE Ask Sts to look at the story again. Tell them to imagine what some of the characters might have said that is not in the story. They say it to the class and the class guesses who might have said it. Encourage Sts to explain why the character might have said it.

5

- With a partner, ask Sts to discuss the questions.

Students' own answers.

6 🔊 13 Workbook Audio script pT105

- In pairs, ask Sts to say what is happening in each picture.
- Then, ask Sts to put them in order.
- Play the audio for Sts to listen and check.

1 D **2** B **3** E **4** A **5** C

EXTRA SUPPORT Play the audio again. Raise your hand when an answer is given.

7 🔊 13 Workbook Audio script pT105

- Before you play the audio again, tell Sts to read the statements and the different options.
- Play the audio for Sts to complete the task.

EXTRA CHALLENGE Ask Sts to choose the answers before they listen again. Then, play the audio for them to confirm their answers.

2 b **3** c **4** c **5** a

8

- Ask Sts to complete the text with the conjunctions in the box.
- With a partner, ask Sts to compare their answers and discuss any differences.

2 until **3** because **4** so **5** but **6** Although

9

Students' own answers.

> **Note**
> To further exploit the video in class, you could use some or all of the suggested activities from page Tviii.

Dan didn't want to answer lots of questions. He ran.

But the ground was soft after weeks of rain. There was a hole…

Oh no!

Dan was in a dark cave. He pulled out his phone and turned on the light.

Wow! This is incredible.

Somebody stood here and painted these, probably thousands of years ago.

Are you OK? You were running, and then I couldn't see you!

I've phoned for help. They'll be here soon.

That's OK. I'm happy to wait here.

'And he was successful in his ambition,' the guide explained. 'Today, you can see his art in galleries around the country. In some of his work, he liked to copy parts of the ancient cave art that he found that day … like this one.'

'You mean … this painting *isn't* very old?' asked Laura.

The guide laughed. 'Look closer.'

Behind the red horse, they could see other things – a bridge and a train.

'I didn't see them at first,' said Ben. 'That's strange.'

'Of course,' said the guide. 'That's what we collect here – strange and interesting things.'

Dan thought about the person who made those paintings – that person was talking to him across the centuries through his art. Dan decided something that afternoon…

I know what I want to do with my life. I'm going to be an artist.

▶ Workbook pages 22–23

The Museum of the Strange · Episode 1

3 Respect

3A Testing

YOU FIRST! Do you like to watch or do experiments? Why do they help us learn?

A laboratory

Vocabulary Practical science nouns

1 a 🔊 2.02 Look at the picture. Read and listen to the article. Are Science lessons at your school the same or different? How?

UK SCIENCE LESSONS

From the age of 11, students in British secondary schools learn how to use equipment such as microscopes, test tubes and petri dishes in scientific tests and experiments. They can see how the theories and ideas in their textbooks work. They wear safety goggles and white coats. Students carry out studies and investigations into cells and different types of specimens. After a test, the students put the cells and specimens under observation so they can see the effects. They then study the results and the information from the test and decide if it was a success.

Labels: safety goggles, cell, equipment, petri dish, test tube, specimen, microscope

b Match the definitions with the highlighted nouns from the article.

1 scientific tests to show that something is true or to discover something new ___
2 thin glass tubes that scientists use ___
3 the act of watching something carefully ___
4 the final situation at the end of a number of actions ___
5 flat glass containers ___
6 the things that you need to do something ___
7 the smallest parts of an animal or plant ___
8 something that makes small things big enough so that you can see them ___
9 special glasses that protect your eyes ___
10 studies of the facts to find out the truth about something ___
11 ideas that explain something ___
12 examples of a type of thing that scientists study ___

c 🔊 2.03 Listen and check, then repeat.

▶ Workbook page 24, exercises 1–3

	Lab report: DNA experiment
Equipment and material:	A ^{1}___ , a sports ^{2}___ , pineapple juice and alcohol for cleaning.
Process:	*Put the alcohol in the ^{3}___ the night before. *Drink a little of the sports drink and move it around your mouth for two minutes to collect ^{4}___ . *Put the liquid from your mouth into the test tube. Add a little ^{5}___ liquid, pineapple juice and the alcohol.
Results:	During a short period of ^{6}___ , we will see white material form on top of the liquid. This is your DNA.

Listening and Writing

2 a 🔊 2.04 Listen to a scientist explaining the experiment above. Complete the lab report.

b Write a lab report about an experiment that you have done or watched in a Science lesson. Use the example above.

3 Over to you! Work in a group. Explain your experiment. Which experiments were the most interesting and why?

> We did this experiment in the science lab last month. We wanted to find out... First, we... Then, we... After that, we... Finally, we...

34 Unit 3 · Respect

3 Respect

Unit objectives

use nouns to talk about practical science

use phrasal verbs to talk about socializing

explain an experiment using words for scientific method

talk about advice, obligation and necessity using modals

talk about permission using *can*, *could* and *be allowed to*

talk about possibility using *can*, *could*, *may* and *might*

use phrases to express advantages and disadvantages about a topic

write a report about social media use

Language

Grammar: modals – advice, obligation and necessity; **permission:** *can*, *could*, *be allowed to*; possibility: *can*, *could*, *may*, *might*

Vocabulary: practical science nouns; phrasal verbs for socializing; the scientific method

Everyday English: expressing advantages and disadvantages

Project: Read all about it!

Culture: Australia under attack

Learn through English: Water (Science)

3A Testing

Supplementary materials

Workbook: pages 24–25, exercises 1–10
Workbook: Grammar summary Unit 3
Photocopiable worksheets: Grammar and Vocabulary, Communication

You First

Ask Sts to think about the experiments they have done in Science classes. Write these questions on the board: 'What experiments did you do?' 'Did you like them?' 'What experiments did you like the most, and why?' 'What did you learn from the experiments?' In pairs, Sts discuss these questions and the ones on page 34.

Vocabulary Practical science nouns

1a 🔊 2·02

- Play the audio for Sts to listen, follow and answer the questions.
- Get feedback from the class.

EXTRA SUPPORT Sts look at the picture. What do they see? Is their Science classroom similar? Encourage Sts to list two similarities and two differences.

EXTRA IDEA Sts write one thing that is the same and one thing that is different about their Science lessons. Sts discuss their ideas with a partner.

EXTRA CHALLENGE Write on a piece of paper one thing that is the same and one thing that is different about your own Science lessons. Ask Sts to guess what they might be.

b

- Give Sts time to complete the task, then check answers.

1 experiments 2 test tubes 3 observation 4 results
5 petri dishes 6 equipment 7 cells 8 microscope(s)
9 safety goggles 10 investigations 11 theories
12 specimens

c 🔊 2·03

- Play the audio for Sts to check their answers.
- Play the audio again for Sts to listen and repeat, paying attention to the stress.

EXTRA SUPPORT Divide the class into two groups. One group matches 1–6, the other group matches 7–12.

➡ Workbook page 24, exercises 1–3

Listening and Writing

2a 🔊 2·04 Audio script pT88

- Give Sts time to read the lab report.
- Play the audio for Sts to listen and complete the report.

1 test tube 2 drink 3 fridge 4 cells 5 washing-up
6 observation

LANGUAGE NOTE DNA (deoxyribonucleic acid) is the chemical in the cells of animals and plants that carries genetic information.

EXTRA SUPPORT Read the script and decide if you need to teach any new lexis before Sts listen.

EXTRA CHALLENGE Sts read and try to complete the lab report before listening.

b

- Give Sts time to write their report, following the example.

EXTRA SUPPORT Sts work in pairs or small groups to write their lab report. They can use a dictionary to help them.

EXTRA CHALLENGE Sts write reasons for their process, using *so* (*that*), as in the audio.

3

- In groups, Sts explain their experiment and decide which experiments were the most interesting.

EXTRA CHALLENGE Sts tell the class about a partner's experiment.

3A

Grammar and Reading Modals – advice, obligation and necessity

4 🔊 **2·05**
- Play the audio for Sts to listen, follow and answer the question.

> James thinks that it is wrong to do experiments on animals, and Lucy thinks that it is sometimes right.

5a
- Give Sts time to complete the sentences, then check answers.

> 1 mustn't 2 must 3 have to 4 don't have to
> 5 should 6 ought to

b
- Tell Sts to complete the rules using the answers they wrote in exercise 5a.
- Get them to compare with a partner, then check answers.

> 1 mustn't 2 must, have to 3 don't have to
> 4 should, ought to

c
- Give Sts time to write sentences about their school using modal verbs and the topics in the box.

EXTRA IDEA With a partner, Sts discuss the rules at their school. Encourage them to explain why the rules exist.

EXTRA CHALLENGE On strips of paper, ask Sts to write sentences about their homes using modal verbs. Each sentence should be on a separate strip. Collect the strips and randomly give them out to the class. Sts then read out the sentence you gave them and try to guess who wrote it; e.g. I have to do the washing up at home. I think that's Michael!

➡ **Workbook** pages 24–25, exercises 4–7
➡ **Photocopiable** Grammar and Vocabulary

Listening and Speaking

6a
- Give Sts time to read the sentences and decide who says them.
- Tell them to refer back to the dialogue in exercise 4 if necessary.

> 1 Lucy 2 James 3 James 4 Lucy

EXTRA IDEA Tell Sts to support their answers with examples from the dialogue.

b 🔊 **2·06** Audio script pT88
- Play the audio for Sts to listen and check their answers.

c 🔊 **2·06** Audio script pT88
- Ask Sts to copy the table into their notebooks.
- Play the audio again for Sts to complete the task.

> **Points in favour:** animals and humans have similar genes; medicine won't improve without testing on animals
> **Points against:** computers can test drugs; some tests show drugs are safe when they're tested on animals, but they aren't safe for humans

EXTRA SUPPORT Play the audio for the Sts. Raise your right hand each time there is a point in favour of medical experiments. Raise your left hand each time there is a point against.

➡ **Workbook** page 25, exercises 8–10

7a
- Ask the class who they agree with.

EXTRA CHALLENGE Tell Sts to defend their opinions, e.g. *I think… because…*

EXTRA CHALLENGE Sts write their own reasons in favour of or against animal testing. Encourage Sts to think of reasons not mentioned yet and ask them to defend their opinions.

b
- Read through the topics with the class.
- Give Sts time to make their notes.

EXTRA IDEA Divide the class into groups. Give two groups the same topic. Ask one group to make an argument for the topic and the other group against it. Groups prepare their arguments to present to each other.

c
- Put Sts in pairs to discuss the topics, saying whether they agree or disagree with their partner's opinions.

EXTRA CHALLENGE Put Sts in new pairs and ask them to report the discussion with their previous partner. Encourage Sts to discuss different opinions.

d
- Get feedback from the class so that Sts can compare with their own opinions.

EXTRA CHALLENGE Hold a class debate. Allow 2–3 minutes for each St to present their argument while the class listens and asks questions. When everyone has spoken, the class votes for or against.

Extra

Sts can either do this in class or as a homework task.

Project Explore

3A

Grammar and Reading
Modals – advice, obligation and necessity

4 🔊 **2.05** Read and listen. What opinions do Lucy and James have on the use of animals in experiments?

Lucy Hey, have you seen the new rules for the science lab?

James Well, we know most of them: we mustn't work in the lab alone, we must wear safety goggles and a lab coat…

Lucy I know, but now there's even a rule about the clothes we have to wear under our lab coats!

James In my opinion, we need another rule – one about using animals and insects in experiments. There are lots of great computer programs for studying Biology, so we don't have to use them at all.

Lucy But studying real animals is one of the best ways of learning about Biology.

James What? It's cruel.

Lucy Cruel? We use dead mice and frogs!

James Yes, but what happens before they arrive at our school? You should look online and discover how science uses animals. It's a big business!

Lucy Well you ought to read about how, thanks to experiments on animals, we can save human lives.

James Look, let's talk later. I'd like to tell you why testing on animals is wrong.

Lucy Fine, and I'd like to explain why it's sometimes right!

5 a Complete the sentences from the conversation.
1 We ___ work in the lab alone.
2 We ___ wear safety goggles.
3 …the clothes we ___ wear under our lab coats!
4 We ___ use them at all.
5 You ___ look online.
6 You ___ read.

b Complete the rules with your answers from exercise 5a.

1 We use ___ to say that you can't do something.
2 We use ___ and ___ to say that it's necessary to do something.
3 We use ___ to say that it isn't necessary to do something. You can choose.
4 We use ___ and ___ to give advice or make recommendations.

c Use modal verbs to write sentences about your school.

school uniform   school meals   classroom   science lab

We don't have to wear a uniform at my school.

They should offer more vegetables and fruit at lunchtime.

▶ **Workbook** pages 24–25, exercises 4–7

Listening and Speaking

6 a Read the sentences. Who do you think says them: Lucy or James?
1 Sometimes scientists have to use animals in experiments.
2 We can use computer programs to do experiments on drugs.
3 Some experiments with animals didn't help scientists discover if drugs were safe or not.
4 Human lives are more important than animal lives.

b 🔊 **2.06** Listen and check.

c 🔊 **2.06** Listen again. What points do Lucy and James use in favour of and against medical experiments on animals?

Points in favour	Points against

▶ **Workbook** page 25, exercises 8–10

7 a Get ready to speak Who do you agree with?

b Make notes in favour of and against the topics.
- doing science experiments at school
- testing new medicines on humans
- using animals to test beauty products

c Over to you! Work with a partner. Discuss the topics. Say if you agree or disagree with each other's opinions.

> In my view, scientists shouldn't use people in their experiments. I think it's dangerous!

> That's a good point, but I think it depends on the type of experiment. I think they should use people when their investigations are about sleep or things like that. That isn't dangerous and the results…

d Compare your opinions with the class.

EXTRA Create an experiment that tests what happens when students don't use social media for a week. What should / shouldn't they do?

Unit 3 · Respect 35

3B Young at heart

YOU FIRST! Do you think there is a right age for some activities? Why? / Why not?

Reading

1 a 🔊 **2.07** Read and listen to the introduction to the article. What are the projects in the article trying to do?

b 🔊 **2.08** Read and listen to the rest of the article. Match the sentences to the project.

Project (A / B / C)...

1 encourages people to take part in a competition
2 puts young and old people together
3 shows what people do on the internet
4 allowed people to enjoy themselves and tell others about their situation
5 helps some people save some money
6 made some people famous

Vocabulary   Phrasal verbs for socializing

2 a Choose the correct words.

1 *come in / cheer up / stay over*: sleep at someone's house
2 *get into / go out / hang out*: become interested in an activity
3 *take sb out / get together / move in*: meet someone
4 *pick up / go out / come in*: leave a place to go and do something interesting
5 *move in / join in / stay over*: start living in a new place
6 *drop by / get into / hang out*: spend time with someone
7 *drop by / go out / take sb out*: visit someone
8 *move in / get together / pick up*: collect someone
9 *join in / stay over / hang out*: participate in an activity
10 *hang out / come in / move in*: enter a place
11 *cheer up / get into / go out*: feel happier
12 *join in / take sb out / drop by*: go somewhere with someone

b 🔊 **2.09** Listen and check, then repeat.

▶ Workbook page 26, exercises 1–3

As YOUNG as you feel

All human beings need to socialize, but it can become more difficult as we get older if we live alone. Although care homes offer a solution, the residents can't always do activities that really interest them because there aren't enough staff. They sometimes feel that they have no freedom and that they are cut off from the rest of society. As a result, some organizations and care homes started setting up projects that connect elderly people with others and encourage them to be active.

A   Your right to party

Alf Carretta wasn't expecting to become a rock star at 90, but he did. Alf and the other 40 members of the pop group The Zimmers made a recording of the famous rock song *My Generation* and it became a hit. The elderly rock stars really got into music, appeared on TV and made more recordings of famous songs such as *You Gotta Fight For Your Right To Party*. However, although The Zimmers were a success, they didn't just want to cheer up their audiences with great performances. They wanted to tell the world about life in some care homes where they weren't allowed to do much more than watch TV or where family could only visit them for a short time. They wanted people to know about elderly people who couldn't go out because they had nobody to meet. They also wanted to show that elderly people could have fun when they were allowed to join in and take part in activities.

B   Care Home Idol

When elderly people are allowed to use their talents or learn new skills, they enjoy the same feelings of satisfaction that we all do. To make sure their residents continue to have those positive feelings, a group of care homes has created a website that copies a popular TV programme, Pop Idol, which allowed viewers to vote for the best new singer on the show. In Care Home Idol, residents can sing, play musical instruments, act or dance. They get together to film their performances, upload them to the website and wait to see how many votes they get by the end of the year. The winners are just as excited as the ones on the TV show!

C   Meet my new flatmate

Many care homes have strict rules about when family and friends can come in and visit residents. Now, however, in some European countries that is changing. University students are moving in to care homes and living there free; in exchange they spend 30 hours a month with the elderly residents. The students and residents play games together or just hang out and chat, with the elderly residents even offering advice to their young friends on relationship problems! Some students teach their older 'flatmates' new skills, including how to paint graffiti! The students' friends can also drop by and even stay over for the night. The idea has been a big success and other countries want to copy it.

These projects aren't simply about picking up elderly people and taking them out for the day. They encourage the residents to learn new things, be creative and feel good about themselves.

3B Young at heart

Supplementary materials
Workbook: pages 26–27, exercises 1–10
Workbook: Grammar summary Unit 3
Photocopiable worksheets: Grammar and Vocabulary, Communication

You First
Sts discuss the question and give their reasons.

EXTRA SUPPORT Ask Sts to discuss these questions about their country *How old do you have to be to drive / vote / leave school? Do you agree with the age? Why? / Why not?*

Reading
1a 🔊 2·07
- Play the audio for Sts to listen, follow and answer the question.

> To connect elderly people with others and encourage them to be active.

EXTRA SUPPORT Read the introduction and decide if you need to teach any new lexis before Sts listen.

EXTRA SUPPORT Sts look at the photo and the title of the article. Discuss what the article is about. Then, Sts read the three headings and continue their discussion.

b 🔊 2·08
- Give Sts time to read the sentences.
- Play the audio for Sts to read and listen to the rest of the article.
- Sts match the sentences to the three projects.

> 1 B 2 C 3 B 4 A 5 C 6 A

EXTRA SUPPORT Pre-teach or elicit any difficult or new vocabulary, e.g. *right, care home, graffiti*, and explain that a *zimmer frame* is a walking aid.

EXTRA SUPPORT Ask Sts to read out a sentence from the article and get the class to guess which project it is about.

EXTRA CHALLENGE Ask Sts to choose a sentence from the article and make it false by changing it slightly, e.g. *Alf Carnetta became a film star at 90.* Get the class to correct the sentence to make it true.

Vocabulary Phrasal verbs for socializing
2a
- Give Sts time to complete the task, then check answers.

> 1 stay over 2 get into 3 get together 4 go out
> 5 move in 6 hang out 7 drop by 8 pick up
> 9 join in 10 come in 11 cheer up 12 take sb out

EXTRA SUPPORT Tell Sts to close their books. Write the phrasal verbs from exercise 2a on the board, with the verbs in one column and the prepositions in another. Ask Sts to match a verb with a preposition to make a phrasal verb from exercise 2a. Get the class to say what it means.

EXTRA CHALLENGE Tell Sts to make a sentence about themselves using one of the phrasal verbs. The sentence can be true or false. Get the class to guess if the sentence is true or false.

b 🔊 2·09
- Play the audio for Sts to check their answers.
- Now play the audio again for Sts to listen and repeat, paying attention to the stress.

EXTRA IDEA Get Sts to repeat the words with different emotions, e.g. if you say 'crying', Sts should repeat the word in a crying voice.

EXTRA CHALLENGE Tell Sts to write a sentence using one of the phrasal verbs. Then, say an emotion and ask a St to repeat the sentence with that emotion.

➡ **Workbook** page 26, exercises 1–3

3B

3a
- With a partner, Sts use phrasal verbs from exercise 2a to talk about a typical weekend.

b
- Put Sts in groups and ask them to tell each other about their weekend, using the phrasal verbs. Remind them to listen carefully to see who used the most phrasal verbs.
- Get groups to decide on the best weekend.

EXTRA IDEA Ask each group to tell the class about the best weekend they have chosen. The class votes on the best weekend. Encourage Sts to explain why.

EXTRA SUPPORT Get Sts to note down some of the sentences while they are listening. This will help them with exercise 3c.

c
- Ask Sts to return to their partner from exercise 3a.
- Ask them to repeat sentences from the weekends they have heard about, but leaving out the phrasal verb for their partner to guess.

EXTRA IDEA Instead of saying the phrasal verb, Sts can say the word 'buzz', e.g. *On Saturday I buzzed with my friends at the shopping centre.*

Grammar Permission: *can, could, be allowed to*

4a
- Give Sts time to look back at the article on page 36 and complete the task.
- Check answers.

1 can (paragraph C) **2** weren't allowed to (paragraph A)
3 are allowed to (paragraph B) **4** could (paragraph A)

b
- Ask Sts to complete the rules, then check answers.

1 can / can't **2** could / couldn't **3** (not) be allowed to

c
- Give Sts time to complete the task.
- Get them to compare with a partner, then check answers.

1 can **2** could **3** couldn't **4** 'm **5** was **6** can't

EXTRA IDEA Ask Sts to adapt the text and make it true for them.

EXTRA CHALLENGE Sts write a similar text about themselves, adding different information.

d
- Put Sts in pairs, **A** and **B**.
- Student **A** looks at page 86, Student **B** looks at page 87.
- Tell them to ask and answer questions to complete their tables. Remind Sts to use the verbs for permission they have learned.
- They then make sentences from the information in the table.

EXTRA SUPPORT Elicit the questions from the class before Sts work in pairs. Write them on the board.

EXTRA CHALLENGE Sts complete the tables for themselves and their dad or mum. Then, in pairs, Sts ask each other questions to complete the tables.

➡ **Workbook** pages 26–27, exercises 4–7
➡ **Photocopiable** Grammar and Vocabulary

Listening and Speaking

5a 🔊 2•10 Audio script pT88
- Play the audio for Sts to listen to the podcast and complete the column about England.
- Tell Sts they need to write the age at which the things become legal in England.

drive a car: 17 **ride a moped:** 16 **start a full-time job:** 18
start a part-time job: 13 **get a tattoo:** 18 **get married:** 16

EXTRA SUPPORT Read the script and decide if you need to teach any new lexis before Sts listen.

EXTRA SUPPORT In pairs Sts complete the column about England before they listen to the podcast.

b
- Play the audio again for Sts to answer the questions.
- Check answers.

1 tractor, moped **2** the weather isn't very good **3** 2 **4** 30
5 early 30s

EXTRA CHALLENGE Get Sts to answer the questions before listening again. Ask them to compare with a partner before checking answers.

> **Note**
> Answering the questions before listening again gives Sts a focus when they do listen: they know what they are listening for.

c
- Give Sts time to complete the second column with information about their country.

EXTRA SUPPORT Sts complete the information individually first. Then, they compare their information with a partner and discuss any differences.

EXTRA IDEA Get Sts to discuss the differences between England and their country. What surprises them the most?

➡ **Workbook** page 27, exercises 8–10

6a
- Give Sts time to write their questions.
- Sts interview their relative or neighbour before the next lesson.

b
- Put Sts in pairs to ask and answer questions about each other's relative / neighbour.
- Then ask them to compare their relative's / neighbour's lives with their own.

EXTRA CHALLENGE Sts discuss these questions: *What surprised you the most? How do you feel about the differences?*

Extra
Sts can either do this in class or as a homework task.

Project Explore

3B

3 a Work with a partner. Use the phrasal verbs in exercise 2a to talk about a typical weekend.

> My friends and I got into skateboarding last year, so we often get together at…

b Work in a group. Listen to your classmates. Who used the most phrasal verbs? Whose weekend was the best?

c Over to you! Work with a partner. Repeat sentences from your group with gaps for your partner to guess the correct phrasal verb.

> On Saturdays, I…with my friends at the shopping centre.

> The phrasal verb is…hang out!

Grammar

Permission: can, could, be allowed to

4 a Complete the sentences from the article.
1 The students' friends ___ also drop by…
2 They ___ do much more than watch TV.
3 When elderly people ___ use…
4 Family ___ only visit them for…

b Complete the rules with the words.

(not) be allowed to
can / can't   could / couldn't

To talk about permission, we use:
1 ___ in the present
2 ___ in the past
3 ___ in the present and the past

c Complete each gap with one word.
Now that I'm 15, I ¹___ go out more than I ²___ when I was younger. Two years ago, I ³___ go to a party because it finished late, but now I ⁴___ allowed to stay out later. Last Saturday I ⁵___ allowed to stay at a friend's house until 11 p.m.! However, I still ⁶___ come back on my own and I have to wait for Dad to pick me up.

d You are going to ask and answer about Jack and his dad and complete a table.
Student A Look at page 86.
Student B Look at page 87.

▶ **Workbook** pages 26–27, exercises 4–7

Listening and Speaking

5 a 🔊 2.10 Listen to the podcast. Complete the England column.

	England	My country
drive a car		
ride a moped		
start a full-time job		
start a part-time job		
get a tattoo		
get married		

b Answer the questions about England.
1 Which vehicles can you drive at 16?
2 What's the problem with riding a moped?
3 How many hours can teenagers work on a school day?
4 What percentage of people want to remove their tattoos?
5 What age do most people get married?

c Find information about your country and complete the table.

▶ **Workbook** page 27, exercises 8–10

6 a Get ready to speak Interview an elderly relative / neighbour. Ask them about the things they were and weren't allowed to do when they were your age. Use the words in the box to help you.

drive   leave home   parties   ride a moped   school   work

b Work with a partner. Ask and answer questions. Then compare your relatives' / neighbours' lives with yours.

> Was your aunt allowed to…on her own?

> No, she wasn't. She could…, but only if her brother went, too.

EXTRA Write sentences about the rules in your house.

> I'm not allowed to stay over at a friend's house if I haven't done my homework.

Unit 3 · Respect 37

3C Finding solutions

YOU FIRST! How scientific do you think you are? When was the last time you found your own solution to a problem? How did you feel?

Reading and Vocabulary
The scientific method

1 a Which step is the Science lesson from 3A?

The six steps of the scientific method

1 ASK A QUESTION.
The scientific method begins with making a question about something that you have seen or noticed.

2 DO SOME RESEARCH.
Use different sources such as the internet, a library or experts such as your teachers to find the new information that you need.

3 MAKE A HYPOTHESIS.
A hypothesis is a guess about why something happens or how something works. A good one will help you make a prediction: If I do this, this will happen.

4 TEST THE HYPOTHESIS IN AN EXPERIMENT.
The experiment tests if your prediction is a good one.

5 CARRY OUT A CAREFUL ANALYSIS OF THE DATA.
A careful analysis will see if your data supports your prediction.

6 WRITE A CONCLUSION.
In the conclusion, explain the procedure that you followed and describe the results and your findings.

b Match the highlighted words to the definitions.
1 your opinion about something after you have thought about the information that you have ___
2 what you think will happen in the future ___
3 a possible explanation for why something has happened ___
4 a careful study of new information that you find in an experiment, etc. ___
5 the way of doing something ___
6 information that you discover at the end of a careful study of something ___
7 the different parts of a plan, experiment, etc. ___
8 information, especially facts and numbers, that you collect to study ___
9 a careful study that looks for new information or a new understanding about something ___
10 the places where you get information ___

c 🔊 **2.11** Listen and check, then repeat the words.

▶ **Workbook** page 28, exercises 1–3

Listening and Speaking

2 a 🔊 **2.12** Listen to two friends, Lucas and Ivy, talking about a problem. What is the problem?

b Complete steps 1–5 of the table with a–e.
a Ivy deletes her recent post and apologizes in a new post.
b Ivy has got 43 likes on her new post, 7 positive comments about her apology and a message from Ruby.
c Lucas thinks that if Ivy deletes the first post and apologizes, Ruby might be her friend again.
d Ivy spoke to Olivia and Jenna. Then Ivy looked at her own post on social media.
e Why isn't she talking to Ivy?

Step 1: Observation and question	Ruby isn't talking to Ivy.
Step 2: Research	___
Step 3: Hypothesis and prediction	___
Step 4: Experiment	___
Step 5: Analysis of the data	___
Step 6: Conclusion and findings	

3 a 📝 **Over to you!** Work with a partner. Make notes about the following for step 6 in exercise 2b:
- an analysis of the data from Lucas and Ivy's experiment
- the findings from the experiment

b Work in a group. Compare your notes. Which conclusions do you agree with? Why?

38 Unit 3 · Respect

3C Finding solutions

Supplementary materials
Workbook: pages 28–29, exercises 1–9
Workbook: Grammar summary Unit 3
Photocopiable worksheets: Grammar and Vocabulary, Communication

You First

Sts discuss the questions. Ask *Are you good at solving problems? What makes you good or bad? Think of the last time you had a problem. How did you solve it? Did you solve it scientifically? In your opinion, what is being scientific?'*

Reading and Vocabulary The scientific method

1a
- Give Sts time to read about the six steps.
- Ask Sts what they remember about the Science lesson in **3A**.
- Refer Sts back to the Science lesson in **3A** to answer the question.

Step 4

EXTRA CHALLENGE Ask Sts to justify their answer based on the information in **3A**.

b
- Ask Sts to complete the task, then compare with a partner.
- Check answers.

1 conclusion   2 prediction   3 hypothesis   4 analysis
5 procedure   6 findings   7 steps   8 data   9 research
10 sources

EXTRA SUPPORT Ask some Sts to use a dictionary to each find the definition for one of the highlighted words to share with the class.

EXTRA CHALLENGE Ask Sts to use the words to make sentences related to science. Encourage them to use their experience from their Science classes.

c 🔊 2•11
- Play the audio for Sts to listen and check.
- Play the audio again for Sts to listen and repeat.
- Model and drill the pronunciation of the words, paying attention to the stress.

EXTRA IDEA Pause the audio before each word is said. Ask Sts to say the word, then continue the audio for Sts to compare with their pronunciation.

EXTRA IDEA Ask Sts, in pairs, to repeat the words to their partner and help each other with the pronunciation. Then, listen to the audio to improve.

EXTRA CHALLENGE Sts pronounce the words in different voices, e.g. whispering, shouting, singing, etc.

➡ **Workbook** page 28, exercises 1–3

Listening and Speaking

2a 🔊 2•12 Audio script pT89
- Play the audio for Sts to listen and answer the question.

Ivy's friend, Ruby, is angry with Ivy.

EXTRA SUPPORT Tell Sts to look at the photo and ask *Who is in the picture? Where are they? Are they friends? What do you think they are talking about?* The questions establish a context for the listening, which helps Sts to listen better.

b
- Sts complete the table with a–e. Point out that the 'Observation' part of Step 1 has been given, but that they need to find the second part ('Question').

Step 1 e   Step 2 d   Step 3 c   Step 4 a   Step 5 b

EXTRA SUPPORT Sts compare their answers with a partner and discuss any differences. Then, they listen again to confirm their answers.

3a
- Put Sts in pairs and give them time to write their notes. Sts compare their notes and make any changes.

EXTRA SUPPORT Play the audio again for Sts to get any extra information.

b
- Sts share their notes in their group and decide which conclusions they agree with, and why.

EXTRA CHALLENGE Ask groups to present their best conclusion to the class. Ask the class to decide which conclusion they agree with, and why.

EXTRA CHALLENGE Get the group to divide their presentation among all of the Sts in the group. When the group presents to the class, each student takes a turn to speak.

3C

Grammar Possibility: *can, could, may, might*

4a
- Give Sts time to read sentences 1–4 and complete the rules.
- Check answers.

A *may, might* **B** *may not* **C** *can* **D** *could*

4b
- Ask Sts to complete the task, then compare answers with a partner and discuss any differences.
- Check answers.

1 may / might not go   2 can find   3 could post
4 may / might not cook   5 may / might / could be   6 can use

EXTRA CHALLENGE Sts look at the sentences and rules in exercise 4a and write their own sentences using the modal verbs.

EXTRA CHALLENGE Give each student a modal verb on a strip of paper. Get Sts to write a true sentence about themselves using the modal verb. Collect the strips of paper and give them back at random to the class. Ask Sts to guess who wrote the sentence, e.g.
Sam I think Tom might watch a film tonight.
Tom No, it's not me. Ana might watch a film tonight.
Ana …

➡ **Workbook** pages 28–29, exercises 4–6.
➡ **Photocopiable** Grammar and Vocabulary

Speaking

5a
- Give Sts time to read the conversation and answer the questions.

1 Some classmates may feel that others don't always show respect.
2 He's going to write a short questionnaire.

EXTRA SUPPORT Ask Sts to write examples from the dialogue to support their answer.

EXTRA CHALLENGE Discuss the question 'In your experience, do people use social media to be cruel?'

b
- With a partner, Sts read the questionnaire and add two more questions.

EXTRA SUPPORT Ask the class to give examples of some questions for the questionnaire. Write them on the board. Tell Sts they can choose two they like or write their own.

EXTRA CHALLENGE Sts add 'Not sure' to the 'Yes / No' answer for each question. They then ask and answer the questions with their partner. Encourage them to explain why they are not sure.

c
- Tell Sts to decide with their partner which of their classmates they are going to ask, so that you can make sure they don't all ask the same Sts.
- Sts ask their five questions and note down the answers. Encourage them to ask at least ten of their classmates.

Writing

6a
- Put Sts in pairs and give them time to prepare their report, using the framework of the questions.
- Tell them to write complete sentences based on their information, e.g. *13 out of 20 students try not to make jokes online.*
- Encourage them to go back to the grammar and vocabulary from **3C**. Ask *Have you used words from exercise 1? Have you used the grammar from exercise 4?*

➡ **Workbook** page 29, exercises 7–9

b
- Give Sts time to write their report in their pairs.

EXTRA SUPPORT Sts compare their reports with their partner and make any necessary changes.

EXTRA IDEA Tell Sts to make a bar graph to show the result of the questionnaire and include it in their report.

EXTRA IDEA Display the reports in the classroom and let Sts walk around to read them.

c
- Put Sts in groups to compare their findings. Get them to discuss differences and similarities.
- Get feedback from the class.

EXTRA SUPPORT Ask Sts to tell a partner one of their findings. Their partner responds with the result from their questionnaire, and they both discuss the difference or similarity.

EXTRA CHALLENGE Sts discuss any disagreements they have with the results, based on their own experience.

EXTRA IDEA In groups, Sts make a poster about good social media practice, using modal verbs. Display all the posters and let Sts discuss the ideas and agree on the best poster.

Extra
Sts can either do this in class or as a homework task.

T39 Project Explore

3C

Grammar
Possibility: can, could, may, might

4 a Read the sentences from the conversation and complete the rules.
1 People can get angry about anything.
2 It may not have anything to do with you.
3 We could try an experiment.
4 I think you might be friends with Ruby again.

> **A** We use *could*, ___ and ___ to talk about the possibility of something really happening.
> **B** We use *might not* and ___ for the negative. We don't use *couldn't*.
> **C** We use ___ to say things are possible in general.
> **D** We use ___ to talk about making a choice or a decision.

b Complete the sentences with *can, may, might* and *could* and the verb in brackets. More than one answer is sometimes possible.
1 I ___ (not go) to Kate's party tonight.
2 You ___ (find) advertisements everywhere on social media.
3 Hey, we ___ (post) the news on Facebook so everyone can see it.
4 Andy ___ (not cook) anything for dinner tonight.
5 There ___ (be) something interesting to read on the website.
6 You ___ (use) this app to send photos.

▶ **Workbook** pages 28–29, exercises 4–6

Speaking

5 a Read the conversation. Answer the questions.

Lucas I've made an observation that some people use social media to be cruel.
Ivy Not the scientific method again!
Lucas I'm afraid so! I'm going to use it to help me do my project for English.
Ivy Good idea. So your hypothesis is that some classmates may feel that others don't always show respect.
Lucas Unfortunately yes, but instead of doing an experiment, I'm going to write a short questionnaire.

1 What is Lucas's hypothesis?
2 How is he going to test it?

b Work with a partner. Read the questionnaire about social media use. Add two more questions.

What type of social media user are YOU?

The aim of this survey is to help you find out what type of social media person you are. Just answer each question with 'yes' or 'no'.

1 Do you try to avoid making jokes about friends online? **YES / NO**

2 Do you ask your friends if you can upload photos of them to social media? **YES / NO**

3 Do you tell someone who has posted a cruel comment that they should delete it? **YES / NO**

4 ___ **5** ___

If your answers are mostly 'yes', then you probably know that you have to be careful about what you say about people online. However, if your answers are mostly 'no', you need to think about how you're using social media. You probably don't want to hurt anyone's feelings, but you need to be more careful about what you say and upload.

c Work with your partner. Ask the five questions to the other students in the class. Make a note of their answers.

Writing

6 a **Get ready to write** Work with your partner. Prepare to write about your findings. Use the conversation in exercise 5a to help you.
- What was the hypothesis?
- What did you do to find out if the hypothesis is correct?
- What were the answers to your questions?
- What were the findings and the conclusion?

▶ **Workbook** page 29, exercises 7–9

b Write your report.

> We wanted to find out if some people can be cruel on social media. We wrote a short questionnaire and...

c Compare your findings with other students.

EXTRA Write a class contract for using social media. Say what may / might / could happen because of what people write on social media.

> Be careful when you write jokes; people might feel hurt by them.

> Tell people about things that are happening at school; other students could find the information useful.

Unit 3 · Respect 39

3D Emil's petition

YOU FIRST! How can people raise awareness of issues that affect them? What ways of raising awareness do you know?

contact the media

sign a petition

1 Read the newspaper report. How can people fight to save the park?

Norton council has given permission to build a new shopping centre on Merton Park. Local people were very surprised to hear the news and have promised that they will fight to save the park. Apart from being popular with parents with young children, many sports teams use the park to play their matches at the weekends. According to…

2 a 🔊 2.13 ▶ Read and listen. How successful is the activity that the friends choose to do?

Liza Oh no! They want to turn the park into a shopping centre!

Danny What park? This park?!

Liza Yeah! It says that the arguments in favour are more shops, more people and more business!

Erika What about the arguments against?! Like, no green areas or nowhere for children to play!

Danny We have to do something about this!

Oliver Let's demonstrate! 'Save our park! Save our park!'

Erika We definitely shouldn't do that.

Oliver Why's that? It'll be a laugh!

Erika Er…well, one disadvantage is that it will annoy everybody. No, we need a petition.

Oliver A petition? That'll fail!

Liza Hmmm, I think that would work. It's a great way to show people we care.

Erika And it'll be really useful for explaining our position, too.

Danny Yeah, I'd go along with that. Let's give it a go.

2 Later

Erika Thank you…There's one more.

Danny But we still only have 37 people. This isn't working!

Liza Hey guys, check this out! I told Emil about the park. He's already built a website *and* started an online petition! He says he does this kind of thing all the time!

> **Twitter** @Emil15
> I had an idea. Check this out:
> http://petition4us.com/saveourpark
> 1 Sept 2019

@saveourpark
Save Merton Park
Sign now | Comment | Share
Petition votes: 0 0 8 3 4/5

Danny He's got 835 people already!

Liza I know and look – there are comments!

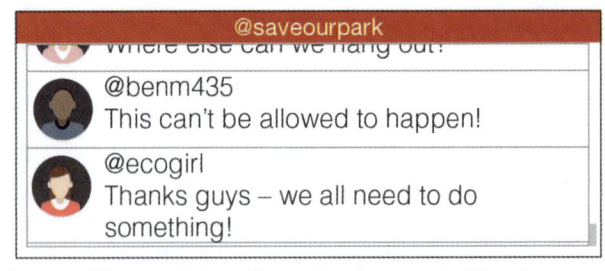

@saveourpark
Where else can we hang out?
@benm435 This can't be allowed to happen!
@ecogirl Thanks guys – we all need to do something!

Liza 'This can't be allowed to happen', 'Thanks guys – we all need to do something!' This is brilliant!

Danny I guess a benefit of doing it online is that you can reach loads of people.

Erika And quickly, too! I knew a petition would be a good idea!

Oliver Yeah, Emil's petition. Not yours!

Danny Oh, come off it, Oliver!

Oliver OK, OK – it was a good idea.

Liza And the best thing is we might actually save our park!

40 Unit 3 • Respect

3D Emil's petition

Supplementary materials
Workbook: pages 30–31, exercises 1–7
Photocopiable worksheets: Everyday English, Pronunciation
Online Practice

> **Note**
> The story can be used in class as a reading and listening task, a video task or both.

You First

Sts discuss the questions. Ask *What issues affect you? How did you hear about them? Do you talk to anyone else about them? Do you do anything about them?*

EXTRA SUPPORT Ask Sts to think of two issues that they feel strongly about. Elicit and write some of the issues on the board. Decide on the three most important issues for the class. With a partner, ask Sts to discuss ways of raising awareness of those issues.
Discuss as a class how to raise awareness of the issues in the school, their community, country and the world.

EXTRA IDEA Ask Sts to think of advertisements that raise awareness of issues. Then, in small groups, have Sts act out an advertisement to raise awareness of their issue.

1

- Give Sts time to read the newspaper report and answer the question.

EXTRA SUPPORT Ask *What is the issue?* (*a new shopping centre on Merton Park*) *How did local people react?* (*surprised; promised to fight it*) *Who uses the park?* (*parents with young children, sports teams*)

2a 2·13

- Play the audio for Sts to listen, follow and answer the question. Alternatively, show the class the video of the story from the DVD-ROM.

> The petition is not very successful until they decide to do it online.

EXTRA SUPPORT Ask Sts to look at the photos. Ask *Who can you see? Where are they? What are they doing? Look at their expressions, how do you think they are feeling?'*

EXTRA CHALLENGE Sts answer the question based on the photos, before they read or listen.

> **Note**
> To further exploit the video in class, you could use some or all of the suggested activities from page Tviii.

Project Explore   T40

3D

b
- Give Sts time to read the sentences and complete the task.

> 1 F 2 T 3 F 4 T 5 F 6 T

EXTRA SUPPORT Play the audio or show the video again first, or get Sts to find the answers in the text.

EXTRA CHALLENGE Sts correct the false sentences. 1 *The sign says they want to turn the park into a shopping centre.* 3 *Erika thinks a demonstration will annoy people.* 5 *Only 37 people signed the petition.*

c
- Give Sts time to complete the task.
- Get Sts to check with a partner and discuss any disagreements, then check answers.
- Model and drill pronunciation and stress.

> **It'll be a laugh.** = It will be fun. (informal)
> **I'd go along with that.** = I agree. (informal)
> **Let's give it a go.** = Let's try it. (informal)
> **I guess…** = I suppose… (informal)
> **Come off it!** = a colloquial way of saying 'I don't agree' (informal)

EXTRA SUPPORT Ask Sts to find the expressions in the dialogue. Encourage them to see how they are used in context.

EXTRA CHALLENGE With a partner, Sts write a short dialogue using the expressions. The class listens and discusses if they agree with the usage.

➤ **Workbook** page 30, exercises 1–2

3a
- Ask the class to predict what they think will happen next.
- Get feedback.

EXTRA SUPPORT Write Sts' suggestions on the board. It will help them to focus as they listen in the next activity.

EXTRA CHALLENGE Encourage Sts to explain their answers based on the information they already know.

b 2•14 Audio script pT89
- Play the audio for Sts to check their predictions. Alternatively, show the class the video of the story from the DVD-ROM.

EXTRA IDEA Sts answer these questions based on the audio: *How many people have signed the petition? What is the Norton Telegraph? What does the Norton Telegraph want?*

4
- Give Sts time to think about the questions, then discuss with a partner.

EXTRA IDEA Sts discuss the questions in small groups. Each group votes and agrees on an answer.

EXTRA CHALLENGE In groups of five, get Sts to act out a TV talk show about the issue of the park. Each group will need these roles: news commentator, representative for the building company, member of the Norton Council, parent, coach of a sports team. Allow each student one minute to present their case.

Everyday English Expressing advantages and disadvantages

5a
- Give Sts time to read the phrases and find them in the dialogue in exercise 2a.

EXTRA SUPPORT Get Sts to repeat the complete phrase from the dialogue. Play the audio to help them with their pronunciation.

b 2•15 Audio script pT89
- Play the audio, pausing for Sts to listen and repeat.
- Drill the pronunciation.

EXTRA SUPPORT First, ask all Sts to repeat the phrase. Next, ask only the boys and then only the girls. Finally, get the class to repeat in small groups of about 3.

➤ **Workbook** pages 30–31, exercises 3–5
➤ **Photocopiable** Everyday English

Pronunciation Sentence stress

6a 2•16
- Play the audio for Sts to listen and follow.
- Now play the audio again, pausing for Sts to listen and repeat each word.

b 2•16
- Play the audio for Sts to listen again and say which word is stressed in each sentence.

> It'll be a <u>laugh</u>! Come <u>off</u> it! I'd go along with <u>that</u>.
> Let's give it a <u>go</u>. I <u>knew</u> it! This is <u>brilliant</u>!

c
- Sts practise saying the expressions in exercise 6a.

EXTRA SUPPORT Practise first as a class, then in smaller groups, and finally in pairs or groups of three.

➤ **Workbook** page 31, exercise 6
➤ **Photocopiable** Pronunciation

Listening and Speaking

7a 2•17 Audio script pT89
- Play the audio for Sts to listen and answer the question.

> Three

b 2•17 Audio script pT89
- Play the audio again for Sts to identify the advantages of each activity.

> The sports activities would show that the park is a great place to do exercise.
> Making cakes and giving them away would let the members speak to people and explain why they should sign the petition.
> Camping in the park would attract the attention of the media.

➤ **Workbook** page 31, exercise 7

8a
- In pairs, Sts each choose a situation and make notes.

b
- With their partner, Sts explain their suggestions.

Extra

Sts can either do this in class or as a homework task.

3D

b Are the sentences true (T) or false (F)?
1 The sign says the area needs somewhere for children to play.
2 Oliver wants to organize a demonstration.
3 Erika thinks a petition will annoy people.
4 Danny agrees that a petition will allow them to explain their ideas.
5 A lot of people have signed Danny's petition.
6 Emil gives Liza an idea.

c Spoken English What do these expressions mean? How do you say them in your own language?

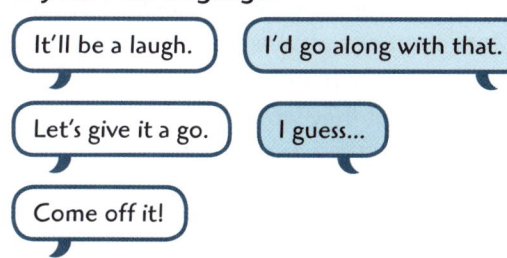

- It'll be a laugh.
- I'd go along with that.
- Let's give it a go.
- I guess…
- Come off it!

▶ **Workbook** page 30, exercises 1–2

3 a What do you think will happen next?

b 🔊 2.14 ▶ Listen and check.

4 Over to you! Do you think the newspaper article will help save the park? Why? / Why not?

Everyday English

Expressing advantages and disadvantages

5 a Look at the useful phrases. Find examples in the dialogue in exercise 2a.

Useful phrases: expressing advantages and disadvantages

One advantage / disadvantage is that…
The arguments in favour / against are that…
A benefit / drawback of doing…is that…
…is a great way to…
…is / isn't really useful for…

Useful phrases: asking for and giving reasons

Why's that?
I think that would work.

b 🔊 2.15 Listen and repeat the phrases. Try to copy the intonation.

▶ **Workbook** pages 30–31, exercises 3–5

Pronunciation Sentence stress

6 a 🔊 2.16 Listen and repeat the expressions in the box.

> It'll be a laugh!   Come off it!
> I'd go along with that.   Let's give it a go.
> I knew it!   This is brilliant!

b 🔊 2.16 Listen again. Which word is stressed in each sentence?

c Practise saying the expressions in exercise 6a.

▶ **Workbook** page 31, exercise 6

Listening and Speaking

7 a 🔊 2.17 Listen. How many new activities do the speakers mention?

b 🔊 2.17 Listen again. What are the advantages of each activity?

▶ **Workbook** page 31, exercise 7

8 a 📋 **Get ready to speak** Work with a partner. Agree on who is A and who is B. Read your situation and make notes about what you want to do.

A

You and your friends have discovered that a cosmetics company in your town uses dogs, cats and rabbits in experiments for new products. The company doesn't want anybody to know and wants to continue the experiments. You want to make the information public and to stop the experiments.

B

Your school wants to replace the unhealthy snacks and soft drinks that it sells in the school canteen with fruit, healthy snacks (such as nuts) and bottles of water. You and your friends want to be able to buy both.

b Explain your suggestions to your partner. Ask your partner to give reasons for their suggestions.

EXTRA Choose an issue that affects your town, region or country. How are you going to raise awareness about the issue?

Unit 3 · Respect   41

3 Revision

Vocabulary Practical science nouns

1 Write the words for pictures 1–5.

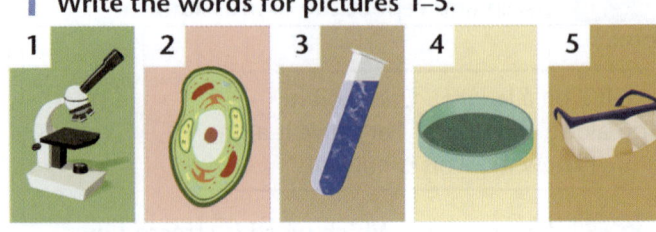

1 2 3 4 5

Phrasal verbs for socializing

2 Complete the sentences with the correct preposition.

1 I hang ___ with my friends at the weekends.
   a over   b up   c out
2 When the sun came out, everyone cheered ___ .
   a up   b in   c out
3 Will your sister join ___ ? We need one more player.
   a over   b in   c together
4 Zoe is staying ___ at her cousin's house tonight.
   a out   b over   c by
5 My classmates dropped ___ to see me when I was ill.
   a by   b up   c out
6 I love Christmas when we get ___ with the family.
   a over   b up   c together

The scientific method

3 Complete the text with the words in the box.

> analysis findings hypothesis
> prediction procedure steps

Before we start an experiment we have to make a ¹___ about the way we think something works and then make a ²___ about what we think will happen because of the experiment. We also have to consider the ³___ and how we're going to do it and the different ⁴___ that we will have to take. When we have finished, we have to make an ⁵___ of the data from the experiment and write a conclusion with our ⁶___ .

Grammar

Modals – advice, obligation and necessity

4 Choose the correct answers.

1 You *should / mustn't* study for the exam tonight.
2 I *don't have to / mustn't* get up early on Saturdays.
3 You *mustn't / ought to* clean your shoes before the interview.
4 We *have to / should* arrive on time for training or we won't be allowed to play on Saturday.
5 You *must / don't have to* try the free offer at the new Italian restaurant.
6 I *must / mustn't* forget to email Sam with some more information for our project.

Permission: *can, could, be allowed to*

5 Correct the underlined mistakes.

1 When I was younger, I <u>didn't</u> allowed to use the computer.
2 I hope I <u>could</u> sleep over at my friend's this weekend.
3 We <u>can't</u> use a dictionary in last week's English exam.
4 My brother is only eight, so he <u>doesn't</u> allowed to go out on his own.
5 Girls <u>were</u> allowed to wear trousers to school now.
6 Last year I <u>can't</u> hang out with my friends in town.

Possibility: *can, could, may, might*

6 Complete the sentences with *can, could, may* and *might*. More than one answer is sometimes possible.

1 Advertisers ___ tell the truth about food products for a change, but they won't!
2 A What are you doing tonight?
   B I'm not sure, but I ___ go to the cinema.
3 A Is the new football computer game available yet?
   B Yes, you ___ buy it online.
4 I ___ not sign the petition. I'm not really sure what I think about the situation.

Everyday English

Expressing advantages and disadvantages

7 Complete the dialogue with the phrases.

> argument in explain why main problem
> one disadvantage reason is Why's that?

A I think a sports day is a great way to let people know about the plans to sell the school sports field.
B ¹___
A The ²___ that people know that keeping fit is important and they want their children to do sport.
B Perhaps, but I think ³___ is that it will be difficult to organize.
A Can you ⁴___ ?
B Well, the ⁵___ with the idea is that sport is popular and a lot of people will come.
A Exactly! That's an ⁶___ favour of a sports day because lots of people want to use it!

Learning to learn Brainstorming

Brainstorming is about producing ideas. When you're brainstorming, you should write down everything that you can think of that is connected to the topic; all ideas are good ideas! When you can't think of any more ideas, read through your list and choose the best ideas for the task.

▶ **Workbook** pages 32–33, exercises 1–8

42 Unit 3 • Respect

Revision

Supplementary materials
Workbook: pages 32–33, exercises 1–8
Online Practice
Unit test 3

Vocabulary Practical science nouns
1

1 microscope 2 cell 3 test tube 4 petri dish
5 safety goggles

Phrasal verbs for socializing
2

1 c 2 a 3 b 4 b 5 a 6 c

The scientific method
3

1 hypothesis 2 prediction 3 procedure 4 steps
5 analysis 6 findings

Grammar Modals – advice, obligation and necessity
4

1 should 2 don't have to 3 ought to 4 have to 5 must
6 mustn't

Permission: *can, could, be allowed to*
5

1 wasn't 2 can 3 couldn't / weren't allowed to 4 isn't
5 are 6 couldn't / wasn't allowed to

Possibility: *can, could, may, might*
6

1 could 2 may / might 3 can 4 may / might

Everyday English Expressing advantages and disadvantages
7

1 Why's that? 2 reason is 3 one disadvantage
4 explain why 5 main problem 6 argument in

Learning to Learn Brainstorming

- Refer Sts to the **Learning to learn** box.
- Emphasize that all ideas are good; there are no right or wrong suggestions.
- Write on the board 'Best things to do on a Sunday morning'.
- Give Sts two minutes to write down their ideas. Who has the most ideas?
- When they have finished, discuss the activity with them. How do they feel about brainstorming? How could brainstorming help them learn?

➡ **Workbook** page 32–33, exercises 1–8

➡ When Sts have finished the **Revision** page, tell them to go to the **Workbook Progress Check** *p.33* and complete the **Your progress** table.

3

My project

Project checklist

Before the lesson
- Ask Sts to bring in photos for their article.

Materials for the lesson
- Photos
- Computers with internet access, or a printer
- Without computer or printer access, Sts can write their article on paper. You will need A3 paper.

You First

Get Sts to discuss the issues that are important to them at the moment. How do the issues affect them? What can they do to solve them?

EXTRA SUPPORT Draw three columns on the board. Write 'Issues' at the top of the first column. Elicit the issues from the Sts. At the top of the second column, write 'How they affect us'. Elicit how the issues are affecting the Sts. At the top of the third column, write 'What can I do about it?' Elicit possible actions.

1a
- With a partner, Sts choose a topic from the box or an issue of their own.

b 🔊 2·18
- Play the audio for Sts to listen, follow and answer the question.

> the environment

c
- Give Sts time to read the article and complete the task.
- Check answers.

> **1** B **2** C **3** A

2
- Give Sts time to complete the task, then check answers.

> **1** According to **2** To sum up, **3** Furthermore,
> **4** There is no doubt that **5** However,

EXTRA SUPPORT Sts compare their answers with a partner and discuss any disagreements.

3
- Give Sts time to plan and start writing their article.
- Encourage them to look at the notes to the right of the article about Gorsham to help them make a plan.

EXTRA SUPPORT Write a structure on the board to help your Sts:
First paragraph: Introduce your topic. What is the issue? Who is behind each side? What language do you need?

Second paragraph: Present both sides. What is the position of one side? What is the position of the other side? What language will you need?

Third paragraph: Write a conclusion. Give your opinion. Explain the reasons for your opinion. What language will you need?

4
- Sts complete their article, and either print it out or upload it to the internet.
- If Sts don't have access to a printer or a computer, they can use sheets of A3 paper.
- Sts write a title and add photos to the article.
- Display printed or hand-written articles in the classroom.

EXTRA SUPPORT Tell Sts to share and discuss their article with a partner and make any changes based on their partner's feedback.

EXTRA IDEA Sts make simple posters to advertise where their article can be found online, if that was their choice. Include the posters with the printed articles.

5
- Sts read each other's articles and choose interesting facts.

EXTRA IDEA Sts read the articles and decide which position they agree with, and why. Their reasons should come from the articles.

EXTRA CHALLENGE In groups, Sts act out the different positons in the articles. A reporter interviews a person representing each position. The class listens and decides which position they agree with.

My project

YOU FIRST! What are the biggest issues in the world at the moment? Do they affect where you live? How can we solve them?

An article

Read all about it!

A Although the town of Gorsham may seem a happy place, there is an organization that is not very pleased with local industry and the council. A group of about 50 members of the local community have set up a website that is inviting people to join in and help them save the River Sheldon that runs through the centre of the town. According to the organization, the town council is allowing the local paint factory to pollute the river with chemicals. Of course, the council should be trying to clean it up and turn it into a tourist attraction for visitors and local people.

B If you take a walk along the river, you will see that the organization, Save Our Sheldon, has a point. The river smells terible and it is an unattractive brown colour. Furthermore, there is no wildlife in, on or around it – a definite sign that something is wrong. However, the council is also in a difficult position. The council has ask the paint factory to stop polluting the river, but the factory has replied that the cost of removing and transporting the chemicals would be very high, and people would lose their jobs. Over 400 people from Gorsham work in the riverside factory.

C To sum up, both sides have strong arguments to support their positions, but this newspaper believes that a solution is possible. Many towns have made their factories more environmentally-friendly and cleaned their rivers and they have not lost their industry. There is no doubt that Gorsham ought to be able to do the same.

Audience: Think about who will read your article and choose a topic that will interest them.

Research: Only use correct information. Say in the article where you got the information from.

Notes: Make notes about the information that you want to include. Organize your notes into a paragraph plan.
Introduction: *Gorsham – pollution of River Sheldon
Paragraph 1: *organization Save Our Sheldon – council lets paint factory pollute river
*want river to be an attraction for local people and tourists
Paragraph 2: *river smells / brown colour

Edit: Check that the style is easy to read and that there are no grammar or vocabulary errors.

1
a Get ready to write Work with a partner. You are going to write an article about an important issue. Choose a topic from the box or choose your own topic.

> the environment   caring for the elderly   animal testing
> climate change   school leaving age   advertising to children

b 🔊 2.18 Read and listen to the article. Which one of the issues is it about?

c Answer the questions.
Which paragraph…?
1 presents both sides of the situation
2 offers an opinion
3 introduces the topic

2
Read the Look! box. Match the underlined words in the article to the definitions.

Look! Phrases for articles
1 to introduce what somebody said
2 to introduce a conclusion
3 to introduce extra information
4 to say that something is obvious
5 to contrast earlier information

3
Start writing Plan and write your article. Look at the student's notes about the article on Gorsham to help you.

4
Complete your project Publish your article.
- Decide if you are going to print it or present it online.
- Choose or take good photos to illustrate it.
- Tell your classmates where they can read it.

5
Read your classmates' articles. Choose the most interesting facts from each article.

Unit 3 · Respect

3 Culture

YOU FIRST! What do you think of when you hear the word 'Australia'? What do you think Australia is like?

AUSTRALIA UNDER ATTACK

Australia is home to a group of animals that you won't find anywhere else in the world. Kangaroos, koalas, wombats and emus are just some of the creatures that have become symbols of the country. Australia also has some of the most spectacular countryside and coasts in the world: the outback (the Australian desert), tropical rainforests and incredible coral reefs give Australia one of the most varied environments in the world. However, both the animals and the environment are under attack – under attack from human activity and visiting plants and animals.

ARE WE IN THE SAHARA OR THE OUTBACK?

When you hear the word 'camel', which region of the world comes to mind? Well, if you said the Sahara, think again because the biggest herd of camels in the world is in Australia. At one stage, there were one million of them living wild in the outback. People have introduced approximately 25 different types of animals to the country and some, such as camels, rabbits and foxes, damage the environment and have made some local animals almost become extinct. This has made life difficult for some of the world's oldest communities, the indigenous people of Australia, who have survived the extremely high temperatures and difficult conditions of the outback in the same way for over 60,000 years.

A UNIQUE COASTLINE

The Great Barrier Reef is a series of thousands of small islands that covers more than 2,300 km of the coast of the state of Queensland. The reef is actually alive and it is also home to turtles, dolphins, whales and many different species of tropical fish. Unfortunately, because of global warming and pollution from coastal towns and cities, parts of the reef are beginning to die. Some scientists say that if the temperatures of the oceans don't fall soon, the Great Barrier Reef will all die.

IT ISN'T ALL DESERT

Although Australia is one of the driest countries on the planet, over 16% of the land is rainforest. These rainforests are home to many plants, trees, birds and insects that are unique to Australia. In fact, some of the trees and plants are so old that the Australian rainforests are the planet's real Jurassic Parks! The wet rainforests also stop fires spreading across the country. However, the government has allowed the paper industry to cut down thousands of trees and, as a result, some plants that could survive drought and fire have also disappeared. Naturally, this reduces the ability of the rainforests to stop fires. Furthermore, farmers sometimes introduce plants and trees from other countries, but they burn easily and Australia now has more and more fires every summer.

THE FUTURE

Although human activity has so far damaged a lot of Australia's environment, the Australian Government and voluntary organizations are hoping that people will have a more positive effect in the future. They are encouraging Australians to protect the environment and there are various projects that involve planting more trees in the rainforests and saving the Great Barrier Reef and local animals.

Glossary

varied   herd   indigenous   unique   drought

---

1 a Look at the photos. Name the animals.

b Which of them do you think people introduced to Australia? Read the article and check.

2 Decide if these facts are about the outback (OB), the Great Barrier Reef (GBR) or the rainforest (RF). Give evidence from the article.
1 12,000 different types of insects and 250 different butterfly species live here.
2 The temperatures can reach 50°C in the summer.
3 You can find plants and fruit here that existed when the dinosaurs were on the planet.
4 9,000 different islands form this incredible natural work of art.
5 Some Australian indigenous people continue to live in a traditional way here.
6 More than 1,500 species of fish live here.

3 Over to you! Work with a partner. Write a short list of the plants, trees and animals that are typical of your region. Translate their names into English.

▶ British wildlife under attack

44 Unit 3 · Respect

Culture

Supplementary materials
Photocopiable worksheets: Culture, Culture video

CULTURE NOTES Below are some additional information on Australia you may want to share with your Sts.
Australian wildlife: More than 80% of the plants, mammals, reptiles and frogs can be found only in Australia. Some of the best-known animals are the kangaroo, koala, echidna, dingo, platypus, wallaby and wombat.
Australia has some of the most dangerous animals in the world: the crocodile, the great white shark and the inland taipan (the world's most poisonous snake). However, more deaths are caused by the honey bee than by these creatures. The honey bee isn't poisonous, but 1–2 % of the population suffer an allergic reaction from its sting.
According to the Red List of Endangered Species (July 2018 update), Australia has 106 animals that are critically endangered and 40 that are extinct, making it the fourth-worst country in the world for animal extinctions. Land clearing and urbanization are two of the main causes.
The Outback: The word 'outback' refers to areas in Australia where few people live. The outback covers most of Australia. When tourists mention the outback, they usually refer to the area near Alice Springs and Uluru (Ayers Rock). This region is in the middle of Australia.
The outback has several climate zones and experiences a wide range of temperatures.
Temperatures in the central deserts can be as high as 50°C (120F) in summer, and as low as -10°C (15F) in winter. It does however receive quite a lot of rain. Even the central desert regions get on average 200–250 mm of rain a year.
The Great Barrier Reef: The Great Barrier Reef is one of the seven natural wonders of the world. It is approximately the same size as Italy, Germany, Malaysia or Japan. In fact, it is the largest living structure on Earth, so big that it can be seen from space.
Ten percent of the world's entire fish species live in the Great Barrier Reef.

You First

With books closed, ask Sts what they think of when they hear the word *Australia*. Ask them to tell you what they think Australia is like. Then, ask them to look at the photos. What do they think the article will be about? Next, ask them to read the title. Now what do they think the article will be about?

1a
- Sts look at the photos and name the animals.

A wombat B camel C fox D kangaroo E emu F koala
G rabbit

EXTRA IDEA If you have internet access in your classroom, let Sts search for some of the animals. Then, ask Sts to give one interesting fact about them to the class.

b
- Ask Sts which of the animals in the photos they think are native to Australia, and which were introduced.
- Get them to discuss with a partner, then read the article quickly to check their answers.

Introduced: camel, fox, rabbit

EXTRA SUPPORT Write the names of the animals from the article on the board before you get Sts to answer the question.

2
- Give Sts time to read the article more closely and complete the task.

1 RF ('These rainforests are home to many plants, trees, birds and insects that are unique to Australia.')
2 OB ('the extremely high temperatures')
3 RF ('In fact, some of the trees and plants are so old that the Australian rainforests are the planet's real Jurassic parks!')
4 GBR ('The Great Barrier Reef is a series of thousands of small islands that covers more than 2,300 km of the coast of the state of Queensland.')
5 OB ('in the same way for over 60,000 years')
6 GBR ('The reef is actually alive and it is also home to turtles, dolphins, whales and many different species of tropical fish.')

EXTRA SUPPORT Read the text and decide if you need to teach any new lexis before Sts do the task. Refer Sts to the **Glossary** and make sure they also understand *outback, coral reefs, extinct*.

EXTRA SUPPORT Sts compare their answers with a partner and look for the evidence in the text if there are any disagreements.

EXTRA IDEA Get Sts to explain how these words relate to the topic of the article: *outback, countryside, reefs, herd, indigenous, drought*. E.g. 'One million camels lived in the outback.' Sts look for and tell the class other words that are important in the article.

EXTRA CHALLENGE Sts look up information about the wildlife of Australia online. Sts bring to class one fact they have learned and found interesting. Display their facts and discuss them in class.

3
- Put Sts in pairs to write and translate their list.
- Ask Sts to discuss their lists with the class.

EXTRA IDEA Sts write their list on a map of the area, writing the names near the area where they exist.

EXTRA IDEA Sts research wildlife in danger of extinction in their own country. Following the example of the article on page 44, Sts write their own article to raise awareness of the issue.

▶ Video British wildlife under attack

As an extension to the Culture topic, watch a short film about British wildlife and do the accompanying photocopiable exercises. You can either do this in class or set it as optional homework. The film is available on the DVD-ROM or on the Online Practice.

Project Explore   T44

Learn through English

Supplementary materials
Photocopiable worksheet: Song

Additional subject notes

Water has always been essential for human existence. Before the agricultural revolution, water was needed for drinking and for fishing. With the agricultural revolution, humans began to settle and relied more on farming than hunting for food. Farmers dug wells and ditches to irrigate crops and built walls to protect their farms against floods. Ancient civilizations used water to power mills to grind wheat and also built canals, aqueducts and pipes to transport water. The industrial revolution in the late 1700s triggered the development of new technology in areas such as water supply, sewage disposal, hydroelectric power and pollution control.

The Great Pacific Garbage Patch is often described as being 'larger than Texas', but it cannot be seen from space, as it is often claimed. The Garbage Patch was first discovered in 1997 by yachtsman Charles Moore as he was sailing. Oceanographer Curtis Ebbesmeyer, who is known for having tracked rubber duck bath toys and Nike tennis shoes across the oceans, gave the Garbage Patch its name. There is now a $32 million clean-up campaign which was started by Boyan Slat from the Netherlands. This campaign is called the Ocean Cleanup.

You First

Tell Sts to make a list of reasons for the location of their town or city. Ask them to consider these questions: *Is there a river? Is it on the coast? Does it have a good bay? Is it on a mountain? Does it have good views of the surrounding area? Is it near other big cities?*

1a
- Ask Sts to fold a piece of paper in half. On one side they write advantages of living near water. On the other side they write the disadvantages.

b
- Sts compare their list with a partner and make any changes to their own.

2
- Put Sts in pairs, **A** and **B**, to each read one of the factsheets.
- When they have both finished reading, tell them to make notes about their factsheet to answer the questions listed.
- Sts then use their answers to the questions to tell each other about their factsheet.

Student A's answers
1. close to water
2. everyday life, farming, the economy
3. It provided steam to power the first machines and then became a way to transport products around the world.
4. More than half the world's population was living in cities.
5. how important water is for their survival

Student B's answers
1. on the coast
2. an enormous collection of floating rubbish that covers the Pacific Ocean from near the coast of Japan to the east coast of California in the USA
3. human activities on the coasts of North America and Asia; ships travelling between major cities; fishing nets
4. It breaks into tiny pieces and falls to the bottom of the ocean.
5. It stops the food that fish and turtles eat from growing; populations of these animals become smaller; there's less seafood for humans.

EXTRA SUPPORT Read the factsheets and decide if you need to teach any new lexis before Sts do the task.

3
- With a partner, Sts discuss the phrases and answer the questions.

Note
Here are some ideas behind the phrases:

Water is life: You need water in order to live.

You can't wash dirty water: It is important not to pollute our rivers and lakes, where we get our water from.

Save water and save your future: Saving water now can avoid not having it in the future in times of drought.

Little actions make a big difference: The little things we do to save water can make a big difference when we all do them.

Save the world's blood: Water is as necessary to life as blood is to our bodies.

EXTRA IDEA In pairs, get Sts to write a brief advertisement to convince people to save water. The last line should be one of the phrases in exercise 3.

EXTRA CHALLENGE Get Sts to search online for areas of the world that are having problems with water. In class, Sts present what they found in a two-minute presentation. Sts can use PowerPoint to show some photos. Discourage Sts from writing text on their slides.

🔊 2.19 Song *Message in a Bottle*
- Play the audio for Sts to listen to the song and complete the Song photocopiable worksheet.
- Check answers.

T45 Project Explore

Learn through English

YOU FIRST! Why do you think people chose to create a town or city in the place where you live? What is good about its location?

Water

Water: the essential ingredient

Look at a population distribution map of any country in the world and you'll see that most people live close to water. The world's biggest cities are on rivers or next to the coast. This isn't an accident, of course. Water is essential for everyday life, for farming and for the economy.

Water has been important in creating jobs and, at the end of the 18th century, it was essential in the development of the Industrial Revolution. Water provided steam to power the very first machines that inventor Richard Arkwright created for the clothes industry. The rivers and oceans then became a natural network to send the products from the world's first factories in England around the planet. As a result, coastal and river cities grew larger because of the job opportunities that they offered.

In 2008, for the first time in history, more than half of the world's population was living in cities and nearly all these urban areas are on the coast or by rivers. Cities need water for people's homes, industry, business, tourism and leisure activities. Because of this, cities have started to realize how important water is for their survival. Water helped create cities; we now have to make sure that cities don't cause the disappearance of water.

THE GREAT PACIFIC GARBAGE PATCH

Fourteen of the world's 17 largest cities are on the coast and you can see the negative effects this can have on the oceans by visiting the Great Pacific Garbage Patch. This is an enormous collection of floating rubbish that covers the Pacific Ocean from near the coast of Japan to the coast of California in the USA.

Most of the rubbish consists of millions of pieces of plastic that float on and under the water. Scientists say that 80% of this plastic comes from human activities on the coasts of North America and Asia. The other 20% comes from ships travelling between major cities, and from fishing nets.

With time, the sun breaks the plastic into tiny pieces. The plastic then falls to the bottom of the ocean and stops the food that fish and turtles eat from growing. This means that the populations of these animals become smaller and, as a result, there is less seafood for humans. Fortunately, international organizations are now trying to reduce the patch and make coastal populations aware of the need to protect the oceans.

1 a Make a list of the advantages and disadvantages of living in a city near a coast, river or lake.

b Work with a partner. Compare your lists. Are your ideas similar or different?

2 Work with a partner. Read one of the factsheets. Make notes to answer the questions. Use your notes to tell your partner about your factsheet.

Student A Read about Water: the essential ingredient.
1 Where are the world's biggest cities?
2 What three things do we need water for?
3 How was water important during the Industrial Revolution?
4 What was true for the first time in 2008?
5 What have cities realized?

Student B Read about The Great Pacific Garbage Patch.
1 Where are most of the world's biggest cities?
2 What is the Great Pacific Garbage Patch and where is it?
3 Where does the rubbish in the Great Pacific Garbage Patch come from?
4 What happens to the plastic?
5 What problems does it cause?

3 Work with a partner. What ideas are behind the phrases? Which phrase would you choose to persuade people to save water in your community? Why?

- Water is life!
- You can't wash dirty water!
- Save water and save your future!
- Little actions make a big difference!
- Save the world's blood!

▶ Song 🔊 2.19 *Message in a Bottle*

Unit 3 · Respect

4 Travel

4A Wonders of the world

YOU FIRST! Which are the most famous buildings and monuments in your town, region or country? Why are they well known?

Reading and Vocabulary Buildings

1 a Look at the photos and read the advertisement. Where are these famous monuments?

1. Christ the Redeemer
2. Burj Khalifa Tower
3. The Leaning Tower of Pisa
4. El Castillo, Chichén Itzá
5. The Taj Mahal
6. Petra
7. The Great Mosque of Djenné
8. The Great Wall of China
9. The Moai

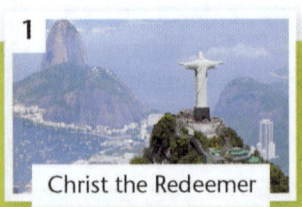

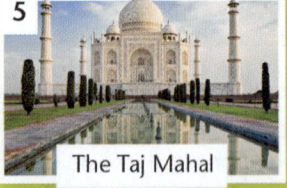

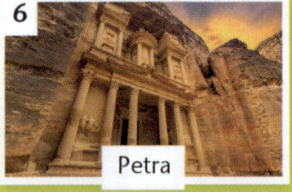

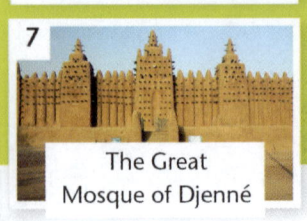

What are the New Seven Wonders of the World?

If you had the time and money to travel, where would you go? Over 2,000 years ago, the world's first tourists, travellers from Greece, had a list of the best places to visit: the Seven Wonders of the World. However, you would be disappointed if you visited them today. Only one of them still exists! If modern travellers made a list, they'd have to choose new places and that's exactly what we want you to do: choose the New Seven Wonders of the World!

b 🔊 **2.20** Listen and repeat the words in the box. Find examples in the photos.

> arch   brickwork   column   dome   floor   pyramid
> ruin   skyscraper   statue   steps   stone   tower

c Complete the descriptions of four places from exercise 1a with the correct form of the words in brackets. Can you name the places?

1. You can see the sea and the desert from the top of this ___ . It's 828 metres tall and has 163 ___ . (floor / skyscraper)
2. This building has four tall ___ . There is one big ___ and two smaller ones on the roof. There is one big ___ at the entrance and a lot of smaller ones in front of the windows. The ___ is white. (arch / brickwork / dome / tower)
3. This ___ has ___ on the four ___ sides so that people can walk to the top. It was a monument to the Mayan god Kukulkan. (pyramid / step / stone)
4. They are repairing these ___ in this famous old city. There are lots of ___ that support the roofs of the buildings. There were ___ of famous people, but they have disappeared. (column / ruin / statue)

▶ **Workbook** page 34, exercises 1–3

Listening

2 a 🔊 **2.21** Listen to two friends, Alex and Daisy. Which three places in the photos do they mention?

b Answer the questions.

1. What do the winners of the competition get?
2. What is interesting about the statues?
3. What do you have to do to visit the towers on the wall?
4. What is a problem with some of the wall?
5. What is special about the Burj Khalifa Tower?

3 a Work with a partner. Make a list of seven wonders in your town, region or country. Only include buildings and monuments.

b Over to you! Work in a group. Read out your list. Explain why you have chosen the buildings. Use some of the words from exercise 1b. Decide on a final list of seven wonders.

> The first monument on the list is the church in the town square. You can visit the tower and see great views of the town, although you have to walk up lots of steps to get there!

46 Unit 4 · Travel

4 Travel

Unit objectives
use words to talk about buildings
use words to talk about train travel
use phrasal verbs to talk about travel
use the second conditional correctly
use comparatives and superlatives correctly
use adverbs of frequency, manner, place and time
talk about a belief or a doubt
write a leaflet for tourists visiting your capital city

Language
Grammar: second conditional; comparatives and superlatives, *too / enough*; adverbs of frequency, manner, place and time
Vocabulary: buildings; train travel; phrasal verbs for travel
Everyday English: expressing belief and doubt
My project: The trip of a lifetime!
Culture: As British as…?
Learn through English: The invention of travel (History)

4A Wonders of the world

Supplementary materials
Workbook: pages 34–35, exercises 1–9
Workbook: Grammar summary Unit 4
Photocopiable worksheets: Grammar and Vocabulary, Communication

You First
Put Sts in pairs or groups to make a list of famous buildings and monuments in their town, region or country. Get feedback, and ask if Sts they know why they are famous.

EXTRA IDEA Ask Sts to think of a building or monument, but not to say what it is. Tell them to say why it is well known and get the class to guess what the building is.

EXTRA IDEA Have a competition. Set a time limit of two minutes for Sts to list all the famous buildings and monuments they can think of. Get feedback.

Reading and Vocabulary Buildings
1a
- Give Sts time to read the advertisement. Ask them to look at the photos and say where the famous monuments are located.

1 Rio de Janeiro, Brazil   2 Dubai, United Arab Emirates
3 Pisa, Italy   4 Yucatán, Mexico   5 Agra, India   6 Jordan
7 Djenné, Mali   8 China   9 Easter Island, Polynesia

EXTRA CHALLENGE Ask Sts, *What would be one of your Wonders of the World, and why?*

b 🔊 2·20
- Play the audio for Sts to listen and repeat the words.
- Ask them to find examples of the words in the photos.

arch – Taj Mahal, Leaning Tower of Pisa, Petra
brickwork – Taj Mahal, Great Wall of China
column – Leaning Tower of Pisa, Taj Mahal, Petra
dome – Taj Mahal
floor – Burj Khalifa, Leaning Tower of Pisa, Taj Mahal
pyramid – El Castillo, Chichén Itzá
ruin – Great Mosque of Djenné, Great Wall of China
skyscraper – Burj Khalifa
statue – Christ the Redeemer, The Moai
steps – El Castillo, Chichén Itzá, Great Mosque of Djenné, Great Wall of China
stone – El Castillo, Chichén Itzá, Petra, Great Wall of China, The Moai
tower – Leaning Tower of Pisa, Great Mosque of Djenné, Great Wall of China

c
- Sts complete the descriptions and name the places.

1 skyscraper, floors (Burj Khalifa)   2 towers, dome, arch, brickwork (Taj Mahal)   3 pyramid, steps, stone (El Castillo, Chichén Itzá)   4 ruins, columns, statues (Petra)

EXTRA CHALLENGE Tell Sts to write a description of one of the other famous buildings in exercise 1a. Remind them to use words from the box. Get them to read out their descriptions for the class to guess what building it is.

➡ **Workbook** page 34, exercises 1–3

Listening
2a 🔊 2·21   Audio script pT89
- Play the audio for Sts to listen to answer the question.

The Moai, the Great Wall of China, Burj Khalifa

EXTRA SUPPORT Read the script and decide if you need to teach any new lexis before Sts listen.

b
- Sts answer the questions. Play the audio again if necessary.

1 A free trip around the world.   2 Nobody knows how they made them or how they moved them.   3 You have to walk up lots of steps.   4 It's a ruin.   5 It's the tallest building in the world.

EXTRA CHALLENGE Ask Sts to answer the questions before they listen to the audio again. Then, play the audio for Sts to check their answers.

3a
- Put Sts in pairs to complete the task.
- Encourage Sts to give a reason for their choices.

b
- Put Sts in groups to compare and decide on a list of seven wonders. Have a class vote on a final list of seven wonders.

Project Explore   T46

4A

Grammar Second conditional

4a
- Give Sts time to read the sentences and complete the rules.
- Check answers.

> 1 unreal or unlikely   2 result   3 past   4 would   5 if
> 6 comma

b
- Ask Sts to complete the sentences, then compare with a partner before you check answers.

> 1 existed   2 didn't invite   3 would have   4 cleaned
> 5 wouldn't be   6 had

EXTRA SUPPORT Ask Sts to identify the verbs in each sentence. Ask *What form are they in?* Write on the board as table headings: '*if* + past simple' and '*would* + infinitive'. Get Sts to complete the table with the verbs. E.g.

if + past simple	*would* + infinitive
existed	would go back
didn't invite	would (you) say
planned	would have

c
- Give Sts time to think about and complete the sentences about what they would do.

EXTRA CHALLENGE Get Sts to make a chain like this:
A If I lived in the Arctic,…
B I would see polar bears.
C If I saw polar bears,…
D I would run away.
E If I ran away,…

➡ **Workbook** pages 34–35, exercises 4–6
➡ **Photocopiable** Grammar and Vocabulary

Listening

5a 🔊 **2·22** Audio script pT89
- Play the audio for Sts to listen and answer the question.

> **Natural wonders:** B the Amazon Rainforest, D Table Mountain
> **Man-made:** A The Golden Gate Bridge, C The Panama Canal, E Sagrada Família

EXTRA SUPPORT Read the script and decide if you need to teach any new lexis before Sts listen.

EXTRA SUPPORT Before they listen, ask Sts to describe the photos and say which are natural wonders and which are man-made. Check that they know what all the photos show. (A *the Golden Gate Bridge*, B *the Amazon Rainforest*, C *the Panama Canal*, D *Table Mountain*, E *Sagrada Família*.)

b
- Give Sts time to read the sentences and see if they can complete them from memory.
- Make sure Sts understand that they can only use one word to complete the gap.
- Ask Sts to check with a partner before you play the audio to confirm.

> 1 monuments   2 Africa   3 longer   4 one   5 mistake

Speaking

6a
- Put Sts in pairs to describe a place in one of the photos for their partner to guess.

b
- Tell Sts to work individually to choose a place they would like to visit, and to make notes about why they would like to visit it.

EXTRA SUPPORT Get Sts to share their ideas with a partner and then make any changes to their notes.

EXTRA IDEA Ask Sts to imagine what they would pack for a trip to their place, and why. E.g. *I would take good walking shoes to visit the Great Wall of China because I would walk a lot on stones.*

c
- Put Sts in groups to recommend their chosen places.
- Sts say why they would / wouldn't want to visit the places.
- Have a group vote for one place to visit.

EXTRA IDEA Put Sts in groups of three. Each group makes a small advertisement for their place and reads it to the class. Have a class vote for the best advertisement.

➡ **Workbook** page 35, exercises 7–9

Extra

Sts can either do this in class or as a homework task.

Grammar Second conditional

4 a Read the sentences from the advertisement. Complete the rules with the words in the box.

If you had the time and money to travel, where would you go?
You would be disappointed if you visited them today.
If modern travellers made a list, they'd have to choose new places.

> comma   if   past   result   unreal or unlikely   would

We use the second conditional to talk about an ¹___ situation or event in the present or future and its ²___ . We form the second conditional with if + ³___ simple + ⁴___ + infinitive. When a conditional begins with ⁵___ , we use a ⁶___ at the end of the if clause.

b Complete the sentences with the correct form of the verbs in brackets.
1 If time travel ___ (exist), I would go back to the Roman period.
2 What would you say if a friend ___ (not invite) you to a party?
3 They ___ (have) fewer problems if they planned their trips.
4 If they ___ (clean) the statue, it would look better.
5 If they repaired the castle, it ___ (not be) a ruin.
6 Harry would be there now if he ___ (have) an app with maps on his smartphone.

c Complete the sentences. Think about what you would do in these situations.
1 If I lived in the Arctic,…
2 If I had a lot of money,…
3 If it was the weekend,…
4 If I spoke fluent English,…

▶ **Workbook** pages 34–35, exercises 4–6

Listening

5 a 🔊 2.22 Listen to Alex and Daisy. Which places in the photos are natural wonders and which are man-made?

A   B   C
D   E

b Complete the sentences with one word or number.
1 Alex would include natural wonders as well as buildings and ___ .
2 Table Mountain is in South ___ .
3 Alex thinks they would need a ___ list if they included different types of wonders.
4 Alex thinks they can only present ___ list.
5 Daisy doesn't want to miss the trip because of a ___ .

Speaking

6 a Get ready to speak Work with a partner. Describe a place in the photos on pages 46–47. Your partner names the place.

> This photo shows a man-made monument. There are some… / It's…

b 📝 Work on your own. Choose a monument, a building or a natural wonder anywhere in the world. Make notes about why you would like to visit it.

c Work in a group. Tell the other students why they should visit the place you chose in exercise 6b. Say why you would / wouldn't want to visit the places they chose. Vote for one place to visit with the group.

> If I could, I'd like to visit Manhattan and go up the tallest skyscraper, the One World Trade Center, to the top floor. We should visit it because…

▶ **Workbook** page 35, exercises 7–9

EXTRA Create a wonder of the world. If you put it in your town, where would you build it? How many columns, arches, steps, etc. would it have? Draw it and name the parts.

Unit 4 · Travel

4B Ticket to ride

YOU FIRST! When was the last time you travelled by train? What are trains like in your country? Do you like travelling by train? Why?/Why not?

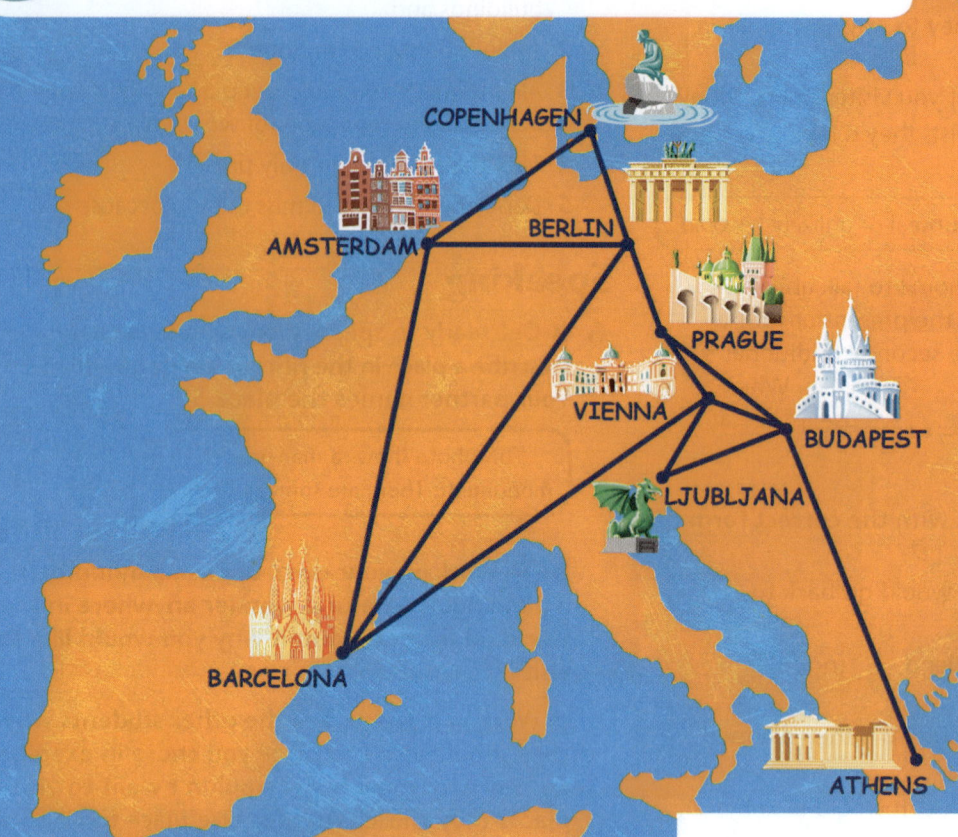

Reading and Vocabulary Train travel

1 a 🔊 **2.23** Read and listen to the webpage about Interrail travel. What will help you enjoy your visits to each place?

HOME | DESTINATIONS | TICKETS | HELP

MAKING INTERRAIL A SUCCESS

If you plan carefully, you'll have a good interrail trip. The first thing to consider is your budget: decide how much money you can spend. You also need to agree the following things with your friends: the dates and an itinerary with a route to the places that you want to visit, and the arrival and departure times for each train journey. When you do this, make sure that you leave enough time for sightseeing when you arrive at each destination and buy a good travel guide so you can read about the monuments and buildings that you're looking at. You should also think about accommodation before you leave. If you're going to stay on campsites or in hostels, you might need to make a reservation so you definitely have somewhere to stay. There's a lot to think about before you go, but a good plan will help you have a great time!

b Complete the definitions with the highlighted words on the webpage.

1 A ____ is a book that gives you information about the places you visit.
2 When you go on a ____ , you go to a place or places and return home again.
3 ____ involves visiting interesting places when you are on holiday.
4 A ____ is an arrangement to keep a hotel room, restaurant table, etc. for you.
5 The ____ is the place that you are going to.
6 ____ is a place to live or stay.
7 Someone's ____ is the moment when they get somewhere.
8 An ____ is a plan with the places you want to visit and a timetable for travelling to them.
9 When you go on a ____ , you travel from one place to another.
10 Your ____ tells you how much money you have got to spend.
11 A ____ is a way for travelling from one place to another.
12 Someone's ____ is when they leave somewhere.

c 🔊 **2.24** Listen and check. Mark the stressed syllable in each word. Then listen again and repeat.

▶ **Workbook** page 36, exercises 1–3

48 Unit 4 · Travel

4B Ticket to ride

Supplementary materials
Workbook: pages 36–37, exercises 1–9
Workbook: Grammar summary Unit 4
Photocopiable worksheets: Grammar and Vocabulary, Communication

You First
Ask Sts to think about their last train journey and how they feel about trains in general. Have a class discussion.

EXTRA IDEA Get Sts to tell a brief story about their last train journey. It can be true or invented. The class listens and says if they believe it or not.

Reading and Vocabulary   Train travel

1a 🔊 2·23

- Play the audio for Sts to listen, follow and answer the question.

a good plan

EXTRA IDEA As added comprehension, write these words and phrases on the board: 'budget', 'dates', 'itinerary', 'arrival and departure times', 'buy a good travel guide', 'think about accommodation'. Tell Sts to rewrite them in the order they appear in the webpage. Sts read and listen to the text to confirm.

b
- Give Sts time read through the definitions and complete them with the highlighted words.
- Get Sts to compare with a partner.

1 travel guide   2 trip   3 Sightseeing   4 reservation
5 destination   6 Accommodation   7 arrival   8 itinerary
9 journey   10 budget   11 route   12 departure

EXTRA CHALLENGE With a partner, Sts put the highlighted words in the order that is important to them when taking a trip. Encourage Sts to explain their suggestions, e.g. *I think accommodation is more important that itinerary, because I like to stay in a comfortable place.*

c 🔊 2·24

- Play the audio once for Sts to listen and check their answers to exercise 3b.
- Play it again for Sts to listen and repeat, and mark the stressed syllables.

1 travel guide   2 trip   3 sightseeing   4 reservation
5 destination   6 accommodation   7 arrival   8 itinerary
9 journey   10 budget   11 route   12 departure

EXTRA SUPPORT Pronounce a word by stressing different syllables so Sts can hear the difference, e.g. *project* as a noun /ˈprɒdʒekt/ and as a verb /prəˈdʒekt/; *bow* /baʊ/ and /bəʊ/; *separate* /ˈseprət/ and /ˈsepəreɪt/; *record* /rɪˈkɔːd/ and /ˈrekɔːd/; *present* /ˈpreznt/ and /prɪˈzent/.

EXTRA IDEA Sts choose a word and stress a different syllable from the one in the audio, and notice the difference.

➡ **Workbook** page 36, exercises 1–3

4B

Listening

2a
- With a partner, get Sts to describe one of the buildings or monuments on the map on page 48 for their partner to identify.

b 🔊 2·25 Audio script pT90
- Play the audio for Sts to listen and make their list of cities.

> **1** Amsterdam **2** Berlin **3** Prague **4** Budapest
> **5** Ljubljana **6** Vienna

EXTRA SUPPORT Read the script and decide if you need to teach any new lexis before Sts listen.

2c
- Give Sts time to read the questions and answer as many as they can from memory.
- Get them to compare with a partner.
- Now check answers or play the audio again for them to listen and check.

> **1** Copenhagen, Vienna **2** in the summer **3** Barcelona and Athens **4** the views **5** sightseeing **6** hostels

EXTRA SUPPORT Divide the conversation into three parts, the first up to 'Look guys…', the second up to 'Me too' and the third to the end. Pause after each part and let Sts answer the questions.

EXTRA CHALLENGE Get Sts to write two sentences from the conversation, one true and one false. Sts say the sentence to the class and the class decides if it is true or false. Confirm any disagreements by playing the audio again.

Speaking

3a
- Tell Sts to choose six destinations from the map and explain why they have chosen them.
- Ask them to plan a route to visit the six destinations.

b
- Put Sts in groups to present their lists and their reasons.
- When everyone has presented, get the group to decide on the six best cities to visit.

c
- Put Sts in pairs, **A** and **B**. Tell Sts **A** to go to page 86 and Sts **B** to page 87.
- Give Sts time to read their information and prepare for the dialogue.
- In their pairs, Sts act out the dialogue at the station. Student **B** starts the dialogue.
- Get Sts to swap roles.

EXTRA SUPPORT Go through how to say some of the times on the timetable: 'oh eight forty-five', 'seventeen oh four', etc.

EXTRA CHALLENGE In pairs, Sts decide on their own trip to Amsterdam and ask for the ticket. Get some pairs to act out their dialogues while the class listens and tells you what time each student will travel and how much the ticket will cost.

Grammar Comparatives and superlatives; too / enough

4a 🔊 2·26
- Ask Sts to complete the sentences based on the dialogue, then compare with a partner. Tell them that all the answers are comparative or superlative adjectives.
- Play the audio for Sts to listen and check their answers.
- Ask the class to tell you which forms are irregular.

> **1** the most expensive **2** cheaper **3** easier **4** more interesting **5** the earliest **6** the best **7** further
> Irregular forms: *the best, further*

EXTRA SUPPORT Sts compare their answers with a partner before listening. Then, they listen to confirm.

b
- Ask Sts to read the sentences and complete the rules.

> **1** *as* + adjective + *as* **2** *not as / so* + adjective + *as*

c
- Sts complete the rules with *before* and *after*.

> **1** before **2** after

d
- Ask Sts to complete the sentences with the words in the box.
- Check answers.

> **1** as **2** too **3** so **4** most **5** more **6** enough

EXTRA CHALLENGE Give Sts one sentence from the exercise. Sts make the sentence true about them, e.g. *I've never eaten a pizza as good as the one from D'Angelo's.*

➡ **Workbook** page 36, exercises 4–6
➡ **Photocopiable** Grammar and Vocabulary

Writing

5a
- Ask Sts to imagine they are planning two possible options for a trip, one costing very little, the other with a bigger budget.
- Sts work with a partner and write sentences using the adjectives in the box.

b
- Put Sts in groups to compare their sentences.

➡ **Workbook** page 37, exercises 7–9

c
- Give Sts time to plan a journal entry for the last two places they visited.
- Remind them to use comparatives and superlatives and the vocabulary from exercise 1b.

EXTRA SUPPORT Write on the board: 'Places I visited', 'Accommodation in each place', 'Sightseeing in each place'. Elicit some sentences from Sts comparing two places and write them on the board.

Extra

Sts can either do this in class or as a homework task.

Project Explore

4B

Listening

2 a Work with a partner. Look at the map on page 48. Describe one of the buildings or monuments. Can your classmate identify it?

> This place is a ruin. It has lots of columns…

b 🔊 2.25 Listen to three friends talking about an interrail trip. List the cities in the order that they plan to visit them.

c Answer the questions.
1 Which two cities do they say are very expensive?
2 When are they travelling?
3 Which two cities have they already visited?
4 What can't you see on high-speed trains?
5 What do they need time for?
6 What type of accommodation do they agree on?

Speaking

3 a Look at the map and make a list of six destinations. Why have you chosen these places? Which route will you follow?

b Work in a group. Present your list and give your reasons. Compare your lists and decide on the best six cities to visit.

> I really want to go to Athens because we could do a lot of sightseeing, but I agree that it's one of the busiest cities.

c You are going to buy and sell tickets for a train journey.
Student A Look at page 86. **Student B** Look at page 87.

Grammar Comparatives and superlatives; too/enough

4 a 🔊 2.26 Complete the sentences from the dialogue. Listen and check. Which forms are irregular?
1 Cities like Copenhagen and Vienna are some of ___ in Europe.
2 Food and accommodation would be ___ than in Copenhagen or Vienna.
3 Travelling to Copenhagen or Vienna after that would be ___ than travelling to Barcelona or Athens.
4 I simply reckon that Copenhagen or Vienna will be ___ .
5 I don't want to get up before 9 o'clock at ___ .
6 I think hostels would be ___ , don't you?
7 Campsites are also ___ from the centre of cities than hostels.

b Read the sentences from the dialogue and complete the rules.

Copenhagen or Vienna will be as busy as Barcelona…
Barcelona and Athens won't be so cheap as you think.

> as + adjective + as   not as / so + adjective + as

1 We use ___ to say that two things are the same.
2 We use ___ to say that two things are different.

c Read the sentences and complete the rules with *before* and *after*.

That's fine if those places are close enough to the capital cities.
They won't be too crowded.

1 We use *too* ___ an adjective to say there is more than is needed or wanted.
2 We use *enough* ___ an adjective to say there is as much as is needed or wanted.

d Complete the sentences with the words in the box.

> as   enough   more   most   so   too

1 I've never eaten a pizza as bad ___ that!
2 The castle is ___ far for a day trip.
3 This travel guide is not ___ good as the one I found online.
4 That museum was the ___ interesting that I've ever visited.
5 That hostel will be ___ expensive than the campsite.
6 The hostel room isn't big ___ for us.

▶ **Workbook** page 36, exercises 4–6

Writing

5 a **Get ready to write** Work with a partner. Write sentences comparing two possible trips you're planning.

> bad   cheap   comfortable   expensive   good

A tent isn't as comfortable as a hotel.
A sandwich is good enough for lunch.

b Compare your sentences in groups.

▶ **Workbook** page 37, exercises 7–9

c Write a short journal entry about the last two places that you visited. Use comparative structures and the vocabulary from exercise 1b.

The last two places that I visited were Salisbury and Leicester. Our accommodation in both places was the same, hostels, but the one in Salisbury was cleaner and more comfortable. Our itinerary was…

EXTRA Write sentences comparing your hometown with a nearby town.

Unit 4 • Travel

4C Off the beaten track

YOU FIRST! Why do you think people like to travel?
Would you like to travel in the future? Why? / Why not?

Reading

1 a 🔊 **2.27** Read and listen to the article. Whose route does the map show?

b What do these numbers in the article refer to?

14   16   17   24   27   54

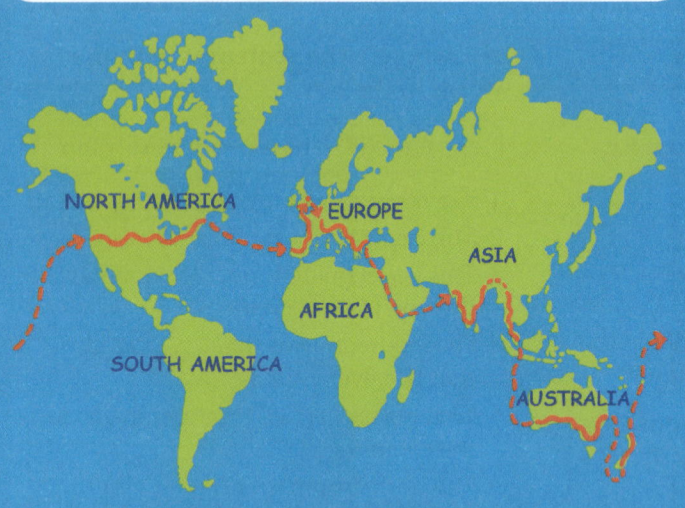

The modern Phileas Foggs

Laura Dekker

14-year-old Laura Dekker's plans to sail around the world alone got her a lot of media attention, but it was usually for the wrong reasons. The authorities in Dekker's home country, Holland, said she was too young to go off on such a journey and she wasn't allowed to leave. Fortunately for Laura, they then decided she could set off when she was 15 if she promised to study while she was sailing. She finally left the Caribbean island of St Maarten and sailed through the Panama Canal and into the Pacific Ocean. Despite her young age, Laura sailed her boat skilfully, thanks to the fact that she was born at sea. Her parents are also enthusiastic sailors and Laura spent the first five years of her life living on a boat, an experience that helped her to sail the world's oceans confidently. She got back to the island of St Maarten after 518 days and, at just 16, she became the youngest person to sail around the world alone. However, she was in trouble again with the Dutch authorities because in one of her blog entries during the trip she explained that she never had time to study!

Everybody has dreamed of **getting away** from the routine of home life and travelling around the world, but only a few of us manage to turn that dream into reality. This week, we look at three young people who were determined to do exactly that.

Lachlan Smart

18-year-old Lachlan Smart **took off** in a small aeroplane from the Sunshine Coast Airport in Queensland, Australia, on the 4th July to fly into the record books. His family and friends **saw him off** then and 54 days later they were there again to welcome him home, as the youngest pilot to fly around the world alone. During his flight, Lachlan **stopped over** at 24 locations in 15 different countries and even had time to visit relatives in Britain. However, when he got back to Queensland, he explained it wasn't always an easy trip. He sometimes experienced language problems with airport staff in different countries and this **slowed him down**. Furthermore, some bad instructions in South Asia almost made him fly into a mountain! Fortunately, however, Lachlan corrected the mistake and he was able to fly safely home to a big celebration.

Tom Davies

18-year-old Tom Davies is a cyclist who always wanted to travel abroad, so going by bicycle seemed to be the obvious way to do it. He left his home in London on the 17th January and crossed Europe and Asia covering 160 kilometres a day at an average speed of 27 km/h, before heading to Australia and New Zealand. He then flew to San Francisco, got on his bike again, crossed the USA and arrived in Boston, where he caught another plane to Lisbon in Portugal to start the last part of the trip. Although he finished each day exhausted, the help and generosity of people that he met on the route helped him to keep going. He also had a few interesting experiences with animals. In Albania he had to **speed up** when a group of wild dogs chased him and he had to do the same in Thailand when a monkey wanted to join him on his bicycle! In Australia he **came across** an emu in the outback that raced him! After seven months' cycling and visiting 17 countries on four continents, he finally got off his bicycle for the last time to celebrate his return home to London with his family and 100 friends and neighbours. He was officially the youngest person to have ever cycled around the world.

c Answer the questions with LS (Lachlan Smart), LD (Laura Dekker) and TD (Tom Davies). Who…?
1 was nearly attacked
2 met members of their family during their trip
3 used more than one type of transport
4 didn't do enough schoolwork
5 didn't always understand what people were saying
6 had a family life that helped them succeed on their trip

Unit 4 · Travel

4C Off the beaten track

Supplementary materials
Workbook: pages 38–39, exercises 1–10
Workbook: Grammar summary Unit 4
Photocopiable worksheets: Grammar and Vocabulary, Communication

You First

Elicit or explain the meaning of *off the beaten track* (*a place where few people go*). Ask Sts to think of two reasons people like to travel. Then, as a class, discuss if Sts would like to travel, and why.

EXTRA IDEA List the most common reasons to travel and ask Sts if any surprise them.

EXTRA CHALLENGE Write on the board, 'Every student should have to travel for one week before starting university.' Discuss this as a class, with Sts giving reasons why it is a good or a bad idea.

Reading

1a 2•27

- Play the audio for Sts to listen, follow and answer the question.

The map shows Tom Davies' route.

EXTRA CHALLENGE Ask Sts why it could not be the other two. (*Lachlan's route would show straighter, unbroken lines because he was flying. Laura's route wouldn't have any lines over land.*)

EXTRA IDEA Get Sts to do some online research on what each person is doing now.

b

- Sts read or listen again to answer the question.
- Get them to compare with a partner before checking answers.

14 – Laura Dekker's age when she was planning to sail around the world
16 – Laura Dekker's age when she finished her trip around the world
17 – the number of countries that Tom Davies visited
24 – the number of locations that Lachlan Smart stopped at
27 – the average km/h that Tom Davies cycled at
54 – the number of days that Lachlan Smart spent travelling

EXTRA SUPPORT Write the name of the person next to the number. This should help Sts focus when reading or listening about that person's trip.

c

- Give Sts time to read the article again if necessary, and answer the questions.

1 TD **2** LS **3** TD **4** LD **5** LS **6** LD

EXTRA IDEA Get Sts to write two more similar questions based on the article. Ask the class to guess who the questions are about.

EXTRA CHALLENGE Ask Sts to imagine something that the three people might have said to themselves during their journey. Get the class to guess the person. Ask Sts to explain their answers with information from the text, e.g. *I wonder what that town down there is.* (*Lachlan, because he flew a plane.*)

EXTRA IDEA Ask Sts to write down one or two cloze gap sentences based on the article. Then get Sts to write their sentences, with the gaps, on the board. The class reads the sentences and looks for the information in the texts. e.g. 'Tom Davies had a few interesting experiences with ____.' (*animals*)

EXTRA CHALLENGE Ask Sts why they think the article is called 'The Modern Phileas Foggs'. (*Because they all travelled around the world, like the famous character in the book 'Around the World in 80 Days' by Jules Verne.*)

Hold a class discussion. If you have internet access in your classroom, let Sts search for the answer. If not, have Sts find the answer for the next class.

Project Explore

4C

Vocabulary Phrasal verbs for travel

2
- Give Sts time to complete the sentences and compare with a partner before you check answers.

> 1 took off 2 got back 3 slow down 4 gone off
> 5 get away 6 came across 7 stopping over 8 speed up
> 9 set off 10 see, off

EXTRA SUPPORT Put Sts in pairs to look at the highlighted phrasal verbs in the article and discuss what they mean. Encourage them to use the context to help them.

EXTRA IDEA Get Sts to write their own sentences using the highlighted phrasal verbs.

EXTRA CHALLENGE Sts write a sentence about someone in the class, using one of the highlighted phrasal verbs. They read it out loud while the class listens and guesses if it is true or not. Then, the student whose name is in the sentence confirms if it is true or not.

➧ **Workbook** page 38, exercises 1–3

Speaking

3a
- Give Sts time to make notes, based on the questions, about the trip on page 50 they would most like to go on.
- Remind Sts to use phrasal verbs from exercise 2.

b
- Put Sts in groups to talk about the trip they have chosen, explaining why they chose it.

EXTRA IDEA Before Sts talk about their trips, get the group to guess which trip each person chose, and why. Encourage Sts to use information from the article.

EXTRA CHALLENGE Tell each St in the group to ask one question about the trip they are listening to.

c
- Sts choose the best trip for the group.
- If Sts can't agree on a trip, encourage them to discuss why not.

EXTRA CHALLENGE Sts write sentences from their notes using the phrasal verbs in the article. Then, get them to say their sentences to the class, substituting the phrasal verb with the word 'buzz'. The class guesses what the phrasal verb is, e.g. *One day I'd like to buzz from here and explore the world.* (*get away*) *Look at that plane. It's ready for buzz.* (*take off*)

Grammar Adverbs of frequency, manner, place and time

4a
- Give Sts time to read the sentences and complete the task.
- Check answers.

> 1 time 2 place 3 frequency 4 frequency 5 manner
> 6 manner 7 frequency 8 place

EXTRA SUPPORT Write these headings on the board: 'Adverbs of frequency', 'Adverbs of manner', 'Adverbs of place', 'Adverbs of time'. Elicit examples for each one.

b
- Give Sts time to read and complete the rules.

> 1 before 2 after 3 after 4 end 5 after 6 end

c
- Ask Sts to read the sentence and complete the rule.

> before

d
- Give Sts time to order the sentences.
- Ask Sts to say what type of adverb is in each sentence.

> 1 Mike drives his dad's car confidently. (manner)
> 2 I had dinner with Kate in Manchester on Monday evening. (place, time)
> 3 You can usually buy food on the train. (frequency)
> 4 Lisa waited patiently for the bus. (manner)
> 5 Sam's cousins never travel abroad. (frequency)
> 6 Our train arrives at the station at midnight. (time)
> 7 Frank was sometimes late for breakfast. (frequency)
> 8 Mara read the exam questions slowly. (manner)

EXTRA IDEA Ask Sts to write two sentences about themselves, using adverbs. Then, ask them to write their sentences on the board, mixing up the words, as in the exercise. The class puts the words in the correct order.

EXTRA CHALLENGE Say *adverb of time* and get Sts to say an adverb, e.g. *on Monday*. Sts then say a sentence with the adverb. Once they understand the activity, let one of the Sts say *adverb of manner*. Another St then says an adverb of manner, e.g. *quietly*. Sts think of sentences with that adverb.

➧ **Workbook** pages 38–39, exercises 4–7
➧ **Photocopiable** Grammar and Vocabulary

Writing

5a
- With a partner, Sts think about what they would recommend to a tourist visiting their capital city.
- Give Sts time to write down places to visit, monuments to see, how to get around and an interesting itinerary.

EXTRA SUPPORT Ask Sts to define the word 'itinerary'.

b
- Give Sts time to write their leaflet. Remind them to use phrasal verbs and adverbs.

EXTRA SUPPORT Show Sts different types of leaflets. Ask *What do you find in a leaflet?* (*photos, map, names of places, an itinerary*, etc.) Next, Sts organize their leaflet. They can use one of the leaflets as a model. Finally, Sts write their leaflet based on an itinerary.

c
- Display the leaflets around the class for Sts to read and decide which is the most interesting.
- Ask them to explain their reasons for their choices.

EXTRA CHALLENGE Sts make a leaflet aimed at teenagers for their town.

➧ **Workbook** page 39, exercises 8–10

Extra

Sts can either do this in class or as a homework task.

Project Explore

4C

Vocabulary Phrasal verbs for travel

2 Complete the sentences with the correct form of the highlighted phrasal verbs in the article.
1 Flight A98T ___ from Paris at 08.17…
2 It was 11 p.m. when we ___ home after the school trip…
3 Could you ___ please! I can't run that fast!
4 Ann's not here. She's ___ with her friends…
5 We've decided to go to the Scottish Highlands for a few days to ___ from the noise of London.
6 I ___ these old silver earrings when we were at a market in Florence.
7 They are ___ in New York for a night when they fly from London to Los Angeles.
8 If you want to win the race, you need to ___!
9 My parents have just ___ on a cruise around the Mediterranean that will last for two weeks.
10 My grandparents come to ___ me ___ at the bus stop every morning when I go to school.

▶ Workbook page 38, exercises 1–3

Speaking

3 a Make notes about one of the trips on page 50 that you would most like to go on. Use the phrasal verbs in exercise 2 in your answers.
- Which trip would you like to go on?
- Why would you like to do it?
- What do you admire about the person who did it?
- What would you do differently?

cycling trip – good fun – go at your own speed – meet people – see nature

b Work in a group. Say which trip you have chosen and why.

c Choose the best trip for the group.

Grammar

Adverbs of frequency, manner, place and time

4 a Read the sentences from the article. Decide if the highlighted adverbs are adverbs of frequency, manner, place or time.
1 His family and friends saw him off **then**.
2 They were there again to welcome him **home**.
3 It wasn't **always** an easy trip.
4 He **sometimes** experienced language problems.
5 He was able to fly **safely** home to a big celebration.
6 Laura sailed her boat **skilfully**.
7 The school bus is **always** on time.
8 Tom Davies is a cyclist who always wanted to travel **abroad**.

b Complete the rules with *after*, *before* or *end*.
1 Adverbs of frequency tell us how often we do something. We put adverbs of frequency ¹___ the main verb, or ²___ the verb *be* or auxiliary verb.
2 Adverbs of manner describe how we do something. They come ³___ the main verb or at the ⁴___ of the sentence.
3 Adverbs of place and time tell us where and when we do something. They usually come ⁵___ the main verb or at the ⁶___ of the sentence.

c Read the sentence and choose the correct answer to complete the rule.
I went home early.

When we use adverbs of place and time together, the adverb of place comes *before / after* the adverb of time.

d Put the words in the correct order to form sentences. Then say if the adverb is an adverb of frequency, manner, place or time.
1 his dad's / Mike / car / confidently / drives.
2 Kate / in Manchester / I / on Monday / with / had / evening / dinner.
3 buy / on the train / can / You / food / usually.
4 for the bus / patiently / waited / Lisa.
5 never / abroad / Sam's / travel / cousins.
6 at midnight / train / Our / at the station / arrives.
7 was / for breakfast / sometimes / late / Frank.
8 slowly / Mara / the exam questions / read.

▶ Workbook pages 38–39, exercises 4–7

Writing

5 a Get ready to write Work with a partner. Think about tourists visiting your capital city.

destinations itineraries sightseeing transport

b Write a leaflet for tourists visiting your capital city. Explain the things that they can do. Use the phrasal verbs from exercise 2 and adverbs.
Welcome to…!
Your first visit should be to the old town. Get up early so you can set off before it gets crowded.
There is a market in the main square at the weekends and you might be able to come across some…

c Read the leaflets that other students have written. Which is the most interesting? Why?

▶ Workbook page 39, exercises 8–10

EXTRA Write sentences for a travel competition for a trip you would love to make.

Unit 4 · Travel 51

4D Hard to believe

YOU FIRST! Why do you think people are interested in the topics of time and space travel? Would you like to be able to travel through time or space? Why?/Why not?

1 a 🔊 2.28 ▶ Read and listen. Why does Oliver want to study?

1

Erika	What are you guys up to?
Liza	I'm sure that's him!
Danny	Really?
Liza	Yeah! I'm certain that it is!
Danny	Oliver! He's...he's in the library.
Erika	Who? Oliver? Are you having me on?! I'm not really sure he knows what a library is.
Liza	Check it out!
Erika	That is definitely Oliver.
Liza	What is he doing in there?
Danny	I can't believe that he's studying! He already thinks he knows it all!
Erika	It is *very* unlikely that he's studying. He's up to something!

b Complete the sentences with the names *Oliver*, *Liza*, *Danny* and *Erika*.
1 ___ finds ___ and ___ outside the library.
2 ___ is working in the library.
3 ___ asks ___ about what he is doing.
4 ___ doesn't believe ___ is going to travel to another planet.
5 ___ and ___ find the idea of travelling to Mars difficult to understand.
6 ___ knows a lot about space travel.

2 Spoken English What do these expressions mean? How do you say them in your own language?

- What are you up to?
- Are you having me on?
- Hang on a minute!
- Says who?
- I can't get my head around this.
- You bet we could!

▶ **Workbook** page 40, exercises 1–3

2

Erika	What are you up to?!
Oliver	Shhh! I'm trying to study.
Erika	It's hard to believe *you* are studying! Why?
Oliver	Because I'm going to Mars.
Erika	Really? When? Today?
Oliver	I'm not joking.
Liza	Whoa – hang on a minute, Oliver. OK, I believe you're studying, but I doubt you're going to Mars!
Oliver	It's possible!
Danny	Says who?
Oliver	NASA. They say it's very likely we'll be able to fly there by the 2030s.
Liza	Sorry. I can't get my head around this.
Danny	Me neither. You're saying that humans could reach Mars in 15 years' time...
Oliver	There's no doubt we can.
Danny	...and that you want to be one of them?
Oliver	Yep.
Erika	So it is possible we could go, too?
Oliver	You bet we could!
Erika	That is so cool! Let *us* have a look!
Danny	Yes, let's see!

3

Danny	Have you seen this? Oliver made it.
Liza	What is it?

52 Unit 4 · Travel

4D Hard to believe

Supplementary materials
Workbook: pages 40–41, exercises 1–9
Photocopiable worksheets: Everyday English, Pronunciation
Online Practice

> **Note**
> The story can be used in class as a reading and listening task, a video task or both.

You First
Ask Sts to think of films that are based on travelling in time and space. Did they like them? What happened? The *Back to the Future* films are a good choice for a discussion of time travel. Recent films about space travel include *Gravity*, *Interstellar*, *The Martian*, *First Man*.

Give Sts time to answer the questions. Sts discuss their ideas with a partner, then share with the class.

EXTRA CHALLENGE In pairs, Sts discuss the positive and negative points of travelling through time and space.

1a 🔊 2·28 ▶
- Ask Sts to look at the photos. Ask *Who do you see? Where are they? What do you think is happening?*
- Play the audio for Sts to listen, follow and answer the question. Alternatively, show the class the video of the story from the DVD-ROM.

He wants to go to Mars in 15 years' time.

> **Note**
> NASA – The National Aeronautics and Space Administration (The United States space agency)

b 🔊 2·28 ▶
- Give Sts time to complete the task. Play the audio / video if necessary, or tell them to find the answers in the text.

1 Erika, Liza, Danny 2 Oliver 3 Erika, Oliver
4 Liza, Oliver 5 Liza, Danny 6 Oliver

EXTRA IDEA To check comprehension, write these words on the board: 'library', 'study', 'Mars', 'NASA', '2030s', '15 years'. Get Sts to relate the words to the conversations.

2
- Individually, Sts find the expressions in the conversations, then discuss what they mean.

What are you up to? = What are you doing? (informal)
Are you having me on? = Are you joking with me? (informal)
Hang on a minute! = Wait, I don't understand. (informal)
Says who? = Who says it is? (informal; implies disbelief)
I can't get my head around this. = I don't understand this. (informal)
You bet we could! = Of course we could. (informal)

- Get the class to agree on the meaning of the expressions.
- Encourage Sts to refer back to the conversation to defend their answers.
- Model and drill the pronunciation of the expressions, paying attention to the stress.

EXTRA SUPPORT Ask Sts to think of similar expressions in their own language.

EXTRA IDEA With a partner, Sts write a short conversation using one or more of the expressions. Then, they act it out for the class.

> **Note**
> To further exploit the video in class, you could use some or all of the suggested activities from page Tviii.

➡ **Workbook** page 40, exercises 1–3

4D

3a
- Ask the class to discuss what they think will happen next. Encourage Sts to use information from the conversation to support their answers.

EXTRA IDEA Write Sts' predictions on the board. Have a class vote on what is most likely to happen next. Sts explain their answers with information from the conversation.

b 🔊 2·29 ▶ Audio script pT90
- Play the audio for Sts to listen, follow and check their predictions. Alternatively, show the class the video of the story from the DVD-ROM.

c 🔊 2·29 ▶ Audio script pT90
- Play the audio or video again for Sts to listen and answer the questions.

> 1 A headset with an image of Mars 2 He has entered a competition. 3 He has to write an essay and do a project about Mars. 4 A trip to NASA 5 They think it's beautiful.

Everyday English Expressing belief and doubt

4a
- Give Sts time to read the phrases and find examples in the conversations on page 52.

EXTRA SUPPORT With a partner, Sts say the complete sentence from the conversation which contains the phrase. Their partner answers with the next line.

EXTRA CHALLENGE In groups of three, Sts write a short dialogue.
Student **A** writes a sentence with an expression of belief.
Student **B** responds with an expression of agreement.
Student **C** responds with an expression of doubt.

b 🔊 2·30 Audio script pT90
- Play the audio for Sts to listen and repeat the phrases, copying the intonation.

EXTRA CHALLENGE Pause after each phrase. Choose one student to make a new sentence with the phrase, e.g. *I'm sure it's going to rain today.*

➡ **Workbook** pages 40–41, exercises 4–7
➡ **Photocopiable** Everyday English

Pronunciation /aɪ/ /i/ /j/

5a 🔊 2·31
- Play the audio once for Sts to listen and follow.
- Play it again for them to listen and repeat the words.

b
- Ask Sts to write the words in the correct column.

c 🔊 2·32
- Sts listen and check their answers.

> /aɪ/ guy, try, why
> /i/   library, really, unlikely
> /j/   you

EXTRA IDEA Sts add two more words to each column. Sts share their words with a partner.

➡ **Workbook** page 41, exercise 8
➡ **Photocopiable** Pronunciation

Listening and Speaking

6a 🔊 2·33 Audio script pT90
- Sts look at the pictures and name the different forms of transport (1 *Flying car*, 2 *hoverboard*, 3 *Passing clouds*, 4 *Teleportation machine*, 5 *Bicycle tunnels above cities*, 6 *Electric car*). How do they think the transport works?
- Play the audio for Sts to listen and answer the question.

> hoverboard (picture 2)

EXTRA SUPPORT Read the script and decide if you need to teach any new lexis before Sts listen.

b
- Sts listen again and answer the question.

> Because it would have to be very powerful to carry someone above the ground

EXTRA CHALLENGE With a partner, Sts discuss their opinions of the hoverboard. Encourage them to give reasons for their opinions. Then, discuss as a class.

7a
- Give Sts time to make their mind maps like the one for picture 3, Passing clouds. (*The other transport forms shown are 1 Flying car, 4 Teleportation machine, 5 Bicycle tunnels above cities, 6 Electric car.*)

EXTRA SUPPORT With a partner, Sts discuss Passing clouds based on the mind map. How would it actually work? Then, discuss as a whole class. Does everyone agree?

EXTRA IDEA Sts make notes on one form of transport they think will be developed in the future, one that won't, and one they are not sure about.

EXTRA CHALLENGE If you have internet access in your classroom, Sts can search for another future form of transport and make a mind map for it. Then, they can present it to the class with their opinions.

➡ **Workbook** page 41, exercise 9

b
- With a partner, Sts talk about their three forms of transport.
- Encourage them to use expressions from exercise 4a to express their opinions.

EXTRA IDEA In small groups, Sts present their forms of transport. The group votes for the best one, the one most likely to succeed. Then each group presents their best idea to the class. Have a class vote on the best one. Encourage Sts to explain their reasons using expressions from exercise 4a.

Extra
Sts can either do this in class or as a homework task.

4D

3 a What do you think will happen next?

b 🔊 2.29 ▶ Listen and check.

c 🔊 2.29 ▶ Listen again. Answer the questions.
1. What has Oliver made?
2. Why has he made it?
3. What two other things does he have to do?
4. What is the prize?
5. What do Danny and Liza think of Oliver's work?

Everyday English
Expressing belief and doubt

4 a Look at the useful phrases. Find examples in the dialogue in exercise 1a.

Useful phrases: expressing belief
I'm sure (that)…
I'm certain (that)…
It's (very) likely (that)…
There's no doubt (that)…
That is definitely/clearly (+ noun/adjective)

Useful phrases: expressing doubt
I doubt (that)…
I'm not really sure (that)…
It's (very) unlikely (that)…
I can't believe (that)…
It's hard to believe (that)…

b 🔊 2.30 Listen and repeat the phrases. Try to copy the intonation.

▶ Workbook pages 40–41, exercises 4–7

Pronunciation   /aɪ/   /i/   /j/

5 a 🔊 2.31 Listen and repeat the words in the box. How is the letter 'y' pronounced?

| definitely   fly   guy   library   really |
| try   unlikely   why   yes   you |

b Put the words from exercise 5a in the correct column.

/aɪ/	/i/	/j/
fly	definitely	yes
___	___	___

c 🔊 2.32 Listen and check.

▶ Workbook page 41, exercise 8

Listening and Speaking

6 a 🔊 2.33 Listen. Which form of transport do Amy and John talk about?

b Why doesn't Amy think it will work?

7 a 🏳 Get ready to speak Make mind maps with notes about what you think of three of the possible forms of transport for the future.

Passing clouds
- winds move the clouds
- big balloons connected together
- passengers enjoy the journey
- friendly to the environment
- passengers sit or stand on the top
- passengers use ladders to get on

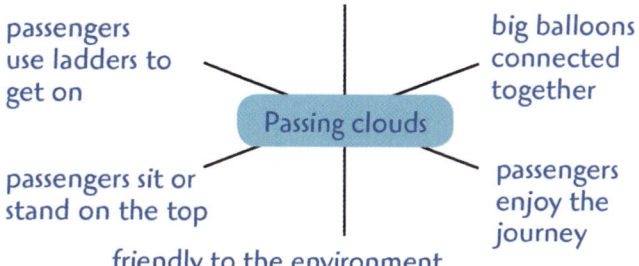

▶ Workbook page 41, exercise 9

b Work with a partner. Talk about the three forms of transport. Express your beliefs and doubts.

> I can't believe that anyone would want to travel on passing clouds.

> There are bound to be some people who would enjoy the experience.

EXTRA Make suggestions for alternative forms of personal transport.

Unit 4 · Travel 53

4 Revision

Vocabulary Buildings

1 Write the words for photos 1–6.

1 _ o _ u _ _   2 _ _ a _ _ _ _   3 _ _ _ p _

4 a _ _ _   5 _ _ m _   6 _ _ _ n

Train travel

2 **Choose the correct answers.**

My parents are taking us on a ¹*trip / journey / travel guide* of a lifetime this summer: we're going to the USA for three weeks! My dad is on the internet all the time, planning our ²*reservation / destination / route* around the country and making hotel ³*accommodation / reservations / budgets*. He's also buying tickets for the most famous monuments and museums so ⁴*journeys / budget / sightseeing* will be easier. He's made ⁵*an itinerary / a travel guide / an arrival* for the three weeks and we already know what we will do from the day of our ⁶*arrival / departure / sightseeing* at JFK airport in New York to the day we leave!

Phrasal verbs for travel

3 **Complete the sentences with the prepositions.**

> across   away   back   down   off   over

1 My grandparents took us to the airport and saw us ___ .
2 We had a great time, but I was quite pleased to get ___ home.
3 We came ___ this great pizzeria while we were sightseeing in Manhattan.
4 When we flew to Australia we stopped ___ in Singapore for a night.
5 The coach was really old and it slowed ___ every time it went up a hill.
6 My mum says she's looking forward to getting ___ and having a holiday.

Grammar Second conditional

4 **Match the sentence halves. Complete them with the correct form of the verbs in brackets.**

1 If I ___ (be) rich,
2 We would ___ (go) camping
3 If we ___ (have) a travel guide,
4 If we ___ (not sleep) so much,
5 We would ___ (not be) late

a if we ___ (have) a tent.
b we ___ (do) more sightseeing.
c if Jack ___ (be) faster.
d I ___ (travel) around the world.
e we ___ (know) the name of the monument.

Comparatives and superlatives

5 **Correct the underlined mistakes.**

1 The bedroom isn't big <u>too</u> <u>enough</u> for everybody.
2 Their hostel isn't as <u>nicer</u> as ours.
3 The hostel was <u>so</u> good as it looked on the website.
4 The town centre was too <u>busier</u>.
5 The campsite is the <u>most small</u> that I've ever seen!

Adverbs of frequency, manner, place and time

6 **Cross out the adverb in the wrong position.**

1 ~~There~~ Zoe left her bag there.
2 Anna read perfectly the poem perfectly.
3 I never have never lived in London.
4 Alex went last month abroad last month.
5 Owen often isn't often late for training.

Everyday English

Expressing belief and doubt

7 **Choose the correct answers.**

1 I'm ___ that the trip will be a success.
   a bound   b sure
2 I'm ___ that we'll all use electric vehicles.
   a no doubt   b certain
3 There's ___ that we will win the match.
   a no doubt   b bound
4 It's very ___ that people will use flying cars.
   a clearly   b unlikely

> **Learning to learn** English in the real world
>
> The internet is great for studying and practising English. You can use it to follow your hobbies and interests in English, too.
> Remember: stay safe online.

▶ Workbook pages 42–43, exercises 1–7

54 Unit 4 · Travel

Revision

Supplementary materials
Workbook: pages 42–43, exercises 1–7
Online Practice
Unit 4 test

Vocabulary Buildings
1

> 1 column 2 statue 3 steps 4 arch 5 dome 6 ruin

Train travel
2

> 1 trip 2 route 3 reservations 4 sightseeing
> 5 an itinerary 6 arrival

Phrasal verbs for travel
3

> 1 off 2 back 3 across 4 over 5 down 6 away

Grammar Second conditional
4

> 1 was / were, would travel, d   2 go, had, a   3 had, would know, e   4 didn't sleep, would do, b   5 not be, was / were, c

Comparatives and superlatives
5

> 2 nice 3 as 4 busy 5 smallest

Adverbs of frequency, manner, place and time
6

> 1 Zoe left her bag *there*.
> 2 Anna read the poem *perfectly*.
> 3 I have *never* lived in London.
> 4 Alex went abroad *last month*.
> 5 Owen isn't *often* late for training.

Everyday English Expressing belief and doubt
7

> 1 b 2 b 3 a 4 b

Learning to Learn English in the real world

- It is important that Sts know how to be safe online. Ask Sts to look up internet safety. Then, tell them to make a poster that you can use in the school, advising other Sts how to be safe on the internet.
- Ask Sts to look back at the topics in the unit (wonders of the world, travelling in Europe, modern adventurers and going to Mars). Ask them to look up one of the topics online. Ask them to bring to class something they learned and found interesting.
- Ask Sts to think of one of their hobbies or interests. Then, tell them to look it up online. What did they learn that they didn't know?
- Have a class discussion. Ask *How do you use the internet? What language do you usually use? How often do you use English? Can the internet help you study? Can you use the internet to improve your English? How?*

➡ **Workbook** pages 42–43, exercises 1–7

➡ When Sts have finished the **Revision** page, tell them to go to the **Workbook Progress Check** *p.43* and complete the **Your progress** table.

4

My project

Project checklist

Before the lesson
- Get some guides with itineraries from a travel agent.
- Get a map of Europe showing cities, rivers and mountains.
- Organize for Sts to be able to use computers, with access to the internet.
- If you cannot organize for computer access, Sts could do the internet research as homework before the lesson. Alternatively, they can bring travel information from a travel agent or other resources to the lesson.

Materials for the lesson
- Computers with internet access
- Map of major European cities

You First

Ask Sts to think about the last time they planned for something, and then answer the questions. With a partner, Sts talk about the most important things when planning. Do they agree? Then, have a class discussion. Write their points on the board in order of importance.

EXTRA CHALLENGE Sts must agree on the order of importance. Sts try to persuade their classmates to change their minds if they disagree.

EXTRA SUPPORT Guide their discussion with questions: *When was the last time you went on a trip? Where did you go? Who did you go with? Who planned it? What did you have to do before the trip?*

1a
- Give Sts time to decide which of the things they need to plan in advance of their trip, and write them in order of importance.

EXTRA CHALLENGE Sts write why the items are important, e.g. *Documents are the most important because you can't travel without them. Knowing what the weather is going to be like is important to decide which clothes to take.*

b
- Tell Sts to compare their lists with a partner and discuss any differences.

EXTRA IDEA Sts decide if they would be able to travel together based on their planning.

EXTRA IDEA Put Sts in groups of about four to discuss their lists. Then, they decide if they would be able to travel together.

2a 🔊 2·34 Audio script pT90
- Get Sts to read through all the questions before they listen.
- Play the audio for Sts to listen and complete the task.

> h, i, b, f, a, g, c, j, d, e

EXTRA SUPPORT Read the script and decide if you need to teach any new lexis before Sts listen.

EXTRA SUPPORT As you play the audio, raise your hand when an answer is being given.

EXTRA SUPPORT Play the audio in different sections to give Sts time to put the question in order:
1 From the beginning to 'some sightseeing and to relax, too.'
2 From 'Where will you stay in each place?' up to 'they'll all be free, too.'
3 From 'What will you eat?' to the end.

EXTRA IDEA Get Sts to answer the questions according to the interview.

b
- Give Sts time to try and remember which topics they heard about, then play the audio again for them to listen and check.

> accommodation, budget, food, sightseeing, souvenirs, transport

EXTRA SUPPORT Ask Sts to look at the topics in exercise 1a. Then play the audio again for them to answer the question.

EXTRA CHALLENGE Sts discuss if they agree with the people's plans in the interview, giving their reasons based on their experience and information in the interview.

3
- Give Sts time to read the information in the **Look!** box and complete the task.

> 1 adjective 2 adverb 3 adverb 4 adjective 5 adverb
> 6 adjective 7 adverb 8 adjective

EXTRA SUPPORT Write on the board:

'Adjectives – before a noun'
Give or elicit an example. (*I'm sure it will be an exciting film.*) Sts underline the noun and draw an arrow to the adjective.

'Adjectives – after *be*'
Give or elicit an example. (*I hope the film will be exciting.*) Sts underline the verb and draw an arrow to the adjective.

'Adverbs – after a verb'
Give or elicit an example. (*They ran wildly through the park.*) Sts underline the verb and draw an arrow to the adverb.

'Adverbs – after a verb and object'
Give or elicit an example. (*He ate his lunch quickly.*) Sts underline the verb and circle the object. Then, they draw an arrow to the adverb.

4a
- Sts work with a partner to plan their interrail route.
- Tell them to make notes on the items suggested.

EXTRA SUPPORT Before they plan, play Track 2.34 from exercise 2a again. Tell Sts to listen and note down information about the bulleted items.

b
- Put Sts in new pairs to interview each other about their trips. Then, they decide if they want to go on their partner's trip.
- Encourage them to give reasons for their decision.

EXTRA SUPPORT In pairs, Sts think of some questions to ask about their partner's trip. They can use some of the questions from exercise 2a.

My project

4

YOU FIRST! Are you good at planning things, or do you prefer to let other people to do it? When you plan to do things with your friends, what are the most important things to think about?

PLANNING AN INTERRAIL TRIP   *The trip of a lifetime!*

1 a You are planning an interrail trip. Which things should you plan before you leave? Write them in the order of importance.

> accommodation   budget   charging your mobile
> clothes   documents   entertainment   food   photos
> sightseeing   souvenirs   transport   weather

b Work with a partner. Compare your lists. Do you agree / disagree?

2 a 🔊 2.34 Listen to an interview. Put the questions in the order that you hear them.
a Why have you chosen these cities?
b Where will you go after that?
c How will you get around in each city?
d What will you eat?
e What will you bring back as souvenirs or presents?
f When are you going?
g Where will you stay in each place?
h Have you decided on your route yet?
i Where will you go first?
j How much money do you think you'll need?

b Which of the topics from exercise 1a do they mention in the interview?

3 Read the Look! box and do the task.

Look! Adverbs and adjectives with the same form

Some adjectives and adverbs have the same form. Adjectives come before a noun or after the verb *to be*. Adverbs come after the verb or after the verb and its object. Decide if the underlined words are adjectives or adverbs.
1 Hopefully the trains won't be late!
2 Everybody's happy to go to the museums late.
3 You can enter some museums and galleries free.
4 There are also free tours.
5 We don't really want to walk far.
6 Some of the campsites are far from the city centres.
7 We'll try hard to save some money.
8 After a lot of hard work, we've finally agreed on one.

4 a Work with a partner. Plan an interrail route around Europe. Choose six places. Make notes about the following:
- the reason for visiting these places
- accommodation
- transport
- food
- budget

b Work with another partner. Interview each other about your interrail trips. Would you like to join your new partner's trip? Why? / Why not?

Unit 4 • Travel   55

4 Culture

YOU FIRST! What are the colours of the national flag of your country? What is the piece of music that they play at national events? Do you know why they chose the colours or the music?

AS BRITISH AS...?

🇬🇧 **FISH AND CHIPS** Potatoes arrived in Britain from South America in about 1580 and Portuguese and Spanish immigrants brought a recipe for fried fish with them in the 17th century. However, it wasn't until about 1860 that the two ingredients were sold together to form Britain's favourite takeaway meal: fish and chips. Historians argue about who had the idea of offering the two foods together. However, the first person to open a fish and chip shop was Joseph Malin, an immigrant from Eastern Europe who arrived in London in 1860. To make it as easy as possible for his customers to carry the hot food, he put pages from newspapers around it. It obviously worked because many shops still sell fish and chips this way today, but they use white paper instead.

🇬🇧 **MARKS AND SPENCER** Ask someone in Britain what the country's most popular department store is and they will probably answer 'Marks and Spencer'. However, although many people think of Marks and Spencer as typically British, it was an immigrant from the Belarusian city of Slonim that started the company. Michael Marks arrived in Britain in the 1880s and he went to live in Leeds, in the north of England. After travelling around local villages to sell goods, in 1884 he had enough money to start a business. He asked an English accountant, Tom Spencer, to join him and the two businessmen opened a stall, Marks and Spencer, at Leeds market. The stall was a success and they soon opened 36 shops across the north of England. Today, there are about 1,000 Marks and Spencer stores in the UK. It was the first British store to make £1 billion profit.

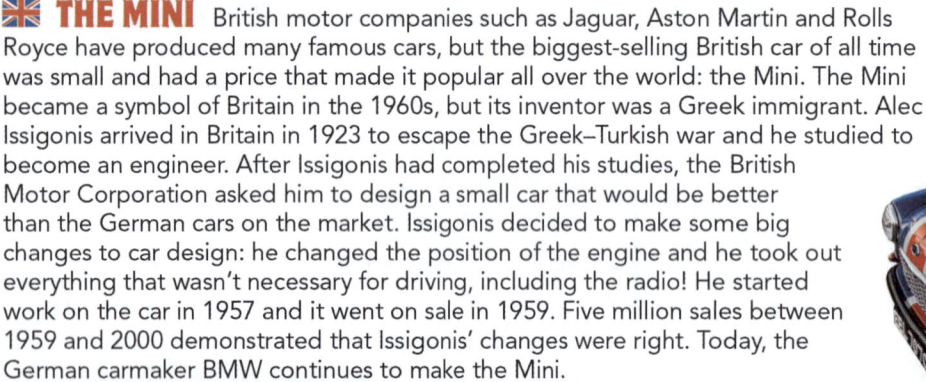

🇬🇧 **THE MINI** British motor companies such as Jaguar, Aston Martin and Rolls Royce have produced many famous cars, but the biggest-selling British car of all time was small and had a price that made it popular all over the world: the Mini. The Mini became a symbol of Britain in the 1960s, but its inventor was a Greek immigrant. Alec Issigonis arrived in Britain in 1923 to escape the Greek–Turkish war and he studied to become an engineer. After Issigonis had completed his studies, the British Motor Corporation asked him to design a small car that would be better than the German cars on the market. Issigonis decided to make some big changes to car design: he changed the position of the engine and he took out everything that wasn't necessary for driving, including the radio! He started work on the car in 1957 and it went on sale in 1959. Five million sales between 1959 and 2000 demonstrated that Issigonis' changes were right. Today, the German carmaker BMW continues to make the Mini.

1 Look at the photos. Do you know other symbols for Britain?

2 Work in groups of three. Read one of the texts. Ask and answer the questions about the other texts and complete the table.

	Fish and chips	Marks and Spencer	The Mini
What is the symbol?	a takeaway meal	a department store	a car
Who created it?			
Where did they come from?			
When did they create it?			
What is the situation today?			

Glossary
department store accountant
stall engine

3 a Over to you! Write a list of symbols for your country.

b Work in groups of three. Compare your lists and say if you think they are good symbols for your country.

Unit 4 · Travel   Baseball

Culture

Supplementary materials
Photocopiable worksheets: Culture, Culture video

CULTURE NOTES Below are some additional details about the three topics mentioned in the lesson.

Fish and chips
Fish and chips were served wrapped in newspaper until the 1980s. This kept prices low, but in the 1980s it was ruled unsafe for food to be touching newspaper ink. Now fish and chips are wrapped in a layer of white paper.

Fish and chips are not as unhealthy as you might think. An average portion of fish, chips and peas contains only **7.3**% fat. However, one portion can contain about 1,110 calories.

Over 250 million fish and chip meals are sold each year in the UK. The record number of fish and chip portions sold in one day is 12,406 at Marini's in Glasgow. The record was set in 1999.

Marks and Spencer: Some interesting numbers
M&S started selling avocadoes for the first time in 1968.
M&S started selling sandwiches in 1981.
M&S recycled 11 million Christmas cards in 2007–2008.
M&S has received 300 awards for its cheeses.
M&S sells about 13 million strawberries during the peak summer week.

The Mini
The production of the original Mini ended in 2000. The company had sold a total of 5,387,862 cars. New models are now being produced.

The designer of the Mini car, Sir Alec Issigonis, didn't like the window, because it needed to be rolled up and down.

In the 1970s, the Mini cost about £600. But if you want to get one of them today, it will cost a lot more than that.

The manufacturing plants for the Mini car were as follows: Cowley and Longbridge in England, Australia, Italy, Belgium, Spain, Portugal, Uruguay, South Africa, Venezuela, and the former Yugoslavia.

There are around 469 Mini clubs in the UK, and 260 more in other countries. These clubs organize events around the world for Mini car owners. The British elected the Mini as the most popular British car ever.

You First
Sts discuss the questions. If you have internet access in your classroom, have a student look up the information. If not, let Sts look up the information at home.

1
- Tell Sts that the three photos are of things that some people consider to be symbols for Britain.
- Ask if Sts can say what they are.
- Ask Sts to think of other things they identify with Britain, e.g. sports teams, royal family, etc.

EXTRA IDEA Get Sts to choose three things that identify their country to the world. Have a class vote for the top three. Sts can expand on these when they do exercise 3.

2
- Go around the class and give each student one of the texts to read.
- Give Sts time to read their text.
- Put Sts in groups of three (one from each text) to ask and answer questions to complete the table.

> **Fish and chips:** Joseph Malin / Eastern Europe / 1860 / shops sell fish and chips wrapped in white paper today
> **Marks and Spencer:** Michael Marks and Tom Spencer / Marks was from Slonim in Belarus, Spencer was from England / 1884 / there are about 1,000 Marks and Spencer stores in the UK
> **The Mini:** Alec Issigonis / Greece / 1957 / the German carmaker BMW continues to make the Mini

EXTRA SUPPORT Read the text and decide if you need to teach any new lexis before Sts begin. Refer Sts to the **Glossary**.

EXTRA IDEA Sts discuss the most interesting thing they learned from their text and explain why.

EXTRA IDEA Sts read all three texts. They choose one sentence to share with the class. The class guesses what it is about.

EXTRA CHALLENGE Write some words from the texts on the board. Sts say how the word is related to information in the text, e.g. 'Joseph Malin' (*first person to open a fish and chip shop*); 'immigrant' (*It was an immigrant that started the company.*); '1960s' (*The Mini became a symbol of Britain.*).

3a
- Tell Sts to write a list of things that they think are symbols for their country.

b
- Put Sts in groups of three to compare their lists, explaining why they are good symbols.

EXTRA CHALLENGE Each group chooses only three symbols. Then, they present their symbols to the class. Sts make a small speech to convince their classmates to choose their symbols. The class votes on the top three.

▶ Video Baseball
As an extension to the Culture topic, watch a short film about baseball and do the accompanying photocopiable exercises. You can either do this in class or set it as optional homework. The film is available on the Teacher's Resource Centre or on the Online Practice.

Learn through English

Additional subject notes

Key dates in early human migration

1–1.5 million years ago: The first evidence of humans using fire to cook food.

60,000–70,000 years ago: The first instance human migration from Africa across the Red Sea. Sea levels were 70 metres lower at this time, so crossing the Red Sea could have been possible.

50,000 years ago: A small group of humans landed in northern Australia. The ocean crossing from Asia to Australia is one of humanity's greatest early achievements.

12,000 years ago: The start of agriculture, which sowed the seeds of civilization. The Fertile Crescent, today's Middle East, is widely considered to be a key location in the development of farming and agriculture. This development meant there was a reliable supply of food throughout the year, and this made permanent settlements possible.

The wheel

Many human inventions were inspired by the natural world. For example, paper was inspired by wasp nests, and the idea for Velcro came from burrs – seeds with little hooks that can catch on fur, hair, or clothing. The wheel, however, could not have been inspired by nature, as there are no living things that use wheels. This makes the invention of the wheel a remarkable example of early human ingenuity. Wheels were used as potter's wheels in in Mesopotamia in around 3500 BC, 300 years before they were used for chariots. There is evidence that wheelbarrows first appeared in classical Greece around 600–400 BC, then in China four centuries later and in Europe in the medieval period. Although wheelbarrows were very expensive to make, they could pay for themselves in just three or four days by reducing labour costs.

You First

Give Sts time to discuss the questions. Elicit ideas and write any useful vocabulary on the board.

EXTRA SUPPORT Have a competition. Set a time limit of two minutes for Sts to write as many different means of transport as they can. Get feedback and award points as follows: 1 point for each form of transport they thought of; 3 points for a form of transport that only three Sts or fewer thought of; 5 points if no other St thought of it. Write their ideas on the board.

1
- Tell Sts to look at the pictures. Elicit the different types of transport.
- With a partner, Sts answer the questions about their own means of transport.
- Get feedback.

EXTRA SUPPORT Read the text and decide if you need to teach any new lexis before Sts begin. Refer Sts to the **Glossary**.

EXTRA SUPPORT First, Sts list all the means of transport they use. Encourage them to think about a normal week: Where do they go? How do they get there? What if they had to walk and use no other mode of transportation? How would their life change? Finally, Sts share their information with a partner.

2a 🔊 2·35
- Play the audio for Sts to listen, follow and complete the task.

g, c, d, b, e, f, a

b
- Sts read the article and match the headings to the paragraphs.

1 D 3 C 4 A 5 B

3a
- Sts make a list of things they have used that have wheels. You could set a time limit for this.

b
- Sts compare their lists with a partner and count who has the most examples.

EXTRA IDEA Sts compare their list with their partner and discuss anything they have used, but didn't write. The class then discusses things only a few people wrote. Finally, discuss the question *How important is the wheel in your life?*

EXTRA CHALLENGE At home, Sts research one daily use of the wheel that has not been discussed in class. Sts bring a photo to class. Display the photos and talk about the uses of the wheel. Discuss *How would your life change without the wheel?*

Project Explore

Learn through English

YOU FIRST! What are the main transport routes from your town? Which ones would you use for transporting goods? Why?

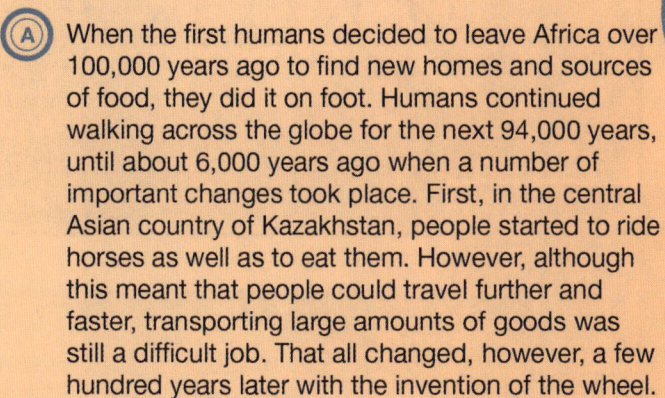

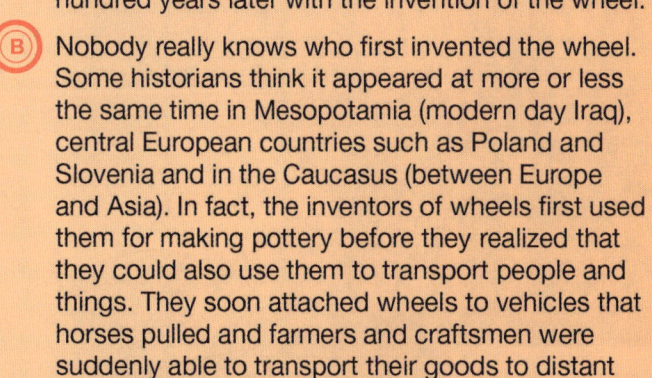

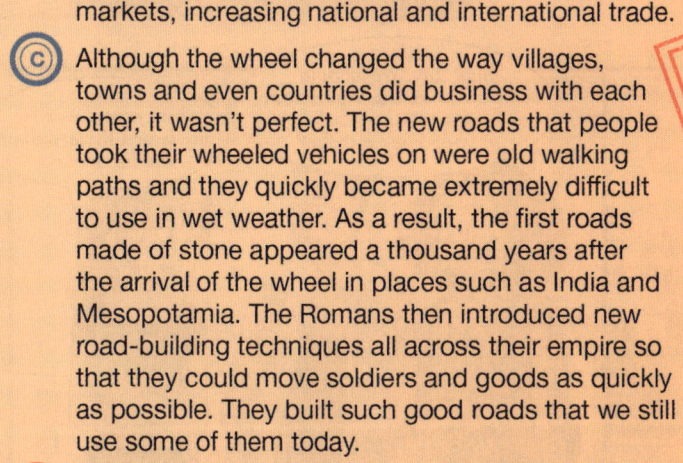

The invention of travel

A When the first humans decided to leave Africa over 100,000 years ago to find new homes and sources of food, they did it on foot. Humans continued walking across the globe for the next 94,000 years, until about 6,000 years ago when a number of important changes took place. First, in the central Asian country of Kazakhstan, people started to ride horses as well as to eat them. However, although this meant that people could travel further and faster, transporting large amounts of goods was still a difficult job. That all changed, however, a few hundred years later with the invention of the wheel.

B Nobody really knows who first invented the wheel. Some historians think it appeared at more or less the same time in Mesopotamia (modern day Iraq), central European countries such as Poland and Slovenia and in the Caucasus (between Europe and Asia). In fact, the inventors of wheels first used them for making pottery before they realized that they could also use them to transport people and things. They soon attached wheels to vehicles that horses pulled and farmers and craftsmen were suddenly able to transport their goods to distant markets, increasing national and international trade.

C Although the wheel changed the way villages, towns and even countries did business with each other, it wasn't perfect. The new roads that people took their wheeled vehicles on were old walking paths and they quickly became extremely difficult to use in wet weather. As a result, the first roads made of stone appeared a thousand years after the arrival of the wheel in places such as India and Mesopotamia. The Romans then introduced new road-building techniques all across their empire so that they could move soldiers and goods as quickly as possible. They built such good roads that we still use some of them today.

D The wheel dramatically changed the way humans move, but it also allowed us to build all types of incredible machines. Wheelbarrows, windmills and clocks all use wheels to work and the Industrial Revolution depended on the wheel. Even in our digitized world, we still use wheels in devices such as 3D printers. Without doubt, the wheel is one of the most important inventions of all time.

Glossary

| source | craftsman | empire |
| pottery | technique | wheelbarrow |

1 Work with a partner. What forms of transport do you use most frequently? Why do you use these forms of transport? If you had to walk everywhere, would you be able to do everything that you have to do?

2 a 🔊 2.35 Read and listen to the article. Put the pictures a–g in the order of the article.

b Match the headings to the paragraphs. There is one extra heading.
1 Wheels are everywhere
2 From road to railways
3 If it rains, stay at home
4 Travelling was hard work
5 An international invention

3 a Make a list of all the things that you have used today that have wheels.

b Work with a partner. Compare your lists. Who has the most examples?

Unit 4 · Travel

The Museum of the Strange   Episode 2

1 🔊 2.36 ▶ Read and listen to the story.

'Shall we leave now?' Ben whispered to Laura. 'This place is *weird*!'

But it was still raining outside and the museum guide was waiting for them at the door to the next room.

'Are you ready?' he asked. 'I think you're going to like the exhibits in our second room.' The sign over the door said THE PRESENT.

This room was as full as the first one, but all of the exhibits seemed to be things from everyday life in the modern world.

'I don't understand,' said Laura. 'Why have you got a smartphone in the museum?'

'Just think…' said the guide. 'If you lived only a few years ago and someone showed you a smartphone, it would look like magic to you!'

Ben was looking at a school notebook. It was open to a page with lots of writing in pencil. There were advanced mathematical formulas and sketches. Ben couldn't understand any of it.

'What about this?' he asked. 'What is it?'

'That is one of the most important documents ever,' said the guide. 'It belonged to a girl called Maddy. She was a brilliant child, but to her older sister she was just an annoying little sister…'

Maddy's big sister was called Jen and she was very different from Maddy.

"I can't believe we've got another History essay to write. 300 words on 'If time travel existed, what moment in history would you visit?'"

"I know. I'd visit Roman times and watch the gladiator games!"

"It's a nice day. We should share our ideas. We're near your house, Jen – can we sit in your back garden?"

"OK, but remember – my weird little sister will be around."

Jen was right. Soon Maddy walked out towards the shed at the bottom of the garden.

"Hello Maddy. What have you got there?"

"Just equipment I need for a science experiment."

Jen and her friends continued to talk, while Maddy worked in the shed.

58 The Museum of the Strange • Episode 2

The Museum of the Strange Episode 2

Supplementary materials
Workbook: pages 44–45, exercises 1–8
Online Practice
Progress test 2

Note
The story can be used in class as a reading and listening task, a video task or both.

EXTRA SUPPORT Pre-teach or elicit from the pictures the meaning of *weird, sketches, documents, annoying, essay, shed, flash* and *whispered*.

1 2·36
- Elicit how Episode 1 of the story ended.

Ben and Laura heard the story of Dan, who became a famous artist after he discovered some cave paintings.

- In pairs, get Sts to look at the pictures on pages 58–59 and predict what they think will happen in Episode 2. Elicit some ideas, but don't tell Sts if they are right at this stage.
- Play the audio for Sts to listen and follow. Alternatively, show the class the video of the story from the DVD-ROM.
- Ask Sts how similar their predictions were to what happens.
- Give Sts time to retell the story about Maddy and her sister in pairs. You could write the words from the pictures on the board to help, i.e. '1 essay, time travel'; '2 back garden, weird little sister'; '3 shed, equipment'; '4 talk, worked'; '5 strange noise, flash'; '6 jumped, worried'; '7 time machine, two minutes'; '8 could travel, greatest moment'; '9 came back, everything'; '10 present, disappeared.'

EXTRA SUPPORT Play the audio again for Sts to listen and follow again before doing the task. They could also retell the story with their books open, using the pictures to help.

EXTRA CHALLENGE Tell Sts to close their books. In pairs, Sts take turns to say what happened in pictures 1–10, e.g. *Jen and her friends have got an essay on time travel to write.*

- Elicit parts of the story from different pairs.

➡ **Workbook** pages 44–45

Notes
The story can be further exploited by doing the tasks from these pages in the **Workbook**. These can be done in class or set as homework.
The tasks in the **Workbook** review the following language points covered in **Units 3–4** in the **Student's Book**:
- Modal verbs (*p. 35*)
- Second conditional (*p. 47*)

1
- Sts choose the correct answers to the questions.

2 b **3** a **4** c **5** b **6** a

2
- Sts complete the diary with words from the box.

2 annoying **3** equipment **4** experiment **5** flash **6** shed
7 could **8** strangest **9** disappeared **10** time

EXTRA SUPPORT Sts look back at the story and check their answers.

EXTRA CHALLENGE In pairs, Sts say a word from the exercise. Their partner says a sentence about the story using the word, e.g. *Essay: Jen and her friends have to write a history essay about time travel.*

3
- Sts match the sentence halves.
- Then, they match the sentences to the correct speaker.

2 c, C **3** e, D **4** a, B **5** d, A

EXTRA IDEA In pairs, Sts take turns to say something one of the characters says in the story. Their partner guesses who said it. Sts use the story to confirm their answers.

4
Students' own answers.

5
- Sts choose the correct words to complete the rules for time travellers.

2 mustn't **3** can't **4** should **5** ought to **6** must

EXTRA IDEA Sts write two more rules for time travellers.

EXTRA CHALLENGE With a partner, Sts discuss if they agree with all the rules. Then, Sts share their ideas with the class.

6 24 Workbook Audio script pT106
- Play the audio for Sts to listen and put the pictures in the correct order.

1 b **2** e **3** d **4** a **5** e

EXTRA IDEA Get Sts to write sentences about the pictures, and then use them to retell the story.

7 24 Workbook Audio script pT106
- Before playing the audio, tell Sts to read and answer the questions.
- Play the audio for Sts to confirm their answers.

1 The look (of surprise) on Jen's face was funny.
2 There were only two pyramids.
3 The battery level / power was low.
4 They were afraid / terrified and then angry.
5 She (had) waited for hours.

Project Explore T58

8
- In pairs, Sts discuss the questions.
- Discuss Sts' ideas as a class.

> Students' own answers.

EXTRA SUPPORT For question 2, elicit from the class some things from modern life. Write them on the board.

EXTRA IDEA In pairs, Sts role-play a conversation between them and a time traveller, comparing the future with the present.

> **Note**
> To further exploit the video in class, you could use some or all of the suggested activities from page Tviii.

Comic panels

Panel 1: But suddenly there was a strange noise and a flash of light. "What was that? It came from the shed. Is your sister OK?" "Wait! Where is she? Where's Maddy?"

Panel 2: Jen jumped up quickly. She didn't always like her little sister, but she cared and now she was worried. "Oh Maddy! What have you done?"

Panel 3: But then there was a second flash of light. "I've done it! I've built the world's first time machine. I have just travelled two minutes into the future!" "What? Is this a trick?"

Panel 4: "Wait, Phil. Where are you going?" "Remember that History homework? Well, if I could travel to any moment in history, I'd see the greatest moment in the history of science."

Panel 5: "And that's what I have done. I came back to see the world's first time machine. It's going to change everything." "And now I have to return to my present."

Panel 6: Then he pushed a button on a tiny machine, and disappeared forever.

When the guide finished, Laura shook her head. 'It's just a story, isn't it? I mean, time travel isn't real. There are no real time machines.'
The museum guide looked surprised. 'Aren't there?' He opened the glass case and reached for the notebook. 'I paid a lot of money for this. Oh well…'
He threw the notebook into the rubbish bin. Then he began to walk to the next room.
'Come along, please…We've saved the best until last.'

'This place just gets stranger and stranger,' Ben whispered.
Laura looked up at the sign over the door to the third room. It said THE FUTURE.
What could be in there?

> Workbook pages 44–45

The Museum of the Strange • Episode 2

5 Heritage

5A Surviving the test of time

YOU FIRST! Which personal objects have you had for a very long time? Why do you think you are still using them?

Listening

1 **a** Work with a partner. Look at the photos. Which inventions do you think people will still use in 100 years' time? Why do you think we will continue to use them?

b 🔊 3.02 Listen to a lecture. Choose the correct answers.

1 Some of the best examples of technology are things that have ___
  a recently been invented.
  b existed for years.
  c incredible designs.

2 When Professor Stevenson mentions one example of technology, his students think it is ___
  a funny.
  b a well known one.
  c a mistake.

3 The bucket was invented ___ years ago.
  a 1,000   b 500
  c 5,000

4 ___ invented the chair.
  a The Greeks
  b Nobody knows who
  c The Egyptians

5 Today, everyone can afford a chair thanks to changes in ___
  a the design.   b materials.
  c society.

Vocabulary — Verbs and dependent prepositions

2 **a** 🔊 3.02 Listen again. Match the prepositions to the verbs. Use some prepositions more than once.

about   at   for   in   into   on   to   with

1 speak ___
2 listen ___
3 think ___
4 search ___
5 laugh ___
6 look ___
7 explain ___
8 succeed ___
9 agree ___
10 divide ___
11 depend ___
12 belong ___

b Choose the correct prepositions to complete the sentences.

1 We didn't look *in/to/at* all the paintings in the exhibition.
2 Our teacher divided the class *with/into/about* four groups.
3 That tablet doesn't belong *to/for/with* you!
4 I like listening *about/to/with* podcasts about science.
5 If you have a problem, speak *on/into/to* your teacher.
6 What do you think *about/in/on* the new desks?
7 I don't agree *for/with/about* you about the future of TV.
8 He didn't like it when we didn't laugh *on/at/with* his jokes.
9 How did the search *into/for/about* a new mobile phone go?
10 Everything depends *into/with/on* my exam results.
11 We succeeded *on/in/for* persuading John to come with us.
12 The story that he explained *at/to/on* me didn't seem true.

▶ **Workbook** page 46, exercises 1–3

Speaking

3 **a** Get ready to speak Write a list of the three most important objects that belong to you. Make notes to answer the questions. Use the verbs and prepositions on this page.

• What do you use them for?
• Do you need them to do something useful?
• How long have you had them? Were they presents?

b Over to you! Work with a partner. Explain to each other your three objects from exercise 3a.

Well, the first object is my mountain bike. It belonged to…

c Work in a group. Choose the most important of your three objects. Compare your objects and decide which are the most interesting/surprising.

Unit 5 • Heritage

5 Heritage

Unit objectives
- use prepositions with verbs correctly
- use compound nouns correctly
- use nouns to talk about modern life
- talk using the passive form of verbs
- use defining and non-defining relatives clauses with relative pronouns, adding commas where necessary
- categorize items into countable and uncountable nouns
- use phrases to agree or disagree
- write a report

Language
Grammar: the passive; defining and non-defining relative clauses; countable and uncountable nouns and determiners
Vocabulary: verbs and dependent prepositions; compound nouns; modern life nouns
Everyday English: agreeing and disagreeing
My project: Celebrations in Barcelona
Culture: Irish heritage
Learn through English: Techniques from literature

5A Surviving the test of time

Supplementary materials
Workbook: pages 46–47, exercises 1–8
Workbook: Grammar summary Unit 5
Photocopiable worksheets: Grammar and Vocabulary, Communication

You First
Sts make a list of personal objects they have had for a long time and think about why they still have them.

EXTRA SUPPORT Elicit from Sts some of their favourite possessions. Briefly discuss why they are important to them. Ask them to individually write down which personal objects they have had for a long time.

EXTRA CHALLENGE Sts think of personal objects that were important to them but they no longer use. Why don't they use them? Briefly discuss how long they usually keep a personal object.

Listening
1a
- Put Sts in pairs to look at the photos and answer the questions.

EXTRA SUPPORT Ask Sts to name the inventions in the photos (*games console, analogue watch, television, car, smartphone / mobile phone, tablet*). Write them on the board.

EXTRA IDEA Sts write the inventions in order of usefulness to them and society today. Then get them to discuss their answers with a partner.

b 🔊 **3·02** Audio script pT91
- Play the audio for Sts to listen and complete the task.

1 b **2** a **3** c **4** a **5** b

EXTRA SUPPORT Read the script and decide if you need to teach any new lexis before Sts listen. Make sure Sts understand *bucket*.

EXTRA SUPPORT Sts predict the answers before they listen and compare with a partner.

EXTRA CHALLENGE Sts discuss which is the more useful invention, the chair or the bucket.

Vocabulary Verbs and dependent prepositions

2a 🔊 **3·02** Audio script pT91
- Play the audio again for Sts to listen and complete the task.

1 to **2** to **3** about **4** for **5** at **6** at **7** to **8** in
9 with **10** into **11** on **12** to

EXTRA CHALLENGE Ask Sts to try to remember how each verb and preposition was used in the lecture, and write a sentence. They needn't write the exact sentence.

b
- Give Sts time to complete the task.
- Get them to compare with a partner before you check answers.

1 at **2** into **3** to **4** to **5** to **6** about **7** with **8** at
9 for **10** on **11** in **12** to

EXTRA SUPPORT Give sentences 1–6 to half of the class and 7–12 to the other half. Sts complete their sentences.

EXTRA CHALLENGE Get Sts to write true sentences about themselves using the verbs and prepositions from exercise 2a.

➡ **Workbook** page 46, exercises 1–3

Speaking
3a
- Give Sts time to make their lists, answering the questions and using the verbs and prepositions.

b
- With a partner, Sts explain what their three objects are and why they chose them.

EXTRA CHALLENGE Sts explain why their object is important without mentioning the object. Their partner guesses what it is.

c
- Put Sts in groups. Each student presents their most important object to the group. The group then chooses the most interesting or most surprising object.

Project Explore T60

5A

Reading

4a
- Give Sts time to read the museum guide and answer the question.

The bucket: materials have changed, but not the design
The shoe: the design used to be the same for both feet
The chair: materials have changed, but not the design

b
- Give Sts time to complete the task.

1 wood 2 materials 3 leather 4 printers 5 Historians
6 design

c 🔊 3·03
- Play the audio for Sts to listen and check.

EXTRA IDEA Ask Sts *Which invention do you think has made the most progress? Which is most useful to you now? Which could be improved even more? How?*

Grammar The passive

5a
- Give Sts time to read the sentences and complete them.

1 *be*, participle 2 *by*

b
- Sts complete the table with sentences A–J from the museum guide.

present simple: B, J
past simple: D, E, F, H, I
future simple: C, G

EXTRA SUPPORT Write the present simple sentences on the board. Ask Sts to identify and circle the main verb. Then, get them to identify and underline the auxiliary verb. Ask *What tells you this is the present simple?* (*the auxiliary verb 'be'*) Do the same with the past simple and the future simple. Finally, get Sts to find the pattern in the passive (*be* + past participle).

EXTRA CHALLENGE Sts write the sentences in their notebooks. What pattern can they see in the passive? Discuss the pattern as a class.

c
- Give Sts time to complete the task, then compare with a partner before you check answers.

2 Trousers were invented in Asia about 3,000 years ago.
3 Chocolate was imported to Europe by the Spanish in the 16th century.
4 How many journeys are made on the London underground every day?
5 Astronauts will be sent to Mars by the government in 2030.
6 Solar panels will not be installed (by him) on the school roof.

EXTRA CHALLENGE Get Sts to write their own sentences in the passive. The class listens and says if it is present simple, past simple or future simple. You could also ask Sts to write sentences in each form and then read one to the class.

EXTRA CHALLENGE Divide the class into three groups. Give Group 1 the present simple, Group 2 the past simple and Group 3 the future simple. Sts write their own sentences in the tense they were given, then read their sentences out loud. The listening groups change the sentence to their tense, e.g.
Group 1: *The most expensive cars are made in Italy.*
Group 2: *The most expensive cars were made in Italy.*
Group 3: *The most expensive cars will be made in Italy.*

➡ **Workbook** pages 46–47, exercises 4–6
➡ **Photocopiable** Grammar and Vocabulary

Listening and speaking

6a 🔊 3·04 Audio script pT91
- Ask Sts to look at the photos and describe the different objects. Encourage them to think of materials, colours, size and what the object is used for.
- Make sure Sts understand that *a number of* means *several*.
- Play the audio once for Sts to answer the question.

3 a fridge

EXTRA SUPPORT Read the script and decide if you need to teach any new lexis before Sts listen.

b
- Play the audio again for Sts to complete the task.

1 It was invented in the 19th century.
2 It's usually made of plastic, metal, and some glass.
3 It's usually covered in white metal.
4 Bigger ones are sold in America.
5 It will be connected to our mobile phones in the future.

EXTRA IDEA Sts write sentences about one of the other objects in the photos, but without naming it. Then, Sts say their sentences for the class to guess the object. Sts get one point for each sentence they say without the class guessing the object.

7a
- With a partner, Sts choose a common object and answer the questions.

b
- Put Sts in new pairs to present and guess each other's objects.

EXTRA CHALLENGE Sts think of different objects that are popular today. Then, they write a sentence about how the object will be used in the future. Discuss ideas as a class.

➡ **Workbook** page 47, exercises 7–8

Extra

Sts can either do this in class or as a homework task.

5A

Reading

4 a Read the museum guide. How have the objects changed over the years?

b Complete the museum guide with the words in the box.

> design   historians   leather   materials   printers   wood

Inventions that have survived the test of time!

THE BUCKET

The bucket has been around for at least 5,000 years. ^A The first buckets were usually made of animal skins or ^1 ____. Today, ^B they are made of ^2 ____ like plastic and metal. In the future, ^C new materials will be used, but the design will probably stay the same.

THE SHOE

Experts believe ^D the first shoes were worn 40,000 years ago. ^E They were made of soft ^3 ____ from animal skins. Until 1850, ^F shoes weren't shaped differently for each foot, so there was no difference between left and right. Shoes in the future will be made by 3D ^4 ____, but ^G will they be designed by people or computers?

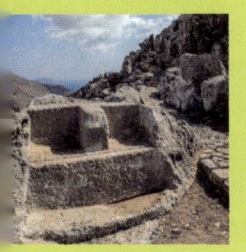

THE CHAIR

^5 ____ think ^H the chair was invented by the Greeks over 5,000 years ago. ^I It was used by rich Egyptians as a symbol of power. Today, ^J lots of different materials are used to make chairs, but the ^6 ____ hasn't changed a lot.

c 🔊 3.03 Listen and check.

Grammar The passive

5 a Read the sentences from the guide. Complete the rules for the passive with the correct words.

The chair was invented by the Greeks.

Lots of different materials are used.

> by   participle   be

1 We often use the passive when the action is the most important thing. It's formed with the present / past / future simple form of the verb ____ and the past ____.
2 We don't always need to say who does the action. If we do, we use the preposition ____.

b Which tense are sentences A–J? Complete the table.

The passive	
present simple	
past simple	A,
future simple	

c Make the sentences passive. Use *by* if necessary.

1 How many hamburgers do Americans eat a year?
   How many hamburgers are eaten by Americans every year?
2 They invented trousers in Asia about 3,000 years ago.
3 The Spanish imported chocolate to Europe in the 16th century.
4 How many journeys do people make on the London underground every day?
5 The government will send astronauts to Mars in 2030.
6 He won't install solar panels on the school roof.

▶ **Workbook** pages 46–47, exercises 4–6

Listening and speaking

6 a 🔊 3.04 Listen to Julia and Tom. Which object does Julia describe?

1   2   3   4

b Answer the questions.

1 When was it invented?
2 What is it usually made of?
3 What is it usually covered in?
4 Where are bigger ones sold?
5 What will it be connected to?

7 a **Get ready to speak** Work with a partner. Choose a common object. Answer the questions about it.

* What is it used for?
* When or where was it invented?
* What is it made of?
* Where is it used?
* How will it be developed in the future?

b **Over to you!** Work with a new partner. Present and guess your objects.

▶ **Workbook** page 47, exercises 7–8

EXTRA Describe the unusual uses that are made of objects at home.

> I know hairdryers are sometimes used to dry wet clothes.

Unit 5 · Heritage

5B Globalization

YOU FIRST! Where were the things that you use at home and at school made? Which things were made locally and which things were made globally, in another country?

Reading

1 a 🔊 3.05 Read and listen to the forum posts. Which posts are positive about globalization?

b Use the names from the forum. Who says…?
1 we can learn about ourselves by studying languages
2 we get too much entertainment from one country
3 what we eat should be included in the essay
4 they aren't happy about what you can find in shops
5 free movement helps us learn about each other

Vocabulary Compound nouns

2 a Complete the sentences with the highlighted words.
1 I hate our ____ where people buy things that they don't really need.
2 Toronto is the city with the most ____ in the world with people from 200 different cultures!
3 My dad has worked for a few ____ and he's often travelled to their offices in other countries.
4 We crossed lots of ____ when we went on our interrail trip across Europe.
5 Everybody needs to know something about ____ because we all depend on computers.
6 ____ such as TV, radio and newspapers doesn't have as much power as it used to.
7 I prefer a ____ such as a concert to watching TV.
8 My sister went on a ____ for a month to Slovakia.
9 The internet is the best example of a ____ that allows people everywhere to communicate.
10 In the past, poetry was part of ____ , but today few people are interested in it.
11 There's an online job advertisement about some interesting ____ in Lisbon.
12 Shops all over the world sell the same ____ .

b 🔊 3.06 Listen and check, then repeat.

▶ Workbook page 48, exercises 1–3

Speaking

3 a Work with a partner. Make a list of examples of the things in the box that you can find in your town, region or country.

> cultural activities   cultural diversity
> global brands   mass media
> multinational companies   popular culture

b Work with another pair. Compare your lists. Which ones are the most well known? Why?

c Which forum posts do you agree with?

GlobalGirl22
Globalization essay 22nd April 17.18

Hey guys, I need your help. I've got to write an essay about the effects of globalization on culture. Any ideas? Please reply 🙂

TheFoxes16
Globalization essay 22nd April 17.42

It depends on what you mean by 'culture'. Is shopping a cultural activity? If it is, then I don't think globalization is good for the town where I live: Leicester in the UK. There's no variety in the shops; it's all global brands. It's really boring! Not long ago, there were local shop owners whose knowledge of their products was incredible. And of course you could find bookshops! Multinational companies aren't interested in culture; they just want to create a consumer society.

InterrailMan
Globalization essay 22nd April 17.59

If shopping is culture, then travelling definitely is! It's great that there are fewer international borders and that moving is easier than it used to be. That's good for employment opportunities, but it also encourages cultural exchange. My sister, who finished school last June, spent a year working in Germany and Poland and she learned a lot about the two countries.

SnowMan
Globalization essay 22nd April 18.35

I'm glad your sister had a great time, InterrailMan, but globalization doesn't promote cultural diversity in popular culture. Last weekend, nearly all the films here in Helsinki were made in Hollywood! It's the same with online TV series and pop music; most of it is American. Don't get me wrong; I like American culture, but some variety would be nice!

DownUnder44
Globalization essay 22nd April 19.04

I've lived in Australia, where we speak over 150 languages, for over ten years. I think that globalization is actually making people around the world more interested in our languages. There are more and more people who realize that we can learn a lot about human history by studying languages – and thanks to mass media and information technology, we can preserve them. There's also a growing global network which defends these languages; that wouldn't be possible without globalization!

GlobalGirl22
Globalization essay 22nd April 19.23

Thanks for some great ideas, guys – both positive and negative! TheFoxes16, whose post asks what we mean by culture, makes a good point. I'll include food and cooking, which I think is part of culture, like shopping and travelling. My hometown is full of international fast food restaurants. Anyway, next time you need some help, I'll be there for you! Thanks! 🙂

Unit 5 · Heritage

5B Globalization

Supplementary materials
Workbook: pages 48–49, exercises 1–8
Workbook: Grammar summary Unit 5
Photocopiable worksheets: Grammar and Vocabulary, Communication

You First
Sts think of things around the house and school and where they were made. Sts consider if they were made locally or globally.

EXTRA SUPPORT Elicit things from the class that they use at school. Write about three on the board. Sts continue the list individually. Then, they decide if the things were made locally or globally.

EXTRA IDEA Sts compare their list of things with a partner and agree on three things that were made locally and three things that were made globally.

EXTRA CHALLENGE Sts describe one of their things without saying the name. The class guesses what it is.

Reading

1a 🔊 3·05
- Play the audio for Sts to listen, follow and answer the question.

InterrailMan, DownUnder44

b
- Give Sts time to complete the task, then check answers.

1 DownUnder44 2 SnowMan 3 GlobalGirl22
4 TheFoxes16 5 InterrailMan

EXTRA SUPPORT Sts find another sentence from the forum posts. The class guesses who said it.

EXTRA CHALLENGE Sts write a sentence that one of the people from the forum might say, e.g. *There are no local shops on our high street*. The class guesses who might have said it and explains why.

EXTRA CHALLENGE Sts think of another topic for the essay (e.g. technology, food, fashion, local traditions, etc.) Then, Sts discuss if it is positive or negative, and why.

Vocabulary Compound nouns

2a
- Give Sts time to complete the sentences with the highlighted words in the text.

2b 🔊 3·06
- Play the audio for them to listen and check.
- Play the audio again for Sts to listen and repeat, paying attention to the stress.

1 consumer society 2 cultural diversity 3 multinational companies 4 international borders 5 information technology 6 Mass media 7 cultural activity 8 cultural exchange 9 global network 10 popular culture
11 employment opportunities 12 global brands

EXTRA SUPPORT Divide the class in two. Give one half sentences 1–6 to complete and the other half sentences 7–12. When they have completed their sentences, ask Sts to say them out loud to the class. Sts from the other group listen and decide if the sentences are correct. Discuss any disagreements.

➡ **Workbook** page 48, exercises 1–3

Speaking

3a
- Put Sts in pairs to complete the task.

b
- Sts then compare with another pair and discuss which things are most well known, and why.

EXTRA SUPPORT Ask Sts to look at the expressions for giving opinions on page 15. Sts then use these expressions to give their opinions to the class.

EXTRA CHALLENGE Divide the class into five groups and give each group one of these topics: global brands, multinational companies, cultural exchange, popular culture, mass media. Get each group to list some examples for their topic. Finally, each group decides the effects of globalization in relation to their topic and presents them to the class. Sts agree or disagree, and say why.

c
- Sts decide which forum posts they agree with.

EXTRA IDEA Sts write their own answer to GlobalGirl22. Display their answers in the classroom and let Sts read them. Which do they agree with, and why? Using Post-it notes, Sts write their opinion and stick it on the text.

5B

Grammar Defining and non-defining relative clauses

4a
- Give Sts time to read the sentences and complete the rules.
- Check answers.

> We use *who* for people, *where* for places, *which* for things, and *whose* for possessions.

b
- Give Sts time to read the rules for defining and non-defining relative clauses.
- Sts match them with the sentences from exercise 4a.

> **A:** 1, 3   **B:** 2, 4

EXTRA CHALLENGE With a partner, Sts discuss the difference between the two clauses before doing the next exercise.

c
- Tell Sts to find the four underlined sentences in the forum posts and decide which kind of relative clause each contains.

> **Defining:** I don't think globalization is good for the town where I live. / There's also a growing global network which defends these languages.
> **Non-defining:** My sister, who finished school last June, spent a year working in Germany and Poland. / TheFoxes16, whose post asks what we mean by culture, makes a good point.

Note
Tell Sts to look at the non-defining relative clauses and remove the relative clause between the commas. Does the sentence still make sense? Reinforce that non-defining relative clauses add something extra to the sentence.

d
- Sts complete the sentences with *who*, *which*, *where*, and *whose*, adding commas where necessary.

1 That's the art teacher **whose** paintings are going to be in the exhibition.
2 My eldest brother**, who** lives in Prague**,** speaks four languages.
3 The Four Seasons pizza**, which** is my favourite**,** was first eaten in Naples, Italy.
4 We went to the fast food restaurant **where** we ate last weekend.
5 Her wedding dress**, which** was made a famous designer**,** cost €3,000!
7 Aberdeen**, where** my dad was born, is on the east coast of Scotland.

e
- Put Sts in pairs. Tell them to use relative clauses to describe the people and things in the box for their partner to identify.

EXTRA SUPPORT Write on the board: 'It's a multinational company. It makes computers and smartphones.' Ask Sts to combine the sentences using a relative clause. Ask Sts to guess the company (*Apple*).

EXTRA SUPPORT Get Sts to write a specific name for the items in the box (e.g. for an actor: Tom Cruise). Ask them to write two sentences about the person / item, e.g. *He's an American actor. He starred in the Mission Impossible films.* Ask them to combine the two sentences using a relative clause. Sts then say their sentences to the class for them to guess who it is.

▶ **Workbook** pages 48–49, exercises 4–6
▶ **Photocopiable** Grammar and Vocabulary

Speaking

5a
- Give Sts time to read and answer the questions.

b
- Sts work with a partner to compare and discuss their answers.
- Ask Sts *Who is more global? Who is more local?*
- Sts discuss if it is possible to replace the global things with things made locally or not, and why this might be.

EXTRA IDEA Have a class discussion. Write these questions on the board and ask: 'Which things are better locally?' 'Which things are better global?' 'Why do you think this is?'

EXTRA IDEA Sts create an advertisement to support local products. They should say what the product is and why it is better locally. Sts act out the advertisements for the class. The class decides if the advertisement is convincing, and why or why not.

Writing

6a
- Tell Sts they are going to write a report based on their answers to the quiz in exercise 5a.
- Give Sts time to make notes based on the example.

b
- Now tell Sts to write sentences based on their notes. Encourage them to write at least two sentences for each question.
- Tell Sts to use relative clauses and organize their sentences into paragraphs as in the example.
- Finally, Sts write a conclusion for their report.

c
- Sts read some of their classmates' reports and decide if the class is more global or local.
- Sts give reasons for their answers based on the reports.

EXTRA IDEA Ask 'global' Sts to stand on one side of the classroom. Then, ask 'local' Sts to stand on the other side. Sts on each side take turns to say why it is important to be global or local.

EXTRA IDEA Sts research any local products that have become global. What is their global message? Why do Sts think they became global?

Extra
Sts can either do this in class or as a homework task.

T63 Project Explore

5B

Grammar
Defining and non-defining relative clauses

4 a Read the sentences. Complete the rules with the highlighted words.
1 There are more and more people who realize that we can learn a lot.
2 I'll include food and cooking, which I think is part of culture, like…
3 There were local shop owners whose knowledge of their products was…
4 I've lived in Australia, where we speak over 150 languages, for over 10 years.

> We use ___ for people, ___ for places, ___ for things and ___ for possessions.

b Read the rules for defining and non-defining relative clauses. Match the sentences from exercise 4a to the rules.

> A A defining relative clause gives us information to identify the noun.
>
> B A non-defining relative clause adds extra information about the noun. We use commas. We can't use *that*.

c Find the four underlined sentences in the forum on page 62. Which ones are defining relative clauses and which are non-defining?

d Complete the sentences with *who, which, where* and *whose*. Add commas if necessary.
1 That's the art teacher ___ paintings are going to be in the exhibition.
2 My eldest brother ___ lives in Prague speaks four languages.
3 The Four Seasons pizza ___ is my favourite was first eaten in Naples, Italy.
4 We went to the fast food restaurant ___ we ate last weekend.
5 Her wedding dress ___ was made by a famous designer cost €3,000!
6 Aberdeen ___ my dad was born is on the east coast of Scotland.

e Work with a partner. Use relative clauses to describe the people and things, then identify them.

> an actor   a capital city
> a global brand   a TV series
> a multinational company   a singer

▶ **Workbook** pages 48–49, exercises 4–6

Speaking

5 a Get ready to speak Answer the questions in the questionnaire.

Are you global or local?
Find out with our quiz!

Where were your clothes made?
○ a locally   ○ b in Europe   ○ c in another continent

Which fashion styles do you follow?
○ a local styles   ○ b national styles   ○ c international styles

Where is the food that you eat produced?
○ a locally   ○ b in Europe   ○ c in another continent

Where do you eat out with friends or family?
○ a at places that offer local dishes
○ b at places that offer international dishes
○ c at multinational fast food restaurants

What is your favourite type of music?
○ a local folk songs
○ b national pop music
○ c international pop music

Where was your favourite TV series made?
○ a locally   ○ b nationally   ○ c in another country

b Work with a partner. Compare your answers. Who is more local / global? Can you replace the global things with local things? Why? / Why not?

> I don't like the clothes which are made locally because…

Writing

6 a Get ready to write Prepare a report on your answers to the quiz.
- Make notes on the answers that you gave to the quiz.

> trainers – global brand – made in Vietnam

▶ **Workbook** page 49, exercises 7–8

b Write the report.
- Organize your notes into paragraphs using relative clauses.
  Clothes   *My trainers, which were made in…, are…*
  Food   *The places where I often eat…*
  Popular culture   *The pop groups which I listen to most are…*
- Write a conclusion.   *In conclusion, I'm a person who's…*

c Read some of your classmates' reports. Do you think your class is local or global? Why?

EXTRA Think of local products that could become global brands. What images and messages would you use?

Unit 5 · Heritage   63

5C Modern life

YOU FIRST! What do you think are the big differences between the lives of a teenager today and the teenager of 100 years ago? Whose life is/was better? Why?

Vocabulary Modern life nouns

1 a Match the words to the pictures.

> advertising   business   data
> entertainment   graffiti   housework
> leisure   litter   news   pollution

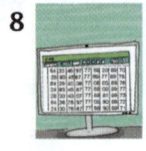

b 🔊 3.07 Listen and check, then repeat.

▶ **Workbook** page 50, exercises 1–3

Reading

2 a Read the first text and complete the mind map. Then read the other texts and make mind maps.

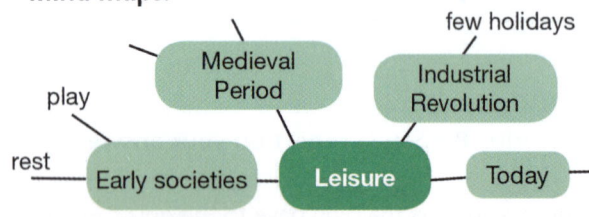

Leisure

In very early societies, people didn't have much work. People hunted for food, cooked, made clothes, etc. when necessary and then had time to rest and play. As societies became more organized, we started to work more. Most people had little time for leisure. Five hundred years ago, in the Medieval Period, only a few rich people had time for activities such as hunting and writing and reading poetry. With the arrival of factory work and the Industrial Revolution in the 18th century, there were few holidays for workers but working conditions slowly improved. Today, most people who have jobs have some time for leisure activities. In fact, our consumer society has turned leisure into a money-making industry.

GRAFFITI

The first examples of graffiti appeared on walls in Ancient Greece and Rome over 2,000 years ago. A little graffiti from that time has survived and shows that people wrote their names, poems and even advertisements. Modern graffiti first appeared in New York in the 1960s. Some experts in graffiti have named a Greek-American, Demetrius, as the first modern graffiti artist. Demetrius worked as a messenger and travelled all over the city on the subway. On every journey he used to write 'Taki 183' on the trains and station walls. Soon, others copied him and more colourful graffiti started to appear. Today, many graffiti artists show their work in art galleries and graffiti has become part of popular culture.

ADVERTISING

Modern advertising started with the arrival of weekly newspapers in Britain in the 18th century. More and more people could read and all newspaper owners realized they could earn money from sales and by charging for each advertisement. With the arrival of the radio, the cinema and TV in the 20th century, advertising became a form of industry. Today, no important TV programme or film is made without money from advertising. Furthermore, local government and private businesses make money by allowing advertising to appear on public transport and in public places. The internet has also introduced new forms of personalized advertising and posters in shopping centres and city streets will soon be digital. It seems that modern life would be impossible without any advertising.

b Put the history of leisure in the correct order.

A Only the wealthy had free time.
B People's work situation got better.
C People only worked when they had to.
D People work and have free time.

Speaking

3 a Work with a partner. Write two more questions with words from exercise 1a.

How do you find out about what is in the news?
How much leisure time do you have?
How much graffiti is there in your neighbourhood?
What kind of advertising annoys you?

b Work with a different partner. Ask and answer the questions.

> I use social media and I also read my mum's newspaper when...

> We don't get a newspaper at home, so we watch the news...

Unit 5 · Heritage

5C Modern life

Supplementary materials
Workbook: pages 50–51, exercises 1–8
Workbook: Grammar summary Unit 5
Photocopiable worksheets: Grammar and Vocabulary, Communication

You First
Write on the board: 'school', 'family', 'friends', 'fun' and get Sts to think about those aspects of their life now. Then, ask them to think about the life of a teenager for those aspects 100 years ago. Get feedback, and write some ideas on the board.

EXTRA IDEA Sts discuss the differences with a partner. What are the three most important differences? Discuss as a class.

EXTRA CHALLENGE Sts decide on the most important difference for them. The class votes on the most important, but they cannot vote for their own.

Vocabulary Modern life nouns

1a
- Give Sts time to complete the task.

b 🔊 3·07
- Play the audio once for Sts to listen and check.
- Now play the audio again for Sts to listen and repeat the words, paying attention to pronunciation and stress.

> 1 litter 2 housework 3 graffiti 4 advertising 5 pollution
> 6 business 7 entertainment 8 data 9 leisure 10 news

EXTRA IDEA Sts choose one of the pictures and say a sentence, e.g. *Cars can cause this*. The class guesses the picture. If the class can't guess, the student can say another sentence, e.g *It is bad for your health*.

➡ **Workbook** page 50, exercises 1–3

Reading

2a
- Point out that mind maps can help Sts remember information in a text.
- Sts read the texts and make a mind map for each text.
- Sts compare their mind maps in pairs, discuss any differences and make any necessary changes.
- Ask *What surprised you the most in each text?*

> **Suggested answers**
> **Leisure**
> Medieval Period: a few rich people hunting, reading and writing poetry
> Today: money-making industry
> **Graffiti**
> First graffiti: Ancient Greece, Rome, names, poems, advertisements
> Modern graffiti: New York, 1960s
> First modern graffiti artist: Demetrius, subway, 'Taki 183'
> Today: art galleries, popular culture
> **Advertising**
> 18th century: weekly newspapers, GB
> 20th century: radio, cinema, TV
> Today: make money, public transport, public places, the internet, digital

EXTRA SUPPORT Get Sts to underline the important information in the texts. Then tell them to write one or two words for each line or branch on the mind map.

EXTRA IDEA Ask Sts to retell the information in the texts using only their mind maps. Does it help? How could they improve?

b
- Sts read the text about leisure again and put the events in the order they happened.

> C, A, B, D

EXTRA IDEA Sts write complete sentences about leisure using the words in the mind map.

EXTRA SUPPORT Sts say a sentence from one of the texts. The class listens and says which text it's about.

EXTRA CHALLENGE Sts write two questions for each text. The class listens to a question and finds the answer in the text.

EXTRA IDEA Divide the three texts among the class. Sts take one important sentence from the text and write it on the board, leaving a space for an important word, e.g. 'Modern advertising started with the arrival of weekly _____'. Sts read the texts to complete the sentences.

EXTRA CHALLENGE Sts say an important word from one of the texts. The class says what the word is about, e.g. *Subway, Demetrius travelled all over the city on the subway*.

Speaking

3a
- Give Sts time to read the questions.
- In pairs, they write two more questions, using the words in exercise 1a.

b
- Sts work with a different partner and answer all six questions.

EXTRA IDEA Take a class vote: Which word from exercise 1a is most important in Sts' lives? Discuss the three most important and why.

Extra
Sts can either do this in class or as a homework task.

5C

Grammar Countable and uncountable nouns and determiners

4a
- Sts write the nouns in the correct column of the table.

Countable: advertisement, expert, holiday, journey
Uncountable: advertising, graffiti, time, work

EXTRA SUPPORT Sts think of two more examples of countable and uncountable nouns and add them to the table. Then, Sts compare with a partner. Do they agree? Encourage Sts to discuss any differences.

EXTRA SUPPORT Sts use a dictionary to see if the nouns are countable or uncountable. How does the dictionary indicate if it is countable or uncountable?

b
- Sts complete the rules with the words in the box.

1 numbers   2 plural   3 ideas   4 never

c
- Refer Sts to the examples in the table, the underlined phrases in the texts and the Grammar summary for **Unit 5** in the **Workbook**. Explain that Sts should put a tick in each column which corresponds to the correct usage of the determiners, e.g. *every journey, each advertisement, no sound*.
- Give Sts time to find the 14 underlined phrases in the texts and tick the correct column.
- Now refer Sts to the Grammar summary and ask them to find five phrases which will allow them to add five more ticks to the table (*no* + plural noun: *no major films*; *no sound*; *any* + plural noun: *any colour films*; *all* + uncountable noun: *all graffiti*; *most* + uncountable noun: *most advertising*).
- Check answers.

	+ singular countable noun	+ plural noun	+ uncountable noun
every	✓		
each	✓		
no	✓	✓	✓
any		✓	✓
some		✓	✓
all		✓	✓
most		✓	✓
much			✓
many		✓	
few / a few		✓	
little / a little			✓

d
- Give Sts time to read the rule and choose the correct answers.

1 Few   2 a little   3 little   4 a few

EXTRA CHALLENGE Give each student one word from the first column of the table. Sts make a sentence using the word and a noun of their choosing. The class listens and says if it is countable or uncountable.

➡ **Workbook** page 50, exercises 4–6
➡ **Photocopiable** Grammar and Vocabulary

Listening

5 🔊 **3·08** Audio script pT91
- Ask Sts what they think is happening in the photo, but <u>don't</u> confirm any answers yet.
- Play the audio for Sts to listen and complete the notes.

1 laugh   2 fish   3 steal   4 river   5 karate   6 successful

EXTRA SUPPORT Read the script and decide if you need to teach any new lexis before Sts listen.

EXTRA IDEA Write the following sentences on the board and elicit answers from the Sts to complete the gaps.
'According to the speaker, most advertisements are _____.' (*boring*)
'There isn't much _____, but there's a lot of _____.' (*dialogue, action*)
'All the bears look _____.' (*real*)
'The fisherman _____ and _____ away.' (*wins, walks*)

EXTRA CHALLENGE Ask Sts what part of the advertisement they liked best. Encourage them to explain why.

EXTRA CHALLENGE Sts think of an advertisement they really like. They tell the class, following the notes for exercise 5.

Speaking

6a
- Put Sts in pairs and give them time to make their notes.
- Tell them to use the ideas in the box and the questions to help them.

EXTRA SUPPORT Sts could work in groups of three or four to make their notes and prepare their lecture, and then pair up to share the presentation.

➡ **Workbook** page 51, exercises 7–8

b
- With their partner, Sts prepare a short lecture on their subject.

EXTRA SUPPORT Sts practise presenting their lecture to their partner and make any necessary changes.

c
- Put Sts in groups so that they aren't with their previous partner.
- Give Sts time to each present their lecture to the group.
- When a student has finished, the group asks questions about his / her lecture.

EXTRA CHALLENGE Sts write two questions for the group to answer after listening to their lecture.

Extra

Sts do the activities in pairs in class.

5C

Grammar
Countable and uncountable nouns and determiners

4 a Are these nouns from the texts countable or uncountable? Put them in the correct column.

> advertisement   advertising   expert
> graffiti   holiday   journey   time   work

Countable	Uncountable

b Complete the rules with the words in the box.

> ideas   never   numbers   plural

Countable nouns are things that we can count using ¹___ . They have a singular and a ²___ form. Countable nouns often refer to physical objects. Uncountable nouns are things that we can't count. Uncountable nouns include food and liquid, ³___ and qualities. They ⁴___ have a plural form.

c Complete the table. Use the underlined phrases from the texts and Grammar summary in the Workbook.

	+ singular countable noun	+ plural noun	+ uncountable noun
every	✓		
each	✓		
no			✓
any			
some			
all			
most			
much			
many			
few / a few			
little / a little			

d Read the rule and choose the correct answers.

> We use *few* and *little* to stress that something is very small. *Few* and *little* usually have a negative meaning. *A few* and *a little* are more positive.

1 I felt sorry for Zoe. *A few / Few* people came to see her graffiti exhibition.
2 We had *a little / little* time between exams so we went for a coffee.
3 My sister's company is in trouble. There's *a little / little* money coming in.
4 You were in the USA for *a few / few* weeks – wow!

▶ Workbook page 50, exercises 4–6

Listening

5 🔊 3.08 Listen and complete the notes about the advertisement.

> My favourite advertisement
>
> Reason for enjoying the advertisement: it made me ___.
> The product: tinned ___
> What happens? The advertisement shows a fisherman who wants to ___ some fish that a few bears have caught in a ___. One of the bears and the fisherman have a ___ fight.
> Conclusion: Few advertisements are so funny, but perhaps it's not a ___ advertisement.

Speaking

6 a Get ready to speak Work with a partner. Make notes about an important aspect of modern life. Use the ideas in the box to help you.

> communication   entertainment   exercise
> school   shopping   social media   travel

- Why is it important?
- What important event(s) has / have happened in this area?
- How would our lives be different without it?

▶ Workbook page 51, exercises 7–8

b Work with a partner. Prepare a short lecture on your subject.

c Work in different group from your partner. Give your lecture. Ask questions about the other lectures.

> I'm going to start this lecture by talking about one of the most important...

EXTRA Make a list of five things in modern life that you think it would be difficult to live without. Compare your list with a partner's. Do you have similar or different ideas?

Unit 5 • Heritage

5D Stereotypes

YOU FIRST! What do adults think of young people? Are their opinions correct?

1 a 🔊 3.09 ▶ Read and listen. List the stereotypes about girls, boys and teenagers that are mentioned.

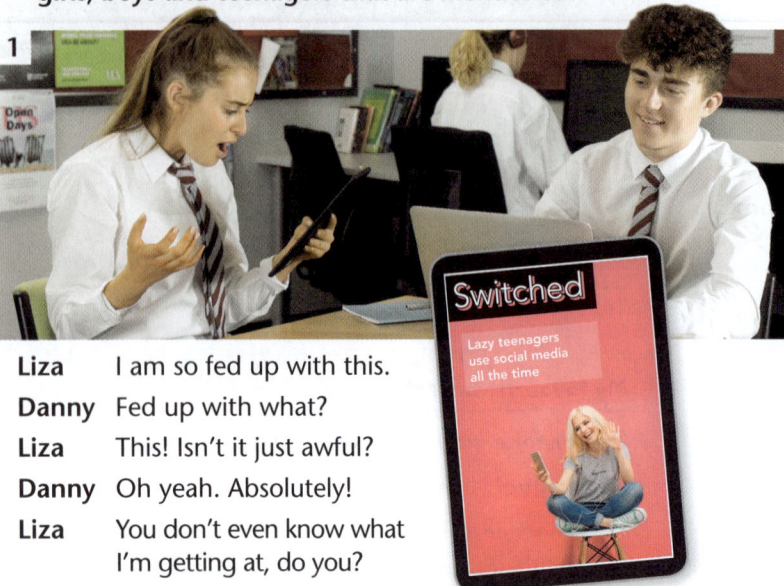

Liza I am so fed up with this.
Danny Fed up with what?
Liza This! Isn't it just awful?
Danny Oh yeah. Absolutely!
Liza You don't even know what I'm getting at, do you?
Danny Er no…not exactly.
Liza This article! It's just full of stereotypes. Girls only wear pink and talk about make-up…sport is just for boys…and every teenager in the world is on social media all the time!
Danny That's so true!
Liza It isn't, Danny. It's a stereotype. A lazy stereotype!
Danny Yeah, you're right about that, but…
Liza But what, Danny? But it's no big deal?
Danny No, I wouldn't say that. But magazine articles are always written about what's popular.
Liza So girls *do* only talk about make-up? Whose side are you on?
Danny I'm not on anybody's side! I'm just saying, you can't always change these things.
Liza Can't I? Well, I…completely…disagree!
Danny I'm not sure tweeting the magazine will help…
Liza Really? Five tweets already – looks like most people completely agree with me. Ha! Look at this one. 'More people need to say this! Boys don't get it!' Spot on! Just what I was thinking!
Danny No, that's not always true.
Liza Isn't it?

Switched — Lazy teenagers use social media all the time

Danny No way! Anyway, I thought we said teenagers don't use social media all the time.
Liza Oh, forget it!
Danny Where are you going?
Liza To put my make-up on.
Danny Really?
Liza No, not really! As you said, you can't change things…if you don't try. I'm going to try.

Oliver …and he was the one that said it first! Hey, it's Liza. Hi Liza! Come over here!
Danny Don't!
Oliver What?
Danny Nothing.
Liza Hi Oliver. Hi Danny.
Oliver Hey! Erika said you're a writer now!
Liza Oh…yeah. *Switched* magazine want me to write an article for them. Danny?

b Answer the questions.
1 Why is Liza angry about the article?
2 What does Danny say about magazine articles?
3 What does Danny say Liza can't change?
4 How does Liza know some people agree with her?
5 What is Liza going to do?
6 What has a magazine asked Liza to do?

2 Spoken English What do these expressions mean? How do you say them in your own language?

- I'm fed up with…
- You don't know what I'm getting at
- It's no big deal
- Whose side are you on?
- Spot on!
- Forget it!

▶ **Workbook** page 52, exercises 1–3

Unit 5 · Heritage

5D Stereotypes

Supplementary materials
Workbook: pages 52–53, exercises 1–8
Photocopiable worksheets: Everyday English, Pronunciation
Online Practice

> **Note**
> The story can be used in class as a reading and listening task, a video task or both.

You First

Sts think about the questions and discuss. Ask them to think of three important adults in their lives, and what their opinions of young people are or might be. Encourage Sts to think about how life was different for those adults. Now ask Sts to imagine that they are one of those adults. They share their opinion with the class in the first person and the class guesses who the adult is. Discuss the opinions as a class.

1a 3•09

- Ask the class if they know what a stereotype is. Can they guess from reading the word? Is it similar in their own language?
- Sts then look it up in the dictionary and discuss different stereotypes.
- Play the audio for Sts to listen, follow and make their lists. Alternatively, show the class the video of the story from the DVD-ROM.

> Girls only wear pink and talk about make-up, sport is just for boys, and every teenager is always on social media.

EXTRA SUPPORT Before they listen, ask *Who do you see in the first photo?* (*Danny and Liza*); *Where are they?* (*In the IT room at school*); *What are they doing?* (*Liza is looking at a tablet, Danny is on a laptop.*); *How do they feel?* (*Students' own answers.*)

b

- Give Sts time to answer the questions.
- Play the audio again for Sts to listen and check.

> 1 She's angry because it is full of stereotypes.
> 2 He says they are always about what's popular.
> 3 She can't change what magazines write about.
> 4 She sees some tweets.
> 5 She is going to try to change the situation.
> 6 *Switched* magazine has asked her to write an article.

EXTRA CHALLENGE Sts defend Liza or Danny's point of view, even if they don't completely agree with them.

EXTRA CHALLENGE Sts make a list of other stereotypes people have about girls, boys and teenagers. Encourage them to think about the opinions they discussed in **You First**. Then, discuss as a whole class.

2

- Give Sts time to complete the task, then check answers.

> **I'm fed up with…** = I'm annoyed with… (informal)
> **You don't know what I'm getting at** = You don't understand the point I'm making (informal)
> **It's no big deal** = It's not important (informal)
> **Whose side are you on?** = Who do you agree with? (informal)
> **Spot on!** = completely accurate (informal)
> **Forget it!** = This shows the speaker is annoyed, and doesn't want to talk about it any more. (informal)

EXTRA SUPPORT Sts find the expressions in the conversations. How do the people feel when they say them?

EXTRA CHALLENGE With a partner, Sts think of a stereotypical opinion people have. This could be about boys, girls, or teenagers, or you could encourage Sts to think of opinions people have about other subjects. Sts write a similar conversation based on the opinion, using some of the expressions. They act out the conversation for the class. The class listens and discusses the opinion.

> **Note**
> To further exploit the video in class, you could use some or all of the suggested activities from page Tviii.

▶ **Workbook** page 52, exercises 1–3

5D

3a
- Elicit some ideas, but don't confirm anything yet.
- Encourage Sts to use information from the conversations to support their answers.

b 🔊 3•10 ▶ Audio script pT92
- Play the audio for Sts to listen and check. Alternatively, show the class the video of the story from the DVD-ROM.

> They're going to write an article about teenagers and social media.

c 🔊 3•10 ▶ Audio script pT92
- Play the audio again and give Sts time to complete the task.
- Check answers, getting Sts to correct the false answers and asking how they know the others are true.

> 1 F (He says 'I know, I know I was wrong.')
> 2 T (She asks if he'll lend her a hand.)
> 3 F (He says 'Oh. I'd love to!)
> 4 F (He suggests an article about teenagers and social media, which was the subject of their argument.)

EXTRA CHALLENGE Hold a class debate. Write on the board: 'Teenagers today have an easy life.' Divide the class in two and tell one half to argue for the statement and the other half to argue against it. Give Sts time to prepare their arguments. Ask a few pairs to present them to the class.

Everyday English Agreeing and disagreeing

4a
- Give Sts time to find examples of the phrases in the conversations on page 66.

EXTRA SUPPORT With a partner, Sts say the complete sentence from the dialogue with the phrase. Their partner answers with the next line.

EXTRA CHALLENGE In groups of three, Sts make a short dialogue.
Student A: Say a sentence with an opinion about girls, boys, or teenagers.
Student B: Agree, using a phrase from the list.
Student C: Disagree, using a phrase from the list.

b 🔊 3•11
- Play the audio for Sts to listen and repeat the phrases, copying the stress and intonation.

EXTRA CHALLENGE Give each student a phrase from the list so that all Sts have a phrase. Say an opinion, e.g. *Teenagers are generally lazy. / Boys are better at science than girls.* Sts respond to the opinion with their expressions.

➤ **Workbook** page 52, exercises 4–6
➤ **Photocopiable** Everyday English

Pronunciation Word stress

5a 🔊 3•12
- Play the audio for Sts to listen and repeat.
- Give them time to decide on the stress and the number of syllables.

> al<u>rea</u>dy, <u>any</u>way, <u>ar</u>ticle, com<u>plete</u>ly, dis<u>agree</u>, e<u>xact</u>ly, maga<u>zine</u>, <u>me</u>dia, <u>po</u>pular, <u>teen</u>ager

b
- Ask Sts to write the words in the correct column.

c
- Play the audio for Sts to listen and check.

> 1 article, media, popular, teenager
> 2 completely, exactly
> 3 magazine

EXTRA IDEA Sts add two more words to each column. Sts share their words with a partner.

➤ **Workbook** page 53, exercise 7
➤ **Photocopiable** Pronunciation

Speaking

6a
- Give Sts time to read the comments. Ask them if they have heard of the three people.
- Then, in pairs, Sts discuss and answer the questions.
- Encourage Sts to give reasons for their opinions.

> **Note**
> The speakers are being ironic and not literally meaning what they say.
> Oscar Wilde (Irish poet and playwright) is joking with the idea that young people usually think they know everything. Only when you get older do you realize how little you really know.
> Margaret Mead (American anthropologist) is saying that it is good to retain child-like qualities even though no one else is aware of them.
> George Bernard Shaw (Irish-British playwright) is playing with the idea that youth is a wonderful time, but that young people don't appreciate it.

EXTRA IDEA Sts do some research about the people in the photos. If you have internet access in your classroom, divide the class into three groups. Each group researches one person. Then, groups share the information they discovered.

EXTRA SUPPORT Ask *Do you think the young know everything? Is it better to stay young? What does it mean to stay young? Do young people appreciate being young?*

b
- With their partner, tell Sts to read the stereotypes and add three more to the list.

c
- Ask pairs to discuss their list and decide on the worst three, giving their reasons.

d
- Sts work with another pair and compare lists.
- Sts choose three stereotypes to present to the class.

EXTRA CHALLENGE Divide class into small groups. Ask Sts in each group to think of a situation involving stereotypes. They act out the situation for the class. The class guesses and discusses the stereotype.

➤ **Workbook** page 53, exercise 8

Extra
Sts can either do this in class or as a homework task.

5D

3 a What do you think will happen next?

b 🔊 3.10 ▶ Listen and check.

c 🔊 3.10 ▶ Listen again. Are the sentences true (T) or false (F)?
1 Danny still thinks he was right.
2 Liza wants Danny to help her.
3 Danny isn't keen on helping.
4 Oliver suggests something that Liza and Danny haven't thought about.

Everyday English Agreeing and disagreeing

4 a Look at the useful phrases. Find examples in the dialogue in exercise 1a.

Useful phrases: agreeing
I (completely) agree (with you).
You're right about that.
That's so true!
Absolutely!

Useful phrases: disagreeing
I (completely) disagree (with you).
No way!
I wouldn't say that.
No, that's not always true.

b 🔊 3.11 Listen and repeat the phrases. Try to copy the intonation.

▶ **Workbook** page 52, exercises 4–6

Pronunciation Word stress

5 a 🔊 3.12 Listen and repeat the words in the box. How many syllables are there in each word? Which syllable is stressed?

> already   anyway   article
> completely   disagree   exactly
> magazine   media   popular   teenager

b Put the words from exercise 5a in the correct column.

1 Ooo	2 oOo	3 ooO
anyway	already	disagree
___	___	___

c 🔊 3.13 Listen and check.

▶ **Workbook** page 53, exercise 7

Speaking

6 a Work with a partner. Read the comments. What do they mean? Do you think they are negative or positive about youth and young people?

Oscar Wilde: I am not young enough to know everything.

Margaret Mead: I was wise enough never to grow up, whilst fooling people into believing I had.

George Bernard Shaw: Youth is wonderful. It is a crime to waste it on children.

b Work with a partner. Read the stereotypes about teenagers. Add three more.

http://www.teentimetalk/mylife/stereotypes

Stereotypes about teenagers that need to disappear…NOW!
- Teenagers don't know what real music is.
- Teenagers love themselves and spend all day taking selfies.
- Teenagers are too young to understand anything about life.
- Teenagers never help anyone.
- Teenagers' favourite pastime is lying on a sofa.

c Work with a partner. Discuss the stereotypes in exercise 6b and the ones that you have added. Decide on the three that you think are the worst and say why.

d Work with another pair and discuss your lists. Are any of the stereotypes the same? Choose three and present them to the class.

▶ **Workbook** page 53, exercise 8

EXTRA Write five stereotypes about elderly people. Why do you think these stereotypes exist?

Unit 5 · Heritage 67

5 Revision

Vocabulary Verbs and prepositions

1 Complete the text with the correct prepositions.

Last week, I spoke ¹___ my uncle who had lived with the Piraha people in the Amazon jungle in Brazil. It was incredible to listen ²___ his stories about how these people live and think ³___ the world. He explained ⁴___ me that teenagers like me don't go to school, but go hunting and searching ⁵___ food in the jungle. He said the Piraha people teach their children to depend ⁶___ themselves to survive because life in the jungle is hard.

Compound nouns

2 Match a word from A to a word from B to form a compound noun.

A consumer   cultural   employment
   global   mass   popular

B brand   culture   diversity   media
   opportunity   society

Modern life nouns

3 Match the words to the situations.

business   entertainment   housework
litter   news   pollution

1 Jack, please do the washing up.
2 Pick that up and put it in the bin!
3 The president is in Paris this week.
4 That film was great. I really enjoyed watching it.
5 We're hoping to open a new office.
6 Don't swim in the river. It's a strange brown colour!

Grammar The passive

4 Complete the sentences with the correct passive form of the verb in brackets.

1 Who ___ *Hamlet* ___ (write) by?
2 Electric cars ___ (drive) by everybody in the future.
3 Hats ___ (not wear) very often these days.
4 When ___ the World Wide Web ___ (invent)?
5 A lot of tea ___ (drink) in Ireland every year.
6 Global brand trainers ___ (not make) at our local factory after next year.

Defining and non-defining relative clauses

5 Complete the text with the relative pronouns. Add commas where necessary.

where   which (x3)   who   whose

BerlinBaby
Globalization essay 22nd April 21.09

There is a lot of cultural diversity in Berlin ¹___ I live and it's great. There are lots of restaurants ²___ serve food from all over the world and you can listen to musicians ³___ songs talk about their culture; much more interesting than the usual pop songs ⁴___ we sing! My brother ⁵___ lived in Australia for three years played a didgeridoo in a concert here. A didgeridoo ⁶___ is an Aboriginal instrument makes a very unusual sound and it's fantastic!

Countable and uncountable nouns and determiners

6 Choose the correct answers.

1 Give a leaflet to ___ student in the group.
  a every   b all   c some
2 I'm afraid I haven't got ___ money and can't come on the trip.
  a few   b much   c a little
3 ___ graffiti is not art in my opinion.
  a No   b Any   c Most
4 The exhibition is on ___ months.
  a most   b all   c any
5 There are ___ tickets left. How many would you like?
  a few   b no   c a few
6 ___ story comes from a different culture.
  a Some   b Each   c Many

Everyday English Agreeing and disagreeing

7 Match the sentence halves.

1 I completely disagree   a about that.
2 I was just going   b not always true.
3 That's so   c with you.
4 No, that's   d say that.
5 I wouldn't   e to say that.
6 You're right   f true!

Learning to learn Expanding ideas

Adding information makes our writing more interesting. On page 69, the writer tells us that Castellers are human towers. The writer then answers questions which a reader might have about Castellers: where they build them, when they first built them, how they build them, etc. If you answer *what, when, where, how, who* and *why* questions in your writing, your readers will find it much more interesting.

▶ **Workbook** pages 54–55, exercises 1–9

68 Unit 5 · Heritage

Revision

Supplementary materials
Workbook: pages 54–55, exercises 1–9
Online Practice
Unit test 5

Vocabulary Verbs and prepositions
1

> **1** to **2** to **3** about **4** to **5** for **6** on

Compound nouns
2

> consumer society   cultural diversity   employment opportunity
> global brand   mass media   popular culture

Modern life nouns
3

> **1** housework **2** litter **3** news **4** entertainment
> **5** business **6** pollution

Grammar The passive
4

> **1** was, written **2** will be driven **3** aren't worn
> **4** was, invented **5** is drunk **6** won't be made

Defining and non-defining relative clauses
5

> There is a lot of cultural diversity in Berlin, ¹**where** I live, and it's great. There are lots of restaurants ²**which** serve food from all over the world and you can listen to musicians ³**whose** songs talk about their culture; much more interesting than the usual pop songs ⁴**which** we sing! My brother, ⁵**who** lived in Australia for three years, played a didgeridoo in a concert here. A didgeridoo, ⁶**which** is an Aboriginal instrument, makes a very unusual sound and it's fantastic!

Countable and uncountable nouns and determiners
6

> **1** a **2** b **3** c **4** a **5** c **6** b

Everyday English Agreeing and disagreeing
7

> **1** c **2** e **3** f **4** b **5** d **6** a

Learning to learn Expanding ideas

- On the board, write a simple sentence about one of your hobbies. Then, ask Sts to write questions for information to expand on the sentence. Encourage Sts to ask questions using *who, what, where, when, why* and *how*.
- Answer the questions and ask Sts to make notes. When Sts have the information from their questions, ask them to write a paragraph about your hobby with the new information.
- Next, divide Sts into groups. In each group, one student says a sentence about their hobby or interest. Other Sts in the group ask questions to get more information. Then, Sts write a short paragraph about the hobby / interest.
- Ask each group to read their paragraphs and decide on the best one. They can make changes if they want. Then, each group reads their paragraph to the class.
- Finally, discuss how using question words can help Sts add information to their texts.

▶ **Workbook** pages 54–55, exercises 1–9
▶ When Sts have finished the **Revision** page, tell them to go to the **Workbook Progress Check** *p.55* and complete the **Your progress** table.

5

My project

Project checklist

Before the lesson
- Get some photos of celebrations from your town or region.
- Get some brochures so Sts can see examples.
- Organize for Sts to be able to use computers with access to the internet.
- If you cannot organize for computer access, Sts could do the internet research as homework before the lesson. Alternatively, they can bring information about the celebrations to the lesson.

Materials for the lesson
- Computers with internet access.
- Without computer access, Sts can create their report on paper. You will need A3 paper.

You First

Have a whole-class discussion about the different celebrations in the Sts' town or region. Encourage them to talk about how they and their family and friends participate in the celebrations.

EXTRA SUPPORT Starting in January, ask Sts to think through the year, noting down the celebrations in the order they happen. Then, guide the discussion with questions that will help them focus: *When does the celebration take place? Who participates in it? Why is it celebrated? What do people do in the celebration?*

EXTRA IDEA Choose three of the local celebrations mentioned by Sts in **You First**. Take a piece of poster paper for each one and display them in the classroom. Ask Sts to describe the celebration and write notes on the poster paper in the form of a mind map. They will be able to use these mind maps when doing their own projects.

1a
Ask Sts to describe the large photo on the page. *What is happening? What time of the year do you think it is? Why? Who is participating? What do you think is the meaning of the activity?*
- Tell Sts to read the report quickly to find the answers to the questions.
- Check answers.

1 Castellers   2 St George's Day

b
- Give Sts time to read the report again and complete the information.
- Get Sts to compare with a partner, then check answers.

1 23rd April   2 book   3 autumn   4 hundred

c
- Put Sts in pairs, **A** and **B**. Tell Sts **A** to go to page 86 and Sts **B** to page 87.
- Give Sts time to read their information.
- Now tell them to ask and answer the questions.

EXTRA IDEA Sts read their texts and answer these questions: *What did you find most interesting? What surprised you? Would you like to participate in this celebration? Why?* You may want to write the questions on the board.

2a
- Give Sts time to make their list.
- Encourage them to use the celebrations they discussed at the beginning of the lesson.

b
- Sts compare their lists with a partner. Then, they choose two celebrations.

c
- Give Sts time to make their notes and organize them into paragraphs, using the report as a model.

EXTRA IDEA Sts start their report by describing their photos first. Ask *What do they see? Who is participating? What are they doing? What time of year is it? How does it relate to the meaning of the celebration?*

d
- Tell Sts to check their texts and decide where to place their photos.
- Now Sts make their final reports, either on a computer or on paper.
- Encourage them to use the report in on page 69 and the work they have done in the unit so far to help them.

e
- Ask Sts to present and share their reports.
- Get class feedback in answer to the questions.

EXTRA IDEA Tell Sts they are going to promote the celebrations for tourists to their town or region. Choose from these ideas:

Brochure
1 Show Sts examples of brochures.
2 Give them paper for their brochure.
3 Sts decide where they will put photos, titles and text.
4 Sts write their texts for the celebration.
5 Tell them their brochures could be in a tourist office or in shops in the city for tourists to pick up. They are encouraging tourists to stay for the celebration.
6 The class votes for the best brochure.

Poster
1 Tell Sts they are going to make posters for the tourist office and shops around their region.
2 Give Sts paper to make their poster.
3 Sts organize their poster. What photos will they use? Where will they put them? What will they write?
4 Remind Sts to use a catchy slogan in bigger letters.
5 Display the posters in class.
6 The class votes for the best poster.

Presentation
1 Tell Sts they are going to make a PowerPoint presentation about the celebrations.
2 Remind them that people do not have a lot of time to stop and read, so their presentations have to be attractive and brief (5–10 slides).
3 Sts decide on the photos they will use and then write a brief text for each photo.
4 Sts present their slide show to the class and the class votes on the best presentation.

T69   Project Explore

My project

YOU FIRST! What are the most popular celebrations in your town or region? What happens during these celebrations? Do people from other towns come to take part?

A report

CELEBRATIONS

Report: the celebrations of Barcelona
There are a few celebrations that take place in Barcelona during the year. In the following report, we will look at two of the most famous events.

Saint George's Day
We share Saint George's day, 23rd April, with many places, but the way we celebrate it in Barcelona is very special. The rose has become a symbol of St George's Day and here all the men are expected to buy a rose for their girlfriends or wives and the women have to buy a book for their partners. Many of the city's streets become crowded with flower and book stalls and there is a great atmosphere. The day is such a success that UNESCO has turned it into World Book Day all around the world.

Castellers
Castellers are human towers and the Catalan word 'castell' means castle. Human towers were first built in the 18th century in a small town not far from Barcelona and today you can see them at different events in Barcelona and towns near the city from the spring until the autumn. They also travel the world and appear at international events. There are almost 100 people in a human tower group, although only a few of them actually form part of the tower. Most of the group stay on the ground to form the base. The base needs to be strong because the tower can have as many as nine or ten levels!

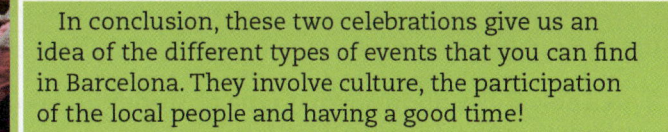

In conclusion, these two celebrations give us an idea of the different types of events that you can find in Barcelona. They involve culture, the participation of the local people and having a good time!

1 a Read the report about festivals and celebrations in Barcelona.

Which celebration…?
1 also takes place in towns near Barcelona
2 has been made international by UNESCO

b Complete the information.

Event: St George's Day Date: ^{1}____
What happens: All the men buy a rose for the women and all the women buy a ^{2}____ for the men.

Event: Castellers Date: From the spring to the ^{3}____
What happens: Groups of nearly a ^{4}____ people form human towers that can have as many as nine or ten levels.

c Exchange information about two more celebrations in Barcelona.
Student A Look at page 86.
Student B Look at page 87.

(What is it called?)   (When does it take place?)

2 a Get ready to write Make a list of the most important festivals and celebrations that take place in your town or region.

b Work with a partner. Compare your lists. Choose two for your report.

c Start writing Make notes about when the events take place and what happens. Organize your notes into paragraphs.

d Complete your project Check your texts and arrange the photos with them to make your report.

e Present and share the reports. Which events did you not know about? Would you like to go to them? Why? / Why not?

Unit 5 · Heritage

5 Culture

YOU FIRST! Which are the most popular stories in your heritage? Who are the main characters and heroes in these stories?

Irish heritage

A nation of storytellers

The Irish are well known for being great storytellers. Bram Stoker invented Dracula, Jonathan Swift created Gulliver and Oscar Wilde gave us Dorian Gray, just a few of the great characters that have entertained the world's readers. However, the Irish are not just good at telling tales with pen and paper; they also tell a good tale through other art forms and this week, we look at two of them.

Folk music

For a lot of music lovers there is only one group when they think of Irish music: the Dubliners. In 1962, a group of friends were playing Irish folk music in a pub in Dublin, when they decided to form the group. They have played together since then and celebrated their fiftieth anniversary in 2012. The Dubliners have always sung traditional songs such as *I'll Tell Me Ma*, *Spancil Hill*, *The Black Velvet Band* and *Molly Malone*. The songs are really short stories about important events in people's lives that are often very moving and sometimes quite amusing.

Glossary

| tale | moving |
| folk | mythology |

Dance

Traditional dancing was uncool in Ireland until Irish TV created *Riverdance* for the *Eurovision Song Contest* that took place in Dublin. The dance was so incredibly successful that young Irish people suddenly wanted to go to dancing classes and people all around the world continue to go to see the *Riverdance* show. Dance has always been an important part of Ireland's mythology and history and the show depicts this. It celebrates the power of nature and reflects the themes that historians believe that the Irish celebrated at dances at important historical sites such as Tara, 4,000 years ago.

1 a Look at the photos. What type of stories do you think these art forms can tell?

b Read the text. Choose the correct answers.
1. Bram Stoker, Jonathan Swift and Oscar Wilde were *authors/characters*.
2. The Dubliners *were/weren't* already playing together when they decided to form a group.
3. Thanks to *Riverdance*, young people *lost interest/became interested* in Irish dancing.

2 a 🔊 3.14 Listen to an explanation about the meaning of the popular Irish song *Molly Malone*. What do you think 'chorus' means?

b Complete the sentences about the song. Use one or two words.
1. It seems that the writer based the song *Molly Malone* on the young girls that ___ around Dublin in the ___ .
2. The song tells us that Molly was ___ and she ___ fish.
3. As part of the chorus the song adds a few lines that explain ___ that Molly shouted.
4. The song then ends sadly because Molly ___ ill and ___ of ___ .
5. I like the song because the writer tells a ___ with just a few words.
6. Go to an Irish ___ and you'll see how much ___ like ___ !

3 a Over to you! Prepare a short presentation about a story in your heritage.

b Work in a group. Give your presentations.

Unit 5 · Heritage

▶ Dublin

Culture

Supplementary materials
Photocopiable worksheets: Culture, Culture video

CULTURE NOTES Below are some additional details about the three topics mentioned in the lesson.

A nation of storytellers: *Dracula* was first published in 1897. The book's original title was *The Undead*. It paved the way for vampire lore in popular culture. More than 100,000 novels and 200 films have been made about the vampire Dracula.
Swift's satirical novel *Gulliver's Travels* was first published in 1726 and it has never been out of print since then. The full title of the novel is: *Gulliver's Travels or Travels into Several Remote Nations of the World, In Four Parts*, by Lemuel Gulliver, First a Surgeon, then a Captain of Several Ships.
The Picture of Dorian Gray by Oscar Wilde was published in 1890. The book was very controversial when it was first published, causing quite a stir in British society. Wilde's wife said, 'Since Oscar wrote *Dorian Gray*, no one will speak to us.'

Folk music: *Spancil Hill* is a true story about an Irish immigrant in California who dreams of returning to his homeland to be reunited with his first and only love.
I'll Tell Me Ma is a children's song sung to accompany a children's playground game.
Black Velvet Band illustrates the trial and subsequent unjust exile of an Irishman to an Australian penal colony. He becomes involved with a young woman who steals a watch and places it in his pocket. He appears in court the next day, and is sentenced to seven years penal servitude in Australia.
Molly Malone is a popular song set in Dublin, which has become the unofficial anthem of the city. There is a statue of Molly Malone in Suffolk Street, and 13th June is known as Molly Malone Day.

Dance: *Riverdance* began at the Eurovision Song Contest in 1994. This theatrical show has been seen by over 25 million people and has been played in 46 countries across six continents.

You First

Sts think of popular stories in their country and answer the questions. Encourage Sts to discuss what the stories say about their heritage and history.

1a
- Sts look at the photos and answer the question.

b
- Give Sts time to read the text and complete the task.

1 authors 2 were 3 became interested

EXTRA SUPPORT Read the text and decide if you need to teach any new lexis before Sts do the task. Refer Sts to the **Glossary**.

EXTRA IDEA Find a video online that shows how to do Irish step dancing as performed by *Riverdance*. Have your Sts try it.

2a 🔊 3·14 Audio script pT92
- Play the audio for Sts to listen and answer the question.

The chorus is the part that is repeated throughout the song.

EXTRA SUPPORT Read the script and decide if you need to teach any new lexis before Sts listen.

EXTRA SUPPORT Sts discuss the meaning of *lyrics* and *chorus* before listening. Then, they listen to confirm.

EXTRA IDEA Find a recording of the song on the internet and play it for the class. You could also give them the lyrics:

In Dublin's fair city
Where the girls are so pretty
I first set my eyes on sweet Molly Malone
As she wheeled her wheelbarrow
Through the streets broad and narrow
Crying 'cockles and mussels, alive, alive, oh!'
Chorus:
Alive, alive, oh
Alive, alive, oh
Crying 'cockles and mussels, alive, alive, oh!'
She was a fishmonger
And sure, t'was no wonder
For so were her mother and father before
And they wheeled their barrow
Through the streets broad and narrow
Crying 'cockles and mussels, alive, alive, oh!'
(Chorus)
She died of a fever
And no one could save her
And that was the end of sweet Molly Malone.
But her ghost wheels her barrow
Through streets broad and narrow
Crying, 'Cockles and mussels, alive, alive, oh!'

b
- Give Sts time to read and complete the sentences.
- Sts listen again to check their answers.

1 sold fish / shellfish, 17th century 2 beautiful, sold
3 the words 4 became, died, a fever 5 sad story
6 rugby match, people, singing it

3a
- Give Sts time to prepare their short presentation.

b
- Put Sts in groups to present their stories.

EXTRA IDEA Discuss what Sts' stories say about the heritage of their country or region.

EXTRA CHALLENGE Sts collect traditional stories from their parents, grandparents and elderly people in their community. They write them in English and provide a title and an illustration for their stories. The class makes a book of the traditional stories.

EXTRA CHALLENGE Have a storytelling session. Sts bring in their traditional stories and read them to the class.

▶ Video Dublin

As an extension to the Culture topic, watch a short film about Dublin and do the accompanying photocopiable exercises. You can either do this in class or set it as optional homework. The film is available on the DVD-ROM or on the Online Practice.

5

Learn through English

Supplementary materials
Photocopiable worksheet: Song

> **Additional subject notes**
> **Simile**
> Similes work by comparing or inferring the same qualities in two different objects. Similes work by using *like* or *as... as*, e.g. *It's like a jungle out there. She's as gentle as a lamb.*
>
> **Metaphor**
> Metaphors work by describing an object as if it is something else. Metaphors often use *is / are*, e.g. *It's a jungle out there. She's a lamb.*
>
> **Hyperbole**
> The word 'hyperbole' comes from Greek, meaning excess. Hyperbole relies on the humorous effect of exaggeration, e.g. *I'm so hungry I could eat a horse.* Hyperbole is the opposite of understatement.

You First

Ask Sts to discuss how they can make their writing more interesting. Get them to compare how they write in English with how they write in their own language.

EXTRA SUPPORT Sts discuss the difficulties they have writing in English. With a partner, Sts make a list of three difficulties. Discuss the difficulties as a class, finding solutions for each.

1a

- Put Sts in pairs to complete the task.

> 1 B   2 E   3 D   4 F   5 A   6 C

EXTRA SUPPORT Ask Sts to quickly look at the pictures and ask what they can see in each one.

EXTRA IDEA Ask Sts to think of two different things they can see in each picture. Then, Sts say what they saw to the class. How many things can they say without repeating any?

b

- Sts read the sentences and decide which are types of comparisons.

> Sentences 1, 3, 4, and 5 are types of comparisons.

EXTRA SUPPORT Sts go back to the sentences with types of comparisons and decide what is being compared. Sts confirm with a partner and discuss any differences.

EXTRA CHALLENGE In pairs, Sts explain the meaning of the comparisons in sentences 1, 3, 4 and 5. Discuss their ideas as a class.

2 3·15

- Play the audio for Sts to read and listen to the text.
- Ask them to match two sentences from exercise 1a to each of the three literary techniques mentioned.

> **simile:** 3, 4   **metaphor:** 1, 5   **hyperbole:** 2, 6

EXTRA SUPPORT Sts read and listen to each text to match the sentences before moving on to the next one. With a partner, they confirm their answers and discuss any differences.

Write these examples on the board. Ask Sts to think of others.

Simile: 'as big as an elephant', 'as quiet as a mouse', 'as black as coal'

Metaphor: 'The snow is a white blanket.', 'Life is a rollercoaster.', 'Their home was a prison.'

Hyperbole: 'I'm so hungry I could eat a horse.', 'My sister will kill me if she finds out that I told you.', 'His brain is the size of a pea.'

EXTRA IDEA: Ask Sts to think of contexts in which they would use the similes, metaphors and hyperbole from exercise 1a. Then, Sts share their ideas with the class. Encourage them to explain why.

EXTRA CHALLENGE Sts think of common similes, metaphors and hyperbole in their own language. Ask them to translate the sentences into English. They can use a dictionary to help them.

3a

- Give Sts time to read the sentences and use one of the literary techniques from the text to improve them.

> **Suggested answers**
> 2 The animals in the zoo are prisoners.   3 Our brains are the computers of our bodies.   4 I'm dying / desperate for some new trainers.   5 The man was as tall as a skyscraper.   6 The bus was like a sauna.

EXTRA SUPPORT Ask Sts to look at the pictures and make notes about what they can see.

b

- With a partner, Sts compare their sentences.
- Discuss any differences and decide on the sentences they like best.

3·16 Song *With a Little Help from my Friends*

- Play the audio for Sts to listen to the song and complete the Song photocopiable worksheet.
- Check answers.

Learn through English

5

Techniques from literature

YOU FIRST! How can you make your writing more interesting? What techniques do you use in your language?

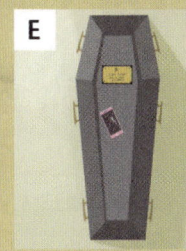

A B C D E F

1 a Work with a partner. Match the sentences (1–6) to the pictures (A–F).
   1 This city is a jungle.
   2 Sara would die without her smartphone.
   3 My dad was as brave as a lion!
   4 Your eyes are like stars.
   5 Laughter is music to my ears.
   6 We had to wait for a bus forever!

   b Which sentences are types of comparisons?

2 🔊 **3.15** Read and listen to the text. Match two sentences from exercise 1a to each literary technique.

Literary techniques

Simile

Similes talk about similarities between things. Of course, there may not be any obvious similarity between the two things, but the writer uses simile to try and create an image in the reader's mind. Similes are formed by using *like* or comparative structures such as *as…as*. There are lots of well-known similes and the comparisons that they make are often funny.

Metaphor

A metaphor is a way of describing something by saying it is *another* thing. A metaphor forces the reader to try and see the similarities that the writer suggests exist between the two things. Many of the common expressions that we use every day are metaphors.

Hyperbole

Hyperbole describes the language a writer uses to make something or someone seem better, worse, or more or less important than they really are. Hyperbole is used to make a situation appear dramatic or funny, so the reader is not expected to take it seriously. We can often find hyperbole in funny stories, comedy films and advertising.

3 a Use one of the literary techniques to improve each sentence. Use the pictures to give you ideas.

1 The teacher asked us to be quiet very often.
   The teacher asked us to be quiet a thousand times.

2 The animals in the zoo don't have any freedom.

3 Our brains control everything that we do.

4 I really need some new trainers.

5 The man was very tall.

6 I was very hot on the bus.

b Work with a partner. Compare your sentences. Which do you think are the best?

▶ **Song** 🔊 **3.16** *With a Little Help from my Friends*

Unit 5 · Heritage 71

6 Our world

6A Online hoaxes

YOU FIRST! How do you know that the information that you read and see on the internet is true? How can you check that a website is trustworthy?

Reading and Vocabulary
Digital media

1 a Look at the photos in the three articles. Match the titles (1–3) to the articles (A–C).
1 Lonelygirl15
2 The Derbyshire fairy
3 The onion charger

b Work in groups of three.
Student A Read about The Derbyshire fairy.
Student B Read about Lonelygirl15.
Student C Read about The onion charger.

c Ask and answer questions about your article.
1 What was the hoax?
2 What did the creators use to make their hoaxes?
3 How did people find out about the hoax?
4 How did people respond to the hoax?
5 Why do you think they created the hoax?

2 a Match the highlighted words in the article with the definitions.
1 the act of watching an online video
2 a person who has a blog that shows mostly videos
3 something or someone that isn't real
4 a short film that people share online quickly
5 a visit to a webpage
6 methods of doing activities in a better way
7 a place where visitors can write their opinions
8 TV, radio and newspapers
9 people who support or admire another person a lot
10 someone with a special skill, talent, etc. that attracts attention on the internet

b 🔊 3.17 Listen and check, then repeat.

▶ Workbook page 56, exercises 1–3

A ____

Artist Dan Baines thought that nobody believed in fairies. Small creatures with special powers that usually live in woods or big gardens, fairies only ever appear in children's folk stories. However, Dan decided to create a modern folk tale and he made a model of a fairy and took some photos of it. He then posted the pictures on his website and he said that a man had found a dead fairy in the countryside. He also said that medical experts were examining the body and they believed that it was real. His site soon received thousands of hits and the photos quickly appeared in the mainstream media such as newspapers and on other websites. After a few days, Baines admitted that it was a hoax, but he was surprised to discover that some people didn't believe him. He received hundreds of emails from people who said they had also found dead fairies!

B ____

16-year-old Bree Avery was just like any other young YouTube vlogger, or so people thought. Sat alone in her bedroom, she told the world that her life was boring at that moment. Bree was nice and her video blogs managed to get about 50,000 views a week, not exactly an incredible number for YouTube. Things changed, however, when Bree said that her parents hadn't allowed her to go hiking the weekend before with her best friend Daniel. She told viewers she was upset about that and then talked about her parents' strange ideas. Bree's problems suddenly attracted half a million views and some loyal followers expressed their support for her in the comments section under the video. Others, however, started to think that Lonelygirl15 was a fake and when Bree's parents mysteriously disappeared, they were sure of it. An online investigation discovered that Bree was really actress Jessica Rose and the whole Lonelygirl15 blog was part of an internet 'show', but this news didn't end Bree's blog. In fact, 'Bree' became an online sensation and made 400 more blogs.

C ____

Thousands of people, a number of TV shows and scientists from Cambridge University have all tried it. They've all taken a white onion, made a hole in it and then left it in a bowl full of a sports drink for 30 minutes. Why? Because according to a viral video with more than 10 million views on the HouseHoldHacker website, the onion becomes a charger for an MP3 music player or a mobile phone. The video explained that you had to connect the onion to the MP3 player with a USB cable and said that it would charge the player for 15 to 20 minutes. However, there was one small problem; it was a hoax! That didn't worry the creators of the video because they received a lot of attention. The channel posts videos of various life hacks to everyday problems and they have become very popular, even when they are hoaxes!

6 Our world

Unit objectives
use words to talk about digital media
use nouns to talk about shopping
use adjectives to talk about shopping
talk using reported speech
talk using reported commands and requests
use subject and object questions correctly
use phrases to give instructions
write a review of a website or an app

Language
Grammar: reported speech; reported commands and requests; subject and object questions
Vocabulary: digital media; shopping nouns; fashion adjectives
Everyday English: giving instructions
My project: Create a video
Culture: Small nations, sporting giants
Learn through English: Be active!

6A Online hoaxes

Supplementary materials
Workbook: pages 56–57, exercises 1–9
Workbook: Grammar summary Unit 6
Photocopiable worksheets: Grammar and Vocabulary, Communication

You First
Ask the class to discuss the two questions based on their experience. Get Sts to list the sites and social media they usually use on the internet. Discuss *What do you use them for? Do you pass on the information they read and see? Who do you pass it on to?* Then ask Sts to talk about a time when they believed something on the internet that wasn't true.

Reading and Vocabulary Digital media
1a
- Give Sts time to look at the photos. Then, ask them to match the titles to the articles.
- Check answers.

1 B   2 A   3 C

EXTRA SUPPORT Ask Sts to describe the three photos. What do they see? Encourage them to explain their answers.

b
- Put Sts in groups of three and tell each St in the group to read one of the articles.

c
- When everyone has finished reading, tell Sts to read through the questions.
- Then, in their groups, Sts ask the questions about each text to the student who read it.

EXTRA SUPPORT Get Sts to answer the questions about their own text before working with their group. Ask Sts to find the sentence in the article which gave them their answers.

The Derbyshire fairy: 1 a man had found a dead fairy **2** a model of a fairy and some photos **3** websites and newspapers **4** some people didn't believe it was a hoax **5** Students' own answers.
Lonelygirl15: 1 the life of Bree Avery **2** a video blog (vlog) **3** from an online investigation **4** her blog became more popular **5** Students' own answers.
The onion charger: 1 an onion left in a sports drink can charge an electronic device **2** an onion, a bowl, a sports drink, a USB cable, an MP3 player, a website channel **3** through a website channel **4** they received a lot of attention **5** Students' own answers.

EXTRA SUPPORT Sts find the sentence in the article to defend their answers. Discuss any disagreements.

2a
- Give Sts time to read the other two articles, then match the highlighted words with the definitions.

EXTRA SUPPORT Divide the ten definitions into two groups. Give 1–5 to half the class, and 6–10 to the other half. Discuss the answers as a class. Encourage Sts to use the context to help them with the definitions.

EXTRA CHALLENGE Before Sts do exercise 2a, write the highlighted words on the board. Find out which ones Sts already know. Then, ask Sts to explain the highlighted words based on their personal experiences on the internet. Then move on to exercise 2a.

b 🔊 3•17
- Play the audio once for Sts to listen and check.
- Play the audio again for Sts to listen and repeat, paying attention to pronunciation and stress.

1 view(s) **2** vlogger **3** fake **4** viral video **5** hit(s)
6 life hacks **7** comments section **8** mainstream media
9 loyal followers **10** online sensation

EXTRA CHALLENGE Ask Sts to write a sentence based on their own experiences using one or more of the highlighted words.

➡ **Workbook** page 56, exercises 1–3

Project Explore   T72

6A

Speaking

Note
Sts will need internet access to complete exercise 3a. They can make notes on the website or vlog at home and then do the exercise in class.

3a
- Give Sts time to think of a website or vlog and make their notes in answer to the questions.
- Remind Sts to use the vocabulary from exercise 2a.

b
- Put Sts in groups to tell each other about their website or vlog, and then categorize them.

c
- Get Sts to present their websites and vlogs for each category to the class.
- Have a show of hands to choose the best three.

EXTRA IDEA Sts say which website or vlog presented was most interesting, entertaining or useful without mentioning the name of the website or vlog. The class guesses which one it is.

Grammar Reported speech

4a
- Give Sts time to find the examples of reported speech in the articles on page 72 and complete the sentences.
- Check answers.

1 He said that a man had found a dead fairy in the countryside.
2 He also said that medical experts were examining the body.
3 She told the world that her life was boring at that moment.
4 Bree said that her parents hadn't allowed her to go hiking the weekend before…
5 She told viewers she was upset about that.

b
- Tell Sts to imagine what the people in exercise 4a actually said and complete the direct speech sentences.

1 'A man has found a dead fairy in the countryside.'
2 'Medical experts are examining the body.'
3 'My life is boring at the moment.'
4 'My parents didn't allow me to go hiking last weekend.'
5 'I am upset about this.'

c
- Give Sts time to compare the reported and direct speech sentences and complete the rules. Draw their attention to the **Look!** box.
- Check answers.

1 tenses 2 pronouns, adjectives 3 Adverbs, *this*

EXTRA SUPPORT Sts look at the sentences in exercise 4a and write down the verb, e.g. *He said that a man had found a dead fairy in the countryside.* Then Sts look at the sentences in exercise 4b and do the same, e.g. *A man has found a dead fairy in the countryside.* Ask them to identify the tenses. Can Sts see a pattern? Sts explain the rule in their own words.

EXTRA IDEA Put Sts in groups of four. Tell each student to write a direct speech sentence using the following tenses:
Student 1: present perfect
Student 2: present continuous
Student 3: present simple
Student 4: past simple
Sts then rewrite each other's sentences in reported speech. Encourage Sts to underline the verbs in both of their sentences, direct and reported speech. Sts discuss their sentences and address any disagreements.

▶ **Workbook** pages 56–57, exercises 4–6
▶ **Photocopiable** Grammar and Vocabulary

Speaking and Writing

5
- Put Sts in pairs to complete the task.

EXTRA SUPPORT Before you put them in pairs, tell Sts to make a list of the smartphone apps and websites they use, and make notes in answer to the questions.

EXTRA IDEA With their partner, Sts write a short advertisement for their favourite website or app, and present it to the class. Have a class vote for the best one.

EXTRA CHALLENGE With their partner, Sts decide on two apps or websites to present to the class. The class listens and Sts discuss any new apps or websites they didn't know about and are going to try.

▶ **Workbook** page 57, exercises 7–9

6a
- Give Sts time to plan a review of the websites and apps, based on their partner's answers.
- Tell them to follow the instructions to write their review.

EXTRA IDEA Show Sts some examples of reviews from smartphone apps or sites. Get Sts to point out the features of the review and descriptions.

b
- Put Sts in groups to read out their reviews and discuss the questions.

EXTRA IDEA After a student has read their review, the group asks questions about the site or app. They decide if the review is useful or not.

EXTRA CHALLENGE Sts add their own opinions to the reviews they listen to, based on their own experience or something they have heard.

EXTRA IDEA Sts talk about online safety. What should they consider before they go online? What shouldn't they do online? Sts make a poster about being safe online to display in the classroom.

EXTRA CHALLENGE Sts talk about things they have read online that they didn't like. Sts think about who wrote it, why they wrote it and why they didn't like it.

Extra
Sts do the activities in pairs in class.

6A

Speaking

3 a Study a website that you visit frequently or a vlog that you follow. Make notes and answer the questions about the site or vlog. Use the vocabulary from exercise 2a.
- Who organizes the site/vlog?
- Who or what is it for?
- Where does the information on the site/vlog come from?
- How often is the site/vlog updated?

   I'm a subscriber to a vlogger who presents a weekly vlog on sport. The vlog is organized by...

b Work in a group. Tell each other about your websites/vlogs. Put the websites/vlogs that you have talked about in different orders:
- the most interesting
- the most entertaining
- the most useful

c Present the websites/vlogs for each category to the class. Choose with the class the best three websites/vlogs.

Grammar Reported speech

4 a Complete the examples of reported speech (underlined) from the articles.
1 He said that a man…
2 He also said that medical experts were…
3 She told the world that her life…
4 Bree said that her parents…
5 She told viewers…

b Complete the original direct speech for exercise 4a.
1 'A man…'
2 'Medical experts…'
3 'My life…'
4 'My parents…me to go hiking last weekend.'
5 'I…about this.'

c Compare the reported and direct sentences. Complete the rules for reported speech.

> adjectives   adverbs   pronouns   tenses   this

1 The ___ change in reported speech and move back in time.
2 The subject ___ (*I, you,* etc.) and possessive ___ (*my, your,* etc.) sometimes change.
3 ___ of time and other words (such as ___, which becomes *that*) can also change.

Look!

We often introduce reported speech with *say* and *tell*. We follow *tell* with a personal object (the person that we are speaking to). We don't follow *say* with a personal object.

He also told me that medical experts were examining the body.

He also said that medical experts were examining the body.

▶ **Workbook** pages 56–57, exercises 4–6

Speaking and Writing

5 Work with a partner. Ask your partner about their use of smartphone apps and websites. Take notes of what they say.
- Which apps/sites do you usually use or follow?
- Which apps/sites are the best? Why? What are the good points?
- Which apps/sites are the worst? Why? What are the weak points?

▶ **Workbook** page 57, exercises 7–9

6 a **Get ready to write** Write a review of the websites/apps based on your partner's answers.
- Organize your review into three short paragraphs:
  introduction – name of the website/app
  user's opinions – what did the user tell you about the website/app?
  conclusion – will you use/follow it or not?
- Use some of the vocabulary from exercise 2a.
- Use reported speech.

b Work with a group. Read your review to your group. Who uses the same websites as you and your partner? Do they agree?

   In this review, we are going to talk about…

   Dara told me that the app was good for…

EXTRA Interview another student about the last time they wrote something online. Use reported speech to tell the class about it.

   I made a holiday vlog when I…

   Marta said she had made a holiday blog when she…

Unit 6 · Our world

6B Shopping

YOU FIRST! Do you like shopping? Why?/Why not? Where do you go shopping? Who do you go shopping with?

Vocabulary and Reading Shopping nouns

1 a Read the online forum. What are the advantages and disadvantages of shopping online?

b Work with a partner. Answer the questions.
- Do people in your family shop online? Why?/Why not?
- Are you allowed to shop online? Why?/Why not?

2 a Match the words to the definitions.

> alterations   bargain   brand
> changing room   consumer   discount
> outfit   receipt   refund   rip-off   sales   size

1 the place where you try on clothes in a shop
2 a person who buys products or services
3 a set of clothes that you wear for a particular occasion
4 something that is not worth the money that you pay for
5 a thing that you buy for a really good price
6 money you get back when you return something to a shop
7 the time when most shops sell things for a cheaper price
8 small, medium, large and extra large
9 a type of product that is made by one company
10 changes that you ask a shop make to your clothes
11 a piece of paper that shows that you have paid
12 the amount of money taken off the usual price

b Work with a partner. Compare your answers.

c 🔊 3.18 Listen and check, then repeat.

d Work with a partner. Describe some of the places and things in the photos. Use the words in exercise 2a to identify them.

> It's a place where people try on new clothes.

> It's the…

e 🔊 3.19 Complete the forum with the correct form of the words from exercise 2a. Then listen and check.

▶ Workbook page 58, exercises 1–3

Sassy10
bargain hunting May 2nd 18.32

It's party time, but I've got nothing to wear! I've had all my clothes for years and I need a new ¹____. The problem is… I can't afford it! Can someone help me find a ²____?

TeKn0123
re: bargain hunting May 2nd 18.36

Shop online. Things cost less and if you have a problem, you can return the product and they'll give you a ³____.

NBAJack
re: bargain hunting May 2nd 18.39

My brother told me to be careful with websites that offer famous ⁴____ at low prices. He bought a pair of basketball boots and they've fallen apart after only two weeks! He asked them to return his money, but they haven't replied to his email! They didn't even send a ⁵____ with the boots. What a ⁶____!

FashionVictim
re: bargain hunting May 2nd 18.41

You're taking a risk buying clothes online. What if you get the ⁷____ wrong? It's better to go to a shop and use their ⁸____. If you ask them, some shops will also make ⁹____ quickly. I bought a dress at a local shop and asked them to shorten it and it was ready the same day!

Jules
re: bargain hunting May 2nd 18.44

Online is great for buying electronics. You can get big ¹⁰____ and if you live in a small town like me, it means you can buy brands that aren't in the local shops. You can also find things that are difficult to find in shops. I bought a mobile phone from a Chinese website; I asked them to send me a yellow one and I had it in two days!

LadyStyle
re: bargain hunting May 2nd 18.47

I can't shop online because my parents told me not to use their credit cards! I go to markets. Some of the clothes are second-hand, but they're in great condition. I got a leather jacket that I haven't taken off since I bought it!

Sassy10
re: bargain hunting May 2nd 18.56

Sounds cool!

TomTom9
re: bargain hunting May 2nd 18.59

Wait for the ¹¹____ after Christmas and at the end of the summer holidays! My sister told me to arrive early and it was good advice! We were first in the queue and found some really good bargains!

BestMates
re: bargain hunting May 2nd 19.02

Don't be a ¹²____! Borrow clothes from your friends! I've had a friend's hoodie and jacket for a fortnight and she's wearing my sweaters at the moment. It costs nothing!

Unit 6 · Our world

6B Shopping

Supplementary materials
Workbook: pages 58–59, exercises 1–9
Workbook: Grammar summary Unit 6
Photocopiable worksheets: Grammar and Vocabulary, Communication

You First

Have a class discussion about shopping based on the questions.

EXTRA IDEA Ask Sts who like shopping to stand to the left in the classroom and Sts who don't like shopping to stand to the right. Then, ask each group to stand in a line based on who likes shopping the most and who likes shopping the least. Sts talk to each other to decide where to stand. Finally, Sts discuss shopping in relation to each other, explaining why they like it or don't like it.

EXTRA CHALLENGE Sts talk about their best and worst shopping experiences.

Vocabulary and Reading Shopping nouns

1a

- Give Sts time to read the online forum and answer the question. Tell them to ignore the gaps.

> **Advantages:** things cost less, and you can return goods for a refund; good for buying electronics, especially if you live in a small town where you can't buy brands that are not in the local shops; you can find things that are difficult to find in shops
> **Disadvantages:** websites that offer low prices might not be honest; it's risky to buy clothes online because they might be too big or small; you have to have a credit card

EXTRA SUPPORT Write on the board: 'Online Shopping'. Ask Sts if they have shopped online. What was the experience like? Then, write on the board, 'Advantages / Disadvantages'. With a partner, Sts discuss two advantages and two disadvantages of online shopping. Then, as a class, Sts say their advantages and disadvantages. Write them on the board in note form. Finally, Sts read the online forum to check their list against the advantages and disadvantages mentioned in the forum.

EXTRA IDEA Sts take turns to say a sentence from the online forum. The class says who wrote the sentence and confirm with the text.

b

- Put Sts in pairs to answer the questions.
- Get some feedback.

EXTRA IDEA Sts discuss if teenagers should be allowed to shop online. What are the reasons for and against?

2a

- Give Sts time to complete the task.

EXTRA SUPPORT Give sentences 1–6 to half of the class and 7–12 to the other half. Sts complete their sentences, then share with the class. Discuss any differences.

b

- Get Sts to work together to share their ideas and the reasons for their choices.

c 🔊 3·18

- Play the audio for Sts to listen and check.
- Play the audio again for Sts to listen and repeat.

> **1** changing room **2** consumer **3** outfit **4** rip-off
> **5** bargain **6** refund **7** sales **8** size **9** brand
> **10** alterations **11** receipt **12** discount

- Drill the pronunciation and stress of any difficult words, e.g. *alterations* /ˌɔːltəˈreɪʃnz/, *discount* /ˈdɪskaʊnt/, *refund* /ˈriːfʌnd/, *receipt* /rɪˈsiːt/.

d

- Ask Sts, in their pairs, to describe the photos, using words from exercise 2a.

EXTRA CHALLENGE With a partner, Sts create a story for two of the photos, using five words from exercise 2a for each photo. Sts tell their stories to the class.

e 🔊 3·19

- Give Sts time to complete the task, then compare with a partner.
- Play the audio for Sts to listen and check.

> **1** outfit **2** bargain **3** refund **4** brands **5** receipt
> **6** rip-off **7** size **8** changing rooms **9** alterations
> **10** discounts **11** sales **12** consumer

EXTRA CHALLENGE Sts say who they agree with in the online forum and why. Encourage Sts to use examples from the text and their own ideas and experiences. They can agree with more than one person.

➡ **Workbook** page 58, exercises 1–3

6B

Listening and speaking

3a 🔊 3·20 Audio script pT92
- Play the audio for Sts to listen to the teenager and answer the question.

a tablet

EXTRA SUPPORT Read the script and decide if you need to teach any new lexis before Sts listen.

b
- Give Sts time to answer the questions.
- Check answers, or play the audio again for Sts to listen and check.

1 at a computer shop in town   2 for about a year
3 It had a 25% discount and people online said it was good.
4 It's got a good screen, a big memory and it's fast.

EXTRA IDEA Play the audio again. Write these statements on the board, and ask Sts if they are true or false.
'He bought it with his dad.' (*True – 'I went with my dad…'*)
'It was the latest model.' (*False – 'They were about to replace the one that I bought with a new model…'*)
'The online reviews were good.' (*True – 'everybody said it worked well…'*)

4a
- Give Sts time to think about their best possession, then answer the questions in exercise 3b about it.

EXTRA SUPPORT Get Sts to change the questions so that they are for them, e.g. *Where did you buy it?* Write the questions on the board if necessary.

b
- Put Sts in groups to describe their favourite possession and ask and answer the questions.

EXTRA CHALLENGE Ask Sts to describe their possession without saying what it is. Other Sts listen and guess the possession.

Grammar Reported commands and requests

5a
- Give Sts time to read the pairs of sentences and complete the task.

1 command   2 command   3 request   4 request

b
- Ask Sts to answer the questions about the sentences in exercise 5a.
- Get them to compare with a partner, then check answers.

1 b   2 a   3 b   4 b

EXTRA SUPPORT Get Sts to write the reported commands and requests in their notebooks or on the board. Ask them to circle the reporting verb in each sentence. Then, ask them to underline the word that comes after the reporting verb. Finally, Sts circle the main verb. What pattern can they see?

c
- Give Sts time to complete the task.

2 He told me not to remove the price tag before trying on the dress.
3 I asked him to give me a discount.
4 She told me not to take more than four items into the changing room.
5 I asked her to help me find a suitable computer.
6 He told me to download the operating program at home.

EXTRA CHALLENGE Sts write two sentences, one command and one request. Sts say one sentence to the class. The class reports the sentence.

➡ **Workbook** pages 58–59, exercises 4–6
➡ **Photocopiable** Grammar and Vocabulary

Speaking

6a
- Ask Sts to look at the photos. Give them two minutes to write words they associate with each one. Encourage them to write words that are unique to each photo.
- Put Sts in pairs. Give them time to make notes about their campaign using the words in the box. You may wish to write up some ideas about what sort of things an advertising campaign might include.

EXTRA IDEA With a partner, Sts discuss how each shop is different from the others.

b
- Put Sts in new pairs to compare their campaigns.
- Tell them to make notes about any similarities and differences.
- Then, Sts decide on their best ideas and rewrite their campaign.

c
- Ask pairs to present their campaigns to the class.
- Have a class vote on the best campaign and ask Sts to explain their choice.

EXTRA IDEA Divide the class into three groups. Give each group one of the photos (1–3). Groups write an advertisement for their shop.

EXTRA CHALLENGE Groups create a radio advertisement or a TV advertisement. Encourage Sts to see that the TV advertisement is more visual and should have more action. Encourage them to use their own clothes and accessories in their advertisements. Sts act out their advertisements to the class. The class votes on the best one. Groups cannot vote for their own advertisement.

➡ **Workbook** page 59, exercises 7–9

Extra

Sts do the activities in pairs in class.

Listening and Speaking

3 a 🔊 **3.20** Listen to a teenager describing his best bargain. What is it?

b Answer the questions.
1 Where did he buy it?
2 How long has he had it?
3 Why did he buy it?
4 Why does he like it?

4 a Make notes about the best possession that you have. Answer the questions in exercise 3b.

b Work in a group. Describe your favourite possession. Who bought it? What is special about it?

Grammar   Reported commands and requests

5 a Read the reported sentences from the forum and their direct forms. Which sentences are reported commands and which are reported requests?

1 My brother told me to be careful.
  'Be careful!'
2 My parents told me not to use their credit cards.
  'Don't use our credit cards!'
3 He asked them to return his money.
  'Can you return my money?'
4 I asked them to send me a yellow one.
  'Could you send me a yellow one?'

b Answer the questions about the sentences in exercise 5a.
1 Which reporting verb do we use in reported requests?
  a tell   b ask
2 Which reporting verb do we use in reported commands?
  a tell   b ask
3 What tense comes after the reporting verb in reported requests and commands?
  a past simple   b infinitive
4 Where do we use *not* in a negative reported command?
  a after the infinitive   b before the infinitive

c Complete the reported commands and requests.
1 'Can you show me a pair of trainers?'
  I asked him *to show me a pair of trainers*.
2 'Don't remove the price tag before you try on the dress.'
  He told me ____ .
3 'Could you give me a discount?'
  I asked him ____ .
4 'Don't take more than four items into the changing room.'
  She told me ____ .
5 'Can you help me find a suitable computer?'
  I asked her ____ .
6 'Download the operating program at home.'
  He told me ____ .

▶ **Workbook** pages 58–59, exercises 4–6

Speaking

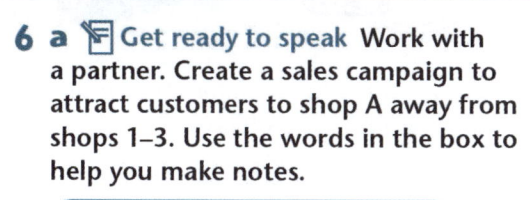

6 a Get ready to speak   Work with a partner. Create a sales campaign to attract customers to shop A away from shops 1–3. Use the words in the box to help you make notes.

> discount   display   lighting
> music   opening hours   posters
> price   sales   special offers

b Work with a new partner. Compare your campaigns. Make notes about the similarities and differences. Create a new campaign based on your best ideas.

c Present your campaign to the class. Which campaign do you think is the best? Why?

▶ **Workbook** page 59, exercises 7–9

EXTRA How do shops in your town try to persuade people to spend money in them? Are there differences between different types of shops? Make a list of five shops and the ways they try to persuade people to spend money in them. Compare your list with a partner's.

Unit 6 · Our world   75

6C Fashion

YOU FIRST! Why do people follow fashion? Do you think image is important? Why? / Why not?

Vocabulary Fashion adjectives

1 a Look at the pictures. Use the adjectives to talk about them.

1
2
3
4
5
6
7
8
9
10

casual   colourful   comfortable   ethnic
glamorous   old-fashioned   practical
smart   trendy   vintage   well dressed

b Replace the underlined words with the adjectives in exercise 1a.

1 You should wear clothes that are <u>suitable for the occasion</u> when you go walking in the countryside.
2 These shoes are <u>really nice</u> to wear.
3 My grandad never wears <u>informal</u> clothes.
4 Mum always looks <u>clean and tidy</u> for work.
5 Ewan's jeans are <u>not modern at all</u>.
6 All the family will be <u>in their best clothes</u> for the wedding.
7 Sean wears <u>very modern, fashionable</u> clothes.
8 Lara loves buying <u>old style</u> clothing.
9 Alice's dress is <u>from a culture that is different to ours</u>.
10 Mara was wearing a very <u>attractive, special</u> dress at the party.
11 Jack's wearing an interesting <u>bright yellow, green and blue</u> jersey!

c 🔊 3.21 Listen and check, then repeat.

▶ Workbook page 60, exercises 1–3

Listening and Speaking

2 a 🔊 3.22 Listen to a quiz show. Which items from the pictures do they talk about?

b Answer the questions.

1 How many questions can the teams ask?
   a two   b three   c five
2 Who invented the Hawaiian shirt?
   a a Chinese person   b a Hawaiian
   c a Japanese person
3 What type of clothing is a kimono?
   a smart   b casual   c trendy
4 Which material didn't the Japanese use to make zori sandals?
   a wood   b plastic   c leather
5 Who looked glamorous in aviator sunglasses?
   a soldiers   b fans of vintage clothing
   c actors

c 🔊 3.23 Which country connects the items of clothing? Listen to the team's answer and check.
   a China   b Japan   c America

3 a Think about a piece of clothing that you really like wearing. Make notes for a short description using the adjectives from exercise 1a.
- Describe it (material, colour, pattern, etc.).
- How long have you had it for?
- Why do you like wearing it?

b Work with a partner. Describe your piece of clothing and explain why you like it. Then listen to your partner's description and guess which piece of clothing it is.

> I've had them for over a year and I only take them off to go to bed! They're really comfortable and practical and although they're supposed to be for sport, I wear them for everything!

> Let me see...your trainers!

76   Unit 6 · Our world

6C Fashion

Supplementary materials
Workbook: pages 60–61, exercises 1–8
Workbook: Grammar summary Unit 6
Photocopiable worksheets: Grammar and Vocabulary, Communication

You First
In pairs, ask Sts to discuss the current fashion trends in their country. Encourage them to consider what is in fashion for men and women. Ask them if they follow the fashion trends.

EXTRA IDEA Divide the class into those who believe fashion is important and those who don't. Ask each group to consider three reasons to defend their position. Encourage them to consider the importance of image in different situations: job, school, being with friends, weekdays, weekends, going out at the weekend, etc.

Vocabulary Fashion adjectives

1a
- Put Sts in pairs or groups to talk about the pictures.
- Point out to Sts that they can use more than one adjective to describe each picture.

EXTRA SUPPORT In pairs, Sts name the items in the pictures. Write the words on the board if necessary.

EXTRA IDEA Give Sts 30 seconds to look at the pictures. Then, ask them to close their books and write down as many as they can. Give one point for each picture they remembered. Give one extra point for each word that is spelled correctly.

EXTRA CHALLENGE Ask Sts to talk about the pictures without saying the object, e.g. *In my opinion it's / they're practical and comfortable.* The class has to guess the object.

b
- Tell Sts to replace the underlined phrases with the adjectives in exercise 1a.
- Get to compare their answers with a partner.

c 3·21
- Play the audio for Sts to listen and check.
- Play the audio again for Sts to listen and repeat.

1 practical   2 comfortable   3 casual   4 smart
5 old-fashioned   6 well-dressed   7 trendy   8 vintage
9 ethnic   10 glamorous   11 colourful

EXTRA IDEA With a partner, Sts describe what they are wearing as if it were a fashion show. Then, Sts walk as if they were in a fashion show as their partner describes what they are wearing. You may want to show some video clips from Fashion TV for Sts to get the idea and really act it up.

EXTRA CHALLENGE Sts look up the definitions of the adjectives in the box. Then, using the definitions, Sts say a sentence with the definition, e.g. *Maria is wearing a blouse with a lot of bright colours.* (*Maria is wearing a colourful blouse.*)

EXTRA CHALLENGE Sts use the adjectives in the box to describe the kind of clothes that they like to wear.

➡ **Workbook** page 60, exercises 1–3

Listening and Speaking

2a 3·22 Audio script pT92
- Play the audio for Sts to listen to the quiz show and answer the question.

(Hawaiian) shirt, sunglasses, sandals, flip-flops, dress

EXTRA SUPPORT Read the script and decide if you need to teach any new lexis before Sts listen.

EXTRA IDEA Ask Sts to describe the photo. What do they see? What is the situation? Are there similar shows in their country?

b
- Play the audio again for Sts to answer the questions.

1 c   2 a   3 a   4 b   5 c

EXTRA IDEA Ask Sts to answer the questions before they listen. Then, play the audio for them to check and confirm.

c 3·23 Audio script pT92
- Ask Sts which country they think connects the items of clothing.
- Then play the audio for Sts to listen and check.

c

EXTRA IDEA

1 Play the audio again for Sts to write the three questions that are asked on the show. (*Who invented the three items? Why did they invent these items? Who used them?*)
2 Divide the class into three groups and give each group one of the questions. Ask Sts to write the following three items under their question: flip-flops, aviatior sunglasses and Hawaiian shirts.
3 Play the audio for Sts to listen and write the answer to their question.
4 Ask groups to compare the information they have for each item.

3a
- Give Sts time to think about their item of clothing and make their notes.
- Encourage them to use the adjectives from exercise 1a.

b
- With a partner, Sts describe their piece of clothing, without naming it, and explain why they like it. Their partner guesses the piece of clothing.

6C

Grammar Subject and object questions

4a
- Give Sts time to read the rules and the questions.
- Then they decide if the question words refer to the subject or the object.
- Get Sts to compare with a partner, then check answers.

3 SQ   4 OQ   5 SQ   6 OQ   7 OQ

EXTRA SUPPORT Gets Sts to look for the auxiliary verb in each question, e.g. *Which jeans did you buy?* If there is one, they should write it down. Remind them that the questions with an auxiliary verb are object questions, so they should write *OQ*.

b
- Explain that Sts should write a subject and an object question for each sentence, using the words in brackets.
- Tell them to write *OQ* or *SQ* after each question.
- Check answers.

1 Which bus did Luke catch? OQ
   Who caught the number 44 bus? SQ
2 Who texted Sara about the party? SQ
   What did Adam text Sara about? OQ
3 What took place at school yesterday? SQ
   Where did a surprising event take place yesterday? OQ
4 Which bus goes into town? SQ
   Where does the number 44 bus go? OQ
5 Who did Chloe email last night? OQ
   Who emailed Sam last night? SQ
6 What did Harry buy last weekend? OQ
   Who bought some new trainers last weekend? SQ

EXTRA SUPPORT Do the first one with the class and elicit the questions. Write the questions on the board, and underline the auxiliary verb. Then elicit OQ or SQ. Get Sts to write the other questions in pairs.

EXTRA IDEA Get Sts to write four answers about themselves, two for subject questions and two for object questions. Then in pairs, their partner should look at their answers and try to guess the correct questions.

➡ **Workbook** pages 60–61, exercises 4–6
➡ **Photocopiable** Grammar and Vocabulary

5a
- Ask Sts to read the conversation and answer the question. Tell them not to worry about items 1–4 yet.

a suit

EXTRA IDEA Ask Sts to say what helped them decide the item of clothing.

b
- Ask Sts to read the conversation again and choose the correct answers.

1 buys   2 wears   3 do people wear   4 goes

c 🔊 3·24
- Play the audio for Sts to check their answers.

EXTRA IDEA Play the game with the class. One St thinks of an item of clothing. The class can ask five questions, then they must make a guess as to what the item is. Alternatively, Sts can ask the four questions in the conversation.

Speaking

6a
- Give Sts time to read the comments under the photos and answer the questions.
- Get feedback from the class.

b
- With a partner, Sts give their opinions on the comments, saying what they agree and disagree with.

EXTRA IDEA Tell the class the school is considering enforcing a dress code for the students. Discuss the pros and cons of this idea. Then, tell them the school has allowed Sts to write the dress code. Divide them into groups and have each group write the dress code for boys and girls. Discuss the ideas as a class.

EXTRA CHALLENGE

1 Bring three photos to class of teenagers in different types of clothes. Make the photos very different. Consider the words in exercise 1a, casual, trendy, glamorous, etc.
2 Divide the class into three groups and give a different photo to each group.
3 Ask each group to describe the person's clothes, and what they think their personality might be like.
4 When the groups are finished, ask them to pass their photo to the next group and repeat the procedure. Do this for the three photos.
5 Discuss the differences and similarities in the descriptions. First, discuss the descriptions of the clothes. Then, discuss the descriptions of the personalities.
6 Finally, based on their descriptions, discuss what clothes can say about us.

➡ **Workbook** page 61, exercises 7–8

Extra
Sts can either do this in class or as a homework task.

6C

Grammar Subject and object questions

4 a Read the rules. Then decide if the highlighted question words from the quiz are asking questions about the subject (SQ) or the object (OQ).

> Questions with *who*, *what* and *which* can be subject or object questions.
>
> In object questions, when we want to find out about the object, we use the auxiliary verb *do / does / did*.
>
> Who did the designer speak to?
>
> **The designer (subject) spoke (verb) to a model (object).**
>
> In subject questions, where we want to find out about the subject, we DON'T use auxiliary verbs.
>
> Who spoke to a model?
>
> **The designer (subject) spoke (verb) to a model (object).**

1 Which jeans did you buy? (OQ)
2 Who bought the black jeans? (SQ)
3 Which place connects these three items of clothing?
4 What do you think, guys?
5 Who invented the three items?
6 Which country does Hawaii belong to?
7 Who did he say invented aviator glasses?

b Write subject and object questions for the answers. Use the words in brackets. Then write *OQ* or *SQ* after each question.

1 Luke caught the number 44 bus.
 (Which bus / Luke) ___
 (who / number 44 bus) ___
2 Adam texted Sara about the party.
 (Who / Sara) ___
 (What / Sara) ___
3 A surprising event took place at school yesterday.
 (What / at school) ___
 (Where / a surprising event) ___
4 The number 44 bus goes into town.
 (Which bus / into town) ___
 (Where / the number 44 bus) ___
5 Chloe emailed Sam last night.
 (Who / Chloe) ___
 (Who / Sam) ___
6 Harry bought some new trainers last weekend.
 (What / Harry) ___
 (Who / some new trainers) ___

▶ **Workbook** pages 60–61, exercises 4–6

5 a Which item of clothing are they talking about?

Adam Guess the item of clothing I'm thinking of.
Kate OK, first question: who ¹*does buy / buys* them?
Adam Well, I suppose everybody can, but they are sometimes expensive.
Kate OK, so they aren't really for teenagers. Who ²*does wear / wears* them?
Adam Both men and women wear them, but I would say more men than women.
Kate I see. When ³*do people wear / people wear* them?
Adam Some people wear them for work, but others only wear them for special occasions.
Kate Right. What ⁴*does go / goes* with them?
Adam Erm, a nice shirt and a smart pair of shoes…oh, and most men also wear a tie.
Kate That last clue has made it really easy! It's a…

b Read and choose the correct answers.

c 🔊 3.24 Listen and check.

Speaking

6 a **Get ready to speak** Read the comments and answer the questions.

- Are they good or bad advice? Why?
- Could they be good and bad advice in different situations? When?

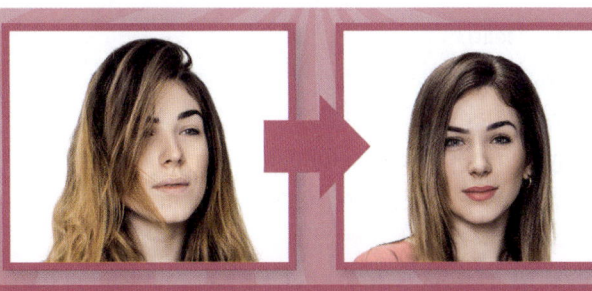

> Change your image and dress better. Buy some new clothes and change your hairstyle.
>
> Change the way you see your image. Don't be critical and don't compare yourself to others. Think about your positive points as a person.

b Work with a partner. Give your opinions on the comments. What do you agree and disagree on?

> In my opinion, I think the way we look is important, so I agree with the first comment.

> I'm not sure. I think we have to be happy about ourselves, but the media…

▶ **Workbook** page 61, exercises 7–8

EXTRA Who decides what we should wear? Write a short list of the things / people that influence fashion and style in your country.

Unit 6 · Our world

6D Life hacks

YOU FIRST! What do you do if you have a problem with one of your devices? Who do you ask for advice about repairing it? Where can you get information about repairing a device?

1 a 🔊 3.25 ▶ Read and listen. Who does Danny phone?

Erika Hello?
Danny Erika, you've got to help me!
Erika Danny? What's with the strange number?
Danny I'm using my mum's phone. I dropped mine in the sink!
Erika Oh no! Have you dried it? The first thing you should do is dry it…immediately.
Danny Yeah, I've done that, but it still isn't working. What am I going to do? It's got all my notes for Wednesday's exam!
Erika I don't know – maybe ask Liza?
Danny I don't want to. It's late and she's studying for the same exam. I know, I'll try Oliver.

2

Oliver Hello?
Danny Hi, it's Danny.
Oliver What's up?
Danny I dropped my phone in water.
Oliver Wet phone, eh? That's not good.
Danny No, it isn't!
Oliver But don't worry – I've had a brainwave. I had this problem with a hard drive, so I know what to do.
Danny You do? Oliver – you've made my day!
Oliver OK, before you begin, turn off the phone.
Danny I've done that.
Oliver Excellent. Now start by drying it.
Danny I've done that, too!
Oliver Very good. The next step is to put the phone in a plastic bag…
Danny OK.
Oliver And when you've done that, wrap it in a towel.
Danny Right…
Oliver Finally, put the towel in the freezer.
Danny Really?
Oliver Yes. For thirty minutes. Trust me!
Danny If you say so.

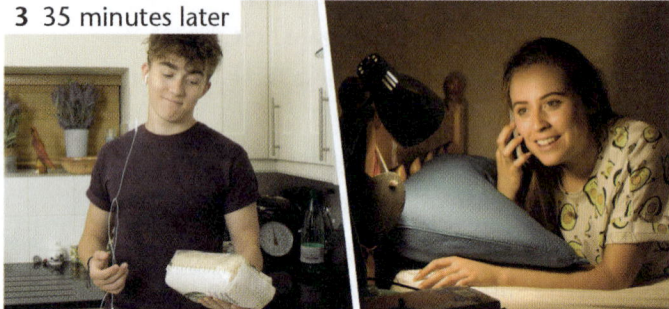

3 35 minutes later

Liza Hello?
Danny Liza, it's Danny. I'm so sorry for waking you up, but I dropped my phone in water. Then I asked Oliver for help and now it's worse than ever!
Liza Danny – don't worry!
Danny Sorry – it's just all my exam notes are on that phone. I don't know what to do.
Liza It's OK. Let me think – do you have any rice?
Danny Yes…
Liza So…turn the phone off and after that, you should dry it. The last thing you do is put it in rice and leave it overnight.
Danny What?! Are you serious?
Liza Give it a go. You've got nothing to lose!
Danny That's true!

b Answer the questions.
1 Why is Danny using his mum's phone?
2 What was on his phone?
3 What does Oliver tell Danny to do?
4 How long should Danny put his phone in the freezer?
5 What does Liza tell Danny to do?
6 How long should Danny leave his phone in rice?

6D Life hacks

Supplementary materials
Workbook: pages 62–63, exercises 1–8
Photocopiable worksheets: Everyday English, Pronunciation
Online Practice

> **Note**
> The story can be used in class as a reading and listening task, a video task or both.

You First
Ask Sts to think about any problems they have had with their devices. Have a class discussion about who they ask for advice about repairing them and where they can get information about repairing devices.

EXTRA SUPPORT On the board, list the problems Sts have had with their devices. Then, next to each problem, write some possible solutions. Discuss these in relation to Sts' experiences.

1a 🔊 3·25 ▶

- Play the audio for Sts to listen, follow and answer the question. Alternatively, show the class the video of the story from the DVD-ROM.

His three friends: Erika, Oliver and Liza

EXTRA SUPPORT Read the conversations and decide if you need to teach any new lexis before Sts listen or watch.

EXTRA IDEA Ask Sts to look at the photos for conversation 1. Ask *Who do you see? Where are they? How does Danny feel? What do you think Danny was doing before he called Erika? Why do you think he feels that way? What are they going to talk about?'*

Before listening to conversation 2, ask Sts to look at the photos. Ask *Where is Danny now? What is he doing? Who is he talking to? How do you think he feels now?'*

Before listening to conversation 3, ask Sts to look at the photos and ask *Where is Danny? Who is he talking to? What time do you think it is? How does he feel now?'*

b
- Give Sts time to answer the questions.
- Get them to compare with a partner before you check answers. You could play the audio or video again for them to confirm.

1. Because he dropped his phone in the sink.
2. His notes for Wednesday's exam
3. He tells him to turn it off, dry it, put it into a plastic bag, and then into the freezer.
4. For 30 minutes
5. She tells him to turn the phone off, dry it and put it into rice.
6. All night

EXTRA IDEA Ask Sts if this has ever happened to them. What did they do? Were they able to solve the problem?

EXTRA CHALLENGE Discuss the two solutions from the conversations. *Why might you put the phone in the freezer?* (To freeze the water, but it doesn't really work because when you take the phone out of the freezer, the ice melts and you're back to the original problem) *Why might you put the phone in rice?* (The rice will absorb the moisture and restore your phone. However, not everyone agrees that this works.)

> **Note**
> To further exploit the video in class, you could use some or all of the suggested activities from page Tviii.

6D

2
- Give Sts time to complete the task.
- Get the class to agree on the meaning of the expressions.
- Model and drill the pronunciation of the expressions, paying attention to the stress.

> **If you say so.** = OK, but I don't really believe you. Here it means 'I'll do it, but I'm not sure it will work.'
> **I've had a brainwave.** = I've had a really good idea. (informal)
> **Let me think.** = Wait a minute.
> **What's with…?** = Explain about… Here, it means 'Why are you calling from a strange number?' (informal)
> **You've got nothing to lose.** = You might as well do it. (informal)
> **You've made my day!** = You've made me really happy today. (informal)

EXTRA SUPPORT Ask Sts to find the expressions in the conversations. How do the people feel when they say them?

EXTRA CHALLENGE With a partner, Sts write and act out a conversation based on a problem with a digital device. Ask Sts to include advice on how to solve the problem. The class listens and decides if it is good advice or not.

➡ **Workbook** page 62, exercises 1–3

3a
- Ask the class what they think will happen next, and get feedback.
- Encourage Sts to use information from the conversations to support their answers.
- You could write their predictions on the board.

b 🔊 **3·26** ▶ Audio script pT93
- Play the audio for Sts to listen, follow and check their predictions.
- Ask them if Liza is pleased.

> Yes, she is.

Everyday English Giving instructions

4a
- Give Sts time to find the examples and decide who says them.

> The first thing you should do is dry it. = Erika
> Before you begin, turn the phone off. = Oliver
> Start by drying it. = Oliver
> The next step is to put the phone in a plastic bag. = Oliver
> When you've done that, wrap it in a towel. = Oliver
> Finally, put the towel in the freezer. = Oliver
> After that, you should dry it. = Liza
> The last thing you do is put it in rice. = Liza

b 🔊 **3·27** Audio script pT93
- Play the audio for Sts to listen and repeat the sentences, paying attention to the correct intonation.

EXTRA CHALLENGE Put Sts in pairs. Get them to use the phrases in **Everyday English** to write the instructions for finding and downloading an app onto their smartphone. Tell Sts their instructions should be for someone who has just started using a digital device.

➡ **Workbook** pages 62–63, exercises 4–6
➡ **Photocopiable** Everyday English

Pronunciation /ʌ/ /uː/
5a 🔊 **3·28**
- Play the audio once for Sts just to listen.
- Now play it again for them to listen and repeat the words.

b
- Ask Sts to write the words in the correct column.

> /ʌ/ studying, trust
> /uː/ true, you

c 🔊 **3·29**
- Play the audio for Sts to listen and check.

EXTRA IDEA Sts add two more words to each column. Sts share their words with a partner.

➡ **Workbook** page 63, exercise 7
➡ **Photocopiable** Pronunciation

Listening
6 🔊 **3·30** Audio script pT93
- Ask Sts to look at the photo and discuss what they see. Ask *Who are they? Where are they? What do you think they are talking about?*
- Play the audio for Sts to listen and complete the task.
- Play the audio again for Sts to check their answers.

> 1 channel 2 lucky 3 doctor's 4 sight 5 parents
> 6 mobile

➡ **Workbook** page 63, exercise 8

Speaking
7a
- Elicit or explain that a *life hack* is a strategy or technique to manage your time and daily activities more efficiently.
- With a partner, Sts choose a life hack, following the instructions. There are many very good examples to be found on the internet.

b
- Put Sts in groups to describe and explain their life hack.

EXTRA IDEA Groups choose the two most useful life hacks for their classmates to use.

c
- Ask groups to tell the class about their life hacks.
- Have a class vote to choose the three life hacks that would be most useful to them, and explain why.

EXTRA CHALLENGE Ask Sts to discuss what problems the life hacks help them with. Then, ask Sts to think about problems they have in learning English. Are there any life hacks that could help them? If you have internet access in your classroom, Sts could do a search online, or research it at home and bring their ideas to class.

Extra
Sts can either do this in class or as a homework task.

6D

2 Spoken English What do these everyday expressions mean? How do you say them in your own language?

- If you say so.
- I've had a brainwave.
- Let me think.
- What's with...?
- You've got nothing to lose.
- You've made my day!

▶ **Workbook** page 62, exercises 1–3

3 a What do you think will happen next?

b 🔊 3.26 ▶ Listen and check. Is Liza pleased?

Everyday English Giving instructions

4 a Look at the useful phrases. Find examples in exercise 1. Who says them?

The first thing you should do is (+ infinitive)
Before you begin, (+ imperative)
Start by (+ -ing)
The next step / thing is to (+ infinitive)
When you've done that, (+ imperative)
Finally, (+ imperative)
After that, you should (+ infinitive)
The last thing you do is

b 🔊 3.27 Listen and repeat the sentences. Try to copy the intonation.

▶ **Workbook** pages 62–63, exercises 4–6

Pronunciation /ʌ/ /uː/

5 a 🔊 3.28 Listen and repeat the words in the box. How are the <u>underlined</u> letters pronounced?

l<u>o</u>se   n<u>o</u>thing   st<u>u</u>dying   tr<u>ue</u>   tr<u>u</u>st   y<u>ou</u>

b Put the words from exercise 5a in the correct column.

/ʌ/	/uː/
n<u>o</u>thing	l<u>o</u>se
___	___

c 🔊 3.29 Listen and check.

▶ **Workbook** page 63, exercise 7

Listening

6 🔊 3.30 Listen to two teenagers talking about watching TV series. Complete the sentences.

1 Poppy's parents have become subscribers to a video-on-demand ___ .
2 Liam thinks Poppy is ___ .
3 Liam went to the ___ .
4 The doctor said he would have problems with his ___ .
5 Liam's ___ have stopped using the channel.
6 Liam promised not to use his ___ to watch series.

▶ **Workbook** page 63, exercise 8

Speaking

7 a Work with a partner. Think of or research a life hack.

Choose a life hack that...
- is useful for your classmates
- is easy to do and practical
- doesn't involve spending money

b Work in a group. Explain your life hack.
- Explain when the life hack is useful.
- Describe the materials that are needed.
- Use the expressions for instructions to explain how to do it.

c Listen to the life hacks that other groups have presented. Which three life hacks do you think are the most useful? Why?

EXTRA Research and describe a life hack that an older member of your family uses.

Unit 6 · Our world

6 Revision

Vocabulary Digital media

1 Choose the correct answers.

It's very difficult to be a successful ¹*loyal supporter/ vlogger* and get thousands or even millions of ²*views/hits* for your videos, but everyone agrees that nobody becomes an ³*online sensation/mainstream media* without working very hard at it. They also say that you can't be ⁴*viral/fake* and you have to really believe in what you are doing if you want people to become ⁵*subscribers/ life hacks* to your ⁶*comments section/channel*.

Shopping nouns

2 Complete the sentences with the words.

> alterations   changing room
> outfit   receipt   sales   size

1 I don't want to spend so much on a dress and then pay for ___ .
2 My mum has bought a lovely blue ___ for my brother's wedding.
3 Sam has lost the ___ , so he can't ask for a refund.
4 I like the colour, but it's too big. Have you got one in a smaller ___ ?
5 Let's go next week when the ___ are on and we'll get a discount.
6 I left all the clothes that I tried on in the ___ .

Fashion adjectives

3 Choose the correct adjectives for each comment.

1 It looks good and you can wear it on lots of different occasions.
2 The colours and design are very Indian.
3 The jacket has a 1940s American pilot design.
4 Anyone wearing it will look like a rainbow on legs!
5 That style is so last year that I don't think anyone will wear it now!

1 A ethnic   B casual   C practical
2 A comfortable   B ethnic   C smart
3 A vintage   B glamorous   C trendy
4 A trendy   B practical   C colourful
5 A casual   B old-fashioned   C well dressed

Grammar Reported speech

4 Use the words in brackets to finish the dialogues.

1 A Andy has a website. (blog)
  B Really? I thought he said *he had a blog*.
2 A Class 4A will go to the museum. (the theatre)
  B Really? I thought the teacher said ___ .
3 A I'm a subscriber to a sports channel. (film channel)
  B Really? I thought you said ___ .
4 A Rachel loves watching crime series. (dramas)
  B Really? I thought she said ___ .
5 A We're revising for a Maths exam. (History exam).
  B Really? I thought Liam said ___ .

Reported commands and requests

5 Answer the questions with the words in brackets.

1 What did Tom ask you to open? (window)
  Tom asked me to open the window.
2 What did they ask the audience to switch off? (mobile phones)
3 What did the librarian tell us to do? (be quiet)
4 What did Lilly ask you to buy? (popcorn)
5 What did the teacher tell us not to do? (be late)

Subject and object questions

6 Choose the correct answers.

1 Which shirt *does cost/costs* €30?
2 Who *did buy/bought* a new dress?
3 Who *did your sister see/did see*?
4 What *did Mara say/said Mara*?
5 Which book *do you want/want you*?
6 What *did happen/happened* at the shopping centre?

Everyday English Giving instructions

7 Complete the sentences with the words.

> before   done   last   should   start   thing

1 The first ___ you should do is switch it off.
2 When you've ___ that, dry the inside.
3 ___ by opening the back of the computer.
4 The ___ thing you do is switch it on.
5 After that, you ___ clean the screen.
6 ___ you begin, check you've got some glue.

Learning to learn Flashcards

Use flashcards to revise. Write a new word on one side and a definition and a translation on the other. For grammar, write the structure on one side and an example on the other.

bargain
something that you buy for a really good price

▶ Workbook pages 64–65, exercises 1–9

80 Unit 6 · Our world

Revision

Supplementary materials
Workbook: pages 64–65, exercises 1–9
Unit test 6
Online Practice

Vocabulary Digital media
1

1 vlogger   2 views   3 online sensation   4 fake
5 subscribers   6 channel

Shopping nouns
2

1 alterations   2 outfit   3 receipt   4 size   5 sales
changing room

Fashion adjectives
3

1 C   2 B   3 A   4 C   5 B

Grammar Reported speech
4

2 Class 4A would go to the theatre   3 you were a subscriber to a film channel   4 she loved watching dramas   5 you were revising for a History exam

Reported commands and requests
5

2 They asked the audience to switch off their mobile phones.
3 The librarian told us to be quiet.
4 Lilly asked me to buy her some popcorn.
5 The teacher told us not to be late.

Subject and object questions
6

1 costs   2 bought   3 did your sister see   4 did Mara say
5 do you want   6 happened

Everyday English Giving instructions
7

1 thing   2 done   3 Start   4 last   5 should   6 Before

Learning to learn Flashcards

- Encourage your Sts to use flashcards to help them learn and revise their English.
- You could get Sts to create a set of class flashcards and use these cards regularly for revision.
- Below are some suggestions for revising vocabulary and grammar, and also for improving reading.

Vocabulary

1 Ask your Sts to look at the words in the box on page 74, exercise 2a.
2 Give them twelve small cards and tell them to write one word on each card.
3 Then, ask them to write the definition on the other side.

They can use these cards to test themselves on how well they have learned the words. Tell your Sts they can write a definition like the ones in exercise 2a, or they can write a sentence using the word, or they can draw a picture.

Grammar

1 Ask your Sts to look at exercise 5c on page 75.
2 Give them six cards and tell them to write one sentence per card in direct speech.
3 On the other side of each card, ask them to write the reported command or request.

To use the cards, Sts look at the sentence in direct speech and say the sentence in reported speech, or vice versa. Sts can play against each other, gaining one point for every sentence they get right.

Reading

1 Ask Sts to look at any of the texts on the **Culture** pages and to choose eight words that they found difficult.
2 Give them eight cards and tell them to write a word on each card.
3 Then, give them another eight cards and tell them to write the sentence from the text that contains the word. They can also write a definition, if it's easier to remember.
4 Next, ask Sts to put their cards face-down on the table so they can't see the sentence or definition.
5 Now, on their own or with a partner, tell them to play Pelmanism, turning over two cards at a time to try and find a match. Set a time limit of one minute. How many cards can they match?

➧ **Workbook** pages 64–65, exercises 1–9

➧ When Sts have finished the **Revision** page, tell them to go to the **Workbook Progress Check** p.65 and complete the **Your progress** table.

6

My project

Project checklist

Before the lesson
- Look for a YouTube video on how to create an online video. Choose a video that will help your Sts make their own video.
- If you cannot organize for computer access, Sts could watch the YouTube videos mentioned in exercise 1a as homework before the lesson.
- Arrange to have a video camera (or more than one), either from the school or one belonging to a student. Sts may be able to use the camera on their mobile phones.

Materials for the lesson
- Video cameras
- Computers with internet access

You First

Ask Sts to think of their favourite online video and what they like about it. Would they recommend it? Why? / Why not?

EXTRA SUPPORT With a partner, Sts choose their favourite online video. Then, they prepare to talk about it, thinking of these questions: *What is it about? Who made it? Is it professional or made by an amateur? How long is it? Why do you like it?*

1a 🔊 3•31 Audio script pT93
- Ask Sts to look at the pictures. What do they see? What are the people doing?
- Play the audio for Sts to listen and complete the task.

C, E, B, D, A

b 🔊 3•31 Audio script pT93
- Play the audio again for Sts to complete the information in the infographic.

1 idea 2 vlog 3 review 4 memory 5 practise 6 text

EXTRA IDEA Ask Sts if they have ever made a video. Did they follow the instructions on the infographic? Was their experience the same? If not, how was it different? Do they find the instructions helpful?

2
- Refer Sts to the **Look!** box.
- Give Sts time to complete the task.

1 so 2 such 3 such 4 so 5 so 6 such

EXTRA SUPPORT Ask Sts to identify the adjectives and the nouns that come after *so* and *such* in the sentences, e.g. 1 *exciting*, 2 *a friendly face*.

EXTRA CHALLENGE Ask Sts to write four more sentences, two with *so* and two with *such*. Then, with a partner, Sts check that their sentences are correct. Get feedback and discuss any disagreements.

3a
- Put Sts in groups to create an online video.
- Give them time to decide what type of video they are going to create.

EXTRA SUPPORT For groups that are unsure about what video to create, tell them to look at the ideas in the infographic.

EXTRA SUPPORT Encourage Sts to think about specifics when deciding on their video:
Where are they going to film?
Who is going to be in it?
How are they going to capture the sound?
When will they film it? (if not during class time)
Will they be able to meet in order to film?
These considerations will help them avoid problems later in the project.

b
- Groups plan their video. Encourage groups to be as specific as they can. This will help them when they are filming.

EXTRA SUPPORT Ask Sts to map out their filming using this table:

Scene	People	Setting	Actions	Sound / Music
1				
2				
3				
4				

People – Who is being filmed, if anyone?
Setting – Where is it being filmed?
Actions – What is happening in the film?
Sound / Music – How will the sound be captured? How will the music be put into the film?

c
- Sts record their video. This could be done outside of class or school time. Make sure Sts plan for this with a date and time. If it is difficult for them to meet, they should change their idea for the videos.

d
- Sts edit their video.

EXTRA SUPPORT Get Sts to show you their edited videos before they present to the class. You could give them some advice or suggestions.

4
- Sts present their videos to the class. The class watches and makes comments about the videos.

EXTRA IDEA Create 'Oscar' categories for the videos: best video, best actor / actress, best sound / music, best location, etc.

5
- Get Sts to write a short review of one of the videos they have seen.

EXTRA CHALLENGE Sts act out their review as if it were a TV programme.

EXTRA CHALLENGE The class interviews one of the groups about their film-making, as if it were a news programme. The class could also interview one of the 'Oscar' winners.

My project

YOU FIRST! What is your favourite online video? What do you like about it? Why would you recommend it?

CREATING A VIDEO

HOW TO CREATE A VIDEO

Think of an ¹____!

Look at a website to see what is popular. You could:
- create a ² ____ about something that interests you
- do a how-to video and show people how to do a dance/move, etc.
- present a video of photos and videos of school, friends or family to music
- do a ³ ____ of a product, film, place that you have visited, etc.
- do some acting

Recording equipment → **Recording** → **Editing**

- Use a smartphone with a big enough ⁴ ____.
- Use a webcam for a vlog.
- Use a free editing program.
- Add music, ⁶ ____ or images to your video.

- Check you have everything you need.
- Make sure there is enough light.
- Rehearse and ⁵ ____ before you record.

← Upload your video

1 a 🔊 3.31 Listen to a tutorial about creating a video. Put the pictures in the order that you hear.

b 🔊 3.31 Listen again and complete the information in the infographic.

2 Read the Look! box and complete the sentences with *so* and *such*.

Look! *so* and *such*

We use *so* and *such* to emphasize an opinion. We use *so* with an adjective and *such* with an adjective + a singular or plural noun.

Most people don't need one that is so professional.
Don't use one that has such a small memory that you can't store your recording.

1 The new video is ___ exciting, but it's very long!
2 The dog in the video has ___ a friendly face.
3 The video had ___ a strange name that I can't remember it!
4 This week's vlog is great, but it's ___ short!
5 The explanation was ___ complicated that I couldn't understand it!
6 The presenters are ___ perfect people that they aren't believable.

3 a Work in a group. Create a video. Decide on the type of video that you want to make.

b Plan the video.
Decide the following together:
- the setting
- the content
- the music, text and images

c Record the video.

d Edit the video.

4 Present your video to the class.

5 Over to you! Write a short review of one of the other videos that you have seen.

Unit 6 · Our world

6 Culture

YOU FIRST! Do you think some countries are better at sport than others? Why? / Why not? Which countries are the most successful at sport at the moment?

Glossary
sprinter   compete
inspire   train

Small nations, sporting giants

Sporting nations fact file: Jamaica
Population: 2,950,210
Capital: Kingston
Major sports: athletics, cricket, football, basketball

Sporting nations fact file: New Zealand
Population: 4,790,390
Capital: Wellington
Major sports: rugby, cricket, sailing, football

THE GLOBAL SPORTS BLOG

This week, I'm reporting on two nations that are small geographically, but giants in the world of sport: Jamaica and New Zealand. If we divide a country's population by the points it obtains for its sporting achievements, then these two island nations are regularly the best in the world. Let's look at what makes the people of these nations such sporting champions.

Jamaica – a nation of sprinters

Jamaicans love athletics! Every international championship is followed closely in the media and youngsters are inspired by every Olympic gold medal success to become athletes, too. The nation's schools encourage children to take part in athletics at a very early age, and secondary students compete in the world's biggest athletics championship for schools: The Champs. The interest in the competition is incredible and the event is watched by 30,000 people in the stadium and thousands more on TV. The winners can receive huge contracts to represent the world's biggest sportswear manufacturers. Some are also offered the opportunity to study and continue doing sport with excellent coaches at some of the best universities in the world. What could be more motivating than that?

New Zealand – home of the All Blacks

The New Zealand rugby team, the All Blacks, is considered to be the best sports team in the world. It has won over 75% of all the games it has ever played, more than any other team in the history of sport. Rugby is the country's national sport and the best children start to train in children's teams, called the Small Blacks, when they are just five years old. Crowds of 7,000 watch matches between secondary schools and they are reported in the mainstream media. The same schools also go on international tours and the students get experience of playing against teams in Argentina, France and Britain.

---

1 a Read the introduction. Answer the questions.
1 What are the similarities between Jamaica and New Zealand?
2 What calculation is used to show that Jamaica and New Zealand are great sporting nations?

b Work with a partner. Ask and answer the questions about each text.
1 When do children start to do the sport?
2 What competitions are organized for school students?
3 How interested are people in these competitions?

2 Work with a partner. Ask and answer questions about an interesting fact.
Student A   Look at page 86.
Student B   Look at page 87.

3 a Over to you! Work with a partner. Write a paragraph for a sports blog about a sport that your country is good at.
Include the following:
- the age when children start playing it
- competitions that school students play in
- public interest
- other factors
- photos of sporting events

b Work with a different partner. Read your blog to them. Have you chosen the same or different sports? Do you agree with the information that they have included?

---

82   Unit 6 · Our world

▶ Parkrun

Culture

Supplementary materials
Photocopiable worksheets: Culture, Culture video

CULTURE NOTES Below are some additional notes that you may want to share with your Sts.

Jamaica: The Jamaican Flag has a diagonal cross with four triangles. The diagonal cross is gold. The top and bottom triangles are green. The triangles on either side are black. Black represents the strength and creativity of the people; gold is for the natural wealth and beauty of sunlight; green stands for hope and agricultural resources. The Jamaican flag is the only national flag in the world that does not feature the colours red, white, or blue.

Usain Bolt (pictured waving the Jamaican flag) is a Jamaican sprinter. He holds the world record for the 100 metres, 200 metres and the 4 x 100 metres relay races. He participated in three Olympic Games and many people consider him to be the greatest sprinter of all time.

New Zealand: The New Zealand Flag has a blue field with the Union Jack to the left and four red stars with white borders to the right. The Union Jack is a symbol of the close relationship between New Zealand and the United Kingdom (it used to be a British colony and is now a member of the Commonwealth of Nations – an organization of 52 countries that used to be part of the British Empire). The four stars represent the Southern Cross in the Crux constellation. This shows the location of New Zealand in the South Pacific Ocean and can only be seen in the southern hemisphere. The colour blue represents the sky and the sea.

New Zealand sports teams often display the silver fern as their national symbol. You can see this in the photo of the All Blacks rugby team. The fern comes from the popular New Zealand tree.

You First

Sts discuss the questions and their reasons. Ask Sts to think of countries that are good at sports. Guide them to think of countries in the Olympics, international sports like football, rugby, basketball, tennis, etc. Then, ask them what they know about Jamaica and New Zealand. Have they heard of Usain Bolt or the All Blacks? Finish the discussion by talking about why they think these countries are so successful in international sports.

EXTRA SUPPORT Ask Sts to look at the photos. What do they see? Do they know what the sports are? (*rugby, athletics*)

1a

- Ask Sts to read the introduction to the text and answer the questions.

1 They are small countries, but they are good at sport.
2 You divide the number of inhabitants in each country by the points obtained in sporting achievements.

b

- In pairs, Sts ask and answer the questions about each text.

1 **Jamaica:** At a very early age.
  New Zealand: At the age of five.
2 **Jamaica:** The world's biggest athletics championship for schools: The Champs.
  New Zealand: Rugby matches between secondary schools and international tours.
3 **Jamaica:** It's a major national event watched by 30,000 people in the stadium and thousands more on TV.
  New Zealand: Rugby matches between secondary schools are reported in the mainstream media and crowds of 7,000 go to watch them.

EXTRA SUPPORT Read the texts and decide if you need to teach any new vocabulary before Sts do the task. Refer Sts to the **Glossary**.

EXTRA IDEA Ask each St to read one of the texts and answer the questions. Then, Sts discuss their answers with a partner and compare both countries, discussing the differences and similarities.

EXTRA SUPPORT Ask Sts to read out a fact about one of the countries. The class listens and says which country it is about.

EXTRA IDEA Ask Sts to read each text and answer these questions: *What surprised you most about each country? How does sports in these countries compare to yours?*

2

- Put Sts in pairs, **A** and **B**. Tell Sts **A** to go to page 86 and Sts **B** to page 87.
- Ask Sts to read their interesting fact.
- Sts then tell each other about their interesting fact using the information in the instructions.

EXTRA IDEA Ask Sts to discuss if they found the facts interesting. Why? / Why not?

EXTRA CHALLENGE If you have internet access in your classroom, ask Sts to find another interesting fact about sports in Jamaica and New Zealand. Then, have Sts discuss their facts with the class.

3a

- Put Sts in pairs to write their paragraphs.
- Tell Sts to consider the items on the list.

EXTRA SUPPORT If you have internet access in your classroom, let Sts look up the information online for their blog.

EXTRA CHALLENGE Sts write a report to increase the participation of young people in a sport in their country. They can consider the items on the list in exercise 3a.

b

- Ask Sts to work with a different partner.
- Sts reads their blog and answer the questions.

▶ Video Parkrun

As an extension to the Culture topic, watch a short film about Parkrun and do the accompanying photocopiable exercises. You can either do this in class or set it as optional homework. The film is available on the DVD-ROM or on the Online Practice.

Project Explore T82

Learn through English

Additional subject notes
Physical activity, or exercise, can be defined as any movement of the body that uses muscles, increases your heart rate, makes you breathe faster and uses up energy. The average adult should do between 75–150 minutes of exercise per week, and can include anything from walking to playing competitive sport.

Scientists have argued that exercise is key for maintaining your physical health, and improving your mental well-being. This means being in 'a positive social and mental state', which allows you to deal with the ups and downs of life, take on challenges and making the most of opportunities that give you a sense of purpose and value. They argue that exercise can help people with mild depression and anxiety by causing chemical changes in your brain, which can help to positively change your mood. For example, going for a quick walk can increase mental alertness, energy and positive mood.

You First
Sts discuss how much exercise they do every week, and whether they enjoy it or not. Get them to give their reasons.

EXTRA IDEA Sts discuss how active they are. Then, they line up from most active to least active. Encourage Sts to talk to each other so they know where to stand. Then, encourage them to talk to the students next to them. Why do they think they are more or less active?

Reading
1a
- Ask Sts look at the photos. What can they see? Do they do these activities?
- Give Sts time to complete the table with the amount of time they spend on each activity.

b
- Tell Sts to compare their table with a partner.
- Ask pairs to discuss if they need to change anything and what activities they need to do more or less of.
- Get feedback.

EXTRA IDEA With their partner, Sts write an ideal balance of activities for the week. Then, Sts discuss their ideas with the class.

2a
- Give Sts time to read the leaflet and answer the question.
- Encourage Sts to find the information in the text to defend their answer.

c
('But we also know that not everybody loves doing it! Just thinking about having to run, swim or do exercise in a gym class can be enough to make some people want to go and lie down!')

b
- Tell Sts to match the headings to the paragraphs.
- Check answers.

1 The benefits 2 Getting started 3 Making it a routine
4 Choosing your exercise 5 Final thoughts

EXTRA IDEA Write these gapped sentences on the board. Ask Sts to read the leaflet and complete the sentences.
1 'Moving our bodies causes our _____ to release chemicals that create a feel-good _____ and just ten minutes of working out can leave us feeling _____.'
2 'If _____ hasn't been part of your life for a long time, there is no point _____ for a marathon or signing up for the gym.'
Then, ask Sts to write six sentences from the text, leaving a gap for two or three important words. Tell Sts to give their sentences to a classmate to complete.

3a
- Put Sts in pairs to create an exercise programme for someone who doesn't like organized sport.
- Tell them to take the items on the list into consideration.

b
- Put Sts in different pairs and tell them to explain their exercise programme to their new partner.
- Ask them to decide which exercise programme would be more effective, and why.

EXTRA CHALLENGE Sts present and discuss the different exercise programmes. Then, Sts return to their original pairs and create a leaflet for an exercise programme. Tell Sts their leaflet would be given to people in their community. Tell them they should think about the title, photos, sub-headings and paragraphs. Display the leaflets in class and give Sts time to read them.

Learn through English

6

> **YOU FIRST!** How much exercise do you do every week?
> Do you enjoy doing exercise? Why? / Why not?

Be active!

Move it!

We all know that exercise is good for us, don't we? But we also know that not everybody loves doing it! Just thinking about having to run, swim or do exercise in a gym class can be enough to make some people want to go and lie down! However, did you know that exercise is not all about doing sport or going to a gym? There are other ways that we can keep fit, but before we look at those, let's remind ourselves why keeping fit is actually quite good for us.

1 _____

For a start, exercise is not just about the body. Moving our bodies causes our brains to release chemicals that create a feel-good sensation and just ten minutes of working out can leave us feeling happier. Moreover, regular exercise increases our energy levels and improves the quality of our sleep. Finally, if we combine our exercise with a healthy diet, we will feel and look healthier and feel more confident about ourselves. Sounds like a good deal, doesn't it?

2 _____

Start small! If exercise hasn't been part of your life for a long time, there is no point training for a marathon or signing up for the gym: you will soon give up and go back to your old ways! Walking, jogging or cycling around the local park for ten minutes every day are great ways to develop a fitness habit.

3 _____

Make exercise part of your life and do it at more or less the same time every day so it really becomes part of your daily routine. Make the experience even more enjoyable by downloading some music to your smartphone and move to the beat as you work out! Instead of music, you could try a podcast or even an audio book: this way, you'll exercise your brain as well as your body!

4 _____

Exercise forces your muscles, lungs and heart to work harder, but you don't have to go to a gym or do individual or team sports to give your body a workout. Some people simply stop using private and public transport and walk or cycle everywhere. Others take up activities such as dancing, yoga, swimming or even rock climbing. Choose an activity that not only exercises your body, but that you also enjoy. That way, you'll never give it up!

5 _____

It doesn't matter how much we exercise, few of us are ever going to achieve athletic bodies like international sports stars, but doing regular exercise isn't about image. It's about being healthier, having more energy and feeling happier. Who wouldn't want that?

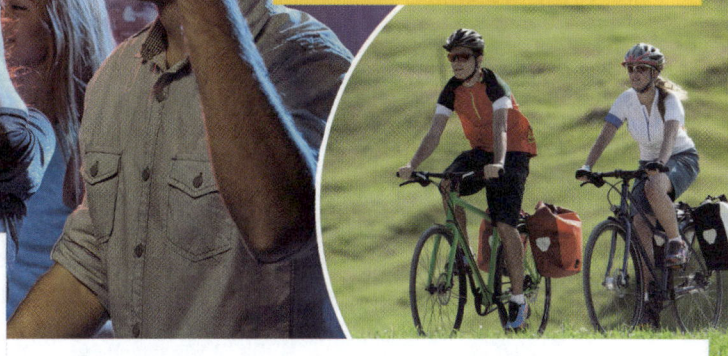

Reading

1 a Complete the table.

How much time do you spend…?	on weekdays	at the weekends
sitting		
lying		
moving		

b Work with a partner. Compare your tables. Do you think you need to change anything? Which do you think you should do more / less of?

2 a Read the leaflet. Who do you think it is for? People who…
a like sport but don't do it
b are very sporty and play organized sports
c don't like sport and are not very active
d want to change sports

b Match the headings to the paragraphs.

> Choosing your exercise   Final thoughts
> Getting started   The benefits   Making it a routine

3 a Work with a partner. Create an exercise programme for someone who does not like organized sport.
Consider the following:
- daily activities that can provide good exercise
- going to and from school
- parks and other open spaces in your town
- social activities
- owning a pet

b Work with a different partner. Explain your programme. Which programme do you think would be more effective? Why?

Unit 6 · Our world

The Museum of the Strange   Episode 3

1 🔊 3.32 ▶ Read and listen to the story.

The third room was very different from the other two. This one was dark and almost empty. The only thing in it was a mirror on one wall.
'I don't get it,' said Laura.
'Go and look in the mirror if you want to see the future,' said the guide quietly.
Laura felt a little afraid, but she was curious to look in the mirror, too. Slowly the two friends walked to the mirror.

At first they couldn't see anything in the dark glass. Then a picture slowly appeared. It became clearer and clearer.
'Look!' said Ben. 'The mirror's showing us the outside of this museum!'
'But it can't be today,' said Laura. 'It's a sunny day.'

Look. The guide is showing more people around the museum.

Everything in the museum is strange and interesting.

And now it's time to see the newest part of our museum – an area all about the world of modern teenagers.

Teenagers have a culture that is very different from ours. Their fashion, their hobbies, their beliefs…

Haha! Look at those terrible dummies!

Ben! It…it's US! We're the dummies. We're part of the museum!

Laura wanted to run, but her arms and legs suddenly felt heavy.
Ben felt as cold as ice. It was hard to speak.
'I…I can't move!'
The museum guide laughed quietly. 'Here at the museum, we collect strange things and teenagers are the strangest thing of all. This is your home now. It's where you're going to be for a long, long time.'
Laura could not speak. The same thought went around and around in her mind. 'Nobody can help us now. Nobody. Unless…Declan, where are you?'

84   The Museum of the Strange • Episode 3

The Museum of the Strange Episode 3

Supplementary materials
Workbook: pages 66–67, exercises 1–9
Online Practice
Progress test 3

Note
The story can be used in class as a reading and listening task, a video task or both.

EXTRA SUPPORT Pre-teach or elicit from the pictures *mirror*, *curious*, *dummies* and *smash*.

1 3·32
- Elicit how Episode 2 of the story ended.

Ben and Laura heard the story of the invention of time travel.

- In pairs, get Sts to look at the pictures on pages 84–85 and predict what they think will happen next in Episode 3. Elicit some ideas, but don't tell Sts if they are right at this stage.
- Play the audio for Sts to listen and follow. Alternatively, show the class the video of the story from the DVD-ROM.
- Ask Sts how similar their predictions were to what happens.
- Give Sts time to retell the story in pairs. You could write words from the pictures on the board to help, e.g. '2 *mirror, showing*', '4 *newest part, teenagers*', '5 *culture, dummies*', '8 *bored, go inside*', '9 *third room, didn't move*', '10 *mirror, smash, run*', '11 *terrible voice, tall and grey*', '12 *outside*', '13 *knock it down*'.
- Elicit parts of the story from different pairs.

EXTRA SUPPORT Play the audio again for Sts to listen and follow before doing the task. They could also retell the story with their books open, using the pictures to help.

EXTRA CHALLENGE Tell Sts to close their books. In pairs, Sts take turns to say what happened in pictures 1–13, e.g. *Laura and Ben went into the third room*.

➡ **Workbook** pages 66–67

Notes
The story can be further exploited by doing the tasks from these pages in the **Workbook**. These can be done in class or set as homework.

The tasks in the **Workbook** review the following language points covered in **Units 5–6** in the **Student's Book**:
- The passive (p. 68)
- Reported speech (p. 73)
- Reported commands and requests (p. 75)

1
- Sts choose the correct adjectives to complete the sentences.

2 curious **3** sunny **4** strangest **5** bored **6** difficult
7 fantastic **8** best

2
- Sts put the words in the correct order to make sentences.
- Then, they match them to the correct pictures.

2 We're part of the museum! C
3 It's an ugly old building, isn't it? E
4 The mirror's showing us the outside of this museum! A
5 Everything in the museum is strange and interesting. B

EXTRA IDEA Sts choose sentences from the story and put them in the wrong order. Then their partner writes the sentences correctly.

3
- Sts complete the crossword.
- When Sts have completed the crossword, they find the missing word.

2 strange **3** grey **4** teenager **5** trap **6** dummy
7 mirror **8** belief
The missing word is **creature**.

4
- Sts write the sentences in indirect speech.

2 Laura said that she didn't get it.
3 Declan thought that he was in the wrong place.
4 Laura told Ben and Declan to run.
5 Laura said that they would never know about the creature.
6 The man said that they were knocking the building down soon.

EXTRA IDEA Sts take some quotes from the story and write them in indirect speech.

5
- Sts complete the newspaper story with the words in the box.

2 older **3** remember **4** didn't **5** closed **6** empty
7 ruin **8** stopped **9** human **10** found **11** knocked
12 built

6
- Sts discuss the questions with a partner.

Students' own answers.

7 41 Workbook Audio script T108
- Play the audio for Sts to listen and answer the questions.

1 pencils **2** vampires **3** The Museum of Bad Art **4** hair
5 bread

Project Explore T84

3

8 🔊 **41 Workbook** Audio script T108
- Before playing the audio again, tell Sts to read and answer the questions.
- Play the audio for Sts to confirm their answers.

2 Paris **3** the USA **4** human hair **5** bread

9
- Sts discuss the questions with a partner.

Students' own answers.

Note
To further exploit the video in class, you could use some or all of the suggested activities from page Tviii.

Declan was bored so he came to find his friends. When he saw the museum again, he thought he was in the wrong place at first. 'It didn't look like that before,' he thought.
He decided to go inside.

The museum was dark and it wasn't easy for Declan to look around. But then he went into the third room.
'Laura? Ben? What are you doing? What's wrong?'
His friends didn't answer. They didn't move.

Declan couldn't explain it, but there was something strange about that mirror. He knew that he had to smash it.
He picked up the nearest thing, which was a stone on the floor. Then he threw it.
Immediately Laura and Ben could move again.
'Run!' shouted Laura.

They ran.
Declan heard a terrible voice behind them. 'Come back! COME BACK!'
He was near the door when he looked behind him. The thing that he saw was tall and grey, and it was moving fast.
'Don't stop!' shouted Ben.

At last the three friends were outside. It felt fantastic! Declan was shaking. 'What was that thing?' he asked.
Laura looked back at the museum. 'A ghost? A vampire?' she said. 'We'll never know.'

Just then they heard a voice behind them: 'It's an ugly, old building, isn't it? Years and years ago it was a museum,' the man continued. 'Now look at it! But don't worry – we're knocking it down tomorrow!'
Declan laughed. 'That's the best news that I've heard in a long time!'
'And look,' said Laura with a smile. 'It's stopped raining!'

THE END

▶ Workbook pages 66–67

The Museum of the Strange · Episode 3

85

Student's Book audio scripts

Unit 1

1.07 p9 Exercise 8
Friend Jake, how long have you played basketball for the school team?
Jake I've played for the team for two years.
Friend Have you ever played another sport?
Jake No, I've never wanted to. I love basketball and I think it's a great team sport. I've learned a lot about team work from playing it!
Friend Ruby, have you decided to do any new after-school activities this year?
Ruby Yes. I've just joined a chess club.
Friend I've never liked chess. I find it hard to concentrate!
Ruby I've played it since I was a child and I've always liked it. I love the way it really makes you think.
Friend Maybe that's my problem.
Friend Lucy, how long have you done gymnastics?
Lucy I've done it since I started primary school.
Friend You obviously enjoy it, then!
Lucy Yes, I do. I've become more self-confident since I started and I feel I can do well at other activities, too.
Friend Perhaps I should try it.
Lucy Come to the next training session. You'll love it!

1.09 p11 Exercise 5a & b
I'm fond of dogs, big dogs, but my mum and dad wouldn't let me have one. Then, on my birthday last year, they gave me a surprise present – a dog! But it was a small dog, the smallest dog in the world! I called him 'Tiny' and decided to train him to be a good dog. So one day, I took him outside and we were walking down the street. While we were walking, I was telling him to 'stop' and to 'sit' and things were going really well. Suddenly, however, Tiny saw a dog on the other side of the street and he ran towards him!
Now, my street is really busy, but I didn't think about the danger and I just ran after Tiny. There were cars, lorries, vans and buses moving in all directions, but I didn't care; I wanted to save my dog! Fortunately, I wasn't the only one, because a bus driver who was about to drive right over Tiny stopped and saved his life! Tiny was so shocked that he just looked up at the bus and I took the opportunity to pick him up before he could run off again. I lifted him up and showed him to the bus driver and he smiled. Tiny and I were both shaking!
I walked back home with Tiny in my arms, telling him, 'No, no, you don't run off like that!' However, I knew the real lesson was for me; you don't go out onto a busy street and let your dog, even the world's smallest dog, run free!

1.11 p12 Exercises 2a, b & c
Podcaster Hi everybody and welcome to the *Science Today* podcast! This week we're going to look at the Genographic Project, the project that the *National Geographic* magazine has organized to find out where we all come from! Isn't that cool? So what were we doing before we arrived in the places where we live now? Well, the Genographic Project can tell us! Here's Mara with a very special example!
Mara Most people have heard of Charles Darwin, the famous scientist. Charles Darwin was the man who wrote *On the Origin of Species* and changed the way we think about human identity. He said that humans and animals all have the same ancestors. Well, Charles Darwin died in 1882, but he has a great-great-grandson…that's right, great-great-grandson…Chris Darwin. Chris lived in Britain until he was twenty-five, but then he moved to Australia. Chris works for the Charles Darwin Reserve, a nature reserve that protects plants and animals. When Chris heard about the *National Geographic* project, he wanted to take part, so the National Geographic looked at his DNA. Chris's DNA showed that he and his family were part of the first group of humans to leave Africa about forty-five thousand years ago. They first moved to the Middle East and then they travelled to Europe and survived the Ice Age in the south of Spain before moving to Britain about twelve thousand years ago. Most of the family stayed in Britain, although Chris is now in Australia. Where will they be in forty-five thousand years' time?
Podcaster An incredible story and a good question, Mara! Next up on the podcast, we're going to…

1.13 p15 Exercise 3b
Erika There you are!
Oliver Hi Erika. What's up?
Erika What's up?! I'll tell you what's up. I've just met Miss Hamilton and she's read our project.
Oliver Great!
Erika And she says it's awful. It's the worst she's ever seen.
Oliver Oh.
Erika Oh? Is that all you can say?
Oliver We've got until tomorrow. I'll do it again.
Erika No, you won't! I won't trust you to do it! Danny? Liza? Can I work with you?
Liza Sure. Miss Hamilton said we could have teams of four.
Erika Thanks.
Danny Oliver, do you want to join us?
Oliver OK. *Live Science*? Great! Let's copy that.
Erika Oliver!
Oliver I'm joking! I'm joking!

1.14 p15 Exercise 5b
What do you think about this project for Miss Hamilton?
I'm not sure.
That's a good point.
I see what you mean, but I feel we should be open-minded.
As far as I'm concerned, I already know it all.
That's exactly what I think!
What's your opinion on 'ancestors', 'genes' and 'Neanderthals' as search terms?
Do you think they work?
My view is that we try those first.

1.17 p15 Exercise 7a & b
Danny What do you think of what Oliver did?
Erika As far as I'm concerned, it's just as serious as copying from another student's work.
Danny I see what you mean, but a lot of people are happy to share ideas on their sites and blogs.
Erika I'm not sure about that. I mean, they use the internet to make their ideas public, but I don't think they want people to copy them.
Danny True. That's a good point.
Erika Anyway, Miss Hamilton has given us a list of rules.
Danny Yes, I've seen it. What's your opinion of it?
Erika As far as I'm concerned, it's really useful.
Danny But do you think it's helpful?
Erika Yes, I do and it's easy. If you use an article, you just give the author's name, the date, the title of the article and the address of the website. In my view, it's easy.
Danny Yes, even Oliver could do it!
Erika Exactly! I mean, we don't want people to copy our work, so we shouldn't copy theirs.
Danny That's exactly what I think!

1.19　p18　Exercise 2c

Although Ascension Island is in the middle of the Atlantic Ocean, between the continents of Africa and South America, it was not the kind of place that sailors in the nineteenth century ever wanted to visit. There wasn't any fresh water or plant life on the volcanic island, so ships stayed away. However, when Darwin saw volcanic activity on the island as *The Beagle* returned to Britain, he decided to briefly visit the island and his stay there gave him an incredible idea.

When he returned to London, he discussed Ascension Island with his friend John Hooker and the two men decided to make it into a 'little England'. Every year they sent out plants and trees to the island and sailors from the British Navy planted them. The trees caught rainwater from the air and this helped more plants and trees to grow. Today, there's fresh water on Ascension Island and it's covered in plants and trees. There's also a population of over eight hundred people living on the island, all thanks to Darwin's idea.

It normally takes millions of years to create an environment, but Darwin and Hooker did it in just twenty years. Thanks to their success, scientists visit Ascension Island today looking to answer a question that is going to be very important in the future: could Darwin's idea work on the planet Mars? If astronauts can do the same on Mars, it means that Darwin will have contributed to space exploration as well as to our understanding of our past.

1.20　p19　Exercise 1

For many years, a theory has existed that we're all just six introductions away from any other person on the planet. The Hungarian writer Karinthy Frigyes was the first person to talk about this in his short story from 1929, *Chains*. Since then, mathematicians have shown with computers that it is possible, and social network sites like Facebook also show that we only need a few introductions to meet everybody on the planet. A few years ago, researchers did an experiment with a social networking site that demonstrated that we're all six messages or fewer away from any person on the planet. Scientists are very interested in this theory. Why? Because they can use it to understand how illness and disease move from one person to another and from one place to another. They say that they can also use it to try and stop terrorism. However, although the idea works on computers and with the internet, does it work in the real world?

Unit 2

1.24　p20　Exercise 3a & b

Girl You're going to visit your aunt in Paris next week, aren't you?
Boy Yes, I am.
Girl Well, make sure you go to the Musée des Arts Forains when you're there.
Boy What's that?
Girl It's a fantastic museum of exhibits and rides from old amusement parks in Europe. The best thing about it is that there are activities that you can do and you can even go on some of the rides.
Boy That sounds unusual and great fun. I think I'll take my young cousins to see it.
Girl Good idea! They'll love it. The man who started the museum said that there are lots of museums about wars, but none about people having a good time and laughing, so he decided to set it up.
Boy The more I hear about it, the more I like it! How much time will we need?
Girl We spent nearly three hours there. If you take children, you might need more time because they'll want to go on everything.
Boy So will I!
Girl I did as well. You have to book the tickets on their website and you should do it soon; it's very popular.
Boy I will. I'm sure it'll make me popular with my cousins!

1.25　p21　Exercise 8a

Good evening ladies and gentlemen, and welcome to London's *Magic Circle* show! I can promise you that our four magicians will really entertain you with their incredible magic! Each one of them is going to show you a different type of magic: Agnes from Hungary is an expert with cards; Sam from the United States can make anything disappear…especially from your pockets; Andrea from Argentina can read your minds; and finally Henry from good old London town is going to make things move with the power of his thoughts! I'm confident that they will amaze you with their awesome talents! Now before we start, I'd just like to remind you that we're going to have a break for 15 minutes after the first two acts; being a magician is very tiring work! OK, ladies and gentlemen, take your seats at your tables and let the show begin!

1.28　p23　Exercise 5a & b

Duncan We've all agreed on the plan, but now we need to see if we can follow our timetable and deliver our community project on time. This National Citizen Service project ends on 31 August, so we've got to move quickly. What are you doing this week, Adam?
Adam Well, Eva and I are meeting local business people tomorrow to see if they can help us with the project. Every week the director of the Bilton Savings Bank meets people from community projects to give them advice on raising money and we're going to speak to him. The meeting starts at ten o'clock and after that we're speaking to the manager at the Bilton Garden Centre at midday to see if we can get a special price for the plants and trees.
Duncan OK, that sounds good, but remember that we want plants with flowers that produce strong smells, and trees that are interesting to touch. Maya, what's your job for this week?
Maya I'm giving a presentation with Lucas to the council on Tuesday afternoon. The council holds a meeting on the first Tuesday of every month to listen to ideas for using the buildings and land that the council owns, but isn't using at the moment. As we all know, the council has a piece of land next to the home for the blind that we could use. In fact, the council has told me there won't be a problem, but I still have to follow the rules and do the presentation!
Duncan Well, good luck with that! Now, we've also got to…

1.32　p27　Exercise 3b

Danny Hi guys. What's up?
Liza Hey Danny. How was your sister's wedding?
Danny Er, great.
Erika And the surprise honeymoon destination?
Danny Er…I'd prefer not to talk about that.
Erika Why not?
Danny OK. They said the traffic was really bad…There were too many tourists… And the hotel was lovely, but a lot more expensive than we thought!
Erika So they enjoyed it, then?
Danny Well, they did say it was 'unforgettable'!

Student's Book audio scripts　T87

1.33 p27 Exercise 5b

I'd love to go on a beach holiday.
I'd prefer not to play it so safe.
I'm not very keen on it, but some people love it.
That sounds more interesting than a beach holiday.
I think I'd rather go somewhere quiet for a honeymoon.
I'd rather not worry about money on my honeymoon!
It sounds much better than a beach or skiing holiday.
I'd prefer to just decide on Paris now!

1.35 p27 Exercise 7a

Dad OK Mark, your mum and I have decided that if you pass your exams, we'll take you on a city break!
Mark Wow Dad, that's great. I'd love to do that, but isn't it expensive?
Dad Not really. We can get a low-cost flight and find an apartment on a peer-to-peer travel site.
Mark Well, I'd rather be in the centre of the city we go to. Aren't those apartments often very far from the centre?
Dad I'm sure we could find one that wasn't too far away. Anyway, I'd rather not go to a youth hostel. I think your mum and I are a bit old for that, don't you?
Mark True! Even I'm not very keen on having to share a room with people that I don't know! I suppose an apartment from a peer-to-peer travel site sounds better.
Dad Well, if we want to travel as cheaply as possible, we'll need to arrange things soon.
Mark OK. We can have a look online together this weekend.
Dad Great! Where would you like to go?
Mark I'd love to go to Lisbon or Madrid.
Dad Me too, although I think Madrid sounds more interesting because of all the art galleries and restaurants.
Mark And we can visit Real Madrid's stadium!
Dad Madrid it is, then!

Unit 3

2.04 p34 Exercise 2a

OK, in this experiment we're going to produce some of our own DNA. You can do this experiment anywhere, but we need some equipment such as a test tube and we also need a sports drink, some pineapple juice and a little alcohol that we use for cleaning. First, you have to put the alcohol in the fridge the night before so that it'll be cold. Then, on the day of the experiment, drink a little of the sports drink and wash it around your mouth for two minutes. It has to be for at least two minutes so the salt in the sports drink can collect cells from the inside of your mouth. Then spit a little of the sports drink into the test tube and add some washing-up liquid from the kitchen until the test tube is half full. Now move the test tube so that the liquids mix, but be careful – we don't want soap bubbles! Then add a few drops of pineapple juice and – very, very slowly – a little alcohol. Now, there's a period of observation of a few minutes as we watch a line of white material begin to form on the top of the liquid. That white material is your DNA! It doesn't look like the typical image of DNA that we usually see, does it? That's because the structure of DNA is impossible to see even with the most powerful microscopes. However, with this white material, scientists would be able to learn a lot about you!

2.06 p35 Exercises 6b & c

Lucy So James, why are you against using animals in medical experiments? I mean, I obviously agree that we shouldn't make animals suffer, but sometimes we have to use them.
James That isn't true. Thanks to computers, we don't have to use them any more. Computer programs can test drugs like painkillers and antibiotics.
Lucy But a computer isn't the same as an animal. Animals have genes, similar to ours, and it's useful to see what drugs do to animals before people use them.
James No, we should test drugs for humans on humans. In some experiments with animals, it seemed that the drugs were safe, but later, when people used them, they were really, really bad. The tests on animals didn't help at all.
Lucy We mustn't test drugs on people first! There are always going to be a few mistakes, but without tests on animals, medicine won't improve. I also think human life is more important and we should make sure that any new medical treatment works on animals first.
James I don't know if I agree that human life is more important than animal life. I mean…

2.10 p37 Exercise 5a

Podcaster In this week's podcast we're going to look at something that interests a lot of our listeners: the age when they can do certain activities legally – things like driving a car or even getting married! Most European countries have similar laws, but there are some in England that might surprise you! Here's Sara.
Sara Are you looking forward to the day when you can borrow your parents' car to go out with your girlfriend or boyfriend? Well in England, you'll have to wait until you're 17 to do that. However, if you want to pick up your girlfriend or boyfriend on a tractor, you can do that at 16, although I'm not sure they would be very comfortable and, more importantly, you can't drive on a road until you're seventeen, so you can't take them very far! You could also try a moped at sixteen but the English weather isn't the best for two-wheeled transport. Of course, if you want a moped or a car, you'll need some money to pay for it. You can start a full-time job at the age of eighteen in England, but if you want to start saving earlier, you can do a part-time job at the age of thirteen. However, you can't work for more than two hours on a school day: schoolwork comes first! If you're more interested in your image than in cars, you'll have to wait until you're eighteen to get a tattoo, but there's no minimum age for piercing your ears or other parts of your body. Perhaps the difference is that you can take off earrings, but it's very difficult to remove a tattoo, as thirty percent of English people with tattoos have realized when they try! Finally, what about getting married? Well, if you want to get married when you're sixteen, you can if your parents agree; but if you wait until you're eighteen, you don't need your parents' permission. However, most men and women in England wait until their early thirties to get married, which sounds like a very sensible thing to do!
Podcaster Thanks, Sara! Now up next on the podcast we're going to…

2.12 p38 Exercise 2a

Lucas Hi Ivy, what's up?
Ivy It's Ruby. I think she's really angry with me.
Lucas Are you sure? People can get angry about lots of things. It may not have anything to do with you.
Ivy I know it has! She hasn't spoken to me all day, but I don't know why.
Lucas Why not use the scientific method to find out why?
Ivy What? I'm talking about a problem with my best friend, not a problem with my Science homework!
Lucas Well, the scientific method works for lots of different problems. Sherlock Holmes used it to solve crimes! You've made an observation: Ruby isn't talking to you. And you've asked yourself a question: why isn't Ruby speaking to me? Next you have to do…
Ivy Some research! I sit next to you in Science class, remember?
Lucas Well, have you done any research?
Ivy I've asked Olivia and Jenna, but they don't know anything.
Lucas Have you looked on social media?
Ivy No…that's a good point…Oh no… now I remember.
Lucas What?
Ivy Ruby posted a picture of herself in a new dress at the weekend and I wrote a comment.
Lucas What did you say?
Ivy It was only a joke…no big deal! I wrote, 'Ruby, why are you dressing like an old lady?'
Lucas I think we can make a hypothesis.
Ivy Oh thank you, Sherlock! What am I going to do?
Lucas Well, if you delete the comment and write a new post saying sorry, I think you might be friends with Ruby again. We could try an experiment if you like.
Ivy OK, I'll do it now…I've deleted the message and I'm typing an apology.
Lucas Good, we can make an analysis of the data tomorrow.
Ivy Lucas, I think you're enjoying this experiment. I hope it works or you'll have lost a friend, too!
The next day…
Lucas Hi, Ivy. Right, so where's your phone? I want to see if our experiment has worked.
Ivy Here it is. I've got forty-three likes on my new post, seven positive comments about my apology and…best of all…a message from Ruby! She says we all make mistakes and she wants to meet after school on Monday.
Lucas Looks like I was right about the scientific method! Now there's just the final step.
Ivy Look, your point about using it for problems outside the lab is a good one, but I am not writing a report with a conclusion and findings!
Lucas I suppose not, but the findings would make interesting reading!

2.14 p41 Exercise 3b

Liza …that's right, and over six thousand people have already signed. Thank you. Oh, a photo? Yes, we will! Bye!…That was the *Norton Telegraph*. They've written an article about our petition and they want a photo of us!
Oliver Media coverage! That's great!
Danny You know, it was a great idea to ask Emil, Liza.
Liza Thanks, Danny. Come on!

2.15 p41 Exercise 5b

It says that the arguments in favour are more shops, more people and more business!
Why's that?
One disadvantage is that it will annoy everybody.
I think that would work.
It's a great way to show people we care. And it'll be really useful for explaining our position, too.
I guess a benefit of doing it online is that you can reach loads of people.

2.17 p41 Exercise 7a & b

Danny The online petition has worked well, but we need to try some other activities. Has anybody got any suggestions?
Liza Yes, let's organize a day of sports activities in the park. A benefit is that it would be a great way to show exactly why we want to keep the park: it's a brilliant place for people to do exercise!
Danny That's a great idea. Anyone else?
Oliver Why don't we make cakes and give them away in the centre of town? One advantage is we could explain our reasons to people when we're giving them a cake and then ask them to sign the petition.
Danny OK, any other ideas?
Erika Let's camp in the park for the weekend.
Danny Can you explain why?
Erika I think it would work because if all the members of our sports club spent the weekend in tents in the park, the local media would become interested.
Danny That's a good point. Well, let's choose an idea now…or perhaps we should do more than one!

Unit 4

2.21 p46 Exercise 2a

Alex Why don't we enter the *New Seven Wonders of the World* competition? If we won, we'd get a free trip around the world.
Daisy It sounds great, doesn't it? I think to have a chance of winning, our list should visit all the continents.
Alex Good idea. Where are we going to start? I'd love to visit the Moai on Easter Island in the Pacific Ocean.
Daisy The what?
Alex The Moai. You know, those incredible statues.
Daisy Oh yes, those great big heads. They're really interesting because nobody knows how they made them or how they moved them! OK, and from there we could go to China to visit the Great Wall.
Alex That's a great place, too. The only problem is if we went there, we'd have to walk up all those steps to visit the towers.
Daisy You sound like my grandad! Another problem is that a lot of the wall is a ruin, so we'd have to visit a part where they've repaired it.
Alex Well, we'll worry about that if we win!
Daisy Good point! How about including a modern place – you know, something like a skyscraper?
Alex The Burj Khalifa Tower in Dubai for example? It's the tallest building in the world. It'd be fantastic if we could go to the top!
Daisy It would, but would you want to walk up all the steps?

2.22 p47 Exercise 5a

Alex Just a minute.
Daisy What?
Alex Well, do the places that we choose have to be just man-made – you know, buildings and monuments? If I organized it, I'd include natural wonders as well, like the Amazon Rainforest in Brazil or Table Mountain in South Africa.
Daisy That's a good point. Perhaps it'd be more interesting if the list included both things. It could also have wonders of the industrial world, like the Panama Canal or the Golden Gate Bridge in San Francisco.
Alex That's a good idea, but I suppose if we did that, we'd need a longer list.
Daisy True, or there could be different lists: one for buildings like the Sagrada Família in Barcelona, one for nature, one for industry, and so on.

Student's Book audio scripts T89

Alex Well, I think you can only present one list for the competition, but I'm not sure if the things have to be man-made or if we can suggest natural wonders. Let's check.
Daisy Good idea! I'd hate to miss a trip around the world because we made a mistake!

2.25 p49 Exercise 2b

Jack OK, we've made a list of the destinations for our interrail trip. All we have to do now is decide on the route.
Anna We haven't decided on all the places, have we?
Tom Well, we've agreed on five, but we said we wanted to go to six places. We should think about our budget because cities like Copenhagen and Vienna are some of the most expensive in Europe. If we went to Barcelona or Athens, food and accommodation would be cheaper than in Copenhagen or Vienna.
Jack We're going in the summer, so Barcelona and Athens won't be so cheap as you think. Also we're going to Amsterdam first and then to Berlin. Travelling to Copenhagen or Vienna after that would be easier than travelling to Barcelona or Athens.
Tom And cities like Copenhagen and Vienna aren't as popular as places on the coast in the summer and they won't be too crowded.
Jack Are you joking? Copenhagen or Vienna will be as busy as Barcelona and Athens.
Anna Look guys, I simply reckon that Copenhagen or Vienna will be more interesting. We've all been to Barcelona and Athens with our families. This is a chance to see new things! I think Vienna would be perfect because we could go from Berlin to Prague, then to Budapest and after that to Ljubljana and finish in Vienna. What do you think?
Jack Let me just check the map…so it's Amsterdam first, then Berlin and after that it's…
Anna Prague in the Czech Republic…
Jack I know where Prague is!
Anna …followed by Budapest and then the capital of Slovenia…
Jack Ljubljana! What's this, a test? I got an '8' in Geography, you know!
Anna …and we finish in Vienna, the heart of Europe!
Jack It's the capital of Austria, actually! Well, that sounds good to me.
Tom Me too. OK, so we've got a route. Great! Now, I've got a suggestion: why don't we travel on high-speed trains?

Anna Who wants to travel as fast as they can when they're on holiday? I'd like to enjoy the journey and see the views through the train windows.
Jack Yes, I agree. I think we'll travel quickly enough on normal trains and they won't be so expensive.
Tom Well, at least we should make sure we have time for sightseeing visits to other places in each country.
Anna That's fine if those places are close enough to the capital cities. I don't want to get up before nine o'clock at the earliest. It's a holiday!
Jack Well, we can plan the visits later, but we also have to think about accommodation. Do we want to stay at campsites or hostels?
Anna I think hostels would be the best, don't you?
Tom I agree. Campsites won't be as comfortable as hostels. Campsites are also further from the centre of cities than hostels.
Jack Good, at least we've agreed on that! Let's meet up at the weekend and make some reservations.

2.29 p53 Exercises 3b & c

Danny Have you seen this? Oliver made it.
Liza What is it?
Danny It's a headset – you know, like a virtual reality headset.
Liza Really?
Danny Yeah, he's entered a competition. He has to write an essay about Mars and he has to do a project on it, too. The prize is a trip to NASA. And he said if he won, he'd take us!
Liza Brilliant! Can I see?
Danny Of course. You have to look through…there's an image of Mars and then you can move it around.
Liza Wow! It's beautiful!
Danny It really is, isn't it?

2.30 p53 Exercise 4b

I'm sure that's him.
I'm certain that it is.
I'm not really sure that he knows what a library is.
That is definitely Oliver.
I can't believe that he's studying!
It is very unlikely that he's studying.
It's hard to believe you are studying.
I doubt you're going to Mars.
They say it's very likely we'll be able to fly there by the 2030s.
There's no doubt we can.

2.33 p53 Exercise 6a

Girl Sorry I'm late. The bus was late because of the traffic.
Boy Well, we won't need buses soon. I'm sure that everyone will have hoverboards.
Girl What's a hoverboard?
Boy You know, a skateboard without wheels like in *Back to the Future*.
Girl *Back to the Future*? That's really old, but I know what you mean. Unfortunately, I think it's very unlikely to happen.
Boy Well, I think that there's no doubt that we will see them. They've already developed a prototype.
Girl I hope you're right, but I'm not sure they would work. They would have to be really powerful to carry a person above the ground.

2.34 p55 Exercise 2a

Interviewer Have you decided on your route yet?
Becky Yes, after a lot of hard work, we've finally agreed on one.
Interviewer Where will you go first?
Chris Well, the route we've chosen takes us from our hometown Cardiff to London, but we're not stopping over in London. We'll change trains and catch a train straight to Paris.
Interviewer Where will you go after that?
Becky Right, from Paris we're going to Amsterdam and then on to Berlin, Prague, Vienna, Florence and back to the UK.
Interviewer When are you going?
Chris We're setting off straight after we finish our exams in June. We're hoping that all these places won't be too crowded then…although I imagine some will be.
Interviewer Why have you chosen these cities?
Becky Ah, we've chosen this route because we're both interested in art and we want to spend our time visiting the famous museums and art galleries in these cities, although of course we'll want to do some sightseeing and to relax, too!
Interviewer Where will you stay in each place?
Chris Hmm…as we don't have a very big budget, we've made reservations to stay at campsites and sometimes we'll catch night trains so that we can sleep as we travel.
Becky Hopefully the trains won't be late!

T90 Student's Book audio scripts

Chris Yeah! Some of the campsites are far from the city centres, but you can rent bikes at most of them, so we'll use those to get into town. It won't be as comfortable as staying in a hostel in the centre of the city, but at least we'll have more money for other things.

Interviewer How will you get around in each city?

Becky We'll probably use the same bikes that we rent at the campsites. We don't really want to walk far when we move around the cities, so bikes would be great.

Chris And in Amsterdam, of course, cycling will be part of the experience!

Interviewer How much money do you think you'll need? You know, for visiting places?

Chris We're going to try and visit the museums when it's free or at least cheaper. In some cities, you can enter museums and galleries free at the weekends and there are also free tours of the galleries. The European Night of Museums will also take place while we're in Paris and if we go to the museums late on that night, they'll all be free, too.

Interviewer What will you eat?

Becky We'll probably go to supermarkets to buy food and have picnics in parks and at the campsites…although we'll try hard to save some money so we can eat cakes in Vienna, sausages in Berlin, and pizzas in Florence!

Interviewer What will you bring back as souvenirs or presents?

Chris In my case, my mum has asked for magnets of interesting paintings that I come across at the different art galleries – you know, for the fridge!

Interviewer Well, I hope you have a great trip!

Becky Thanks!

Chris Yes, thanks. We can't wait to get away!

Unit 5

3.02 p60   Exercises 1b & 2a

Teacher When you speak to your friends about technology, you probably talk about modern inventions, don't you? However, in the lecture that we're about to listen to, Professor William Stevenson is going to explain that the word *technology* also has other meanings. Professor Stevenson…

Professor Thank you. Well, let's begin by thinking about what the word *technology* means. Technology is the use of science to search for practical solutions to our problems, so some of the best examples of technology are objects that we have used for important jobs for many, many years. They also have designs that have changed very little. An example which makes my students laugh at me when I first mention it is…the bucket.

Yes, if you look at a bucket, it doesn't seem to match our modern idea of technology, does it? However, when I explain to my students that its design is so good that nobody has succeeded in improving it since it was invented five thousand years ago, they begin to agree with me that it's an example of perfect technology. Over the years, the materials used to make buckets have changed and today they're made of materials like plastic and metal, but they still do the same job.

Another example of near perfect technology is…well, what are you sitting on?

Yes, chairs. Now, the chair isn't as global as the bucket because the world is divided into cultures that sit on the floor and cultures that use chairs. If you use them depends on where you live. However, since the Greeks invented the chair over five thousand years ago, there has been a steady increase in its use.

In Egypt, the first chairs belonged to the wealthiest members of society and they were symbols of power. Today, although the basic design hasn't changed, anyone can afford one, thanks to the use of materials like plastic.

Clothing has also given us some examples of technology that has survived the test of time. The first shoes were worn forty thousand years ago and…

3.04 p61   Exercise 6a

Girl Right, let's see if you can guess what this object is. It was invented in the nineteenth century, but it wasn't sold to the public until the twentieth century. Today, it's usually found in the kitchen and I imagine everyone has one – well, if they have electricity. It's made of a number of materials, including plastic, metal and some glass.

Boy Hmm, is it a microwave?

Girl No, it isn't. I'll give you a couple more clues. It's usually covered in white metal, although other colours are sometimes used. The ones that are sold in America are usually much bigger than the ones that are bought in Europe. In the future, they'll be connected to our mobile phones and they'll tell us when we need to buy milk or eggs or…whatever we need.

Boy I know, I know! It's a…

3.08 p65   Exercise 5

In my opinion, most advertisements are boring, so when one makes you laugh, you take notice. There's one that I think is really funny. The product is fish that comes in a tin and it shows a fisherman who wants to steal some fish that a few bears have caught in a river. There isn't much dialogue, but there's a lot of action. At first, each bear is busy catching fish, but one of them sees that the fisherman is about to steal one. The bear turns around to attack the fisherman, but not as you would expect; the bear uses a few karate moves on the fisherman! How many bears do you know that can do that? This is what makes it so funny! All the bears look real, and you aren't expecting the karate fight. Unfortunately for the bear, the fisherman wins and walks away, leaving it without any fish. Few advertisements have made me laugh so much! Of course, all advertisements are trying to sell something, but I've never bought this product or asked my mum to buy it, so… yes, it's a funny advertisement, but perhaps not a successful one!

3.10 p67 Exercises 3b & c

Oliver …and he was the one that said it first! Hey, there's Liza. Hi Liza! Come over here!
Danny Don't!
Oliver What?
Danny Nothing.
Liza Hi Oliver. Hi Danny.
Oliver Hey! Erika said you're a writer now!
Liza Oh…yeah. Switched magazine want me to write an article for them. Danny?
Danny I know, I know. I was wrong, you were right. I get it.
Liza No, it's not that. I wanted to ask… could you lend me a hand? To think of ideas?
Danny Oh. I'd love to!
Oliver I've got a great idea! It's an article about teenagers…and – get this – social media!…What? It's brilliant!

3.14 p70 Exercise 2a

I'm going to talk about the song *Molly Malone*, one of the most popular songs in Ireland. It seems that the writer based Molly Malone on the young girls that walked around Dublin in the 17th century selling fish and shellfish. The song tells us that Molly was beautiful and that she sold fish because both her parents did, too. As part of the chorus, the song adds a few lines that explain the words that Molly shouted while she was trying to sell shellfish. The song then ends sadly because Molly became ill and died of a fever, but it adds that we can still see the spirit of Molly on the streets of Dublin.
I like the song because the writer tells a sad story with just a few words, but the music and the chorus make it a song that everybody wants to sing. Go to an Irish rugby match and you'll see how much people like singing it!

Unit 6

3.20 p75 Exercise 3a

I've bought a few bargains, but I think my tablet is the best. I went with my dad to buy it in a sale at a computer shop in town and I've had it for about a year. First we went to the computer shop to look at the brands that they had and we saw one that had a twenty-five percent discount. Then I checked it online to see what people thought. They were about to replace the one that I bought with a new model, but everybody said it worked well and they were right. It's got a good screen and my eyes don't get tired from looking at it. It's also got a big memory and is very fast. It really has been a bargain!

3.22 p76 Exercise 2a

Presenter Welcome to *Find the Connection*, the quiz where two teams can ask five questions to help them decide what connects three objects. This week, we start by looking at fashion and the first question is for Emma's team. Are you ready? Which place connects these three items of clothing? They're on the screen now…flip-flops, aviator sunglasses and colourful Hawaiian shirts. Is it A China, B Japan or C America?
Woman 1 Wow, that's a tough one. What do you think, guys?
Man Let's ask about who made them. That might help.
Presenter OK Emma, what's your team's first question?
Woman 1 Who invented the three items?
Presenter That's a good place to start! Well, Hawaiian shirts were invented by a Chinese clothes shop owner, while an American company made the first aviator sunglasses and the Japanese created the first flip-flops.
Woman 1 Right. How about asking about the reason for making them?
Woman 2 Sounds good to me.
Woman 1 OK. Why did they invent these items?
Presenter Some surprising information here. Many people think that Hawaiian shirts are an example of ethnic fashion from the island, but that's not true. A Chinese shop owner in Hawaii had a lot of old-fashioned kimonos, a smart Japanese dress, that nobody wanted, so he cut them up and made them into casual shirts. However, if you lived in Japan, you wouldn't cut up your kimono because it's traditional to wear one for special occasions when you need to be well-dressed. You'd also wear a pair of zori sandals with it. In Japan zori sandals were made of wood or leather, but in other countries they're also made of plastic and called flip-flops. Finally, aviator sunglasses were made for a practical reason: to protect pilots' eyes from the sun when they were flying high in the sky.
Woman 2 It sounds like the answer is Japan to me.
Man Just a minute, who did he say invented aviator sunglasses? It was an American company, wasn't it? And which country does Hawaii belong to?
Woman 1 The USA. It's an American state. Look, why don't we ask about who used these things? We've still got three questions left.
Man Good idea, OK.
Woman 1 Here's our third question: who used them?
Presenter Well, Hawaiian shirts became a must-have item for American soldiers visiting Hawaii and they became very trendy in the fifties. They're still popular today with fans of vintage clothing. It was also American soldiers in Japan during the Second World War that took the comfortable zori sandals home with them. However, when they returned to the USA, they made them from plastic and called them flip-flops. Finally, aviator sunglasses were made for American pilots and they became very popular when film stars started to wear them to look glamorous.
Woman 2 Well, that's clear, isn't it guys? The answer has to be…

3.23 p76 Exercise 2c

Woman 2 Well, that's clear, isn't it guys? The answer has to be…
Woman 1 I think we all agree that it's… America!
Presenter Emma's team says it's America…and it is! Congratulations, you've got your first points! Now it's time for…

3.26 p79 Exercise 3b

Liza Hi Danny.
Danny Hey Liza! I really have to thank you!
Liza What for?
Danny Your rice trick. It worked!
Liza That's great. So you got your exam notes, then?
Danny Yeah…and listen…I was wondering…if I could take you to the cinema. To say thank you.
Liza Yeah, sure. That would be really nice.
Danny Really? Brilliant!
Liza So, are you ready for the exam?
Danny As ready as I'll ever be!
Liza Let's do it!

3.27 p79 Exercise 4b

The first thing you should do is dry it.
Before you begin, turn off the phone.
Start by drying it.
The next step is to put the phone in a plastic bag.
When you've done that, wrap it in a towel.
Finally, put the towel in the freezer.
After that, you should dry it.
The last thing you do is put it in rice.

3.30 p79 Exercise 6

Poppy Hey Liam, guess what?
Liam What?
Poppy My parents have become subscribers to a video-on-demand channel. Now I can watch all the series I want!
Liam Lucky you…
Poppy What do you mean?
Liam You know I kept getting headaches from watching series on my mobile?
Poppy Yes, I remember.
Liam Well, I went to the doctor's and she said if I didn't stop watching on small screens, I'd soon have problems with my sight.
Poppy It's not surprising, is it?
Liam No, I suppose not. But the worst thing is that my parents have cancelled our subscription to the channel! I promised I wouldn't watch on my mobile again, but they wouldn't listen.

3.31 p81 Exercise 1a & b

This first YouTube tutorial on creating an online video is going to look at the basic rules for making an entertaining video.

To begin with, a writer or team of writers need an idea. If there's no content, there's no video! So decide with your team what type of video you want to make. If you can't think of anything, look at a site like YouTube and see what's popular. You could create a vlog about something that you're interested in, explain how to do something such as a dance move or how to play a musical instrument, present a video of photos and films of your school, friends or family with music in the background, or do a review of a product, a film or a place that you've visited. You could even do some acting, but you would really need to prepare that carefully.

OK, once you've decided what your video is going to be about, you have to think about how you're going to film it. Of course, a smartphone comes with a video camera, but make sure you don't use one that has such a small memory that you can't store your recording. If you're going to do a vlog, then the webcam on your computer will do the job.

Next comes the recording. Before you start, check the place where you're going to do the filming. Is everything that you want to film in the right place? Is there enough light? If possible, film during the day so that you have plenty of light; but if you're filming inside, focus lights on the people or scene that you want to record. Then, if you can, rehearse and practise the scene. Obviously, if you decide to film a party or a school concert, you won't be able to rehearse. However, you should try to visit the place where the event will take place and find good places to stand and do the recording.

Now we arrive at the final stage, transferring the recording to your computer and editing it. To do this, you'll need an editing program. Most computers come with a free one but if yours hasn't got one, you'll be able to find one online. You can also buy one, but most people don't need one that's so professional. You can use the program to add music, text or images to your video to make it more attractive to watch. Then, when you and your team are happy with the results, it's time for the big moment: upload your video, show it to the world and see how many views it gets! Good luck!

Student's Book audio scripts   T93

Workbook answer key

Unit 1 Social circles

1A Classmates

1 2 aggressive 3 moody 4 selfish 5 caring 6 jealous

2 2 cruel 3 loyal 4 moody 5 sensitive 6 honest
   7 jealous 8 competitive

3 2 ever, never 3 have, known 4 Since, just
   5 Have, since 6 played, for

4 2 for 3 since 4 ever 5 just 6 never

5 2 Have you ever studied at a different school?
   3 How long has your mum studied English?
   4 How long have you known your best friend?
   5 How long has your family lived in your house?
   6 Have you ever worked out at the gym?

6 Students' own answers.

7 2 F 3 A 4 E 5 C 6 B

8 5, 8

1B Group instinct

1 2 down 3 to 4 in 5 of 6 with

2 2 fancies 3 hates 4 dislikes 5 socialize
   6 get in touch with

3 Students' own answers.

4 2 while, PS 3 when, PC 4 when, PC 5 While, PS
   6 when, PS

5 2 was wearing 3 fell 4 saw 5 were dancing 6 was

6 2 Amy was shopping when she saw the boy she dislikes.
   3 I arrived home while my dad was cooking dinner.
   4 We were living in London when we met Beth.
   5 Ben was reading Lisa's blog post when she phoned him.
   6 Why didn't you visit Brazil while you were travelling in South America?

7 A 6 B 3 C 5 D 2 E 4 F 1

9 2 While, suddenly 3 Next, Meanwhile 4 As soon as
   5 When 6 Finally 7 The following day 8 After that

1C Starting points

1 2 population 3 resources 4 ancestors 5 Migration
   6 genes

2 2 genes 3 habitat 4 migration 5 ancestors
   6 resources

3 2 because 3 but 4 while 5 so 6 Until 7 When

4 2 Although 3 so 4 while 5 until 6 but

5 Students' own answers.

6 2 While 3 so 4 until 5 Although 6 but 7 When

7 2 You can include the dates of their birth and death, a photo and their birthplace and hometown.
   3 You will learn about your family history and the migrations that brought your family to where you live now.
   4 It's more interesting to find information from relatives than from the internet.
   5 It might be useful to use a family tree created by a computer.
   6 You can present it to your family.

8 Students' own answers.

1D A piece of cake

1 2 What's up?, Wow! 3 A piece of cake
   4 you're in for a surprise! 5 Oh, come on!

2
   Asking for opinions: What do you think about…?; What's your opinion of…?; Do you think it works?
   Giving opinions: As far as I'm concerned…; My view / opinion is that…; I feel we should…
   Agreeing and disagreeing with opinions: That's exactly what I think.; That's a good point.; I see what you mean, but…; I'm not sure.

3 2 My view is that 3 That's exactly what I think 4 I'm not sure 5 I feel we should 6 I see what you mean, but…

4 Students' own answers.

5a 2 looked 3 face 4 hopeful 5 careless 6 backache

6a 1 She fancies him. 2 He used Tom's phone.
    3 She'll think it's from Tom. 4 Do you want to go out with me?

6b 2 view 3 common 4 keen 5 never 6 cake

6d 2 nervous 3 button 4 glad 5 exhibition
    6 together

Progress check

1 2 sensible 3 honest 4 self-confident 5 moody
   6 loyal

2 2 e 3 b 4 a 5 d 6 c

3 2 genes 3 habitat 4 resources 5 population
   6 migration

4 2 since 3 ever 4 just 5 never 6 for

5 2 Who were talking to when I saw you in town?
   3 Andy got your text message while he was going home on the bus.
   4 I wasn't studying when my parents came home.
   5 What did you talk / What were you talking about while you were dancing?
   6 We were having lunch when the bell rang.

6 2 so 3 but 4 Until 5 Although 6 While

7 2 a 3 b 4 a 5 c 6 b 7 b 8 a 9 c 10 b

8 2 I'm concerned 3 see what you mean 4 point
   5 shouldn't 6 sure

9 1 I 2 F 3 I

T94 Workbook answer key

Unit 2 New horizons

2A Awesome

1 2 ride 3 scenery 4 exhibit 5 gallery 6 entrance

2 2 show 3 caves 4 tour 5 activities 6 festival

3 2 scenery 3 gallery 4 maze 5 festival 6 show

4 2 will 3 're going to 4 'll 5 will 6 're going to

5 2 are going to fly 3 'm not going to go 4 will find
   5 is going to start 6 'll help

6 2 'll need 3 're going to go 4 're going to visit
   5 'll send 6 'm going to meet

7 Students' own answers.

8 1 see the show at York Dungeon 2 visit York Maze 3 visit York Minster

9 2 E I think we should because it'll get crowded
   3 C We're going to see a show about the Vikings
   4 B I'm sure we'll love it
   5 F We're going up to the roof
   6 A Yes, I think we'll enjoy everything

2B Collaborate

1 2 a 3 d 4 b 5 f 6 c 7 h 8 g

2 2 monitor 3 improve 4 raise 5 protect
   6 collaborate

3 2 protect 3 plan 4 raise 5 organize 6 develop

4 2 FP 3 FP 4 FT 5 FP 6 FT

5 1 'm repairing 2 does the bus leave 3 're meeting
   4 don't have 5 're collecting, 're doing
   6 does the play start, begins

6 2 start 3 're collaborating 4 're giving
   5 are organizing 6 return

7 Students' own answers.

8 2 F 3 F 4 T 5 F 6 T

9 2 Saturday 3 31st 4 teacher 5 school 6 5
   7 Maths 8 8 a.m.

2C Taking a risk

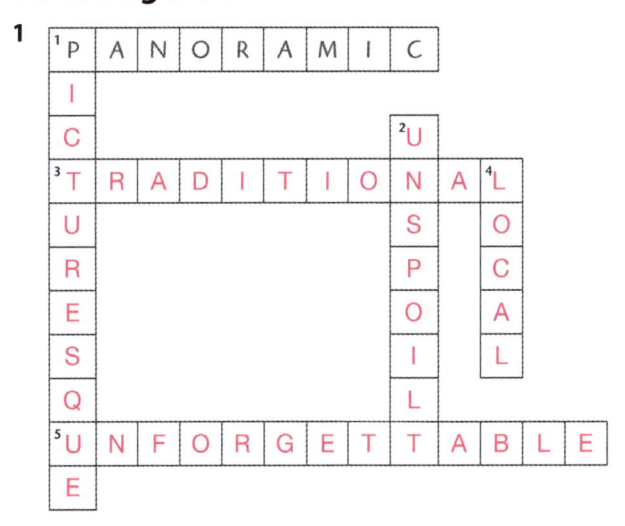

1

	¹P	A	N	O	R	A	M	I	C	
	I									
	C					²U				
³T	R	A	D	I	T	I	O	N	A	L
	U					S			⁴L	
	R					P			O	
	E					O			C	
	S					I			A	
	Q					L			L	
⁵U	N	F	O	R	G	E	T	T	A	B	L	E
	E									

2 2 unforgettable 3 remote 4 colourful 5 crowded
   6 historic

3 2 historic 3 crowded 4 remote 5 local
   6 traditional

4 2 If 3 Unless 4 If 5 Unless 6 unless
   Sentences 1, 2 and 6 give advice and recommendations.

5 2 if 3 Unless 4 Ask 5 want 6 will give

6 2 Unless Ben calls, we won't meet in town.
   3 If you arrive on time, you'll catch the plane.
   4 Unless you're 16, the organizers won't allow you to climb the Via Ferrata.
   5 Unless you wear a hat, the sun will hurt your head.
   6 If John doesn't arrive soon, he won't see the concert.

7 1 Lots of crocodiles. 2 They're six metres long and weigh 800 kilos. 3 You swam with crocodiles and survived.

8 2 A 3 B 4 C 5 A 6 B

9 Students' own answers.

2D Sorted!

1 2 play it safe 3 I reckon 4 pricey 5 No way
   6 no big deal 7 Sorted

3 2 much 3 to 4 not 5 prefer 6 than 7 'd
   8 rather

4 Students' own answers.

5a I'm not keen‿on backpacking.
   It's‿out‿of this world!
   It was‿unforgettable!
   There's‿a man in‿a T-shirt.
   They're waiting for‿a friend.

6a Photo A: the marathon

6b I'd prefer to… 4
I'd rather… 6
I'd prefer not to… 8
I'd rather not… 3
I'm not very keen on… 5
It sounds much better than… 7
That sounds more interesting than… 2

6c 2 The shopping centre will be crowded.
3 She doesn't really know how to play it.
4 Her parents won't let her cycle on busy roads.
5 She doesn't get on well with Danny.

Progress check

1 2 entrance   3 ride   4 cave   5 attraction   6 exhibit

2 2 build   3 collaborate   4 improve   5 planning
6 develop

3 2 crowded   3 local   4 traditional   5 colourful
6 picturesque

4 2 'm going to do my homework.
3 'll bring it tomorrow, I promise!
4 'll go abroad.
5 're going to win this match.
6 will travel in space.

5 2 When are you organizing the voluntary programme?
3 What time does the talk on the safari start?
4 Andy isn't participating in the activities next week.
5 The music festival takes place in the second week of August this year.
6 Our plane doesn't arrive in New York until 1 a.m.

6 2 Unless   3 Go   4 will tell   5 If   6 it rains

7 2 c   3 f   4 d   5 b   6 h   7 a   8 e

8 2 encourage   3 explore   4 learn   5 avoid

The Museum of the Strange Episode 1

1 2 hasn't stopped   3 saw   4 went   5 was sitting
6 offered   7 said   8 gave   9 looked / was looking
10 told

2 1 artist   2 exhibits   3 graffiti   4 bridge   5 cave
7 guide

3 2 Dan didn't have any friends.
3 He was walking in the country, when he saw some children / students from his school.
4 They were sitting on a bridge.
5 One of the kids wanted Dan to spray graffiti on the bridge.
6 Dan ran because he didn't want to answer a lot of questions.
7 He fell into a cave.
8 The paintings in the cave were thousands of years old.
9 That day Dan decided to become an artist.

4 2 I'll give you a tour, of course. A
3 I like art, but I don't like graffiti. B
4 This looks really old. E
5 Someone is coming to get you out. C

5 Students' own answers.

6 1 D   2 B   3 E   4 A   5 C

7 2 b   3 c   4 c   5 a

8 2 until   3 because   4 so   5 but   6 Although

Unit 3 Respect

3A Testing

1 Top row: 5, (1)
Middle row: 3, 6
Bottom row: 2, 4

2 2 investigation 3 specimens 4 experiments
5 observation 6 results

3 2 specimen 3 petri dish 4 microscope 5 cells
6 results

4 2 We have to clean the equipment.
3 You don't have to wear safety goggles.
4 Alice ought to take notes in class.
5 I must go straight home after school.
6 He mustn't be late for the coach.

5 2 have to / must study the theories as well
3 mustn't take equipment from the lab
4 should / ought to take photos on the field trip
5 don't have to read the article

6 2 OU 3 MP 4 NASA 5 OU 6 MP

7 2 They want to study what happens to our bones, muscles and hearts when we do almost no physical exercise.
3 They have to look at images of faces and communicate with virtual worlds.
4 They want to know how our senses react to digital information.
5 They have to visit twice.
6 They want to discover how our brains are organized and how different regions of the brain help us make decisions and learn.

8 The computer game experiment.

9 2 point 3 agree 4 mean 5 sure 6 completely

3B Young at heart

1 2 over 3 out 4 together 5 out 6 up

2 2 joined in 3 cheered up 4 came in 5 got into
6 hang out

3 Students' own answers.

4 2 can't speak 3 can play 4 could stay over
5 could hang out 6 can't drop by

5 2 Students aren't allowed to speak in the library.
3 I'm allowed to play in today's match.
4 We were allowed to stay over at Helen's house last night.
5 My sister was allowed to hang out with her friends every night during the summer holidays.
6 I'm not allowed to visit you tomorrow because I've got to shop for my grandma.

6 2 can't 3 couldn't 4 is 5 can 6 isn't

7 Students' own answers.

8 3, 4, 6

9 2 Did 3 could 4 stay out 5 what 6 when

10 2 They didn't have cars because they were expensive.
3 He can stay out late in the holidays.
4 Grandad's mum thought it would have a bad influence.
5 He worked in a car factory.
6 He says it's great that young people can do more things.

3C Finding solutions

1 2 analysis 3 procedure 4 data 5 conclusion
6 research

2 2 analysis 3 step 4 findings 5 source 6 hypothesis

3 2 sources 3 data 4 findings 5 conclusion
6 procedure

4 2 may / might / could be 3 can / could wear 4 can prepare 5 may not / might not stay over 6 could eat

5 2 may / might 3 can 4 could / can / may / might
5 may / might 6 could

6 Students' own answers.

7 1 Data 2 Conclusion 3 Hypothesis

8 2 six hours a week 3 three hours a week
4 25% 5 The findings support the prediction
6 a variety of materials

9 2 Our analysis, 4 3 To sum up, 5 4 The aim or our survey, 1 5 On the other hand, 6 6 Our hypothesis, 2

3D Emil's petition

1 2 Let's give it a go. 3 I'd go along with that. 4 I guess
6 It'll be a laugh.

3 2 A 3 H 4 J 5 K 6 E 7 I 8 M 9 N 10 C
11 B 12 G 13 L 14 F

4 2 e 3 a 4 f 5 d 6 b 7 g 8 h 9 i 10 c

5 Students' own answers.

6a 2 Let's <u>demonstrate</u>! 3 <u>That</u> would work.
4 That's a <u>good</u> point. 5 That's a <u>great</u> idea!
6 This is <u>brilliant</u>!

7a
Tom: The animals don't have space and the trainers hit them.; They can have much better lives in their natural environments.
Ella: Circuses and zoos look after animals.; Animals are safer in circuses and zoos than in the wild.; I ought to investigate the situation.

7b 2 Lions, chimpanzees and elephants are performing in the circus.
3 Tom thinks that they should organize a demonstration.
4 Children can see wild animals thanks to circuses.
5 Circuses are cruel places according to Tom.
6 The only problem animals have is when people come to hunt them.

Progress check

1 2 safety goggles 3 equipment 4 test tubes
5 results 6 theories

2 2 by 3 over 4 together 5 out 6 out

3 2 predictions 3 a conclusion 4 procedure
5 hypothesis 6 step

4 2 doesn't have 3 shouldn't 4 must 5 has to
6 ought to

5 2 aren't 3 can't 4 could 5 couldn't 6 allowed

6 2 We might not have enough time to do everything.
3 Wear your raincoat because it might rain later.
4 We could go to the cinema or stay at home and download a film.
5 We might go to the beach at the weekend.
6 The summer in Athens can be very hot.

7 1 c 2 b 3 a

8 2 way 3 advantage / benefit 4 benefit / advantage
5 work 6 useful 7 that 8 reason 9 problem
10 against

Unit 4 Travel

4A Wonders of the world

1 2 steps 3 statue 4 arch 5 tower 6 brickwork

2 2 pyramid 3 Stone 4 Ruins 5 A dome 6 floor

3 2 columns 3 towers 4 statues 5 dome 6 steps

4 2 had 3 would volunteer 4 didn't have to
5 would use 6 allowed

5 2 If I were the president, I'd make my town the capital city of the country.
3 Mark would repair your computer if you asked him.
4 Mum and Dad would never take us on holiday if we didn't pass our exams.
5 If my sister Lily had more money, she'd visit Iceland.
6 What would happen if the dome fell down?

6 Students' own answers.

7 2 The date when they built the first monument at Stonehenge.
3 The Skybridge is on the 41st floor.
4 The number of floors that the Petronas Towers has.
5 They painted the domes 200 years after they built the cathedral.
6 St Basil's Cathedral has ten domes.

8 1 5,000 2 500 3 88 4 41 5 10 6 200

9 2 She'd like to touch the stone columns.
3 A shopping centre at the bottom of the towers.
4 The bridge moves because of the wind.
5 He thought it was from a Disney film.
6 A fire destroyed them.

4B Ticket to ride

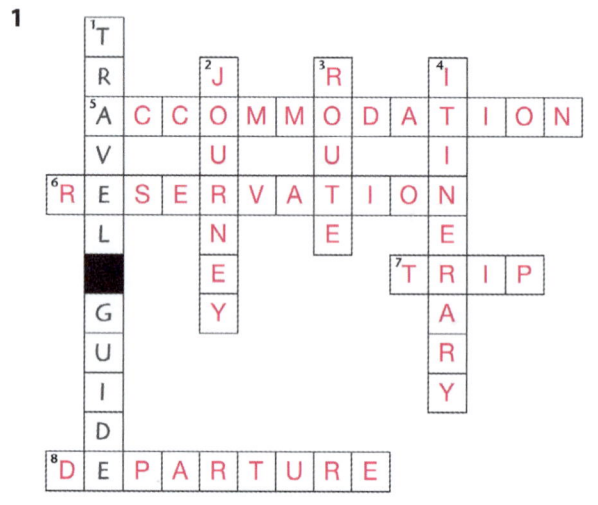

1 Crossword answers:
- 1 down: TRAVEL GUIDE
- 2 down: JOURNEY
- 3 down: ROUTE
- 4 down: ITINERARY
- 5 across: ACCOMMODATION
- 6 across: RESERVATION
- 7 across: TRIP
- 8 across: DEPARTURE

2 2 budget 3 destination 4 sightseeing
5 travel guide 6 journey 7 itinerary

3 2 trip 3 accommodation 4 destination
5 departure 6 arrival

4 2 most 3 than 4 too 5 as 6 enough

5 2 busiest 3 than 4 good 5 tastier 6 as

6 Students' own answers.

T98 Workbook answer key

7 Malmo: cheaper accommodation
Copenhagen: nightlife, more exciting, better sightseeing
Both: interesting for visitors

8 2 C 3 A 4 B

9 Students' own answers.

4C Off the beaten track

1 2 b 3 c 4 b 5 a 6 c

2 2 set off 3 stopped over 4 came across
5 get back 6 went off

3 2 off 3 back 4 off 5 off 6 across

4 2 time 3 frequency 4 manner 5 frequency
6 manner

5 2 carefully 3 always 4 gradually 5 never 6 there

6 2 last Monday 3 quickly 4 home 5 usually
6 beautifully

7 Students' own answers.

8 Cairo, California, Eritrea, Italy, Vietnam

9 2 24 3 175 4 198 5 Africa 6 two
7 18 8 doctor

10 2 last week 3 youngest person 4 the USA
5 study seriously 6 get to know

4D Hard to believe

1 2 Are you having me on? 3 I can't get my head around this. 4 Hang on a minute! 5 What are you up to?
6 Says who?

3 2 Says who? 3 You bet we could! 4 Hang on a minute! 5 What are you up to? 6 I can't get my head around this!

4 2 doubt 3 am 4 clearly 5 really 6 unlikely

5 belief: 3, 4
doubt: 2, 5, 6

6 2 not really sure 3 definitely 4 doubt 5 sure
6 certain 7 hard 8 unlikely

7 Students' own answers.

8a 2 reply 3 spy 4 easy 5 ready 6 deny

8b 2 /aɪ/ 3 /aɪ/ 4 /i/ 5 /i/ 6 /aɪ/

9a 2 Kate 3 Kate 4 Kate 5 Adam 6 Adam

9b 2 He says some people are certain that we'll soon have driverless cars.
3 Kate says we've never seen flying cars.
4 He says a lot of people would prefer to surf the internet or read.
5 Driverless buses and lorries would be good for businesses.
6 Adam says the technology for planes without pilots already exists.

Progress check

1 2 skyscrapers 3 columns 4 ruins 5 Stone 6 domes

2 2 b 3 a 4 b 5 c 6 a

3 2 off 3 back 4 over 5 across 6 up

4 2 lived 3 built 4 exercise 5 didn't want 6 had

5 2 than 3 as 4 enough 5 the 6 too

6 2 at the hotel, at midnight
3 never, in England.
4 often, in the United States
5 loudly, the art gallery
6 sometimes, in the mountains

7 2 e 3 b 4 c 5 d

The Museum of the Strange Episode 2

1 2 b 3 a 4 c 5 b 6 a

2 2 annoying 3 equipment 4 experiment 5 flash
6 shed 7 could 8 strangest 9 disappeared
10 time

3 2 What have you done? (C)
3 Why have you got a smart phone in the museum? (D)
4 This place just gets stranger and stranger. (B)
5 I came back to see the world's first time machine. (A)

4 Students' own answers.

5 2 mustn't 3 can't 4 should 5 ought to 6 must
6 A 4 B (1) C 5 D 3 E 2

7 1 The look (of surprise) on Jen's face was funny.
2 There were only two pyramids.
3 The battery level / power was low.
4 They were afraid / terrified and then angry.
5 She (had) waited for hours.

Unit 5 Heritage

5A Surviving the test of time

1 2 c 3 b 4 b 5 a

2 1 searching 2 spoken, agree, think, look

3 2 to 3 in 4 to 5 for
Students' own answers.

4 2 was sent 3 will be 4 divided 5 will

5 2 is asked 3 is used 4 were designed
5 were not given

6 2 aren't made in German factories
3 will astronauts be sent to Mars by NASA
4 weren't invented by Steve Jobs
5 are new computers designed

7 2 chairs 3 desks 4 essays 5 2010 6 problems

8 Suggested answers
2 basic technology such as a chair can have negative health effects
3 working out a few times is not enough. We have to work out while we're working
4 there were improvements in the exam performances of students who did exercise
5 that students deal with schoolwork better while they are exercising
6 we haven't done anything about it until we are surrounded by technology

5B Globalization

1 2 f 3 a 4 b 5 d 6 e

2 2 multinational company 3 global network
4 consumer society 5 cultural diversity
6 cultural exchanges

3 Students' own answers.

4 2 D 3 ND 4 D 5 D 6 ND

5 2 which is one of the world's best-known global brands
3 who started Apple with Steve Wozniak
4 which sells sports clothes
5 where Jaguar cars are made
6 which he got for his birthday

6 2 who 3 whose 4 which 5 which

7 2 would recommend that 3 In general, on the whole
4 The aim of this report is to 5 my information comes from 6 on the other hand

8 Suggested answer
Introduction
The aim of this report is to look at where the clothes which are found in local shops come from. My information comes from visits that I made to clothes shops for young people in my town.
Clothes shops
In general, clothes shops for young people have famous brands such as [names of brands]. Other typical global brands which are found in clothes shops are [names of brands].
Conclusion
To sum up, clothes shops for young people have global brands and not local products. If you want to buy clothes that are not expensive, I would recommend that you shop at [name of shop].

5C Modern life

1 2 pollution 3 leisure 4 housework 5 news
6 advertising

2 2 graffiti 3 litter 4 advertising 5 business
6 data

3a & b Students' own answers.

4 2 few 3 much 4 each 5 many 6 any

5 2 many 3 All 4 a little 5 every 6 no

6 Students' own answers.

7 A, B, D, E

8 2 Everybody thought that people would soon live on the moon.
3 It was decided that it was exciting, but too expensive.
4 Advances in computers and communications technology made satellites a good business.
5 Data makes money for the owners of satellites.
6 Satellites have provided them with the global network that they need.

5D Stereotypes

1 2 unhappy 3 explain 4 help 5 don't understand
6 support

2 2 I'm fed up with 3 Whose side are you on? 4 Spot on! 5 you don't know what I'm getting at 6 forget it!

4 B disagree C completely D say E right F just
G true H don't I so J way

5 Agreeing: 2 C 3 E 4 F 5 I
Disagreeing: 6 B 7 D 8 G 9 H 10 J

6 Students' own answers.

7a 2 oOo 3 ooO 4 oOo 5 Ooo 6 ooO 7 oOo
8 Ooo 9 ooO 10 oOo

8a 1 A 2 C 3 F

8b 1 He's beginning to think that it's boring.
2 After doing her homework.
3 There is too much violence in some video games.
4 That they play a video game.

8c 1 F 2 T 3 F 4 T

8d 1 it isn't always possible 2 country 3 clothes
4 advertising

Progress check

1 2 f, for 3 a, at 4 e, into 5 b, with 6 c, on

2 2 international 3 Consumer 4 popular
5 mass 6 multinational

3 2 leisure 3 litter 4 advertising 5 entertainment
6 graffiti

4 2 wasn't made 3 is built 4 are caused
5 will be powered 6 will be invented

5a 2 That's the computer shop where I bought my tablet.
3 I spoke to the man who can repair my smartphone.

5b 2 The hamburger, which was invented in Hamburg, Germany, is very popular around the world.
3 The Piraha, whose language is very difficult, live in the Amazon rainforest.

6 2 few 3 Every 4 much 5 All 6 little

7a 2 c, When exactly does the party take place?
3 d, Why did they start a party in Gràcia?
4 b, What did the neighbours decide to do?
5 b, What has the party become?

7b Suggested answers
1 Because a lot of local people leave the city to escape the high temperatures.
2 Every year in the third week of August.
3 To celebrate the return of normal life after the war between France and Spain in August 1817.
4 They decided to decorate their streets.
5 It has become a popular tourist attraction.

8 2 No 3 say 4 disagree 5 with 6 about

Unit 6 Our world

6A Online hoaxes

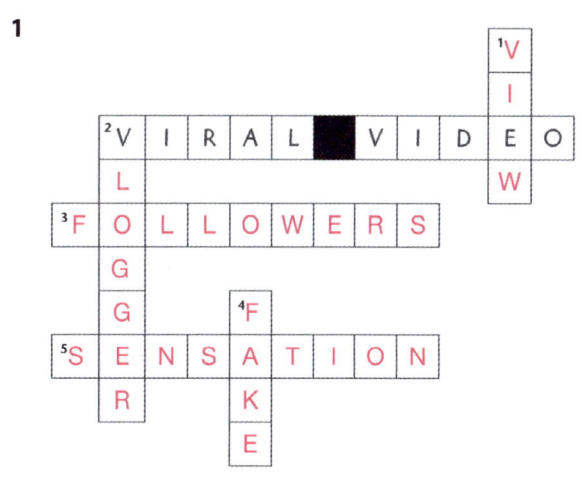

1

[Crossword]
Across: 2 VIRAL VIDEO 3 FOLLOWERS 5 SENSATION
Down: 1 VIEW 2 VLOGGER 4 FAKE

2 2 loyal 3 online 4 viral 5 life 6 comments

3 Students' own answers.

4 2 They told me that they were watching a viral video.
3 Sean said that he would write in the comments section.
4 Ava told us she was waiting for a friend.
5 Nathan said that they had been abroad.
6 Lily told me that her boyfriend was Italian.

5 2 they were annoyed about that.
3 his parents were abroad.
4 she was watching a vlog at that moment.
5 they would prepare a hoax for their vlog.

6 … He said he hoped to receive 3,000 views a day! He told me that his sister would help him make the vlog. He said she worked in mainstream media and knew a lot about making videos. He told me she was working for TV company at that moment and she was making a website.

7 1 B 2 C 3 A

8 2 It is aimed at 3 It offers advice on 4 recommended the site to 5 I particularly like 6 All in all

9 Students' own answers.
Paragraph 1: A
Paragraph 2: B, F
Paragraph 3: C, E

6B Shopping

1 2 receipt 3 size 4 alterations 5 changing room
6 discount

2 2 sales 3 brand 4 bargain 5 rip-off 6 refund

3 Students' own answers.

4 2 asked, R 3 told, C 4 told, C 5 asked, R 6 asked, R

5 2 f 3 e 4 a 5 d 6 b

6 2 told me to clean my shoes
3 told me not to spend too much money
4 asked me to open the window
5 asked to try the jeans on
6 told us / me not to be late for the exam

7 D, B, C, A

8 2 sales 3 discount 4 cheaper 5 touch 6 clothes

9 2 They do it to attract people into the shops and then they might buy something with or without a discount.
  3 The brain forgets about the part after the decimal point.
  4 Because a study has shown that people are more likely to buy something that they have touched and used.
  5 It puts them on big tables.
  6 She has to make a presentation.

6C Fashion

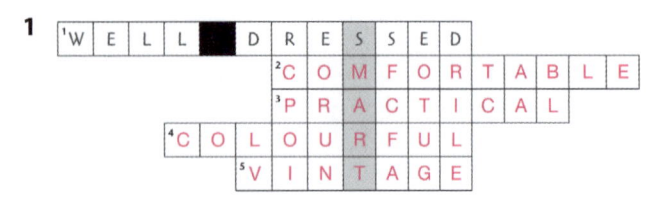

1
1 WELL DRESSED
2 COMFORTABLE
3 PRACTICAL
4 COLOURFUL
5 VINTAGE

2 2 f 3 a 4 b 5 d 6 c

3 Students' own answers.

4 2 b 3 b 4 b 5 a 6 a

5 Possible answers
  2 What did Amy buy last weekend? OQ
  3 What happened at the party? SQ
  4 Who shops online in your house? SQ
  5 Who did you buy a present for? OQ
  6 What did the Americans buy in Hawaii? OQ

6 2 What did the virus cause?
   What caused the computer problems?
  3 Who phoned Eva last night?
   Who did Alfie phone last night?
  4 Which website did the school principal choose?
   Who chose the second website?

7 1 **E** Buy here; look like this!
  2 **B** How it works
  3 **A** A surprising conversation
  4 **D** Telling the truth

8 2 She thought he was a photographer because he said he was responsible for the photos.
  3 She thought she had a problem because she didn't look like the models in the photos.
  4 He thought that everybody knew that advertising photos were changed with digital technology.
  5 It makes them feel bad about their looks.
  6 He was brave because his decision to talk about the tricks of the fashion industry didn't make him popular with the people that he worked with.

6D Life hacks

1 2 if you say so 3 Let me think. 4 What's with
  5 I've had a brainwave 6 You've got nothing to lose

3 2 let me think. 3 give it a go 4 if you say so
  5 you've made my day 6 you've got nothing to lose

4
Beginning: The first thing you should do is…(+infinitive); Before you begin…
The next steps: After that, you should…(+infinitive); The next step / thing is to…(+infinitive); When you've done that…
Finishing: The last thing you do is…; Finally, (+ imperative)

5 2 do 3 When 4 The next thing 5 After
  6 thing to do

6 Students' own answers.

7a 2 touch 3 won 4 through 5 lunch 6 cool

7b 2 /ʌ/ 3 /ʌ/ 4 /uː/ 5 /ʌ/ 6 /uː/

8a E, F, C

8b 1 T 2 F 3 F 4 T

8c D, B, C, A

8d 1 The speaker says it is one of his favourite devices.
  2 It doesn't run out because it doesn't have a battery.
  3 You can use it at the speed you like.
  4 She complains about the use of the word 'device'.

Progress check

1 2 an online sensation 3 subscribers
  4 mainstream media 5 fake 6 loyal followers

2 2 receipt 3 bargain 4 sales 5 changing rooms 6 size

3 2 colourful 3 practical 4 glamorous 5 ethnic
  6 must-have

4 2 would 3 us 4 said 5 were 6 told

5 2 asked 3 us 4 told 5 not 6 to

6 2 did 3 - 4 did 5 do 6 -

7 2 start 3 before 4 step 5 When 6 After
  7 finally 8 thing

9 2 Block those sites 3 Keep out 4 Variety is important
  5 Take a break

The Museum of the Strange Episode 3

1 2 curious 3 sunny 4 strangest 5 bored
   6 difficult 7 fantastic 8 best

2 2 We're part of the museum! C
   3 It's an ugly old building, isn't it? E
   4 The mirror's showing us the outside of this museum! A
   5 Everything in the museum is strange and interesting. B

3

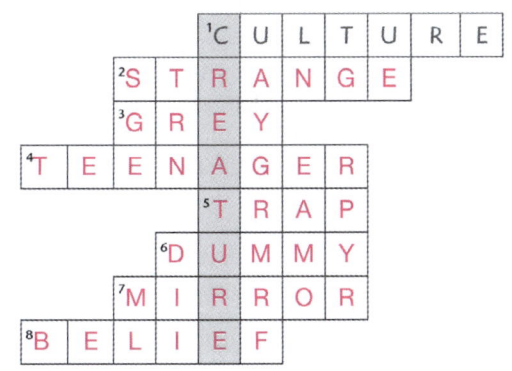

			¹C	U	L	T	U	R	E
	²S	T	R	A	N	G	E		
		³G	R	E	Y				
⁴T	E	E	N	A	G	E	R		
			⁵T	R	A	P			
		⁶D	U	M	M	Y			
	⁷M	I	R	R	O	R			
⁸B	E	L	I	E	F				

4 2 Laura said that she didn't get it.
   3 Declan thought that he was in the wrong place.
   4 Laura told Ben and Declan to run.
   5 Laura said that they would never know about the creature.
   6 The man said that they were knocking the building down soon.

5 2 older 3 remember 4 didn't 5 closed 6 empty
   7 ruin 8 stopped 9 human 10 found
   11 knocked 12 built

7 1 pencils 2 vampires 3 The Museum of Bad Art
   4 hair 5 bread

8 2 Paris 3 the USA 4 human hair 5 bread

Workbook audio scripts

02 p2   Exercise 2

1. Andy doesn't seem to get nervous about anything and so he seemed the obvious person to do the TV interview.
2. Hannah's always saying unpleasant things. She seems to enjoy upsetting people!
3. Mia is the type of friend that will always support you!
4. Oscar is great fun most of the time, but he can be happy one minute and then sad the next for no reason at all!
5. Harry always thinks about other people's feelings and considers how they might feel about things.
6. The shop assistant gave Olivia £10 extra in her change by mistake but instead of keeping it, she returned it.
7. Jenny hates it when her friends do better in exams than her and when they have things she doesn't have.
8. Tom likes to win at everything, even when he plays with his younger brother.

03 p5   Exercises 8 and 9

This story is about a terrible haircut that I had a few years ago. The problem was, my mum wanted me to spend my pocket money at the hairdresser's and I didn't!

Well, I was at my best friend Tom's house. Tom and I had lots in common, especially playing video games. While we were playing a game in the living room, I suddenly realized that his older brother, Alex, was looking at me. Actually, he was looking at my hair. Then he said, 'You know, I can cut your hair for free!' I wasn't very keen on Alex, but I immediately said 'Great!' when I realized I could save my pocket money.

Next, I went to the kitchen with Alex. Meanwhile, Tom continued playing. There wasn't a mirror and I couldn't see what Alex was doing, so when he finished, I went back to see Tom in the living room. As soon as Tom saw me, he started laughing so I ran to the bathroom. When I looked in the mirror, I didn't laugh… I cried! My hair was very short in some places and really long in others. I looked awful!

Finally, I left Tom's house and went home. I expected my mum to be very angry, but she just said, 'People are going to laugh at you,' and she was right. The following day, everybody at school laughed at me! After that, I decided to always go to the hairdresser's, even if I had to pay for haircuts with my pocket money!

05 p9   Exercise 6a

Jack So Ann, what do you think about Sam's joke?
Ann I think it's cruel.
Jack That's exactly what I think. He knows that Lily really fancies Tom.
Ann I know. He used Tom's phone to send the message and she'll believe it was from him.
Jack What did it say?
Ann Do you want to go out with me?
Jack Listen, I've got an idea.

07 p9   Exercise 6d

Lily Hi Tom.
Tom Er, hi Lily.
Lily Thanks for the messages.
Tom Messages?
Lily Yes, you sent me two!
Tom Well, I felt nervous when I was typing. Perhaps I pressed the send button twice!
Lily Ha, ha! Well I'm glad you did.
Tom Good. Did you know that there's an exhibition of Japanese comics on at the art centre?
Lily Yes and I want to see it. Why don't we go together?
Tom That's exactly what I was thinking!

08 p12   Exercise 3

1. Andy wants to go here, but I'm not sure. It's going to be really dark and it will be full of bats!
2. It's a lovely part of the English countryside with lakes surrounded by green hills. There are very few buildings and it's so beautiful to look at.
3. I've wanted to see Van Gogh's work for a long time so it's great that this exhibition is coming here to London. I can't wait to see it!
4. They say it's the biggest in Europe and if you get lost, it can take an hour to get out! I think I'll use my mobile phone to find the way out!
5. There are going to be about twenty rock bands and people are coming from all over Europe to attend. It's going to be awesome!
6. I saw it last year and the artists are brilliant! There are dancers, singers and magicians…something for everyone, really.

09 p15   Exercises 8 and 9

Tom Hey Laura, is it true that your sister is going to participate in a volunteer programme in India in the summer?
Laura Yes, she is.
Tom Wow, that sounds great!
Laura Yes, she's really excited. She flies to Mumbai on Saturday 1st July and she doesn't return until Monday the 31st, the end of the month.
Tom So what's she going to be doing there?
Laura Well, she's going to be teaching primary school children aged five to eleven in a small village. They don't have enough teachers and they need volunteers until they can train more local people.
Tom What's she going to teach?
Laura English and Maths. She arrives on a Sunday and her first class is the next day. She starts at 8 a.m. and finishes at 1 p.m.
Tom That sounds like a lot of work!
Laura It is! And she has to prepare and organize all her classes, but she wants to be a teacher so it'll be a great experience for her.
Tom She's studying education at university next year, isn't she?
Laura Yes. So this trip will show her what teaching is really like!
Tom It will! So what are you doing in the summer?
Laura I'm doing voluntary work as well!
Tom You're not going to India with your sister, are you?
Laura No! I'd love to, but my parents think I'm too young. I'm helping at the youth centre. It needs painting, so I'm using my graffiti skills to paint one of the walls.
Tom Really? That sounds like more fun than teaching English and Maths.
Laura It does to me too, but not to my sister!

12 p19   Exercise 6a

Joe Hey Rebecca, why don't we watch a few episodes of our favourite series this weekend?
Rebecca I don't really want to stay at home. I'd love to go out.
Joe OK, we could go shopping.
Rebecca That sounds more interesting than watching TV, but I'd rather not go to the shopping centre. It'll be crowded. I'd prefer to do something more active.
Joe How about playing tennis?

Rebecca I'm not very keen on tennis. I don't really know how to play it. I'd rather do something that I feel comfortable with.
Joe Well, we could go on our mountain bikes and go for a long ride.
Rebecca It sounds much better than tennis, but my parents won't let me cycle on busy roads.
Joe I know…how about volunteering with Danny and Lily on Saturday? They're giving out water to the runners on the marathon.
Rebecca I'd prefer not to see Danny. I don't get on well with him.
Joe OK, Rebecca – I get the message! But next time, if you don't want to go out with me, just say it!

13 p23 Exercises 6 and 7

The cave paintings at the Lascaux cave, in the southwest of France, are some of the most famous in the world.

Four teenagers discovered the cave in the summer of 1940. They were walking in the country with their dog (called Robot!). When the dog ran ahead and began to sniff at a hole in the ground, the four friends went and investigated. They found a deep hole.

The boys were excited because there was a local story about buried treasure. After they made the hole wider, they climbed down. In the cave below, they discovered lots of ancient paintings on the cave walls. There were paintings of bulls, horses, and other animals.

The boys returned the next day with ropes and lights. As they explored further, they discovered more paintings. One showed a man with the head of a bird.

At first, the boys kept the cave a secret, but after a few days they told one of their teachers. At first, he thought it was a joke. When he finally saw the paintings, he knew how important they were. One of the boys decided to camp in a tent near the cave. He could protect the paintings and also show visitors around. The cave became more and more famous until at last historians learned about the cave. After studying the paintings, they decided that they were around seventeen thousand years old.

14 p25 Exercises 8 and 10

A These experiments sound like a great way to earn some extra money. Which one would you choose?
B As far as I'm concerned, I'd do the video games experiment. I think it would be good fun.
A That's a good point, but they only want people for a few hours, so you wouldn't make much money. In my view, the one to do is the NASA experiment. How often do young people like us get a chance to earn eigtheen thousand dollars.
B I agree, the money is fantastic, but I'm not sure that staying in bed for so long is really the best way to spend seventy days!
A I see what you mean, it would be difficult! Anyway, I'm sure we both agree that the brain experiment doesn't sound like fun.
B I completely agree. What does 'uncomfortable' mean? That sounds like another way of saying painful to me.
A Me too! I suppose the video game experiment is the best one after all!

15 p27 Exercises 8 and 9

Josh So Grandad, have you got a few minutes so I can ask my questions?
Grandad Yes, ask away!
Josh OK, my first one is about the city. You've always lived here, so how has Coventry changed since the 1950s?
Grandad Well, it's changed in many ways, but a big difference was that there was less traffic then. We could play football in the street!
Josh Did your dad have a car?
Grandad No, very few people did. Remember we're talking about seventy years ago, and cars were very expensive.
Josh What things could you do?
Grandad Well, we were allowed to stay out all day and play. We had a black and white TV, but there were only two channels and there were no programmes during the day so there was nothing to do at home.
Josh Could you stay out late at night?
Grandad No, that hasn't changed. You can't stay out late, can you?
Josh Well, I can in the holidays, but not when there's school.
Grandad It was the same for me.
Josh And what about fashion and music? Could you wear and listen to what you wanted?
Grandad Well, in the 1950s, rock and roll was becoming popular and of course there was a rock and roll style, but we weren't allowed to copy it. My mum thought it would have a bad influence on us!
Josh Really? Wow! I can listen to what I like.
Grandad I know and it sounds awful!
Josh So when did you leave school?
Grandad I left at fourteen and I got a job in a car factory.
Josh At fourteen? You can't leave school at fourteen now.
Grandad I know and I think it's a good idea, but times change. I was going out with your grandma when I was seventeen and I left home at eighteen and we got married.
Josh I can't imagine doing that! Do you think things are better now?
Grandad No, but they aren't worse either! Young people can do more things and I think that's great, but I've had a good life and I wouldn't change any of it!
Josh That's good to know.

18 p31 Exercise 7a

Ella Did you see that the circus is coming to Merton Park for Christmas? They've got lions, chimpanzees and elephants that do tricks. It should be great!
Tom What? I think we should get together and organize a demonstration against it.
Ella Why's that?
Tom The reason is that we shouldn't use animals for our entertainment.
Ella Come off it! What's wrong with animals in a circus? The trainers look after them like they do in zoos and they're a great way for children to see wild animals!
Tom Are you joking? They're cruel places. The animals don't have any space to move and the trainers hit them if they don't learn the tricks that they have to do.
Ella But isn't it an argument in favour of circuses and zoos that the animals are safer there than in the wild?
Tom Wrong! They can have much better lives in their natural environments. The only problem they have is when people come to hunt them!
Ella OK, OK, perhaps I ought to investigate the situation a bit more.
Tom I'd go along with that!

Workbook audio scripts   T105

20 p39 Exercises 8 and 9

Podcaster Welcome to this week's edition of The Young Traveller's Podcast. Now, most of our listeners probably haven't had the chance to travel much, but would like to in the future. In fact, we know some have never gone off to another country at all! However, reporter Emma Richards is here to tell us about one young person that has already seen it all. Here's Emma.
Emma Eric Nguyen from the town of Orinda, California, arrived in Asmara, the capital city of Eritrea in the North East of Africa, last week. Eric took off from Italy, and stopped over in Cairo, before he finally landed in the Eritrean capital. It was a long journey and Eritrea is a very difficult country to visit and it can be dangerous, but Eric was happy. Why? Because after visiting Eritrea, Eric, at the age of twenty-four years and a hundred and seventy-five days old, became the youngest person to have visited all the world's a hundred and ninety-eight countries! Eric started travelling at the age of two, when he and his parents moved from Vietnam to the USA, then when he turned eighteen, he started travelling on his own. When he got back home from Eritrea, Eric said he planned to continue travelling, but first he wants to study seriously and become a doctor. After that, he'd like to return to some of the countries he's visited because he was travelling quickly and didn't have time to get to know them. It sounds like Eric will always be a traveller!
Podcaster Indeed it does, Emma! Well, now you know, if you're still not twenty-four, there's a world record for you to break! Next up, we meet the…

23 p41 Exercise 9a

Adam Hi Kate. What are you up to?
Kate My mum's thinking about buying a new car and I'm checking out different models on the internet.
Adam Why is she buying a car? I doubt that anybody will drive their own car soon.
Kate What do you mean?
Adam Well, a lot of people are certain that we'll have driverless cars instead.
Kate Pull the other one! They've talked about flying cars for years, but have you ever seen one? It's hard to believe that people will want driverless cars.
Adam Why not?
Kate People like driving. My mum loves it!
Adam I don't agree. I'm certain that a lot of people would prefer to sit and surf the internet or read in their cars on the way to work instead of worrying about driving.
Kate Who says so?
Adam Well, nobody actually! But if big companies like Google are creating prototypes of self-driving cars, it's because they think there's a market.
Kate Perhaps they're thinking more about lorries and buses. If they didn't need drivers, it would be good for businesses.
Adam But it wouldn't be good for jobs!
Kate That's true!
Adam They're also talking about passenger planes without pilots. The technology already exists.
Kate It's very unlikely that anyone would get on a plane without a human pilot.
Adam That's true! I'm sure that I wouldn't, even if it were free!

24 p45 Exercises 6 and 7

Phil Fuller
This is the audio log of Phil Fuller. I was feeling excited when I left the twenty-first century. I waved goodbye to Jen and then I pressed the button on my time travel machine. I was going home! When I started to disappear I had to laugh because the look of surprise on her face was so funny!

As usual, there was a bright light all around me. But then, when the light stopped, I saw that there was a problem. A big problem! I wasn't home in my own time. I was in the wrong place and the wrong time. I was in the desert and I was looking at two of the Great Pyramids in Egypt! How did I know it was the wrong time? That's easy. Later there was a third pyramid – you can still see three pyramids there today – but at that time, there were only two pyramids!

I was getting nervous. What was wrong with my time machine? I looked at it and saw that the battery level was really low. Oh, oh. This was bad.

I took a deep breath and pressed the button again. A moment later, I was in a new place, and a new time. But again, I wasn't in the right time! And I wasn't alone. There were people looking at me. They were wearing animal skins and carrying spears. They looked terrified…and then they looked angry. They began to run towards me. I don't think they wanted to chat!

My time machine was almost dead. I only had enough power for one more time jump. I pressed the button and closed my eyes. When I opened them again, my friend Kelly was looking at me. 'Where have you been?' she asked crossly. 'I've waited hours for you!' I smiled. 'It's a long story,' I told her.

25 p51 Exercises 7 and 8

Good morning, everybody. I'm going to start this lecture by talking about one of the most important developments in modern life: space travel. Although you might think that space travel will be even more important in the future, our modern lifestyles depend on it today.

Neil Armstrong, who was the first man to walk on the moon, said those famous words, 'one small step for man, one giant leap for mankind' back in 1969. Everybody thought that after that people would soon live on the moon but it didn't happen. Why? Well, money was the reason why the Apollo space program was cancelled. Travelling to the moon, it was decided, was very exciting, but it was too expensive.

However, during the trip to the moon, a lot of technological advances were made, especially in the area of computers and communications technology. Space organizations realized that sending spacecraft which had this technology just a short distance into space, sometimes only as far as three hundred and fifty kilometres away from the Earth's surface, could be a good business. Of course, they weren't thinking about space ships with astronauts; they were thinking about satellites.

Without satellites, globalization would not exist. There are over two thousand of them going around the Earth at this very moment and their owners are making money from today's invisible gold: data. Drivers, pilots and sailors whose vehicles are connected to GPS systems know exactly where they are and can plan their journeys thanks to satellites. Satellites connect mobile phone users and send images from one side of the world to the other in seconds. Space and telecommunications and information technology has proved to be a perfect combination and has provided multinational companies and the mass media with the global network that they need. I think we can say that if there weren't any satellites, many of you would not be wearing the global brands that you are sitting in now!

Let's consider the following example…

28–31 p53 Exercise 8a, b & c

1
A What are you doing tonight?
B I was going to watch a TV series, but I'm fed up with watching rubbish! I'm beginning to think popular culture is boring!
A No way! I like watching TV series after doing my homework. It's a great way to relax.
B No, that's not always true. There's too much violence in some of them and that doesn't help me relax!
A I agree with you that there are some series that are violent, but some of them are really good. Why don't you come round tonight and we can find an interesting one for you?
B I'd like to come round, but finding a good TV series isn't such a big deal. We could play a video game instead.
A Great, but I thought you didn't like popular culture!

2
A Hi Max, are you coming out tonight?
B No Amy, I can't. I've got lots of homework.
A Maybe I can lend you a hand?
B Thanks, but I can do it. It's not difficult! I just wish we lived in the past. You know, when young people went to work instead of going to school.
A No way! I completely disagree with you. Teenagers in the past used to work ten or twelve hours a day on farms or in factories! I much prefer school!
B Well, I've probably worked ten hours today!
A Yes, but it isn't like that every day and you've had time to chat with your mates.
B Yes, you're right about that. I suppose life today does have its good points!

3
A I really think we should buy local products.
B You're right about that, but I don't think that it's always possible.
A What are you getting at?
B Well, for a start, in our country we don't make smartphones, computers or other types of information technology.
A You're right about that, but I was thinking more about clothes.
B The problem is that young people like global brands.
A I wouldn't say that. I don't think they would be so successful without advertising.
B Perhaps you're right, but I think they would be popular anyway.

33 p59 Exercises 7, 8 & 9

Ahmed Hi Isla. How's your project on shopping going?
Isla Great, thanks to my sister's boyfriend, Oliver. He's studying Marketing and Advertising at university and I asked him to give me some information on how shops try to persuade us to spend our money and he's been really helpful.
Ahmed So what have you learned?
Isla Lots of interesting information! For a start, we have to be careful when we see sales signs in shops.
Ahmed Why's that?
Isla Well, the shops often only offer a few bargains and they sometimes put the sales signs above products that don't have any discount at all.
Ahmed That sounds strange.
Isla Well, it's to get people into the shops. Once people start looking at things, they might see something that they like and buy it even if they have to pay full price.
Ahmed That's not very fair, is it?
Isla No, but it's legal. Oliver also told me to always add a one to the number before the decimal point on a price label.
Ahmed Come again?
Isla Well, if a pair of jeans cost €29.99, our brains read the twenty-nine, the number before the decimal point, and forget about the ninety-nine after it. Of course, the price is really €30, but twenty-something sounds cheaper.
Ahmed So that's why the prices of so many products end in ninety-nine.
Isla That's right. Another interesting thing is touch. Do you remember when you were younger and you went food shopping with your parents? I bet they always told you not to touch anything.
Ahmed They did!
Isla Well, clothes and electronics shops want you to touch their products. A study has shown that people are more likely to buy things that they've touched, and in the case of electronics shops, used.
Ahmed So that's why that electronics shop in town has all the laptops and tablets on big tables for people to play with.
Isla Exactly. We should also be aware of friendly shop assistants when we go clothes shopping on our own. They're sometimes trained to chat to customers as if they were a friend and when you come out of the changing room in a new outfit, they'll always tell you that you look great. But they do all of that so that you'll buy something.
Ahmed That one doesn't surprise me! Well, I think your project sounds great and I'm sure the class will love it when you make your presentation.
Isla Thanks, I hope you're right!

36–39 p63 Exercise 8a, b & c

1
A Well, before you begin, find a place where you can use it. Somewhere flat would be a good place to start. After that, you should start moving on it. Don't go too far at first, or too fast. Put one foot on it and push yourself along with the other foot. The next step is to find a park that is made for using it. You'll find lots of other users and you can learn from them by watching…
B I know, I know! I've just had a brainwave! It's a…

2
A The first thing you should do is connect it to your TV and switch it on. When you've done that, you should put in a disk or download the material that you want from a website. The next step is to decide if you want to use it alone or with a friend. You can also use it with someone online. My mum doesn't like me using it with people online, so I use it with my sister or friends. Finally, you give the device instructions about how you want to use it.
B You play with me too sometimes! It's a…

3
A OK, so I'm going to give you the instructions for one of my favourite devices. You start by picking it up and opening it with your hands. You don't need to charge the battery, because it doesn't have one; it never runs out! After that, you can use it at the speed that you like. You use it very quickly or very slowly. You can also go back to the beginning or right to the end. The last thing you do is close it when you want.
B Hey, what's with the use of the word 'device'? It's not a device, it's a…

41 p67 Exercises 7 and 8

A Welcome to *Weird World*, the only travel podcast that tells you about the more…unusual tourist attractions.
B That's right, and today we're going to tell you about some of the strangest museums in the world.
A First on our list is a small museum in the north of England. It's the Derwent Pencil Museum. You heard that right – PENCIL museum!
B As well as exhibits about the history of pencils, it has the biggest colour pencil in the world. It's almost eight metres long!
A Our second museum is about something that is a little scarier than pencils. If you go to Paris, instead of the Eiffel Tower you might visit the Museum of Vampires and Legendary Creatures. It's got lots of exhibits about vampires in books and films. For example, you can see the autographs of every film actor who has ever played the most famous vampire of all…Dracula.
B One thing – this is a small private collection. So to visit the museum, you have to phone and make an appointment.
A OK, our next museum is in the USA. This is an art museum, but it's an art museum that no artist wants to display their work in.
B Why's that?
A You'll understand when you hear the museum's name. It's called the Museum of Bad Art, in Boston. It says it's for art that is 'too bad to be ignored'! So if you're the kind of person who finds bad art funny, this is the place for you!
B And we stay in the USA for our next strange museum. In the town of Independence, Missouri, you can visit Leila's Hair Museum. The museum has samples of hair from famous people – Elvis Presley, Abraham Lincoln, Michael Jackson – but most of the museum is devoted to hair art.
A Hair art?
B That's jewellery and other pieces of art that include human hair.
A Yuck! Why would anyone do that?
B It used to be popular to carry a bit of a loved one's hair with you – your partner's or perhaps a child's. It was to show your love by keeping something of that person close to you.
A OK, what's our last strange museum?
B This one is in the town of Ulm in Germany, and it's the Bread Museum. It contains around sixteen thousand different exhibits, all about bread.
A And lots of bread too, right?
B Wrong! There's no actual bread in the museum because the creators of the museum think that bread is a food that must be made fresh every day. Here's the review one visitor gave the museum online: 'What can you say? It's just a museum about bread.'
A Well, you can't really disagree with that!